American Government
a core approach

fourth edition

Agboaye • Bottrell • Giardino • Jackson • Madani • Saxe

Madani • *General Editor*

Custom Editor:
Staci Powers

Project Development Editor:
Terry Isgro

Marketing Coordinators:
Lindsay Annett and Sara Mercurio

Production/Manufacturing Supervisor:
Donna M. Brown

Senior Project Coordinator:
Melanie Evans

Pre-Media Services Supervisor:
Dan Plofchan

Rights and Permissions Specialist:
Kalina Hintz

Senior Prepress Specialist:
Deanna Dixon

Cover Design:
Amy Wilkins

Cover Image:
Getty Images

© 2006 Thomson Custom Solutions, a part of the Thomson Corporation. Thomson, the Star logo, and Custom Publishing are trademarks used herein under license.

Printed in the
United States of America
1 2 3 4 5 6 7 8 9 08 07 06

For more information, please contact Thomson Custom Solutions, 5191 Natorp Boulevard, Mason, OH 45040.

Or you can visit our Internet site at www.thomsoncustom.com
ALL RIGHTS RESERVED. No part of this work covered by the copyright hereon may be reproduced or used in any form or by any means — graphic, electronic, or mechanical, including photocopying, recording, taping, Web distribution or information storage and retrieval systems — without the written permission of the publisher.

The Adaptable Courseware Program consists of products and additions to existing Thomson Custom Solutions products that are produced from camera-ready copy. Peer review, class testing, and accuracy are primarily the responsibility of the author(s).

For permission to use material from this text or product, contact us by:
Tel (800) 730-2214
Fax (800) 730 2215
www.thomsonrights.com

ISBN 0-759-34943-6

Preface

American Government: A Core Approach, is a joint effort by professors Agboaye, Bottrell, Giardino, Jackson, Madani, and Saxe. Professor Madani serves as editor, coordinator, and liaison with the publisher. The book is an alternative to longer textbooks that file copious facts on the institutions and processes of American government. This is a conversation-based text. Studies have shown that conversational-style textbooks make the subject more readable, more understandable, and more interesting to students. It is hoped that by gradually easing students into the field of government and politics, they will become more interested in the democratic process.

The text does not apply any particular theoretical approach in analyzing American government and politics. It basically introduces the student to the concepts that are essential and helpful in explaining the facts of American politics. The goal is to give students an understanding of key concepts and major issues, and to encourage them to make judgments of their own about major political issues.

The fourth edition provides opportunity to reorganize, add new information, and update the materials about American government and politics. It includes information about the 2004 presidential and congressional elections. Chapter Five has been reorganized and expanded. It includes a new title, Social/Political Movements. We have updated the information on the civil liberties by including and discussing new Supreme Court decisions. In addition, the latest edition includes a computer game.

We wish to acknowledge the help we received from our developmental editor, Staci Powers, for her invaluable technical assistance. Above all, thanks to our students who have supported this text in the past eight years by reading and improving it with their helpful comments.

Hamed Madani
Arlington, Texas
June 2005

About the Authors

Ehi Agboaye is an Associate Professor of Government at Tarrant County College. He received his M.A. in journalism and Ph.D. in political science from the University of North Texas.

Catherine Bottrell is an Assistant Professor of Government at Tarrant County College. She received a B.A. in political science from the University of Texas at Arlington and a juris doctorate from the University of Tulsa College of Law. She is the recipient of the *Who's Who Among American Teachers*.

Anthony Giardino teaches political science and criminal justice at Tarrant County College. He is co-author of *Lone Star Politics*, a widely acclaimed political science textbook about state and local government. He specializes in public policy and due process. Formerly a police administrator, he continues to serve as a consultant, trainer, and advisor for law enforcement agencies.

Andrew Hudson Jackson, a juris doctorate, is an attorney who has taught a variety of courses over the past sixteen years at Tarrant County College, including national and state government, introduction to the legal system, and introduction to legal research.

Hamed Madani received his Ph.D. in political science from the University of North Texas. Before joining the faculty of Tarrant County College as a full-time professor in 1984, he taught at the University of Texas at Arlington and the University of North Texas as a graduate teaching fellow. He is the recipient of the Chancellor's Award for Exemplary Teaching and the *Who's Who Among American Teachers*. Dr. Madani has been teaching courses in the U.S. government, U.S. foreign policy, and state and local governments.

Allan Saxe is a professor of political science at the University of Texas at Arlington. He received his Ph.D. from the University of Oklahoma in political science. He has been teaching courses in national, state, and local politics, and civil liberties. He is recipient of the Piper Professor Teaching Award and various University of Texas at Arlington teaching awards. He is also a political analyst for WBAP Radio in Dallas/Fort Worth and writes a weekly column for the *Arlington Star-Telegram*.

Contents

PREFACE iii

ABOUT THE AUTHORS iv

CHAPTER 1
    Introduction to Political Science 1

CHAPTER 2
    Foundation of American Government and Politics 31

CHAPTER 3
    Federalism 51

CHAPTER 4
    Individualized Participation: Voting, Campaigns, and Elections 71

CHAPTER 5
    Collective Participation: Interest Groups, Movements, and
      Political Parties 103

CHAPTER 6
    American Media in Politics 129

CHAPTER 7
    Congress 159

CHAPTER 8
    Office of the President of the United States 191

CHAPTER 9
    The Federal Bureaucracy 219

CHAPTER 10
    The Judiciary 237

CHAPTER 11
    Civil Liberties in America 253

CHAPTER 12
    Civil Rights: Journey to Full Participation 281
CHAPTER 13
    Public Policy 309
CHAPTER 14
    American Foreign Policy 325
APPENDIX A
Founding Documents 349
    The Declaration of Independence 349
    The United States Constitution 353
    The Amendments to the Constitution 364
    The Federalist No. 10 374
    The Federalist No. 51 381
APPENDIX B
    The Government and the Community:
    A Coordinated Response to Hate Crime in America 385
APPENDIX C
    GLOSSARY 389
INDEX 395
POLITICAL CHAOS 399

Chapter 1
Introduction to Political Science

I seldom think of politics more than eighteen hours a day.
—*Lyndon B. Johnson*

INTRODUCTION

For most Americans the word *politics* has unfavorable overtones; they believe that politicians are corrupt, self-serving, or egotistical. The very mention of politics conjures up the image of "a smooth-talking wheeler-dealer" who uses money to influence votes. Most of us perceive that only those who have "thick skin and a strong stomach" will get involved in politics. One political scientist stated, "At its best, politics is a noble quest for a good order and justice; at its worst, a selfish grab for power, glory and riches."[1]

Despite much of the existing disillusionment with politics, it can be an honorable and noble profession. Participation in politics by citizens of democracy is a duty, a responsibility, and an obligation. By getting involved, we not only promote our own interests but also those of the community as a whole.

Sustaining a democracy such as ours requires informed and interested citizens who can meaningfully take part in the political process. To achieve this goal, a basic familiarity with political science principles and concepts is essential. Understanding the basics of political science will enable the student to better understand and evaluate contemporary political issues and problems facing America. This chapter is designed to achieve that goal.

What Is Political Science?

Political science is one of the disciplines within the social sciences. Social scientists study different aspects of human behavior. Other disciplines within the social sciences include psychology, sociology, economics, and anthropology. Political science examines that aspect of human behavior involving power and authority. According to Harold Lasswell, "The study of politics is the study of influence and the influential."[2] Before we expand on the meaning of the term *political science*, it is essential to elaborate on the genesis of the term *politics*.

The Origin of Politics

As a field of study, politics dates back approximately 2,500 years. European and American scholars generally believe that politics and government originated in ancient Greece. The West is indebted to the ancient Greeks for the genesis of politics, its vocabulary, and the very creation of Western civilization. Western social and political values are Greek in origin. The Greek ideas of politics set the tone and nature of most political thought as embodied in writings during the subsequent 2,500 years.[3]

Among early scholars of classical Greece were Socrates (469–399 B.C.), Plato (427–347 B.C.), and Aristotle (381–322 B.C.). **Socrates** was a noted oral historian and teacher. He did not leave any written work behind. He interacted with his students through direct dialogue of questions and answers, described as the **Socratic method**. This is the pursuit of knowledge through question (thesis), answer (antithesis), and additional question (synthesis).

Socrates lived in fifth century B.C. Athens when democracy blossomed. At this time, Athens had an assembly and a council. The assembly (the legislative branch) was composed of all male citizens, and the council (the executive branch) was chosen by lot from among these citizens. The council prepared legislation for the assembly and administered the day-to-day functioning of the city-state. This type of political arrangement is an example of **direct democracy,** or the **Athenian model** of democracy where qualified citizens act as their own representatives in making decisions for themselves.

Plato was present during Socrates' trial and wrote its detailed account. Plato abhorred Athenian democracy. He left Athens in disgust after the execution of Socrates in 399 B.C., returning later to establish the Athenian Academy in 387 B.C., the prototype of the Western university. Plato viewed democracy as tyranny of majority at the expense of minority. He argued that individuals' unique ideas, like those of Socrates, were suppressed in a democracy. Plato wrote *The Republic* to describe his best political order. His ideal society was not democratic because Plato argued that the wise and virtuous person—the **philosopher-king,** would best conduct government. According to Plato, "Until philosophers become kings or kings become philosophers, there will be no rest from ills for the cities or mankind."[4] This refers to the belief that it is only through wisdom that the good life could be attained.

Portrait of Plato
© CORBIS

Throughout the dialogue, Plato sought to identify the components of a state that best achieves justice. He envisioned a just society as one in which individuals perform functions for which they are best suited by innate qualities and training. He also maintained that political justice could be achieved when philosophers become kings.

Philosophically, Plato was an idealist. He believed that the tangible world is a reflection of ideal forms. In the area of politics, this meant that for Plato objective good and truth (i.e., good and truth that are universally valid without regard to individual self-interest) exist. Furthermore, he believed that properly trained individuals could discern these basic principles.

A major portion of Plato's *Republic* is devoted to a discussion of the concept of an "ideal state." In order to construct it, Plato divides an individual's soul into three functions: appetite, the materialistic nature of people; spirit, the will to fight and endure deprivation and discipline; and reason, the love of wisdom.

Thus, there were three separate classes of people, each corresponding to the division of the soul. The lowest class, (farmers, artisans, merchants, etc.) represented the appetitive function in the republic. They had only practical knowledge, and lacked the wisdom, of how to do things. They were only interested in satisfying the materialistic function of the soul.

The second group was the guardian or auxiliary class. They corresponded to the spirited function of the soul. Among these were police, soldiers, and administrators of the republic. They were brave, had the will to fight, and endured discipline. Members of this class also lacked wisdom.

Corresponding to the reasoning part of the soul, the highest and best class, was the philosopher-kings. They had wisdom and truth. Plato's system of education identified them and subjected them to further training in order to seek out the good life, translating this goal into state public policy by using the auxiliaries.[5] He believed that his ideal state would last as long as people had faith in their leaders. To achieve this, leaders may resort to a "noble lie," a falsehood that is for the good of everyone. (See Table 1.1.)

TABLE 1.1   PLATO'S SYSTEM

Individual or Soul	Virtue	Polis or State
Man of Reason or Gold	Wisdom or Truth	Rulers or Philsopher-King
Man of Spirit or Silver	Courage or Bravery	Auxiliary, Soldiers
Man of Appetite or Bronze	Temperance	Working Class

Aristotle was a student of Plato at the Athenian Academy for 20 years. On Plato's death, he left Athens, lived in Macedonia, and tutored young Alexander the Great (338–323 B.C.), who led the Macedonian and Greek troops and conquered the entire Persian Empire: Asia Minor, Egypt, the Fertile Crescent, and Persia. In 334 B.C., Aristotle returned to Athens and established his own academy, the Lyceum.

Aristotle was an **empiricist,** someone who believes in factual knowledge in his approach to politics. Instead of postulating the existence of ideal forms to be apprehended by rational analysis, Aristotle studied actual political conditions.

He is the author of *The Politics,* the first work to provide an empirical and comprehensive view of different types of regimes. The book is based on the study of 158 constitutions of the Greek city-states of his time. From his empirical data, Aristotle constructed principles that he believed would produce good life and the means for moral improvement for citizens.

The Politics proposed two criteria for distinguishing governments: the end for which governments exist and various kinds of authorities. The first criterion is used to distinguish between political systems in which rulers rule in their own interest (the wrong constitution), and systems ruled in the general interest (the right constitution).

The second criterion is used to distinguish governments according to the number of citizens who are entitled to rule. In this way, he arrived at the familiar distinction among the rule of one, few, and many. By combining these criteria, Aristotle produced six types of governments: three good forms of government and three bad or perverted types of government. (See Table 1.2.) Like Plato, Aristotle classified democracy as a bad form of government. For Aristotle, democracy signified poor ruling in the rulers' own self-interest without regard for the concerns of other social classes.

TABLE 1.2   ARISTOTLE'S CLASSIFICATION

Quantity	Quality	
	Good	Bad
Rule by One	Monarchy	Tyranny
Rule by Few	Aristocracy	Oligarchy
Rule by Many	Polity	Democracy

Aristotle preferred monarchy, provided the monarch was an exemplary individual and ruled in everybody's best interest. Aristotle's best practical regime was **polity**, defined as a moderate democracy where the interests of all social classes are equally promoted.[6]

Both Plato and Aristotle agreed that knowledge is virtue, and that the pursuit of knowledge is good in and of itself. Furthermore, drawing on their experiences with the city-states of their time, both sought the means for achieving harmonious and stable communities. Finally, each placed tremendous value on constructing a moral basis for the good life. A sound civic morality was integral both to a stable political system and a well-rounded personal life.

The Meaning of Politics

The origin of the word *politics* is *polis,* a Greek term for a **city-state**. Before the seventeenth century, the nation-state as we know it did not exist. Territories were divided into a variety of constantly shifting units, including city-states, kingdoms, or empires. Ancient Greece was made up of city-states. The Greeks believed that the task of politics was to organize the *polis* in order to foster human excellence. They considered individuals as part and parcel of city-state. For instance, Aristotle argued that the *polis* was the highest community that aimed at the highest goal—happiness and the good life. People in the *polis* were expected to devote all their behavior patterns to the achievement of this goal. Aristotle did not make any distinctions between the *polis* and individuals. "A man who is not part of *polis* is either a beast or a god." In other words, participation in the *polis* gets to the essence of what it means to be human. Thus, to be detached from the political process is not to be properly human. It was for this reason that politics was the study of life in the *polis* and included all behavior within the *polis*.[7] For Athenians, an individual achieved the good life by participating actively in the civic life of the city-state.

Alternative Definitions of Politics

Two commonly used definitions coined by political scientists David Easton and Harold Lasswell are, respectively, "the authoritative allocation of values" and "who gets what, when, and how." **Values** are those things that have importance and significance to people or things that are good and desirable. There are intangible values that inspire political action. These include liberty, equality, freedom, justice, and patriotism. Or *values* can be defined in terms of the tangible. Tangible values can be a decent house, road, quality health service, or protection from crimes. **Allocation** refers to making choices in order to govern. It refers to the process by which decisions and actions are taken to grant or deny to people. Value allocations are taken as **authoritative** when the decisions are accepted as binding by the people affected by them. The *who* of politics includes voters, candidates, and political parties, etc. *How* refers to the means by which these participants get what they want. It includes bargaining, compromising, and lobbying. *What* refers to the substance of politics—governmental decisions.

The basic difference between the two definitions is the boundary identification. Easton says that only those power relationships binding upon the whole society are political. On the other hand, Lasswell believes that all power relationships are political. Thus, the discussion of politics is not limited to government. One can apply politics to any setting—family politics, university politics, church politics, labor union politics, and so on. Politics, then, exists within any group in society whenever a decision is to be made that will directly affect members of that group. A family's decision to spend their vacation in Tahiti, for example, is a political decision for that family.

Political scientists Herbert R. Winter and Thomas J. Bellows argue that although most American political scientists adhere to Easton's definition of politics, he ignores an important aspect of the political process in his definition—the competition and struggle that occur before an authoritative allocation of values can take place. Therefore, they offer an amended and more complete version of Easton's definition of politics. They define politics "as a struggle between actors pursuing conflicting desires on issues that may result in an authoritative allocation of values."[8]

Politics can also be considered as a process by which people in a society express their opinions about what government should do on particular issues of the time. Government, in turn, may use these opinions to make decisions. People express their opinions by voting, participating in public opinion polls, joining special-interest groups, making speeches, attending political rallies, etc. Individual opinions are based on politics of interest and politics of ideas. **Politics of interest** refers to people demanding different things for themselves from government; **politics of ideas** emphasizes those opinions that will best serve the public good.[9]

The Meaning of Science

The word *science* comes from the Latin word *scientia*, which means organized knowledge as opposed to belief or opinion. The goal of any science is to describe and explain—to answer what, why, and how questions. Science is empirical because it involves phenomena that can be observed or measured.

Most political scientists attempt to follow the rules of the scientific method to establish shared knowledge about the political world. The **scientific method** entails formulating a question with precision, gathering and analyzing empirical evidence that is relevant to the question, and then proposing a generalization or conclusion.

Those who support the scientific study of politics believe that human behavior, though complex, follows regular patterns. Through careful, systematic observation, these patterns can be discovered. In addition, these advocates also point out that because the scientific study of politics is fairly new, lack of progress in the discipline is expected.

According to Anita C. Danker, the use of scientific method by political scientists has resulted in three types of statements. The first is an **observational/evidential** statement that describes the characteristics of what has been observed. For example, in 1992, 518 out of 535 members of the United States Congress were male. In the British Parliament, 550 of the 635 members were male. Danker calls the second type of scientific statement an **observational law.** These are hypotheses based on what has been observed. For example, legislative and executive branches in modern democracies tend to be dominated by males. Finally, the last type of scientific statement is called a **theory,** and it analyzes the data and offers general principles that can be drawn from what has been observed. For example, "Political power in modern democracies is in male hands."[10]

Critics of the Scientific Method

All political scientists are not in agreement about whether the scientific method should be applied to politics. Critics state that political scientists have not agreed on a coherent set of concepts and theories required to provide organization and direction within a fully developed science. They also point out that it is impossible to develop a science of politics because the political world is far too complex and unpredictable for systematic generalizations. Politics is based on the actions and interactions of many individuals and groups. Politics occurs in the midst of many changing conditions that can influence those actions. In addition, these critics fault the scientific method for not helping to answer the crucial normative questions of politics.[11]

Furthermore, these scholars state that the study of politics should also include **normative statements** (e.g., "You should not come late to class."), dealing with passing value judgment on the existing state of affairs in a society. Whereas **empirical statements** are factual statements (e.g., "You came late to class."), normative statements require ethical or moral judgments. Normative statements identify one outcome as better than another.

Thus, the study of politics is fundamentally different from, say, the study of chemical reactions. People do not behave like atoms, and political activities tend to be unique events and cannot be regularly produced in a laboratory.

THE SCOPE OF POLITICAL SCIENCE

Political scientists explore such issues as the following: What are the philosophical foundations of modern political systems? What makes a government legitimate? What is the nature of relations among nations? Who governs, for what ends, and by what means? In addition, political scientists are concerned with who participates in politics, who benefits most from government decisions, who bears the greatest costs, and how these decisions are made.

Most departments of political science in American colleges and universities feature courses grouped into the following subdisciplines: political theory, American government and politics, comparative politics, and international relations. Political theory deals with major concepts, ideas, and values from the ancient Greeks to the contemporary political theorists. They raise fundamental questions about an individual's existence and one's relationship to the political community. American government surveys the origins and development of American government and politics with an emphasis on the Constitution and various political institutions, as well as political processes. Comparative politics focuses on the study of two or more foreign governments, such as a comparative study of democratic societies, the communist governments, or developing nations. International relations studies how nations interact with each other within the framework of law, diplomacy, and international organizations such as the United Nations, the World Bank, and the World Trade Organization.

KEY CONCEPTS IN POLITICS

To better understand politics, one must understand the main concepts related to politics. They are power, influence, authority, and legitimacy. When people have different opinions about what government should or should not do, decision making involves the exercise of power. **Power** is the ability of individuals to control the behavior and actions of others using means ranging from influence to force or coercion. According to Robert Dahl: "A has power over B to the extent that A can get B to do something that B would not otherwise do."[12] Individuals who exercise power must have resources of power. They include wealth, intellectual ability, social status, and charisma.

Influence is the ability to persuade others to accept certain things or behave in certain ways. Bribing, or offering of rewards, is a form of influence. It is free of threat or physical restraint. **Authority** is the right to exercise power. It is the government's power to make binding decisions and to command the obedience of people. Those with authority have power based on a general understanding that they have the right to make decisions, which others must obey. If individuals fail to accept those decisions, the failure is socially unacceptable, because the authority itself is based on a general acceptance of its exercise.[13]

Government's exercise of power involves authority, and there is no limit to the range of activities over which it may exercise authority. Most governments self-impose some limits on their exercise of authority through their constitutions. For instance, the United States Constitution rules out government's exercise of authority over what religion people are to follow. Authority is related to power because the government may back up authority with persuasion or threat of coercion or physical restraint.

The concept of **legitimacy** is very closely related to authority. Legitimacy is defined as general public acceptance of government's right to make and enforce decisions. Legitimacy is a moral or ethical concept which involves a perception of what is right. When authority is based on legitimacy, people feel they have a duty to obey what the government legislates. In other words, governments enjoy legitimacy to the extent that people willingly accept their claim to rule.

Governments may gain and retain legitimacy from their people by providing for them what they want most. This is called **legitimacy by results**. When a particular government exists for a long time, people become accustomed to obeying its laws. This source of legitimacy is **legitimacy by habit**. Another source of legitimacy is **legitimacy by procedures**. The procedures allow citizens to select their leaders and determine the state's policies.[14]

According to the German sociologist Max Weber (1864–1920), governments claim legitimacy based on three main sources: traditional, charismatic, and rational-legal. **Traditional legitimacy** is derived from history and gained through inheritance. During the Middle Ages, feudal relationships between princes and their lords, and between lords and their vassals provided traditional bases of legitimacy. The Saudi and Moroccan monarchies are contemporary examples of traditional legitimacy. Citizen loyalty is to the person in authority. **Charismatic legitimacy** is based on popular admiration of the personal attributes of an individual. For example, people perceived President Gamal Nasser of Egypt (1954–1970) and Mao Zedong of China (1949–1976) as their supermen. Lastly, **rational-legal legitimacy** is based on the electoral process, as in the case of the president of the United States who derives legitimacy from popular election.[15]

Though the elected leader may administratively be a superior to others in the organization, all are equals before the law. The obedience of those in the state or the organization is to the law, not to the personal whims or decisions of the leader.

THE SYSTEMS APPROACH TO POLITICS

Whereas David Easton considers politics to be a system within the larger social environment, Gabriel Almond uses his model to formulate a theory of politics that could be applied to describing actual political systems. A **system** is any combination of interrelated activities that regularly repeat themselves in much the same way. A **political system** is a set of institutions and activities that link government, politics, and public policy. The essence of the systems theory is that the politics of a country can be depicted by the interaction of the political environment with a political system, which processes demands and supports into output. One of the advantages of this model is that it provides a means for understanding how political process takes place in a society. (See Figure 1.1.)

Inputs can be identified as interest articulation, interest aggregation, political recruitment, political socialization, and communications. These are the sources of demands on the political system and support for it. **Demands** refer to actions citizens want government to pursue or reject. These might include demands for better housing or health care or lowering taxes. Interest groups, political parties, and voters casting

FIGURE 1.1 SYSTEMS APPROACH

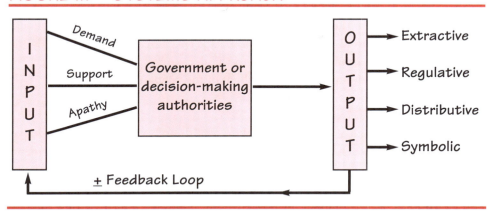

their votes serve as the transmission belts by which demands are fed into the political system so that official decision makers can achieve the needed authoritative allocation of values. Citizens also **support** the system in various ways. These supports would include participating in government, paying taxes, being patriotic, or simply obeying the laws of the state. Moreover, Easton identifies three different levels on which support is given: the political community, the governmental structure, and personnel and policies.

The decision makers are members of government who convert inputs into outputs. In terms of **output**, political systems engage in rule making, rule application, and rule adjudication. Those outputs are the authoritative allocation of values for a society. They use decision as a means of conversion.

These authoritative responses are in the form of extractive, regulative, distributive, and symbolic actions as outputs. **Extractive output** extracts goods, resources, or money from the population. **Regulative output** regulates the behavior of the members of the political system. For example, the decision to install a stop sign at a busy intersection will regulate the driving habits of people. **Distributive output** extracts from one group and gives to another. Social Security is an example of this type of output.

Symbolic output is created for the purpose of being fed back into the system via a feedback loop in order to create a higher level of support or to manage the frequency of demands. Examples include the president lighting the White House Christmas tree or laying a wreath on the tomb of an unknown soldier.

Finally, by **feedback** we mean the impact of the decisions, whether positive or negative, that represent the output of the political system in response to the demands that have been fed into it. The feedback loop helps create new levels of demands and supports. The people can then respond to the decision makers' policies, and the decision makers can alter their policies in light of the people's responses.[16]

Is Politics Inevitable?

Politics would be simple if everyone agreed on who should get what, who should pay for it, and how and when it should be done. But conflict arises from disagreements over these questions. Therefore, politics is inevitable because people do not always agree on the best course of action. Individuals differ in terms of needs, values, abilities, and attitudes. Disagreements follow over moral issues of right or wrong, such as abortion or the death penalty. Individuals may disagree over what problems are the most important to solve. For example, should the federal government spend more money on defense or social programs? In addition, individuals compete for scarce goods and services. Senior citizens want higher Social Security benefits, but workers in their middle twenties would prefer that less money be taken from their paychecks.

People differ on issues because they hold different social values. **Social values** deal with views about what government should do in order to promote the public good. **Public good** is the social choice that represents the best outcome for society as a whole rather than for some subset of the population.

American Ideologies

One's social values determine what kind of ideology that person may embrace. In other words, an important source of preference is ideological in origin. **Ideology** is a coherent set of beliefs guiding people's attitude toward government. In order to make it possible to map ideology in the United States, Thomas Dye has used a two-dimensional framework based on (1) whether people prefer more or less government and (2) whether people prefer government in either social or economic affairs. Four different ideologies emerge from this framework: liberal, conservative, populist, and libertarian.[17] (See Figure 1.2.)

FIGURE 1.2   AMERICAN IDEOLOGIES MAP

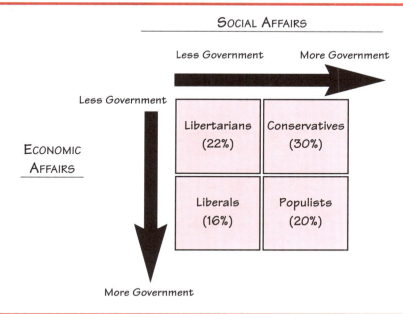

Liberalism

Liberals generally prefer an active, powerful government in economic affairs, but less government to regulate social conduct. Liberals want an active government to regulate business, protect civil rights, and protect consumers and the environment. They oppose government restriction on abortion, school prayer, speech, the press, and protest.

One of the founders of liberalism was Thomas Hobbes (1588–1679). He broke with the notion of using custom and religion as support for political authority and the divine right of the king, and he argued that individuals are rationally capable of forming a government that will protect them from living in a state of nature. Although liberals did not advocate Hobbes' support for absolute political power, they drew heavily on his more general point that government should serve the interests of self-seeking individuals.

John Locke (1632–1704) provided the first coherent and clearly recognizable statement of liberalism. He believed in the natural goodness of man and developed the social **contract theory** of the state. According to this theory, the state gains legitimacy from the consent of the people and government is created to protect individuals' rights to life, liberty, and property.

Contemporary American liberalism is different from what was known in the nineteenth century as classical liberalism. Classical liberals, including Thomas Jefferson and Andrew Jackson, stressed limited government and individualism. They moved into the conservative camp in reaction to the emergence of welfare liberalism, an important strand of contemporary liberalism that advocates increased government intervention in the economy and society.

Modern liberals believe that a strong government is necessary to protect individuals from the inequities of a modern industrial and technological society. They see government as correcting the injustices of the marketplace, not supplanting it.

Conservatism

In contrast, conservatives generally prefer limited governmental involvement in economic affairs and an activist government to regulate social conduct. Conservatives embrace a government that relies on free market to provide and distribute goods and services; keeps taxes low; and minimizes its regulatory activities.

The first modern formulation of the basic tenets of conservative thought is attributed to Edmund Burke (1729–1797). Burke was a leader of the Tories in the English Parliament. These tenets include a belief that there are transcendent values governing society and individual conscience; a conviction that orders and classes are natural developments in any society; a belief that private property is the key to individual freedom; reliance on convention, tradition, and custom as checks on human emotions and rational designs; and suspicion of efforts at reform and change that move too rapidly in the face of social traditions.

Populism

After the American Civil War, farmers suffered through a perpetual economic crisis. Agricultural prices fell and interest rates rose. The targets of liberal reform became railroads and the banks and not the government. Out of this turmoil evolved a new liberal movement known as populism. The populists, who formed their own political party in the 1880s, the **People's Party**, called for further democratization of government through the secret ballot, direct election of senators, and voter initiatives and referenda. They also advocated a strong government to regulate business and provide economic security. In addition, they supported a government to control social conduct. Finally, they believed strongly in tradition, law, and morality in social affairs.

Libertarianism

The political party that espouses libertarian ideology is called the **Libertarian Party**. It was formed by David Nolan in 1971. The Libertarian party's statement of principles begins with this declaration:

> We, the members of the Libertarian Party, challenge the cult of the omnipotent state and defend the rights of the individuals. We hold that all individuals have the right to exercise sole dominion over their own lives, and have the right to live in whatever manner they choose, so long as they do not forcibly interfere with the equal right of others to live in whatever manner they choose.

Libertarians contend that activities of government should be limited—that is, government should not interfere with the free market or promote traditional values. They are against government regulation of the environment, consumer protection laws, and government restriction on abortion. They want to end all subsidies to foreign nations. They favor privatization of many government services, minimal welfare benefits, and low taxes.

WHAT IS GOVERNMENT?

Politics is inevitable because people have different beliefs and opinions on issues. How do we resolve these differences? Peaceful resolution of conflict necessitates the creation of government. **Government** consists of institutions and elected/appointed political officials whose purpose may be to write, enforce, or interpret laws and public policies for a community. At the national level, these institutions are Congress, the president, the courts, and federal administrative agencies or the federal bureaucracy. Key members of the executive and bureaucracy are appointed by the president and confirmed by the Senate of the Congress. In addition, the United States has some 500,000 elected officials, including the president and 535 members of Congress.

Moreover, governments in the United States include the federal government in Washington, 50 state governments, and more than 86,000 local governments. The **goals of government** are to maintain public order, provide goods and services that help the lives of citizens, and protect basic freedoms and liberties. Governmental decisions are different from decisions made by any other institution in at least two ways. First governmental decisions can extend to a large segment of society. Second, the one function that distinguishes the government from all other organizations is its monopoly on the legitimate use of force and coercion in the society.[18] This basically means that people accept the necessity for government to act forcefully.

THE DIFFERENCE BETWEEN GOVERNMENT AND POLITICS

While the words *government* and *politics* are often used interchangeably, government and politics differ. Governments regulate the lives of their citizens. They decide how fast you should drive on the highways, whether you can carry a gun, and whether the parents of a minor must be notified before she has an abortion. On the other hand, politics consists of people acting politically by voting, joining a political party, organizing an interest group, or demonstrating to protest against governmental decisions in order to induce governments to act in ways that will promote their interests over those of their opponents.

Thus, politics is the activity of making decisions about public issues, whereas government is the institution used for making, implementing, and enforcing those decisions.

The Origin of Government

How did governments come into existence? There are at least four alternative theories on the origin of government. **Evolutionary theory** states that government developed as families joined to form clans, which grew into tribes regulated by older males. **Force theory** argues that government originated when strong groups conquered territories and then brought the inhabitants under their control. The third theory on the origin of government is the so-called **divine right**. According to this theory, God gave those of royal birth the unlimited right to govern others. This theory was widely accepted in Europe prior to the eighteenth century. Absolute monarchs claimed to rule as the representatives of God on earth, and as their subjects had to obey the will of God, so they had to obey the will of the sovereign. The last theory, **social contract,** is associated with three European political thinkers: John Locke, Thomas Hobbes, and Jean-Jacques Rousseau. It states that government derives its power from the consent of the people, and government is instituted among people to protect and promote life, liberty, and property.

John Locke and the Social Contract

Among the three, John Locke (1632–1704) is sometimes referred to as the "philosopher of the American Revolution." Locke stated that as a result of the inconvenience of the life in the state of nature, people created a social contract by which they called into being civil society. Once this society was formed, the people then further contracted to create government. Thus, government derived its right to rule from the people (also known as **popular sovereignty**) and not from God (divine right). Government acted to protect people's liberty, especially the right of property. Each citizen was viewed as the recipient of a set of **natural rights**, or **human rights**, owed to that person by the mere fact that the individual was human. Locke called for a limited government that does not infringe on the natural rights of citizens.[19] Natural rights are rights that no person or society can take away.

John Locke provided the first coherent and clearly recognizable statement of liberalism. He believed in the natural goodness of man and developed the contract theory of the state or **social contract**. According to this theory, the state gains legitimacy from the consent of the people, and government is created to protect individuals' rights to life, liberty, and property.

For Americans, the most salient of Locke's ideas are a belief in natural rights, the consent of the governed through the social contract, limited government, the primacy of property rights, and the right to revolt against a repressive government.

These principles are clearly visible in the United States Declaration of Independence of 1776, and they are embodied in the Constitution written in 1787. The Constitution begins with the phrase "We the People," because it is the people who "ordain and establish" the Constitution by their consent. Also, the checks and balances set up by the Constitution are designed to keep the government within limits as much as possible. The Bill of Rights (the first ten amendments to the Constitution) identifies certain individual rights that the government is not allowed to infringe upon.

POLITICAL SOCIALIZATION AND POLITICAL CULTURE

Political Socialization

Whenever a government successfully asserts its claim to rule within a territory, it is said to possess sovereignty. Sovereign states exercise authority; that is, they have the right to exercise power. Moreover, they enjoy legitimacy to the extent that their claim to rule is willingly accepted. A government is legitimate when its citizens believe that they should obey the laws of government, and that its institutions deserve their loyalty. Legitimacy can be given or taken away from an individual politician, government, or country.

Governments work hard to establish legitimacy through **political socialization**, a process by which people acquire their orientation toward the political world. Different institutions are involved in the socialization process. These include one's family, religion, peer group, school, media, and government. They are major sources of political training and indoctrination. For example, American schools teach children that democratic government is good, governmental leaders are legitimate rulers, and citizens should participate in protecting the gains of the Founding Fathers.

Political Culture

Widely shared political values are called political culture. According to Daniel Elazar, three cultures predominate in the United States, each with a regional and ethnic base. The first is the **moralistic political culture**, found in states of the upper Midwest and New England, which are populated by citizens of Scandinavian descent. In this culture, politics is seen as a way of improving life, and people have a strong sense that they should participate. Politics is relatively free of corruption. According to Elazar, "Good government, then, is measured by the degree to which it promotes the public good and in terms of the honesty, selflessness, and commitment of those who govern."[20]

The second type is the **individualistic political culture**, most typical in the Midwest and East, which are populated by descendants of immigrant groups from Eastern and Southern Europe and from Ireland. In these states, the ultimate objective of politics is not so much to create a better public life but rather to get things for yourself and your group. This culture believes that government should perform only limited and essential functions so that individuals can pursue their own private interests. Elazar states that, "The individualistic culture holds politics to be just another means by which individuals may improve themselves socially and economically. In this sense politics is a 'business' like any other that competes for talent and offers rewards to those who take it up as a career."[21]

In the **traditionalistic political culture**, still present in some parts of the South, politics is left to a small elite. Politics is not seen as a way to further the public good but as a way to maintain the status quo. Government's principal function is to preserve that social order and the relative positions of different classes in society. The representatives of the social elite dominate politics. Citizens support conservative ideas, a limited role of government, and a greater orientation by the governing elite to preserve the existing order.

According to Elazar, in some areas, immigration patterns of the twentieth century blurred cultural patterns; a mix of people from all three cultures, for example, populates the West.

How Do Governments Differ?

We can classify governments according to the location of power, who makes decisions, and the way political and economic decisions are made.

Governments Based on Location of Power

The first classification of government will produce three types of government: unitary, federal, and confederal. A **unitary system** concentrates power in the national government. The constituent parts of national government cannot exercise the power independent of national government. They exist to implement decisions made by the national government. In a unitary system, power flows from the national to the constituents. Great Britain, Italy, and France are examples of unitary governments. (See Figure 1.3.)

In a **federal system**, there is division of powers between the national government and member states. The power flows in two directions: from the federal government to its member states and vice versa. For the first time, the federal system was successfully tried in the United States following the adoption of the Constitution in 1788. Other countries with federal systems include Canada, Switzerland, Mexico, Australia, and India. (See Figure 1.3.)

Finally, a **confederal system** is a voluntary association of sovereign states, where major powers belong to member states and the national government has only minor powers. A confederal system is the opposite of a unitary system. Following the adoption of the Articles of the Confederation in 1781, the 13 original states formed a confederal system. Moreover, when the Southern states of America seceded in 1861, they adopted a confederal system. Today, the confederal system only exists at the international organization level (i.e., the United Nations).(See Figure 1.3.)

Governments Based on Who Makes Decisions

We can also distinguish between governments based on who makes decisions. According to this classification, governments fall into two types: authoritarianism and rule by many or democracy. (See Figure 1.4.)

FIGURE 1.3   THE FEDERAL, CONFEDERAL, AND UNITARY SYSTEMS OF GOVERNMENT

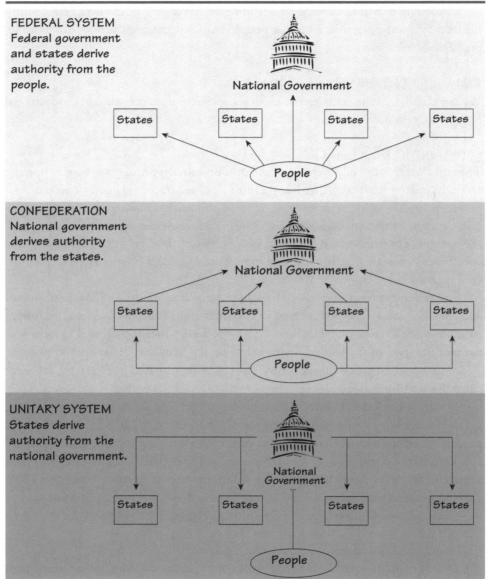

Source: "The Federal, Confederal, and Unitary Systems of Government" from *Politics in America*, 3/e by Thomas Dye. © 1998. Reprinted by permission of Prentice-Hall, Inc., Upper Saddle River, NJ.

Authoritarianism is a system of government in which power rests in the hands of one individual or a few individuals. It rests on the obedience of people rather than their consent. All institutions of government are carefully controlled and censored. Democratic political institutions and processes are banned, and opponents are often imprisoned. An authoritarian government is founded on the basis that its authority does not originate with those over whom it is exercised; instead, some alternative source must be used. These alternative sources of authority include divine right, "might is right," or ancestral lineage. They are divided into two categories: monarchy and dictatorship. Monarchs legitimize their exercise of power through divine right or ancestral lineage. A handful of absolute monarchs are still in existence. Monarchy still prevails in Saudi Arabia, Jordan, and Morocco.

Dictatorship exists where one person or party holds absolute power. Unlike monarchs, dictators do not take on the titles of royalty. They usually use force or "might is right" to acquire power. Dictatorship can be classified into right and left. **Dictatorship of right** seeks to restrict only political aspects of human behavior by not allowing citizens to form opposition groups and political parties. The extreme forms of dictatorship of right are fascism (Benito Mussolini's rule in Italy from 1922 to 1943); and nazism (Adolf Hitler's government in Germany from 1933 to 1945; Imam Khomeini's rule in Iran: 1979 to 1989; and Saddam Hussein's rule in Iraq: 1979 to 2003).

Dictatorship of left is also known as **totalitarianism**. In the totalitarian dictatorship, the ideal leader is glorified. The government seeks to control all aspects of political, social, and economic life. Examples of dictatorships of left are Joseph Stalin's regime in the former Soviet Union from 1928 to 1953 and subsequent regimes until its breakup in December 1991.

A democracy can be classified as direct or indirect. **Direct democracy** (also known as the Athenian model of democracy) allows individuals to make political decisions for themselves. The very term *democracy* is from the Greek *demos*, meaning *people*, and *kratos*, meaning *authority*: democracy is thus rule by the people. Athens of the fifth and fourth centuries B.C. (from 450 B.C. to 350 B.C.) can be described as a democracy. Its democratic institutions consisted of an assembly (the legislature) and a council (the executive). The assembly was made up of only male citizens and the council members (known as the council of five hundred) were chosen by lot from among the male citizens. Athenians thought that if selection was made by vote, the wealthy and well-known candidates would have a better chance of winning an election.

FIGURE 1.4 GOVERNMENTS BASED ON WHO MAKES DECISIONS

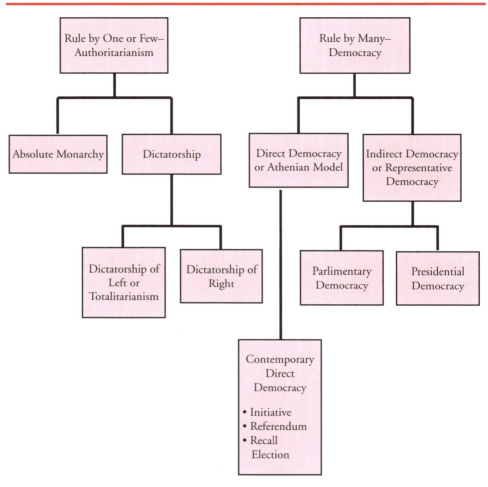

Direct democracy was feasible in Athens because only a limited number of people were qualified to participate in the political process. Slaves, women, and foreigners (those who were not born in Athens but lived there) were not allowed to participate in politics. Therefore, the Athens of classical Greece was quite undemocratic by modern-day standards of democracy. Leon H. Hurwitz argued that, "The Athenian system had the structural facade of democracy but it was not a functional democracy."[22]

Modern examples of Athenian democracy, exercised at local and state levels of government in the United States, include initiative, referendum (or plebiscite), and recall. An **initiative** is a citizen-drafted measure proposed by a number of qualified voters. If approved by popular vote in a **referendum**, it becomes law without government approval. A referendum is a procedure in which a measure is proposed by the government and approved by popular vote. **Recall** is a process for removing elected officials through a popular vote.

At the federal level in the United States, we have *indirect democracy*, known as a **republican** or a **representative democracy**. It is a government that gives individuals the right to elect their representatives, who will then make political decisions on behalf of the voters. The United States has an indirect democracy because in such a large society all citizens cannot assemble and engage in meaningful discussion, debate, and decision making.

The democratic political process is decentralized and flexible. It requires a system of government based on the following principles: majority rule expressed in free, open, competitive, and periodic elections; protection of minority rights against tyranny of majority; guarantee and protection of individual rights to freedom of speech, press, religion, petition, and assembly; and equality before law for all citizens regardless of race, creed, color, gender, or national origin. Democratic systems employ these principles in order to articulate and integrate a wide variety of opinions into decision-making process.

There are two forms of representative democracy: presidential and parliamentary. In a **presidential democracy**, the head of the executive, the president, is elected independent of Congress and is not a member of Congress. In **parliamentary democracy**, the leader of the party with a majority in the parliament will take over the executive branch as the new prime minister. If the incumbent prime minister's party loses a vote on major issues, the prime minister will dissolve the parliament and a new election will take place. (See Figure 1.4.)

Governments Based on Economic Systems

One can classify governments based on their economic systems into capitalism, socialism, and communism or the command economic system.

Capitalism is an economic system in which the major means of production are owned privately and not by the state. The means of production include land, labor, capital, and entrepreneurship. Land includes natural resources. Labor is the productive input of individuals. Capital includes nonhuman productive input, such as financial resources, machinery, and technology. Entrepreneurs are risk takers who have the ability to start a new business or bring a product to the market.

Adam Smith (1723–1790) is the founder of capitalism.[23] Smith argued that the capitalist economy operates according to economic laws that naturally promote prosperity. He likened these laws to an "invisible hand" that guides the self-interested profit motives of individual entrepreneurs into a pattern that produces material benefits for society as a whole. His essential point is that capitalism is based on the principle of **laissez faire** or "let alone," which basically means that there should be a minimum intervention by government in economic affairs. He created an economic system based on free enterprise, free trade, competition, and the pursuit of self-interest or profit that will benefit consumers.

Socialism, also known as democratic socialism, is an economic system in which some major productive resources are owned or controlled by the state. The government owns the nation's transportation, communication, energy, and so forth. (See Table 1.3.) But most means of production are privately owned. The state actively intervenes in the economy in an attempt to attain a high degree of economic equality. Competitive socialist parties have evolved in Germany, France, and the Scandinavian countries. In France and Scandinavia, socialists have won control of governments through the electoral process.

Communism is an economic system based on public ownership of the means of production. The founder of communism is a German economist named Karl Marx (1818–1883).[24] Marx's major works are *The Communist Manifesto* (1848) and *Das Kapital* (1867, 1885, 1894); volumes 2 and 3 were edited by Friedrich Engels and published posthumously. In these books Marx argued that all history has been a class struggle. In each era, one class was pitted against another: master against slave, lord against serf, capitalist against worker—the haves and the have-nots or the **bourgeoisie** and the **proletariat**. Marx argued that the labor of the proletariat was exploited in a capitalist society. Marx gave the name **surplus value** to the difference between the wage paid and the market value of the worker's output. He argued that this difference became the capitalist's profit. Marx predicted that hostilities would build between these two classes until the working class would rise up in a violent revolution. During the transition from capitalism to communism, the working class, using the government, will impose dictatorship of the proletariat.

TABLE 1.3 GOVERNMENT OWNERSHIP OF BASIC INDUSTRIES

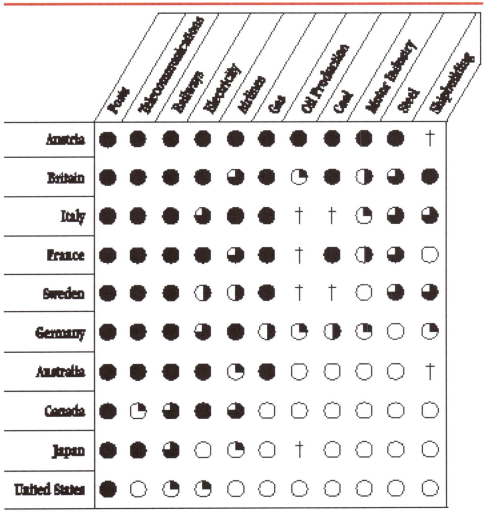

Source: "Frontiers of State" from the article "Privatisation: Everybody's Doing It Differently" in *The Economist*, December 21, 1985, p. 72. © 1985 The Economist Newspaper Group, Inc. Reprinted with permission. Further reproduction prohibited. www.economist.com

The ideal state of communism is based on the slogan "from each according to his ability, to each according to his needs." According to Marx, the end of history will bring triumph of the proletariat over the bourgeoisie, a withering of the state, and the formation of communism—an idealistic, stateless society.

ALTERNATIVE THEORIES OF DEMOCRACY

In order to understand how political conflicts are resolved, we have to determine who governs and for what ends. Over the years, alternative theories have been offered in an attempt to answer this question. These theories include elitism, pluralism, and hyperpluralism.

Elites are those who get most of the values society has available. One of the main proponents of elitism is an American sociologist named C. Wright Mills. He identified three groups that compose the American power elite: the "warlords" in the military establishment, the "corporation chieftains" in the economic sector, and the "political directorate" composed of those in the top positions in the political system. These three groups are the true "power elite" in America. Elite theory assumes the population has little, if any, impact on the decision-making process. Instead of the population making policy through elected officials, elite theorists indicate that all policy decisions are made by the desires of a select few within the society.

Dye and Ziegler summarized the elite theory of decision making as follows:

- Society is divided into the few who have power and the many who do not; only a small number of people allocate values for society; the mass do not decide public policy.
- Elites are drawn disproportionately from the upper socioeconomic strata of society.
- The movement of nonelites to elite positions must be slow and continuous to maintain stability and avoid revolution. Only nonelites who have accepted the basic elite consensus enter governing circles.
- Elites share a consensus on the basic values of the social system and the preservation of the system. They disagree only on a narrow range of issues.
- Public policy does not reflect the demands of masses but the prevailing values of elites. Changes in public policy will be incremental rather than revolutionary.[25]

An alternative approach to understanding who makes decisions in America is also known as **pluralism,** a process whereby policy is influenced by various groups. A **group** is made up of like-minded individuals who interact to pursue a common interest.

Proponents of pluralism argue that power is vested in the hands of a few wealthy but it is reasonably diffused in America. Robert Dahl is strongly associated with the development and defense of pluralism. He has shown that there is never a cohesive, single ruling elite group in the United States. He argues that American politics is that of compromise reached among competing groups with conflicting desires over particular issues. The political process will lead to the political outcome that maximizes everyone's preferences.

Dye and Ziegler state that, "Pluralism, then, is the belief that democratic values can be preserved in a system where multiple, competing elites determine public policy through bargaining and compromise, voters exercise meaningful choices in elections, and new elites can gain access to power."[26]

In recent years, some political scientists and sociologists have argued that hyperpluralism has replaced pluralism. It is pluralism gone sour.[27] **Hyperpluralism** is a situation in which many effective single-issue groups are able to pressure the government to respond to their policy demands. These groups include peace groups, groups on both sides of the abortion issue, environmental groups, etc. Hyperpluralists argue that too many influential groups disable the government, due to the fact that they are so strong that the government is unable to act. According to Edward, when policy makers try to placate many powerful groups, the result is muddled and inconsistent policy. For example, one part of the government can subsidize tobacco farmers while another preaches about the evils of smoking.[28] In short, hyperpluralists argue that groups have become too powerful in the political process as the government attempts to help every existing group, and that this will result in contradictory and confusing policy.

SUMMARY

As a field of study, politics dates back to ancient Greece. Among early scholars of classical Greece were Socrates, Plato, and Aristotle. They considered the *polis*, the city-state, as the perfect community, where one achieves happiness and the good life. Therefore, participation in the *polis* gets to the essence of what it means to be human.

Political science is called science because students of politics use scientific method and empirical analysis to study that aspect of human behavior involving power and authority. Politics is inevitable because people have different preferences, which lead to conflict. The peaceful resolution of conflict necessitates the creation of government. According to John Locke, the primary function of government is to protect and promote life, liberty, and property.

Political scientists offer models to explain how political processes take place in a society. David Easton offers one of those models. He considers politics to be a system whereby input is converted into output by the conversion box. Input is made up of people, output has to do with governmental decisions, and institutions of government occupy the conversion box.

All governments seek legitimacy. To achieve this goal, governments resort to political socialization. It is a process by which people acquire their orientations toward the political world. Widely shared political values are called political culture. Daniel Elazar divides American political culture into moralistic, individualistic, and traditionalistic.

Governments can be classified based on the location of power, who makes decisions, and their economic systems. To understand how we resolve conflicts, we have to determine who governs and for what ends. Both sociologists and political scientists have offered alternative theories of decision making. These theories are elitism, pluralism, and hyperpluralism.

KEY TERMS

- Authoritarianism
- Authority
- Capitalism
- Charismatic legitimacy
- City-State
- Communism
- Confederal system
- Conservatism
- Democracy
- Empirical statements
- Federal System
- Government
- Hyperpluralism
- Ideology
- Influence
- Initiative
- Laissez-faire
- Legitimacy
- Legitimacy by habit
- Legitimacy by procedures
- Legitimacy by results
- Liberalism
- Monarchy
- Normative statements
- Pluralism
- Political culture
- Political Socialization
- Politics

Populism
Power
Rational-legal legitimacy
Recall election
Referendum
Scientific method

Social contract
Social values
Socialism
Traditional legitimacy
Unitary system
Values

INTERNET SOURCES

1. Political Theory:
   http://swift.eng.ox.ac.uk/jdr/index.html
   Information on classical theories of politics can be found in this site, especially major writers whose influence has shaped contemporary political discussion. Examples include ideas of Plato, Aristotle, Machiavelli, and major 19th and 20th century political theories of Marx, Lenin, etc.
2. Political Science Teaching and Research:
   http://www.polmeth.ufl.edu/research.html.
   This University of Florida site has information on political science data sites, research methodologies, political science associations and conferences, government and nongovernmental data sites, academic journals in political science, etc.
3. Major Historical Documents:
   http://infomall.org:80/Showcase/civnet
   Major historical and political documents of international importance, including those of America's founding, can be found in this site. They include commentaries, documents, and resources for important regional and international organizations.

NOTES

[1] Peter H. Merkel, *Political Continuity and Change* (New York: Harper and Row, 1967), p. 13.

[2] Harold Lasswell, *Politics: Who Gets What, When, and How?* (New York: McGraw-Hill, 1936), p. 13.

[3] Leon H. Hurwitz, *Introduction to Politics* (Chicago: Nelson-Hall, 1981), p. 8.

[4] Robert Vavalier, *Plato for Beginners* (New York: Writers and Readers, 1990), p. 128.

[5] Plato, *The Republic* (New York: Oxford University Press, 1968).

[6] Aristotle, *The Politics* (New York: Dover, 1959).

[7] Leon Hurwitz, *Introduction to Politics* (Chicago: Nelson-Hall, 1991), p. 18.

[8] Herbert R. Winter and Thomas J. Bellows, *Conflict and Compromise: An Introduction to Political Science* (HarperCollins, 1992) p. 11.

[9] Steve Kelman, *American Democracy and the Public Good* (Fort Worth, TX: Harcourt Brace, 1996), p. 14.

[10] Anita C. Danker, *The Essentials of Political Science* (New Jersey: Research and Education Association, 1996), pp. 3–4.
[11] James N. Danziger, *Understanding the Political World: A Comparative Introduction to Political Science* (New York: Longman, 1998), pp. 18–20.
[12] Robert Dahl, "The Concept of Power," *Behavioral Science*, 2 (1957): 202–203.
[13] W. Phillips Shiverly, *Power and Choice: An Introduction to Political Science* (New York: McGraw-Haill, 1991), p. 107.
[14] Ibid., pp. 109–112.
[15] Robert J. Jackson and Doreen Jackson, *A Comparative Introduction to Political Science* (Englewood Cliffs, NJ: Prentice Hall, 1997), p. 12.
[16] Herbert R. Winter and Thomas J. Bellows, *Conflict and Compromise: An Introduction to Political Science* (New York: HarperCollins, 1992), pp. 24–36.
[17] Thomas Dye, Tucker Gibson, and Clay Robinson, *Politics in America* (Englewood Cliffs, NJ: Prentice Hall, 1997), p. 50.
[18] Ibid., pp. 4–5.
[19] Robert Heineman et al., *American Government* (New York: McGraw-Hill, 1995), p 22.
[20] Daniel Elazar, *American Federalism: A View from the States* (New York: Harper & Row, 1984), p. 117.
[21] Ibid., p. 115.
[22] Leon H. Hurwitz, *Introduction to Politics* (Chicago: Nelson-Hall, 1981), p. 9.
[23] Adam Smith, *An Inquiry into the Nature and Causes of the Wealth of Nations* (London: Methuen, 1961).
[24] Karl Marx and Friedrich Engels, *The Communist Manifesto* (New York: Penguin, 1985).
[25] Thomas Dye and Harmon Ziegler, *The Irony of Democracy* (Belmont, CA: Wadsworth, 1993), p. 5.
[26] Ibid., p. 11.
[27] George C. Edward, et al., *Government in America* (New York: Longman, 1997), p. 7.
[28] Ibid.

Chapter 2

Foundation of American Government and Politics

If men were angels, no government would be necessary. If angels were to govern men, neither external nor internal controls on government would be necessary. In framing a government which is to be administered by men over men, the great difficulty lies in this: You must first enable the government to control the governed; and in the next place, oblige it to control itself. A dependence on the people is no doubt the primary control on the government; but experience has taught mankind the necessity of auxiliary precautions.

—James Madison in The Federalist No. 51

INTRODUCTION

Because men are not angels, government is a necessity. We need government to keep the peace and to provide for the common good. However, there must be limits on the government's power. Government must not interfere unnecessarily in the lives of its citizens. According to Madison, "a dependence on the people is…the primary control on the government; but experience has taught mankind the necessity of auxiliary precautions." American citizens have a contract with the government that spells out its rights and responsibilities; and the government, in turn, protects the citizens' rights. That contract is the U.S. Constitution. A **constitution** establishes the framework of a government, its powers, and enumerates the rights of the people. This chapter focuses on events leading to the Declaration of Independence and the creation of the first constitution among the 13 newly independent states. It ends with a detailed discussion of the United States Constitution.

BRITAIN AND COLONIAL AMERICA

America began as a British colony governed by a distant ruler. Britain established the first permanent settlement and the first colony in 1607. The town was called Jamestown and the colony was named Virginia—formed by the Virginia Company of the London stock company. The British king granted the supporters of the colony a charter giving them "full power and authority" to make laws "for the good and welfare" of the settlement.

By and large, the colonists were relatively happy to be affiliated with Britain because it brought them prosperity. Britain also granted them some degree of autonomy. For years the colonists thought of themselves as British citizens who lived across the ocean from the mother country. But things changed. Several factors brought the colonial citizens' identity crisis to a head in the mid-1700s: an emerging sense of a continental community, the concept of republicanism, and heavy British regulation of the colonists.[1]

A Continental Community

At first the colonists felt like British citizens abroad in a new country that would be, literally, New England. They built communities, churches, homes, farms, and conducted business together. They built a new country together and over time (1600–1750s) their attitudes about their identities changed. No longer did they feel like British citizens born on American soil, but like American citizens born on American soil. This subtle shift occurred over decades and had an incredible impact on the future of the colonies.

During the **Seven Years' War** (1756–1763)—known in North America as the French and Indian War—and the fight for western expansion, the colonists began to see themselves as different from the British.[2] British soldiers considered the colonial soldiers "riff-raff," and the colonial soldiers considered their countrymen to be lewd and cruel.[3] The dislike of the British soldiers created a sense of colonial identity and heightened thefeeling that the colonists were different from the British.

In the 1750s, the colonial newspapers began to focus more on intercolonial affairs, in part because people wanted coverage of the Seven Years War. It was during this period that newspapers began using the term "Americans" to denote the colonists' common identity and to distinguish them from the British.[4] Living together for decades and fighting together in war gave the colonists a separate sense of identity. They were now different from the British; they were Americans.

Republicanism

At about the same time the colonists were discovering that they were more American than British, several European philosophers and writers were discussing the role of government. Two writers in particular had a profound impact on the future of the colonies: John Locke and Thomas Paine.

These philosophers were staunch opponents of absolute monarchy and in favor of republicanism. Whereas an absolute monarch, like King George III, enjoyed personal authority over his subjects and ruled his realm as his personal possession, citizens for the common good conducted government in a republic.

John Locke is known as the philosopher of the American Revolution. He is also regarded as the early theorist of republicanism and democracy. Locke stated that by nature human beings are equal and therefore nothing can put anyone under authority of anybody else except by his own consent. He argued that government derives its right to govern from the people. Thus, the ultimate source of power is the people. People institute government among themselves in order to protect their lives, liberties, and property.

Thomas Paine (1737–1809), who immigrated to America in 1775, wrote an anonymous pamphlet entitled "Common Sense" in January 1776. The pamphlet helped crystallize the idea of a revolution for the colonists. It denounced King George and the British rule of the colonies. The pamphlet, which sold more than 120,000 copies, called the king a "royal brute" and advocated independence for the colonies. Paine stated that, "We have it in our power to begin the world over again…the birthday of a new world is at hand."[5]

Regulation

In the 1760s, the British government began passing legislation that required increased taxation of the colonists in order to boost governmental revenues to pay for the cost of war and administering the colonies. The colonists considered those pieces of legislation to be unfair. For example, the **Sugar Act** of 1764 placed a costly duty on imported sugar and increased the jurisdiction of some courts wherein no presumption of innocence existed nor the right to a jury trial.[6] The **Stamp Act** of 1765 called for a tax on all paper; the **Declaratory Act** of 1766 granted the British parliament the authority to make laws binding on the colonies in all cases; the **Townsend Revenue Act** placed an import duty on lead, glass, paper, and tea; the **Tea Act** granted a monopoly on all tea imports to the British East India Company; and a series of acts known as the **Intolerable Acts** of 1774 closed the Boston Harbor, protected British officials by sending them home for trial if arrested, and legalized the housing of British troops in private homes.[7]

The colonists, tired of "taxation without representation" and rule by what they now regarded as a foreign government, were encouraged by the words of Locke and Paine, and decided it was time for independence. (See Table 2.1.)

TABLE 2.1 EVENTS LEADING TO THE CREATION OF AMERICA

Event	Date
Mayflower Compact	1620
King George III assumed the throne of England	1760
Stamp Act passed by Parliament	1765
Stamp Act repealed	1766
Townsend Acts; colonists boycott tea	1767
First Committee of Correspondence formed	1772
Tea Act; Boston Tea Party	1773
Coercive or Intolerable Acts; First Continental Congress convened	1774
Fighting breaks out at Lexington and Concord	1775
Declaration of Independence	1776
Articles of Confederation	1781
Treaty of Paris, British recognizes U.S. independence	1783
Constitutional Convention	1787
Constitution ratified	1788
Washington inaugurated	1789

THE DECISION FOR INDEPENDENCE

In the fall of 1774, 66 delegates from 12 colonies (Georgia was not represented) met in Philadelphia. The meeting is referred to as the **First Continental Congress**. They passed the **Declaration of Resolves**, which denounced British rule as violating the rights of the colonists. In addition, the delegates drafted a petition to the king that explained the feelings of the colonists. The petition became known as the **Declaration**

of the Rights and Grievances. The Congress decided to boycott all trade with Britain. They also recommended that each state should consider raising and supporting an army. The delegates also voted to meet again in May of 1775 if the British king did not address the colonies' grievances.

Meanwhile, on April 19, 1775, the first shots were fired at Lexington and Concord in Massachusetts between the Minutemen (colonial militia trained to respond at a moment's notice) and the British soldiers (the Redcoats). In 1776, the **Second Continental Congress**, comprised of delegates from the colonies, met to decide the fate of the emerging nation.

On June 7, 1776, Richard Henry Lee, a delegate from Virginia, rose on the floor of Continental Congress and introduced a resolution of independence: "Resolve, that these United Colonies are, and of right ought to be, free and independent states, and that they are absolved from all allegiance to the British Crown, and that all connection between them and the state of Great Britain is, and ought to be, totally dissolved." Richard Henry Lee's resolution of independence was unanimously approved and a committee was selected to draft the Declaration of Independence.

The Declaration of Independence

The committee selected to draft the Declaration of Independence was made up of John Adams, Ben Franklin, Thomas Jefferson, Robert Livingston, and Roger Sherman. Thomas Jefferson wrote and presented his draft to the committee, who recommended minor changes and forwarded it to the Continental Congress. On the evening of July 4, 1776, the Declaration of Independence, which explained the act of independence, was adopted.

The Declaration of Independence is considered an outstanding American contribution to political philosophy. It is also a revolutionary document because it talks about inalienable rights of individuals at the time when Europe was dominated by monarchy and individuals were considered not citizens but subjects.

The document contains five major sections. (See Appendix A.) The introduction explains why it was necessary to declare independence; Section 2 deals with principles for government; the third lists the wrongs suffered by the colonies at the hand of King George III; the fourth section expresses regrets that the British king had not supported Americans in their efforts toward a peaceful resolution of conflict in order to avoid separation; and the last section announces the creation of a new government for the colonies.

The second part of the document is the most important part. It spells out four significant principles about government: (1) all people are created equal and have certain inalienable rights: "We hold these truths to be self-evident, that all men are created equal, that they are endowed by their Creator with certain unalienable rights, that among these are life, liberty, and the pursuit of happiness"; (2) the purpose of government is to safeguard these inalienable rights; (3) the right of government to rule comes from the people; and (4) the people have the right to change their government.

These four principles about government are based on Locke's ideas in his book, *Two Treatises on Civil Government* (1690). It is for this reason that Locke is considered the philosopher of American Revolution.

The Articles of Confederation

The first document to govern the new nation was the **Articles of Confederation**, adopted by the Continental Congress in 1777, and reflected the nation's fear of a monarchy. It established a **confederal system** of government, which lasted until 1787. A confederal system is a voluntary association of independent states where a national government derives authority from the states. In other words, major powers are vested in the state governments and minor powers are exercised by the national government. (See Figure 1.3 on page 20.)

The Articles of Confederation provided for no central government or executive branch and created a national Congress wherein each state had one vote. The Congress handled the administrative duties of government but could not tax citizens or forbid states from coining their own money, and each state was guaranteed sovereignty.[8] It established 13 independent states that were loosely overseen by a national Congress of limited power. In essence, there were 13 little countries.

This system of governing proved to be unworkable because the states controlled all major powers: the army, taxation, and commerce. In 1787, delegates from 12 of the 13 states convened a **Constitutional Convention**. The delegates had to decide how to establish the power structure of the United States.

The Constitutional Convention of 1787

The Constitutional Convention began its work on May 25, 1787, in Philadelphia. All states, except Rhode Island, sent delegates. Most of the delegates were convinced that it would be impossible to improve the Articles of Confederation by revising it. They therefore voted to draw up a new plan of government. For this reason, the meeting at Philadelphia became known as the Constitutional Convention.

George Washington Speaking at the Constitutional Convention

© CORBIS

The framers had to decide how to establish a workable government: who would be in charge, what type of representative system would be best, what court system would they adopt, and what would be the limitations on this new government.

MAJOR AGREEMENTS AND DISAGREEMENTS

All the delegates agreed on certain basic issues. They favored the idea of limited and representative government. They agreed that the new government should be based on the separation of powers—that is, executive, legislative, and judicial branches. They also agreed that it was necessary to increase powers of the national government at the state's expense. Furthermore, the founders embraced the Lockean principles for government.

Whereas there was near unanimity that a strong national government was necessary, there was less agreement about the structure of such a government. The convention faced a deadlock over several key questions. The first was representation. Should Congress be based on population or should each state be equally represented?

After an extensive debate, two distinct views emerged: the position of the large and populous versus that of smaller states.

The Virginia and New Jersey Plans

The Virginia plan, proposed by **James Madison**, called for a strong national government that would have a bicameral legislature based on population.[9] This new national government would supersede the state governments. The **New Jersey plan** also called for a strong national government but demanded a unicameral legislature comprised of one representative from each state. The point of contention was representation. Small states feared that the Virginia plan, which based representation on population, would leave them underrepresented. After much debate an agreement, called the Great Compromise (or the **Connecticut Compromise**), was reached.

The **Great Compromise** created a bicameral legislature where representation in the House is based on population and that of the Senate on equal bases. Members of the Senate were originally elected by state legislatures. The Seventeenth Amendment to the Constitution later changed this practice; it provides that the Senate shall be composed of two senators from each state elected by the people.

Slavery

Another controversy involved the North and South over the issue of slavery. The U.S. Constitution does deal directly with the issue of slavery. A significant portion of Americans, at that time, owned slaves, and outlawing slavery would have been a controversy that might hinder ratification of the document. The critical question hinged on the proportion of the slaves to be counted in order to determine population for the purpose of representation in the U.S. House. It was decided that slaves would not count as an entire person but rather would count as **three-fifths** of a free person when establishing the population of a state. In addition, Article 1, Section 9, of the Constitution forbids Congress from prohibiting importation of slaves until 1808. The **three-fifths** clause and Article I, Section 9, of the Constitution represent a compromise between the proponents and detractors of slavery.

Ratification

For the new constitution to go into effect, nine out of the 13 states, through special state conventions, had to ratify it. The political debate over ratification lasted until May 29, 1790, when Rhode Island finally approved the Constitution. It, however, actually went into effect on June 21, 1788, when New Hampshire became the ninth state to ratify it. (See Table 2.2.)

TABLE 2.2 RATIFICATION OF THE CONSTITUTION

State and Date	Accept	Reject
Delaware, December 7, 1787	30	0
Pennsylvania, December 12, 1787	46	23
New Jersey, December 18, 1787	38	0
Georgia, January 2, 1788	26	0
Connecticut, January 9, 1788	128	40
Massachusetts, February 6, 1788	187	168
Maryland, April 23, 1788	63	11
South Carolina, May 23, 1788	149	73
New Hampshire, June 21, 1788	57	47
Virginia, June 25, 1788	89	79
New York, July, 26, 1788	30	27
North Carolina, November 27, 1789	194	77
Rhode Island, May 29, 1790	34	32

The Struggle for Ratification

Two organized groups emerged during the ratification of the Constitution: The Federalists and Anti-Federalists. Those who favored ratification of the Constitution referred to themselves as the **Federalists** (advocates of a strong centralized government). They labeled their opponents **Anti-Federalists**. The Anti-Federalists criticized the Constitution for having been drafted in secrecy. They claimed that the document was extralegal, because the convention was authorized only to revise the Articles of Confederation. They further argued that the Constitution took important powers from the states.

The Anti-Federalists' strongest argument, however, was that the Constitution lacked a Bill of Rights without which, they warned, might result in a strong national government that could take away the people's rights. Thus, they demanded a Bill of Rights.

The Federalists, conversely, argued that without a strong national government, anarchy would triumph. They claimed that only a strong national government could protect the country and solve its internal problems. To gain the necessary support, however, the Federalists promised to add a Bill of Rights to the Constitution as the first order of the business under a new government. With such assurance, the Anti-Federalists withdrew their opposition from ratification of the Constitution.

THE FEDERALIST PAPERS

To help win ratification of the Constitution, Alexander Hamilton, James Madison, and John Jay published a total of 85 newspaper articles, under the pen name "**Publius**," or public citizen. A collection of the entire articles is referred to as **The Federalist Papers** and is considered a significant political document in American history, after the Declaration of Independence and the Constitution. Not only did it help to ratify the Constitution, but it is also regarded as the best single commentary and an authoritative explanation of the Constitution. Among Madison's Federalist Papers, numbers 10 and 51 are considered classic political theory documents.

Federal Papers Numbers 10 and 51

Although Alexander Hamilton wrote most of the Federalist Papers, Madison wrote the two most famous articles, numbers 10 and 51 (see Appendix A). *Federalist Paper Number 10* addresses the problem of **factions,** groups of people pursuing benefits for themselves at the expense of other citizens. James Madison raises the question of whether or not people can be talked out of joining factions. No, he answers, for factions are "sown in the nature of man." Humans have a natural lust for domination, an urge to "vex and oppress" each other.

Madison argues that one cannot eliminate the cause of factions, at least not without destroying liberty, but we can control their effects. Here the solution is to have a republic large enough to contain a wide variety of factions; the competition among factions will prevent any single one from taking control.

In *Federalist Paper Number 51*, Madison discusses another means of controlling factions: **checks and balances**. Derived from the writings of the French philosopher, Baron de Montesquieu, checks and balances were designed to protect liberty by keeping branches of government in competition with one another. Government should be divided into three separate branches and each branch should be given partial control over the others.

According to Madison in *Federalist 51*, "If men were angels, no government would be necessary. If angels were to govern men, neither external nor internal control on government would be necessary." Since neither men nor government officials are angels, the difficulty in framing the government lies in "how to enable the government to control the governed, and how to oblige the government to control itself." Madison stated that both difficulties had been solved by the constitutional principles of separation of powers and checks and balances. Based on these two principles, each of the branches of government has its own responsibilities and each branch holds some control over the other two branches—both will permit the existence of freedom and a strong republican government.

A New Constitution

By June 21, 1788, the required nine states had ratified the new Constitution, but the crucial states of New York and Virginia still held out. They gave their approval the following month. North Carolina and Rhode Island, the last two states to ratify, did so within 15 months.

The U.S. Constitution is the world's oldest written and surviving constitution. It was written for a nation with only a few million people. More than 200 years later, it still serves as the basic law for a nation of about 285 million people. A **constitution** is a fundamental contract that establishes the rules of the political game of government. It assigns the powers and duties of governmental agencies and establishes relationship between the people and their government.

The Structure of the U.S. Constitution

The Constitution consists of three major parts: a preamble, seven articles, and 27 amendments. (See Appendix A.)

Preamble

The preamble sets forth the general purposes of American government: to form a more perfect union, establish justice, insure domestic tranquility, provide for common defense, promote the general welfare, and to secure the blessings of liberty to ourselves and posterity.

The Constitution attempted to form "a more perfect union" by establishing a federal system of government. To "establish justice," the Constitution created a Supreme Court and gave Congress the power to establish a federal court system. To "insure domestic tranquility," the government tries to create a safe environment, to protect people's rights, and provide aid when natural disasters occur. On an international level, the government spends billions of dollars on American military to "provide for the common defense." Finally, the government has created entitlement programs in order to "promote the general welfare."

THE ARTICLES

The seven articles in the Constitution are as follows.

Article I: The Legislature

Article I of the constitution establishes the U.S. Congress: the House of Representatives and the Senate. Article I, Section 2, lists the qualifications for House membership and states that the House "shall have the sole power of impeachment," which means that the House is responsible for drafting articles of impeachment. Article I, Section 3, establishes the qualifications for membership in the U.S. Senate and grants it the "sole power to try all impeachments" after the House drafts the articles. Section 7 discusses the process of how a bill becomes a law and grants the House the exclusive power of introducing appropriations bills.

Article I, Section 8, lists the powers of Congress. Among these are the **enumerated or delegated powers**, which enable the U.S. Congress to lay and collect taxes, coin money, and regulate interstate commerce. The last paragraph of Section 8 states that Congress shall have the power to "make all laws necessary and proper for carrying into execution the foregoing powers." This is called the elastic or necessary and proper clause because it expands the enumerated powers of Congress and gives rise to the concept of **implied powers**.

Article I, Section 9, lists the things that Congress is prohibited from doing: abolishing slavery (at least until 1808), granting titles of nobility, passing **bills of attainder** (legislative punishment without a trial), or passing *ex post facto*—or, after the fact—laws. Article I, Section 10, lists the things forbidden to the states: coining money, keeping troops in times of peace, or entering into treaties.

Article II: The Executive

Article II establishes the executive branch of the government; the qualifications for the office of the president, and presidential duties. Section 1 of Article II vests the executive power of the United States in a president who shall serve four-year terms and discusses the method of electing the president. Section 1 provides that if the president vacates the office, the vice president shall become the president. It also provides that the president take an oath of office and states the oath, which is still used today: "I do solemnly swear (or affirm) that I will faithfully execute the Office of President of the United States, and will to the best of my ability, preserve, protect and defend the Constitution of the United States."

Article II, Section 2, provides for presidential power: serving as commander in chief of the armed forces, granting reprieves and pardons for offenses against the United States, making treaties with advice and consent of the Senate, and appointing ambassadors and judges to the Supreme Court also with advice and consent of the Senate. Section 3 requires that the president from time to time give a state of the union address to Congress and that the president shall "take care that the laws be faithfully executed."

Article II, Section 4, provides that the president, vice president, and all civil officers of the United States can be removed from office by impeachment proceedings for "treason, bribery, or other high crimes and misdemeanors."

Article III: The Judiciary

Article III creates the judicial branch of the U.S. government. Section 1 provides that judicial power of the United States "shall be vested in one Supreme Court, and in such inferior courts as the Congress may from time to time, ordain and establish," thus establishing the Supreme Court and laying the groundwork for the federal court system. It also provides that the Supreme Court and other federal court judges hold their office for life ("during good behavior").

Section 2 of Article III establishes the jurisdiction of the Supreme Court and states that trials of all crimes, except in cases of impeachment, shall be by jury. Section 3 discusses the crime of treason.

Articles IV through VII

Article IV, Section 1, requires that states grant **full faith and credit** to other states' legal proceedings, and Section 2 provides that citizens of each state shall be entitled to the same treatment or **privileges and immunities** of citizens of the several states. Section 3 discusses the admission of states into the union, and in Section 4 the United States guarantees to all states protection from invasion and promises a republican form of government.

Article V establishes procedures for proposing and ratifying amendments to the U.S. Constitution. Article VI declares that the U.S. Constitution and all laws made in pursuance thereof are the supreme law of the land otherwise referred to as the supremacy clause and that judges in every state shall be bound thereby. Article VII provides that nine states shall be necessary to ratify the Constitution.

THE AMENDMENTS

Once the Constitution was ratified, the newly elected Congress convened in 1789 and proposed a bill of rights, made up of twelve proposed amendments. Two of the 12 amendments, one enlarging the House of Representatives and the other preventing the members of Congress from raising their own salaries, were not ratified. The latter was eventually ratified in 1992 as the Twenty-Seventh Amendment. The Constitution has been amended 27 times.

The First Amendment

The First Amendment provides for freedom of religion, speech, press, and assembly.

"Congress shall make no law respecting an establishment of religion, or prohibit the free exercise thereof." Congress cannot sanction an official church of the United States or pass laws that elevate the status of one religion over another. The government cannot prohibit citizens from practicing the religion of their choice or pass legislation that would have the same effect.

"Congress shall make no law abridging the freedom of speech." The government cannot pass legislation that has the effect of infringing on free speech. However, speech is not entirely unregulated. Certain types of speech can be outlawed, limited or punished, such as obscene speech, libel, slander, and speech that incites imminent lawless action that is likely to succeed (*Brandenberg v. Ohio*, 395 U.S. 444, 1969).

"Congress shall make no law abridging freedom of the press." The press enjoys tremendous freedom from regulation with very few exceptions. A free press serves as a check on the government.

"Congress shall make no law abridging the right of the people to peaceably assemble, and to petition the Government for a redress of grievances." Citizens enjoy the right to gather together to discuss public policy or the government, to protest, and to complain to the government when necessary. The right to assemble also allows for freedom of association. People can form organizations and join organizations without interference from the government.

The Second Amendment

The federal government may not infringe on a citizen's right to bear arms. However, this amendment has not been incorporated to the states. Thus, states are not prevented from enacting gun control legislation.[10]

The Third Amendment
This amendment prohibits the federal government from housing soldiers in private homes without consent, a practice that occurred with some regularity when the colonies were under British rule.

The Fourth Amendment
Citizens are free from government invasion into their homes, bodies, and belongings unless the government can show a reason for such an intrusion. The Fourth Amendment protects citizens from unreasonable searches and seizures, not from all intrusion, and the government defines what constitutes a reasonable search.

A search warrant must be supported by facts showing that a crime has likely occurred (probable cause) and describing in detail the place to be searched and the things to be seized. This is to protect the citizen from unreasonable government intrusion. In England, the government could issue a general warrant calling for a citizen's arrest and/or search that stated no particular reason for the intrusion. The key phrase in the Fourth Amendment is "unreasonable." This is defined by federal statutes and case law and is constantly changing.

The Fifth Amendment
The first part of the Fifth Amendment regarding indictments has not been incorporated to apply to the states. In federal courts the formal charging instrument is an indictment by a grand jury. This amendment prohibits the government from trying a person for the same crime twice (double jeopardy). However, a person may be held to answer for an alleged violation of the law in both civil and criminal court without violating the double jeopardy prohibition.

The Fifth Amendment also prohibits government from compelling a person to testify in one's own case (ban against self-incrimination), prohibits the federal government from denying a person due process, and provides for compensation to citizens if the government takes private property for public use (eminent domain).

The Sixth Amendment
The Sixth Amendment provides for a speedy and public trial in all criminal prosecutions by a neutral jury within the state and county where the alleged crime occurred. The amendment also provides that the accused shall be informed of the charges against him or her and be allowed to confront witnesses and compel them for the defense (subpoena). The Sixth Amendment also provides that the accused in

a criminal case shall have the right to the assistance of an attorney for his or her defense.

The Seventh Amendment
This amendment provides for jury trials in some federal civil cases.

The Eighth Amendment
The Eighth Amendment prohibits the government from inflicting cruel and unusual punishment. The Eighth Amendment also prohibits the federal government from imposing excessive bail or excessive fines and punishment.

The Ninth Amendment
This amendment states that the listing of rights in the aforementioned amendments does not preclude the existence of other rights retained by the people. In other words, the Bill of Rights is not an exhaustive list of the rights of mankind.

The Tenth Amendment
The Tenth Amendment provides for reserved powers of the states. Power that is not granted to the United States nor denied to the states shall be reserved for the states or to the people.

The Eleventh Amendment (1795)
The Eleventh Amendment bars federal suits against states by citizens of other states or of foreign countries.[11]

The Twelfth Amendment (1804)
The Twelfth Amendment alters the manner by which the president and vice president are selected in the Electoral College. Based on this amendment, members of the Electoral College are given two ballots, one to cast a vote for the president and another to cast a vote for the vice president.

The Thirteenth Amendment (1865)
Section 1 of the Thirteenth Amendment abolishes slavery in the United States and Section 2 provides Congress with the power to enforce the amendment with appropriate legislation.

The Fourteenth Amendment (1868)
Section 1 of the Fourteenth Amendment provides that all persons born or naturalized in the United States are citizens, thus granting citizenship to the former slaves. Section 1 forbids the states from making or enforcing laws that abridge the privileges and immunities of citizens of the United States. The Fourteenth Amendment also prohibits states from denying any person life, liberty, or property without due process and prohibits the states from denying equal protection of the laws to any person.

The Fifteenth Amendment (1870)
The Fifteenth Amendment states that the right to vote shall not be denied on the basis of race, color, or previous condition of servitude (slavery), thus granting male African American citizens the right to vote.

The Sixteenth Amendment (1913)
The Sixteenth Amendment establishes the federal income tax, granting Congress the power to lay and collect taxes on income "from whatever source derived."

The Seventeenth Amendment (1913)
This amendment changes the manner in which U.S. senators are elected. The Seventeenth Amendment requires that the people, not the state legislatures, elect two senators from each state.

The Eighteenth and Twenty-First Amendments (1919 and 1931)
The Eighteenth Amendment, ushered in the era of prohibition, which outlawed the manufacture, sale, or transportation of intoxicating liquor. The Twenty-First Amendment repealed the Eighteenth Amendment.

The Nineteenth Amendment (1920)
The Nineteenth Amendment expands suffrage to include women, stating that the right to vote shall not be denied on account of sex (gender).

The Twentieth Amendment (1933)
The Twentieth Amendment establishes the beginning and ending of terms of office for the U.S. Congress and the president.

The Twenty-Second Amendment (1951)
This amendment sets a two-term limit on the office of the president.

The Twenty-Third Amendment (1961)
The Twenty-Third Amendment allows the District of Columbia electoral votes for the election of president.

The Twenty-Fourth Amendment (1964)
The Twenty-Fourth Amendment bans the use of a poll tax. A poll tax was a fee required by some states before a person could vote.

The Twenty-Fifth Amendment (1967)
This amendment establishes the rules of presidential succession and provides for instances when the resident may become unable to fulfill the duties of office due to disability.

The Twenty-Sixth Amendment (1971)
The Twenty-Sixth Amendment lowers voting age from 21 to 18.

The Twenty-Seventh Amendment (1992)
The Twenty-Seventh Amendment was proposed in 1789 and ratified in 1992, 203 years later. It provides that Congress cannot vote themselves raises in salary that take effect immediately.[12]

SUMMARY
Britain was the first power to colonize America. At first, the colonists felt like British citizens abroad in a new country that would be like a New England. Over the years, American attitudes about their identities changed. Several factors brought the colonial citizens' identity crisis to a head in the mid-1700s, including an emerging sense of a continental community, the concept of republicanism, and heavy British regulation of the colonists.

    The colonists, tired of "taxation without representation," and rule by what was now a foreign government, were encouraged by the writings of Locke and Paine. They declared independence and adopted the Articles of Confederation, which, however, proved unworkable. In 1788, a new constitution was established.

    The framers of the U.S. Constitution created a living document that is adaptable and can thus govern a nation for centuries. The document has to be flexible to keep up with the changing times. In 1787, for instance, it was generally accepted that only white males had voting rights. Subsequent amendments extended suffrage to other groups of Americans when the public demanded change.

KEY TERMS

Anti-Federalist
Articles of Confederation
Checks and balances
Constitution
Constitutional Convention
Declaration of Resolves
Declaration of Rights and Grievances
Declaratory Act of 1766
Delegated power
Federalist
First Continental Congress

Great compromise
Implied Power
Intolerable Acts
Publius
Second Continental Congress
Separation of powers
Stamp Act of 1765
Sugar Act of 1764
Supremacy Clause
Tea Act
Townsend Revenue Act

INTERNET SOURCES

1. Historical Documents:
   a) http://www.nara.gov/
   This site, created by the National Achieves and Records Administration, contains the Declaration of Independence. Other links in this site include such other major historical documents as the U.S. Constitution and debates that occurred when they were written.
   b) http://www.loc.gov
   This Library of Congress site is home to major historical documents such as the Declaration of Independence, the U.S. Constitution, Bill of Rights, etc. and debates associated with their writing.
   c) http://law.house.gov/1.htm
   The U.S. House of Representatives' Internet Law Library maintains this site. It's an excellent source for early American historical documents, especially the Declaration of Independence, Federalist Papers, etc.
   d) http://earlyamerican.com/review/index.html
   The history of 18th century America is maintained in this site. Major political, economic, and social events that took place during this period are detailed in this site.
   e) http://www.let.rug.nl/welling/usa/revolution.html

This site, maintained by the United States Information Agency, contains discussions of major historical events and biographies of those who shaped and influenced them.

NOTES

[1] John M. Faragher et al., *Out of Many: A History of the American People*, 2nd ed. (Englewood Cliffs, NJ: Prentice Hall, 1997), pp. 152–153.

[2] Ibid., p. 152.

[3] Ibid.

[4] Ibid.

[5] Robert A. Devin et al., *America Past and Present*, 2nd ed. (New York: Scott Foresman, 1987), pp. 134–135.

[6] Faragher, *Out of Many*, p. 154

[7] Ibid., p. 162

[8] Steven Kelman, *American Democracy and the Public Good* (Fort Worth, TX: Harcourt Brace, 1996), p. 46, and Faragher, *Out of Many*, p. 188.

[9] Kelman, *American Democracy*, p. 52.

[10] Jethro K. Lieberman, *The Evolving Constitution: How the Supreme Court Has Ruled on Issues from Abortion to Zoning*, (New York: Random House, 1992), p. 477.

[11] Ibid., p. 177.

[12] Ibid., p. 550.

Chapter 3

Federalism

The proposed Constitution, therefore, is, in strictness, neither a unitary nor a confederal, but a composition of both.

—James Madison

INTRODUCTION

Federalism is a system of government in which power is distributed among levels of government within the same geographic territory. In framing the Constitution, the founders were influenced by their experiences with the unitary system of England as well as the confederal system of the Articles of Confederation. They felt that the unitary system was the ideal environment for a tyrant to impose unfair, arbitrary, and capricious policies on a powerless people. They also reasoned that confederation, a system of government in which power is concentrated at the state level, created the ideal environment for a tyrannical majority to impose unjust, arbitrary, and harmful policies on unpopular minorities. To avoid the problems associated with the unitary and confederal systems of government, the framers of the United States Constitution adopted federalism.

This chapter sets forth the constitutional framework of American federalism by closely examining the distribution of powers and the relationships that have evolved overtime within the federal system. Furthermore, it discusses different types of grants that the federal government gives to the states and localities. The chapter concludes with a brief discussion of the advantages and disadvantages of American federalism.

CONSTITUTIONAL FRAMEWORK

Federalism relates to the division of powers among the three levels of government: federal, state and local. (See Figure 3.1.)

FIGURE 3.1 POWERS GRANTED BY THE CONSTITUTION

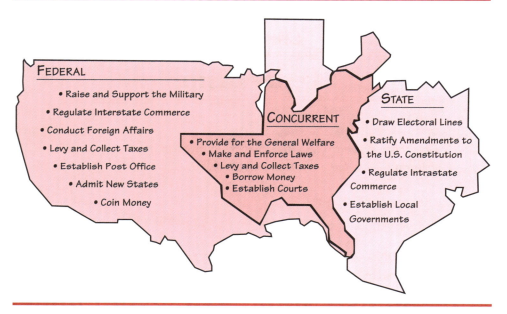

Enumerated, Implied, and Inherent Powers

The Constitution grants the federal government both expressed and implied powers. Most of the powers expressly delegated, also known as enumerated, to the federal government are established in Article I, Section 8, of the Constitution. These **enumerated powers**, a total of 17, include borrowing money, laying and collecting taxes, regulating commerce with foreign nations and among the states, making uniform naturalization laws, establishing post offices, coining money, and declaring war.

The constitutional source of **implied powers** of Congress is also found in Article I, Section 8, Clause 18. This clause reads: "To make all Laws which shall be necessary and proper for carrying into Execution the foregoing Powers, and all other Powers vested by this Constitution in the Government of the United States, or in any Department or Officer thereof."

This clause is sometimes called the "elastic clause" or the "necessary and proper clause," because it gives Congress powers that go beyond its specifically enumerated powers and provides flexibility to our constitutional system. These powers are not specifically mentioned in the Constitution but are "necessary and proper for carrying into execution" the enumerated powers.

The clause was first used in the Supreme Court's landmark case of *McCulloch v. Maryland* (1819)[1] to develop the concept of the implied powers. The U.S. Supreme Court upheld the implied powers granted to the Congress by the "necessary and proper" clause of the Constitution. Specifically, the Court ruled that the federal government had the right to establish a national bank under the power delegated to Congress to borrow money and control commerce.

The last category of powers exercised by the federal government comprises **inherent powers**. These powers derive from the fact that the United States is an independent and sovereign power among nations, and as such, its national government must be the only government to deal with other countries. Thus, only the national government has the power to declare war, to discover and occupy territory, to make treaties with other nations, and to send and receive representatives.

Reserved Powers

The Tenth Amendment to the Constitution states that the powers not delegated to the United States by the Constitution, nor prohibited by it to the states, are reserved to the states, or to the people. These are reserved powers that the national government cannot deny to the states. State powers have been held to include each state's right to police power, public education, and intrastate commerce. Police power gives states the authority to legislate for the protection of the health, morals, and welfare of the people. It also enables states to pass laws with regard to activities such as crimes, marriage, and contracts.

Concurrent Powers

The last type of power consists of concurrent powers. These are powers held jointly by all levels of government. Most concurrent powers are not specifically mentioned in the Constitution; they are implied. Income tax is a good example of concurrent power. In most states, citizens must file tax returns for both the federal and state levels. Other specific examples are the power to regulate commerce, the power to establish courts, and the power to build roads and highways.

Prohibited Powers

Prohibited powers are those that the Constitution denies to any level of government. These prohibited powers are specified in Sections 9 and 10 of Article I. (See Figure 3.2.)

FIGURE 3.2   POWERS DENIED BY THE CONSTITUTION

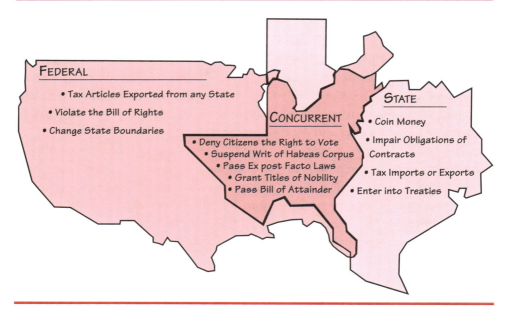

Prohibitions upon the National Government
In some areas, intrusion by the federal government is prohibited under Article I, Section 9. These include barring the federal government from prohibiting the migration or importation of slaves prior to 1808, but allowing a $10 tax on each person, taxing articles exported from any state, suspending the writ of habeas corpus, and changing state boundaries.

Prohibitions upon the States
Prohibitions on the states are contained in Article I, Section 10, of the Constitution.
   Some of the areas of prohibitions are entering treaties, alliances, or confederation, coining money, taxing import or exports, impairing the obligations of contract, and keeping troops or ships of war in time of peace.

Concurrent Prohibitions
Prohibitions on both the national and the state governments are contained in Article I, Sections 9 and 10, of the Constitution. Some of these include the **bill of attainder**, denying citizens the right to vote, **ex post facto law**, and issuing a title of nobility.

The Constitution states that neither Congress nor the state legislatures may enact a bill of attainder. A bill of attainder is a non-judicial determination of guilt. A bill of attainder has come to mean a legislative act declaring an individual guilty of a crime without permitting the individual a trial.

Furthermore, no government may pass an ex post facto law, derived from Latin and meaning "after the deed." The prohibition makes it unlawful for government to declare an act a crime when, at the time committed, it was not unlawful. In other words, it prohibits government from punishing an individual for an action committed before the law was passed. For example, a state may not pass a law prohibiting smoking in public buildings and then arrest all those who smoked during the previous year. It is important to remember that ex post facto laws only apply to criminal law and not civil laws. For example, Congress could pass a law increasing income taxes and apply it retroactively.

In addition, neither the federal government nor the states may suspend the **writ of habeas** corpus except in times of war or rebellion. The phrase is derived from the Latin words *habeas* or "have ye" and *corpus* or "the body." Its literal translation is "you have the body." It requires a law enforcement agent to bring a person in custody before a court of law so that a judge can determine the legality of the detention. Issuance of the writ of habeas corpus does not establish an accused person's innocence or guilt. It only tests whether the individual was accorded due process. If the writ of habeas corpus were suspended, then the government would be able to keep an individual in jail for an indefinite period of time without any legal justification.

Finally, no government may issue **titles of nobility**. This means that no government can bestow a title such as duke, duchess, or prince on an individual in the United States.

RELATIONS AMONG STATES

There are specific constitutional rules that govern relations among the states. They include the **full faith and credit clause**, the **privileges and immunities clause**, the **interstate rendition clause**, and the interstate compacts. The first three clauses are part of Article IV, and the last clause is part of Article I, Section 10.

The full faith and credit clause (Article IV, Section 1) mandates that state courts enforce the civil judgments of the courts of other states and accept their public records and acts as valid. Note that it is the acts of a state, not its laws, that get full faith and credit. Specifically, this clause applies to the enforcement of judicial settlements and judicial awards. For example, a Texas court awards citizen A a $100,000 judgment against citizen B, both Texans. After moving to Oklahoma, citizen B refuses to pay.

According to the full faith and credit clause, citizen A does not have to prove his case all over again and secure a new judgment against citizen B in an Oklahoma court. The Oklahoma court will give full faith and credit to the Texas judgment and will enforce the judgment.

According to the privileges and immunities clause, "The citizens of each state shall be entitled to all Privileges and Immunities of Citizens in the several States." This clause forbids discrimination against the citizens of another state by a state government or by a local unit of government. Therefore, each state is expected to extend the same courteous treatment to citizens of other states as well as the same legal protections.

The interstate rendition clause, found in Article IV, Section 2, asserts: "a person charged in any state with Treason, Felony, or other Crimes, who shall flee from Justice, and be found in another State, shall on Demand of the executive authority of the State from which he fled, be delivered up to be removed to the State having jurisdiction of the Crime."

The preceding process is known as **interstate rendition** or, more commonly, extradition. Despite their constitutional obligation, governors of asylum states have on occasion refused to honor a request for extradition. For example, in 1976 Governor Jerry Brown of California refused to extradite Dennis Banks, a Native American activist, to South Dakota, from which he had fled after being convicted of a felony. The Supreme Court, in the case of *Puerto Rico v. Branstad* (1987),[2] has ruled that the federal courts can compel a governor to extradite a fugitive.

The Constitution also requires that states may negotiate **interstate compacts**. Article I, Section 10, states that "no State shall, without the Consent of Congress, enter into any Agreement or Compact with another State." Although this provision of the Constitution requires that Congress approve interstate compacts, as a practical matter, many agreements on minor matters ignore this requirement. Thus, according to the Supreme Court, an agreement between New Hampshire and Maine, *New Hampshire v. Maine* (1976),[3] locating an ancient boundary, did not require congressional assent. The original intent was to prevent states from forming regional alliances that might threaten national unity.

FEDERAL-STATE RELATIONSHIP

According to Article IV, Section 4, of the Constitution, the federal government is required to guarantee a "republican" form of government within each state and to protect each state against both foreign invasion and domestic violence. The Constitution does not define the republican form of government, but it is that form of government in which sovereignty resides in the people who elect individuals to represent them in political decision making.

National Supremacy

In addition, Article VI is clear on the issue of national supremacy—the states may not pass laws or enact policies that conflict with the Constitution, acts of Congress, or provision of treaties signed between the United States and heads of other states. This clause suggests that when a conflict develops between the powers of the states and the national government, the federal law prevails.

The concept of the national supremacy was confirmed by the Supreme Court, under the leadership of Chief Justice John Marshall, in two major cases: *McCulloch v. Maryland* (1819) and *Gibbons v. Ogden* (1824).[4] In the former, the Court argued that the state of Maryland did not have the power to tax the national bank of the United States, and in Marshall's words, "The power to tax was the power to destroy." Thus, this act clearly violates the Supremacy Clause. (For further discussion of the position of the Supreme Court, see page 59.)

In the case of *Gibbons v. Ogden* (1824), the Court again decided in favor of the U.S. government. The Supreme Court ruled that congressional control over interstate commerce included not only direct dealings in products, as the states argued, but also all commercial intercourse. Thus, the Court denied control over shipping on the lower Hudson River to both New York and New Jersey. It also held that the states could destroy national institutions and federal laws would be subordinate to those of states, undermining the supremacy clause.

FEDERALISM IN HISTORICAL PERSPECTIVE

Despite the distribution of powers in the Constitution, the actual meaning of federalism had to be developed in practice. (For a summary of the evolution of federalism, see Figure 3.3.) This is due to the fact that the Constitution created competing centers of power and the lack of clearly delineated authority between the federal and state governments. For instance, the Constitution does not define the "necessary and proper" clause and does not specifically list any of the states' reserved powers. Thus, federalism has been a contentious dynamic system of government and its allocation of power between the federal government and the states debated and changed over the years.

Dual Federalism (1790–1933)

Federal-state relationships from 1790 to the 1930s usually are defined in terms of dual federalism. It argues that the powers of the federal government are limited to those specifically stated in the Constitution under Article I, Section 8, or the enumerated powers and should not exceed them; all other powers are reserved to the states under the Tenth Amendment. Thus, dual federalism calls for a distinct sphere of governance between the federal government and the states, and it argues that the levels are functionally separate and each is supreme within its own sphere. For example, interstate commerce, defense, and foreign relations are the functions of the federal government, whereas matters of public health and intrastate commerce belong to the states. In other words, it was assumed that the states would continue to do most of the governing of people and that each level of government has a fixed place in the arrangement. This is often described as **layer-cake federalism**.[5]

FIGURE 3.3   THE EVOLUTION OF FEDERALISM

Years	Era	Description
1790–1933	Dual Federalism:	Emphasis on power of federal government limited to delegated powers; states considered themselves sovereign; tension between the federal and state governments over scope of their authorities
1933–1964	Cooperative Federalism:	Greater role of federal government in domestic policies; many centers of powers work together with shared responsibilities
1964–1968	Centralized Federalism:	Federal government defined national problems and set national goals
1969–1974	New Federalism I:	President Nixon attempted to reduce the role of federal government and decentralize federal programs using federal grants
1981–1989	New Federalism II:	President Reagan attempted to reduce federal domestic spending
1996–Present	Devolution Revolution:	Transfer of authority and responsibility from the federal government to the states

The Supreme Court and Dual Federalism

As long as John Marshall was the chief justice (1801–1835), the Supreme Court favored a broad interpretation of the scope of the federal power. *McCulloch v. Maryland* (1819) was the first major decision of the Marshall court to define the relationship between the federal and state governments. The Court unanimously argued that Congress acted constitutionally when its members chartered the Second Bank of the United States in 1816. It stated that although the word "bank" cannot be found in the Constitution, in order to fully implement the authority to levy and collect taxes, issue a currency, and borrow money (examples of enumerated powers of Congress), Congress found it "necessary and proper" to establish the bank.

Furthermore, the Court backed the supremacy of the national government in carrying out functions assigned to it by the Constitution and established the doctrine of the intergovernmental tax immunity: "the power to tax is the power to destroy." The Court held that the Bank of the United States was not subject to taxation by the state of Maryland. This same principle applied to the *Gibbons v. Ogden* (1824) case.

This broad interpretation of the commerce clause has provided a means to enforce civil rights laws and to regulate wages, working conditions, and other areas that seem at first glance far removed from federal jurisdiction.

When Roger Taney (1835–1863), was chief justice, the Supreme Court reemphasized the belief that a separate and equally powerful sphere of governing was the best arrangement. At the same time, the Court decided most cases in favor of states' rights, a term used to imply opposition to increasing the federal government's power at the expense of that of states, within the framework of dual federalism. For example, in *Dred Scott v. Sandford* (1857),[6] the Court held that blacks could not become citizens of the United States and were not entitled to the rights and privileges of citizenship. The Court also ruled that the Missouri Compromise of 1820, enacted by Congress to ban slavery in the territories, was unconstitutional. This was the second time a federal law was declared unconstitutional, following the case of *Marbury v. Madison* (1803).[7]

Cooperative Federalism (1933–1964)

The economic hardships produced by the Great Depression of the 1930s resulted in demands that the federal government have a greater role in domestic policies. Neither state nor local governments had the economic resources to deal with rampant unemployment and a host of other problems facing the nation in 1933. Franklin Delano Roosevelt's promise of a new deal for Americans helped him win the presidential election of 1932. With the introduction of the New Deal programs, the role of the federal government relative to state and local governments expanded dramatically.

This phase in the evolution of federalism is referred to as **cooperative federalism**. Cooperative federalism implies that instead of competing centers of powers, government in the United States is actually made up of many centers that work together to solve the nation's problems. This new phase of federalism is as also referred to as **marble-cake federalism**.[8] The federal government, during this era, used its influence to address increasing problems that had been ignored or were considered within the purview of state governments. This expansion would not have been possible without the ratification of the Sixteenth Amendment in 1913. The Sixteenth Amendment may have been the most significant factor in the development of cooperative federalism. It brought three important changes to taxation: taxation could now be based on income from whatever source derived, without appropriation among the states, and without regard to any census or enumeration.

In addition, the Sixteenth Amendment increased federal revenue at a time when the nation was expanding. Cities and states had little finance to solve their ever-increasing problems. The federal government willingly cooperated with states in areas that had previously been regarded as state matters. States were more than happy to accept federal money for projects through **grant-in-aid programs**—programs through which the federal government shared its revenues with state and local governments. This money was directed at problems that states often could ill-afford to address themselves.

Thus, cooperative federalism assured that all levels of government share responsibility in domestic politics "by making the larger governments primarily responsible for raising revenues and setting standards, and the smaller ones primarily responsible for administering the programs."[9]

Centralized Federalism (1964–1968)

The extension of federal power reached its apex under President Lyndon Baines Johnson through his Great Society programs. These programs included initiatives in health care, public housing, nutrition, welfare, urban development, and other areas reserved previously to state and local governments. The purpose of the program was to improve the lot of the poorest Americans. The Great Society was a term for the domestic policies of the Johnson administration. It was premised on the belief that the new federal programs could solve social and economic problems. This new approach to federalism sometimes is referred to as centralized federalism. The goal was to persuade state and local governments to adopt programs that they might otherwise not have undertaken. The federal government assumed the power to define national problems and set national goals. In reality, centralized federalism was centralized government.[10]

The War on Poverty, the phrase used by the Johnson administration for its Great Society programs, made extensive use of federal grant-in-aid programs. During the 1960s, the federal aid dollars more than tripled, from $7 billion in 1960 to $24 billion in 1970. By 1970, nearly one dollar out of every four spent by state and local governments came from the federal treasury.[11] The federal government now sought to address a wide range of problems in areas ranging from the education of children to training for the unemployed to the needs of the senior citizens. Many of these programs, called redistributive programs, channeled wealth to the poor and the needy.

New Federalism I (1969–1974)

President Richard Nixon stated that the federal government was too large. Therefore, he proposed to return power to state and local governments by increasing their control over federally funded programs. Nixon's attempt to do this was called the new federalism. New federalism was, in essence, a reaction to the excesses of President Johnson's centralized federalism. Nixon wanted to reduce the role of the federal government and largely decentralize federal programs. His strategy included these components. The first was general revenue sharing (GRS). It gave money to the states with "no strings attached" and started during President Nixon's second term. Nixon's second component consolidated groups of categorical grants into a few large block grants—also known as special revenue sharing. Not only would state and local governments have greater discretion over the use of these grants, but the excessive paperwork required for grant applications would be eliminated. President Reagan attacked the GRS for contributing to the increased federal budget, and the program was dismantled in 1986.

New Federalism II (1981–1989)

President Ronald Reagan also expressed a commitment to reduce the role of the federal government over the states. In practice, President Reagan's federalism meant reducing federal domestic spending and letting the states take over programs that used to be provided by Washington. He proposed, for example, that the federal government would assume responsibility for Medicaid, health care for low-income individuals. In return, states would take over food stamps and the Aid to Families with Dependent Children (AFDC). But Congress rejected his proposal. As a result of federal budget cuts, there was a sharp decline in federal aid to the states during the

Reagan years. During 1980s, states experienced an increased demand for basic services such as housing, food, and health care, in response to reductions in federal spending in those areas.[12] In addition, President Reagan was able to further consolidate 76 categorical grant programs into 9 new or reconstructed block grants.[13] States demanded that less control by the federal government and its agencies be exercised over local implementation of programs.

The Devolution Revolution (1996–Present)

This demand for responsibility to be transferred from the federal government to the states is referred to as the devolution revolution. Welfare reform turned out to be the key to devolution. Welfare reform occurred when President Bill Clinton signed the Personal Responsibility and Work Opportunity Reconciliation Act in 1996. It did away with the Aid to Families with Dependent Children (AFCD) program and replaced it with the Temporary Assistance to Needy Families (TANF) program. The law required Congress to appropriate a total of $16.4 billion, in the form of block grants, to the states annually through 2002.

It also placed a lifetime limit of five years on the length of time that a family can receive welfare benefits. (The states can avoid this limit by using their own funds to pay for continued welfare benefits.)[14] In addition, the states have flexibility to determine eligibility and benefit levels for those who receive welfare assistance. The intended purpose of the welfare reform is to move people off welfare rolls and encourage them to take advantage of state-established job-training programs in order to learn skills and be able to find jobs.

The shifting of responsibility from the federal to the state governments may not be the panacea that was advertised. The positive side of devolution is characterized by block grants, great flexibility in the implementation of programs, and a reduction in the number of people receiving welfare assistance through the TANF program. At first glance, this would appear to be a coup for state governments. The inevitable downside of devolution was that due to reductions in federal aid, states faced fiscally stressed budgets. Ultimately, many states had to make the choice between increasing taxes or cutting services.[15]

The Supreme Court and New Federalism

To a significant degree, the federal courts have supported the basic premise of the devolution revolution, which states that the federal government has gone too far in usurping powers that rightly belong to states. It has long been held that when the courts find that Congress has any basis for finding that a regulated activity affects interstate commerce, the statute by the federal government will be valid. For example, in *Garcia v. San Antonio Metropolitan Transit Authority* (1985),[16] the Supreme Court, using the interstate commerce clause of the Constitution, upheld the constitutionality of federally imposed minimum wage and maximum hour provisions on state governments. This trend has been threatened, however, by the Court's decision in *United States v. Lopez* (1995).[17] This case involved the conviction of a student charged with carrying a concealed handgun within 1,000 feet of school property. The majority members of the Supreme Court concluded that local gun control in schools was a state, not a federal, concern.

Furthermore, in *Gonzales v. Raich* (2005), the Court ruled the Bush Administration can block the backyard cultivation of pot for personal use, because such use has broader social and financial implications. This Supreme Court decision invalidated California's medical marijuana law. Critics argue that by granting Congress the authority to regulate small amounts of marijuana grown in a backyard—marijuana not sold and never crossing state lines—makes a mockery of the efforts of the Constitution's framers to place limits on federal powers and thus undermining the devolution revolution.

Critics also blame the Bush Administration for this. They argue that it was the Bush Justice Department that decided to defend use of the federal drug laws to suppress homegrown marijuana. Another example shows the Bush Administration's lack of interest in the devolution revolution is the case of the No Child Left Behind Act. This act reduces state autonomy in education by imposing uniform testing requirements. It uses the threat of organizing school operations if districts do not meet federal standards, all in an area that historically has fallen under the control of states.

Critics argue that the demand for rigid nationwide rules suppresses the ability of states to serve as "laboratories of democracy." Expansion of federal power at the expense of states will retard the innovation that can answer difficult national problems.

FEDERAL GRANT SYSTEM

Federal grants have been in existence throughout American history. One of the early federal grants to the states was the Merrill Land Grant Act of 1862. It gave each state public land and income from the sale of lands earmarked for the establishment of agricultural and mechanical colleges and universities. One of these land-grant universities is Texas A & M University.

At the beginning of the twentieth century, annual federal grants to the states totaled about $6 million; the grants increased to about $100 million in the early

President Johnson after Signing War on Poverty

© Bettmann/CORBIS

1920s and grew to nearly $300 million toward the end of 1930s.[18] Franklin D. Roosevelt's New Deal program noticeably increased the flow of federal dollars to the states. By 1964, the number of federal grant programs increased to 51. As a result of President Lyndon Johnson's Great Society programs, the number of these programs grew to 530 by 1971. The cost of these programs changed from about $24.1 billion in 1970 to approximately $262 billion in 1999.[19]

TYPES OF FEDERAL GRANTS
Categorical Grants
Various federal grants exist. The oldest and the largest is the categorical grant. More than 400 categorical grants are available, which constitute approximately 80 percent of federal aid to the states and localities. Categorical grants earmark funds for specific purposes, usually with strict rules attached—for example, highway construction or the enforcement of the Clean Air Act of 1970. A categorical grant requires a matching grant—the state or local government receiving the grant must pay some percentage of the grant. For some categorical grant programs, the funds are distributed to the state or local governments according to a formula (formula grant) that takes into account the relative wealth, number of needy residents, and the total size of the state's population. The formula is used to make sure that the funds are equitably distributed among the state and local governments.

Project Grants
A project grant is a type of categorical grant. This type of grant requires a state or local government to apply for it with the appropriate federal agency, and it is usually awarded on the basis of competitive applications. The Department of Education, for example, administers project grants involving teacher training in math and science education. Public schools, colleges, and universities submit applications to the agency, which then decides which grant proposals merit funding.

Block Grants
President Johnson created block grant programs in 1966. These programs earmark funds for general purposes. Some examples are community development, criminal justice, and mass transit system block grants. State and local governments have a great deal of flexibility in how the money is actually spent. A county may decide to use its mass transit block grant to upgrade its buses rather than build a light rail system, for example. Because block grants tend to loosen federal control over the states, Republicans, rather than Democrats, favor it. In addition, governors and mayors also prefer block grants because they give the states more flexibility in how the money is spent. Block grant funds are also based on formula. Block grants reached their peak at the end of the 1970s when they constituted about one-quarter of the total grants-in-aid. By the 1990s, block grants accounted for over 10 percent of all federal aid programs. The latest example of a block grant is the welfare program. It became a block grant with the passage of the welfare reform bill in 1996.

General Revenue-Sharing

General Revenue-Sharing (GRS) was a new grant created in 1972 and was considered the most innovative of President Nixon's proposals. This grant went a step further by distributing funds to state and local governments without federal controls. The GRS provided for the distribution of about $6 billion a year to state and local governments. The distribution of the GRS funds was determined by a formula. It gave state and local governments wide latitude on how the funds could be spent. This type of federal fund was very popular with the states because most of them were experiencing fiscal crisis in the 1970s. Due to soaring federal deficit in the 1980s, Congress completely phased out general revenue sharing in 1986 after having distributed about $85 billion over a 14-year period.[20]

STATES AS LOBBYISTS

Both local and state governments now lobby the legislative and the executive branches for favorable funding and policies. This process has been around since the administration of Franklin Roosevelt.[21] This competition among state and local governments for funds has become fierce in recent years. It extends also to competition for private funds. The new wave of competition is the use of tax incentives, labor laws, and public works to attract industry, tourism, and sports franchises.[22] Nearly every state and local government has lobbyists in Washington who push for federal dollars. Many states and cities have combined their efforts at attracting industry. For instance, the Dallas–Fort Worth metroplex in Texas, with the help of the state legislature, has waged campaigns in recent years to keep a General Motors plant in Arlington, Texas (between the two cities), from closing; to attract the Olympics; and to build recreational facilities along the Trinity River. However, they lost in a bid to attract Boeing, the aircraft manufacturer, which instead located in Chicago.

THE ADVANTAGES AND DISADVANTAGES OF FEDERALISM

The federal system has several advantages and disadvantages. One advantage of federalism is the decentralization of power. All political powers are not vested in the federal government. Under federalism, states are given a certain degree of flexibility in terms of adopting and implementing their own policies. For instance, each enjoys flexibility with respect to the types of educational programs, and welfare policies it will pursue. Thus, some states tend to spend more money on public education and social welfare than others.

Another advantage of federalism is that it encourages innovation in governmental activities. That is, state and local communities are considered to be a massive social and political laboratory in which different policies, services, and programs are proposed, adopted and implemented. Successful policies and programs are publicized and incorporated by other state or local governments. For example, California was a pioneer in devising air pollution policies long before other states or even the federal government adopted a comprehensive clean-air act.

Federalism also enhances and promotes the freedom of individual citizens. The decentralization of political power ensures that no one level will be able to establish domination over the others. Furthermore, a citizen or interest group denied access at one level of government could seek redress at another. In addition, decentralization of power also contributes to government efficiency. There would be red tape and massive confusion if the federal bureaucrats in Washington directed every governmental activity in the United States. According to Dye, "Government can become arbitrary when a bureaucracy far from the scene directs local officials."[23]

Despite the advantages of federalism, it has its problems. For example, decentralized government may allow local leaders to derail the national agenda. In other words, decentralized government may provide the opportunity for local NIMBY's ("not in my backyard") to prevent the construction of an airport or public housing in a local community.

In addition, federalism does not allow the costs and benefits of government to be spread evenly across the nation.[24] For example, many states in the Northeast and Midwest pay more in federal taxes than they receive in federal grants, whereas the federal government subsidizes many southern states. This is due to the fact that the per capita incomes and federal tax payments of many northeastern and midwestern states are higher than they are for many southern states.

SUMMARY

The United States is the first country to successfully adopt the federal system of government following the adoption of the Constitution in 1788. Federalism calls for a sharing of power among governmental units. Each unit has its own separate sphere of authority or jurisdiction. The Constitution sets the rules and framework for how power among these units is divided. Article I, Section 8, is the primary source of power for Congress. Its interpretation of the relationship between the federal and state governments in *McCulloch v. Maryland* has set boundaries for much of our later debate on federalism. States derive their power from the Tenth Amendment. The proper role of the federal and state governments has long been controversial.

The key periods of federalism since the Civil War have been called dual federalism, cooperative federalism, new federalism I and II, and the devolution revolution. It is due to the devolution revolution that state governments are more powerful than they were in the 1960s.

Over the years, the federal government has been giving money to the states and localities in the form of categorical, block, project, and general revenue sharing grants. The most restrictive is the categorical; and the least restrictive, the general revenue sharing grant. The latter was dismantled in 1986. The federal government uses specific criteria to disperse the grants, which include formula and matching. The formula criterion takes into account the relative wealth and the total size of the population, while the matching criterion requires states receiving the grant to pay some percentage of the grant.

Today, states compete and lobby for federal money. Local governments, most notably big cities, have joined in this lobbying. Most of them have lobbyists in Washington who push for federal dollars.

Finally, the federal system not only decentralizes political power in order to give states a certain degree of flexibility in terms of adopting and implementing policies, but it encourages innovation in governmental activities. At the same time, the fragmentation of political power may encourage local social and political leaders to derail national programs and agenda.

KEY TERMS

Bill of attainder
Block grant
Categorical grant
Centralized federalism
Concurrent powers
Cooperative federalism
Delegated powers
Devolution revolution

Dual federalism
Ex post facto law
Federalism
Formula grant
Fullfaith and credit clause
General revenue-sharing
Grant-in-aid
Implied powers

Interstate compacts
Interstate rendition
"Layer-cake" federalism
"Marble-cake" federalism
Matching grant
Necessary and proper clause
New federalism
Privileges and immunities clause
Project grant
Reserved powers
War on poverty
Writ of habeas corpus

INTERNET SOURCES

1. States' Information
   a) http://www.nasire.org/ss/STstates.html
   This site, operated by the National Association of State Resource Executives (NASIRE), provides information on sociopolitical and economic information on each of the fifty states in the Union, including their local governments.
   b) http://www.scvol.com/States/
   The National Conference of State Legislatures (NCSL) is responsible for maintaining this site. It provides information on all fifty states' legislatures relative to legislation, budget, and various policy decisions.
2. Local Governments:
   a) http://www.piperinfo.com/state/states.html
   Maintained by the Piper Resources, this site contains vital information on various local governments within the fifty states of the Union.
   b) http://www.capitol.state.tx.us
   This Texas State Legislature site provides information on bills, laws, policies, and links to other useful sources relative to the state.
   http://oyez.at.nwu.edu/cases/subject-index.html#federalism
   This site, among other state-related policies and laws, has information on major federalism and intergovernmental relations cases.
   c) http://www.prairienet.org/~scruffy/f.htm
   Information on states' laws, constitutions, statutes, bills, etc. can be found on this site.

NOTES

[1] *McCulloch v. Maryland*, 4 Wheat 316 (1819).
[2] *Puerto Rico v. Branstad*, 483 U.S. 219 (1987).
[3] *New Hempshire v. Maine*, 426 U.S. 363 (1976).
[4] *Gibbons v. Ogden*, 9 Wheaton 1 (1824).
[5] Morton Grodzins, *The American System* (Chicago: Rand McNally, 1966), pp. 8–9.
[6] *Dred Scott v. Sandford*, 19 Howard 393 (1857).
[7] *Marbury v. Madison*, 5 US 137 (1803).

[8] Morton Grodzins, *The American System* (Chicago: Rand McNally, 1966), pp. 8–9.

[9] Daniel Elazar, *American Federalism: A View From the States*, 2nd ed. (New York: Haper & Row, 1972), p. 6.

[10] Thomas R. Dye, *American Federalism: Competition among Governments* (Lexington, MA: Lexington Books, 1990), p. 7.

[11] Timothy Conlan, *New Federalism: Intergovernmental Reform from Nixon to Reagan* (Washington, D.C.: The Brookings Institution, 1988), p. 6.

[12] Anne Marie Cammisa, *Governments as Interest Groups, Intergovernmental Lobby and the Federal System* (London: Praeger, 1995).

[13] Joseph F. Zimmerman, "Federal Preemption under Reagan's New Federalism," *Publius*, 21 (1991): 11.

[14] Water E. Volkomer, *Ameircan Government* (Englewood Cliffs, NJ: Prentice Hall, 2001), p. 67.

[15] U.S. House Committee on Budget, 1996 Hearing on Federalism, 104th Congress, 2nd Session, March 5.

[16] *Garcia v. San Antonio Metropolitan Transit Authority*, 469 U.S. 528 (1985).

[17] *United States v. Lopez*, 131 L. Ed. 2nd 626 (1995).

[18] U.S. Bureau of the Census, *Statistical History of the U.S.* (Washington, D.C.: U.S. Government Printing Office, 1963), pp. 484–516.

[19] U.S. Bureau of Census, *Statistical Abstract of the United States* (Washington, D.C.: U.S. Government Printing Office, 1999), Table 507, p. 314.

[20] James Q. Wilson and John J. DiIulio, Jr., *American Government: The Essentials*, 8th ed. (New York: Houghton Mifflin, 2001), p. 64.

[21] Anne Marie Cammisa, *Government as Interest Groups, Intergovernmental Lobbying and the Federal System* (Westport, CT: Praeger, 1995).

[22] Joseph F. Zimmerman, *Interstate Relations: The Neglected Dimension of Federalism* (Westport, CT: Praeger, 1996).

[23] Thomas R. Dye, *Politics in America*, 3rd ed. (Englewood Cliffs, NJ: Prentice Hall, 1998), p. 103.

[24] Ibid., p. 104.

Chapter 4

Individualized Participation:
Voting, Campaigns, and Elections

One of the penalties for refusing to participate in politics is that you end up being governed by Inferiors.

—Plato

INTRODUCTION

Political participation refers to those political activities pursued by individuals and groups in order to affect the policies of government and the selection of government officials. Many different forms of participation exist, all with the potential to influence the political process.

Political participation can be divided into two broad categories: conventional (or legitimate) and unconventional (or nonlegitimate). The law allows conventional acts of participation; however, the law does not sanction unconventional political activities. (See Table 4.1.)

Even though scholars have studied different aspects of unconventional political activities, this chapter focuses on conventional political activities. We start with voting—the minimum act in which we can take part.

TABLE 4.1 MODES OF POLITICAL ACTION

Actor	Type	Characteristic Action
Protesters	Revolutionaries	Political Assassination
		Insurgency
		Undertake political violence against the political order
		Riot
		Engage in civil disobedience
		Join in public protest demonstrations
		Attend protest meetings
		Refuse to obey unjust laws
		Protest verbally if government does something morally wrong
Government activists		Candidates for or hold public office
Partisan activists		Contribute money to party, candidate, issue
		Attend meetings, rallies
		Actively work for party, candidate, and issue
		Persuade others how to vote
		Join and support party
Community activists		Active in community organization
		Form group to work on local problems
		Contact officials on social issues
		Work with others on local problems
Communicators		Write letters to media
		Send support or protest messages to political leaders
		Engage in political discussions
		Keep informed about politics
Contact specialists		Contact local, state, or national officials on particular problems
Voters		Vote regularly in elections
Supporters and patriots		Show patriotism by flying flag, attending public parades, etc.
		Express love of country
		Pay all taxes

Source: From *Understanding the Political World: A Comparative Introduction to Political Science*, 4th ed., by James N. Danziger. Copyright 1998 by Addison Wesley Longman Inc. Reprinted by permission of Addison-Wesley Educational Publishers, Inc.

VOTING

An example of individualized political participation is voting. It is an important political act in a democracy. It is an act of consent to be governed. From the standpoint of the voters, voting not only allows eligible citizens to choose between competing candidates and political parties but also provides them the opportunity to influence public policies indirectly. Furthermore, participation in a democracy plays an important role in the self-development of its citizens. Elections are also critical to the continued success of the political system. Voting gives the political system legitimacy and also links individuals to the political system, which will promote stability and obedience to the laws.

Voting also protects individuals and groups from governmental abuse. According to **John Stuart Mill**, "Men, as well as women, do not need political rights in order that they might govern, but in order that they not be misgoverned."[1]

Most voters seek the following benefits from participating in politics: material benefit, such as tax cuts; social benefit, the simple pleasure of working together; civic benefit, the fulfillment of one's duties as a citizen; and policy benefit, the ability to influence governmental decisions.

LIMITS ON THE RIGHT TO VOTE

If elections are to link individuals to their government and its officials, there must exist universal suffrage—the right of all citizens to vote. Not all Americans enjoyed the franchise—the right to vote—in the past. Politics used to be the exclusive domain of the rich. Specific groups of Americans were denied the right to vote; they included nonwhites, the poor, women, and those who did not meet specific religious and age requirements. In the past 200 years, these restrictions have been eliminated.

These restrictions were imposed by the states. The original Constitution, Article I, Section 2, left voting qualifications entirely to the states. It states, "The House of Representatives shall be composed of members chosen every second year by the people of the several states, and the electors in each state shall have the qualifications requisite for electors of the most numerous branch of the state legislature." At the same time, Article I, Section 4, gave Congress the power to regulate only the "time, place, and manner" of federal elections. For example, Congress passed a law in 1872 setting congressional elections on the first Tuesday after the first Monday in November of even-numbered years.

The states took advantage of their constitutional power and imposed a very limited franchise. Since the end of the Civil War, Congress and the federal courts have imposed national standards on state-run elections. A series of constitutional amendments, federal laws, and Supreme Court decisions forced states to conduct elections without discrimination because of race, creed, color, or sex. Even with such laws imposed from the federal level on the states, the registration of voters and the regulation of elections are still primarily state powers.

Constitutional Amendments

The principle changes to voter qualifications have come through amendments. In fact, the greatest number of amendments deal with voting rights. The racial limitation was set aside by the **Fifteenth Amendment** (1870), which legally extended suffrage to black male Americans. However, this right was not fully realized until congressional action was taken during the 1960s and 1970s. Women were enfranchised with the passage of the **Nineteenth Amendment** (1920). However, it was not until 1984 that women were reported voting in the same proportion as men.[2] The last significant extension of franchise came with passage of the **Twenty-Sixth Amendment** (1971), granting the right to vote to those who are 18 years old.

Several other amendments also affected the right to vote. The **Seventeenth Amendment** (1913) gave voters the right to vote for senators directly. Prior to the passage of this amendment, members of the Senate were selected by state legislature. The **Twenty-Second Amendment** (1951) limits presidents from serving more than two full terms, which gives us the ability to reelect a popular incumbent (office holder) president. The **Twenty-Third Amendment** (1961) made it possible for citizens of the District of Columbia to vote for the president by providing them three electoral votes. Finally, the **Twenty-Fourth Amendment** (1964) did away with the poll tax in national elections.

Despite the passage of the Fifteenth Amendment, many states invented legal devices to prevent blacks from voting. These discriminatory laws became known as **Jim Crow laws**. The term is a nickname for a minstrel character. It rose out of the 1820s, a time when white audiences howled at white entertainers who covered their faces with burnt cork and then mimicked the dance steps of American slaves. One of those minstrels devised a dance character supposedly suggesting a dancing crow. The character thus came to be called Jim Crow. These laws included the poll tax law, a literacy test requirement, the grandfather clause, and the white primary.

Voting on Election Day

© David Turnley/CORBIS

The **poll tax** was a fee that had to be paid as condition for voting. It was intended to discriminate against blacks, but had the effect of discouraging poor whites as well. The Court said that a state violates the equal protection clause "whenever it makes the affluence of the voter or the payment of any fee an electoral standard."[3] The **literacy test** was designed to determine a voter's ability to read and to understand documents. A **grandfather clause** stated that anyone who was to vote before January 1, 1867, or whose father or grandfather was qualified at that time, did not have to pass a literacy test. Though the law did not mention race, color, or previous servitude, the selection of a date prior to the adoption of the Fifteenth Amendment had the effect of denying blacks the right to vote. Finally, the **white primary** deprived African Americans the right to participate in the Democratic party primary.

Supreme Court Decisions

The Supreme Court also played and important role in expanding the rights to vote. In 1915, in the case of *Guinn v. the United States*,[4] the Court declared the grandfather clause unconstitutional. In addition, in the case of *Smith v. Allwright* [5](1944), the Court ruled that the white primary violated the Fifteenth Amendment. Two years after the passage of the Twenty-Fourth Amendment, the Court ruled, in *Harper v. Virginia Board of Elections*,[6] that poll taxes were also unconstitutional in state or local elections.

Congressional Actions

Prior to 1924, Native Americans were not considered citizens. The **Indian Citizenship Act of 1924** made all American Indians born in the United States American citizens and gave them the right to vote. The **Civil Rights Act of 1964** is considered a major piece of legislation designed to erase racial discrimination in most areas of American life, including voter participation. It outlawed arbitrary discrimination in voter registration and expedited voting rights suits.

The **Voting Rights Act of 1965** suspended the use of literacy tests adopted by states to discriminate. The act also authorized registration by federal registrars in any state or county where such tests had been used and where fewer than 50 percent of eligible voters were registered.

The **Voting Rights Act of 1970** prohibits the states from disqualifying voters from participating in presidential elections because of their failure to meet state residence requirements beyond 30 days. In 1975, Congress extended the Voting Rights Act for seven years. Among other things, the amended version of the act required bilingual ballots. The 1982 act extends the law for 25 years. The result was a dramatic increase in black voter registration and voter turnout, especially in the South. (See Table 4.2.)

CURRENT REQUIREMENTS FOR VOTING

Today universal suffrage is extended to any individual who is an American citizen, is 18 years of age or older, has a residence, and is a registered voter. Resident aliens are not qualified to vote in any election. Once a resident alien becomes a naturalized citizen, then he or she has the right to vote.

The residency requirement states that a citizen must live in a state's election district for a specific period of time, typically 30 days, before becoming eligible to vote. Texas law, for example, requires residency in a Texas county on the day of election. Residency is required based on the assumption that a voter must have enough time to know the candidates and understand the issues prior to voting.

Registration is required in order to avoid electoral fraud. Except for North Dakota, all states mandate voter registration. Several states will register voters on Election Day. This is known as same-day registration. (See Table 4.3.) A voter remains registered unless he or she moves to another county or state, where the voter must reregister in order to be able to vote in an upcoming election.

TABLE 4.2 EXTENSION OF THE RIGHT TO VOTE

Date	Property	Race	Sex	Age
1790–1850	States drop property qualifications			
1869			Wyoming gives women the right to vote	
1870		Fifteenth Amendment gives blacks the right to vote		
1920			Nineteenth Amendment gives women the right to vote in state and federal elections	
1944		Supreme Court, in *Smith v. Allwright,* outlaws the white primary		
1964		Twenty-Fourth Amendments outlaws the poll tax in federal elections		
1965		Voting Rights Act of 1965 abandons literacy test for those with sixth-grade education		
1966		Supreme Court, in *Harper v. Virginia Board of Elections,* outlaws the poll tax in state and federal elections		
1970		Voting Rights Act Amendments of 1970 outlaw state literacy tests		
1971				Twenty-Sixth Amendment extends the right to vote to those age 18 and older

TABLE 4.3 STATE VOTER REGISTRATION AND DEADLINES

STATE	RESIDENCY REQUIREMENT	DEADLINE
Alabama	None	11 days before the election
Alaska	30 days	30 days before the election
Arizona	29 days	29 days before the election
Arkansas	None	30 days before the election
California	None	15 days before the election
Colorado	30 days	29 days before the election
Connecticut	None	14 days before the election
Delaware	None	20 days before the election
District of Columbia	30 days	30 days before the election
Florida	None	29 days before the election
Georgia	None	5th Monday before the election
Hawaii	None	30 days before the election
Idaho	30 days	25 days before the election
Illinois	30 days	28 days before the election
Indiana	30 days	29 days before the election
Iowa	None	10 days before the election
Kansas	None	15 days before the election
Kentucky	28 days	29 days before the election
Louisiana	None	30 days before the election
Maine	None	Election day registration
Maryland	None	21 days before the election
Massachusetts	None	20 days before the election
Michigan	30 days	30 days before the election
Minnesota	20 days	Election day registration
Mississippi	30 days	30 days before the election
Missouri	None	28 days before the election
Montana	30 days	30 days before the election
Nebraska	None	3rd Friday before the election
Nevada	30 days	5th Saturday before the election
New Hampshire	None	10 days before the election
New Jersey	30 days	29 days before the election
New Mexico	None	28 days before the election
New York	30 days	25 days before the election
N. Carolina	30 days	25 days before the election
N. Dakota	None	None
Ohio	None	30 days before the election
Oklahoma	None	25 days before the election
Oregon	None	21 days before the election

TABLE 4.3 STATE VOTER REGISTRATION AND DEADLINES

State	Residency Requirement	Deadline
Pennsylvania	30 days	30 days before the election
Rhode Island	None	30 days before the election
S. Carolina	None	30 days before the election
S. Dakota	None	15 days before the election
Tennessee	None	30 days before the election
Texas	None	30 days before the election
Utah	30 days	20 days before the election
Vermont	None	2nd Saturday before the election
Virginia	None	29 days before the election
Washington	30 days	30 days before the election
W. Virginia	None	20 days before the election
Wisconsin	10 days	Election day registration
Wyoming	None	30 days before the election

Source: "Voter Registration Requirements and Schedule of PRimary Elections." The State University of New Jersey, Eagleton Institution of Politics. <http://www.eagleton.rutgers.edu/News-Research/NewVoters/VoterRegRequire.html?

In an effort to encourage greater electoral participation, Congress passed the **National Voter Registration Act** in 1993, also known as **"motor voter law."** Under this law, states must let voters register whenever they apply or renew their driver's licenses or make contact with welfare or disability assistance offices. The law also requires states to permit registration by mail.

THE AFTERMATH OF THE 2000 FLORIDA DEBACLE

Following the 2000 presidential election debacle in Florida, many Americans demanded Congress to reform the voting process. In 2002, Congress passed, and President Bush signed, the Help America Vote Act (HAVA). The HAVA requires that states make a number of changes beginning in 2004, including issuing provisional ballots, and creating statewide computerized voter lists. The law is intended to make it easier to vote and harder to cheat. It requires new voters to show identification when voting and creates new criminal penalties for providing false information and for conspiracy to prevent people from voting.

TABLE 4.4   PRESIDENTIAL ELECTION VOTER TURNOUT, 1924–2004

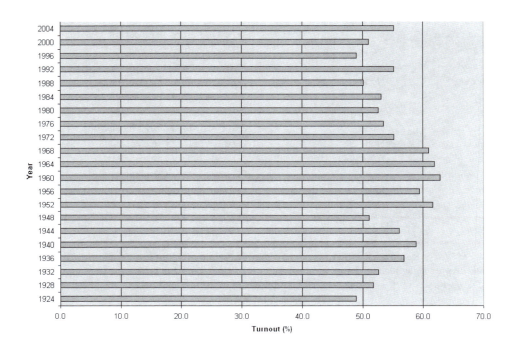

Source: Center for Voting and Democracy, www.fairvote.org.

It also requires that provisional ballots be provided to voters whose eligibility is in question, so they will not be turned away at the polls. Provisional votes are counted, and their eligibility determined later. In addition, the HAVA gave $3.9 billion to states to update voting machines, train poll workers, and educate voters. With these funds many states have obtained electronic voting machines.[7]

THE GREAT AMERICAN VOTER TURN-OFF

Although it is so easy to qualify to vote, voter turnout has declined since the 1960s in the United States. (See Table 4.4.) In 1960, 62.8 percent of eligible voters turned out and voted in the presidential election; by 1988, the figure dropped to 50.1

percent. It rebounded to 55.2 percent in 1992, declined again to 49 percent in 1996, and increased to 51.1 percent and 55 percent in 2000 and 2004, respectively.

According to the U.S. Census Bureau, there were appoximately 220 million qualified voters, but only 121 million Americans cast their vote for president on November 2, 2004. This figure is the largest ever. The 2004 voter turnout in the presidential election represents 15 million more votes than in the 2000 elections. The highest overall presidential vote was recorded in Minnesota at 73 percent, followed by Wisconsin's 71.5 percent and New Hampshire's 67.7 percent. The lowest voter turnout was recorded in Hawaii at 43.8 percent, followed by Texas with 45.6 percent and California's 46.6 percent. (See Table 4.5.)

TABLE 4.5 TURNOUT IN 2004: STATE BY STATE

STATE	PERCENTAGE OF VOTING AGE POPULATION VOTED
Alabama	55.0
Alaska	66.5
Arizona	48.0
Arkansas	51.0
California	46.6
Colorado	61.6
Connecticut	58.8
Delaware	59.6
District of Columbia	56.2
Florida	56.6
Georgia	50.5
Hawaii	43.8
Idaho	58.4
Illinois	60.4
Indiana	54.0
Iowa	66.3
Kansas	58.0
Kentucky	56.9
Louisiana	57.9
Maine	71.3
Maryland	56.8
Massachusetts	58.8
Michigan	63.5
Minnesota	73.0
Mississippi	53.9
Missouri	62.9

TABLE 4.5 TURNOUT IN 2004: STATE BY STATE

State	Percentage of Voting Age Population Voted
Montana	63.0
Nebraska	59.1
Nevada	47.7
New Hampshire	67.7
New Jersey	54.9
New Mexico	53.9
New York	50.0
N. Carolina	54.6
N. Dakota	63.8
Ohio	64.8
Oklahoma	54.9
Oregon	66.4
Pennsylvania	60.0
Rhode Island	51.9
S. Carolina	51.0
S. Dakota	67.4
Tennessee	54.0
Texas	45.6
Utah	56.4
Vermont	64.0
Virginia	56.2
Washington	60.4
W. Virginia	52.8
Wisconsin	71.5
Wyoming	63.0

Source: McDonald, Michael P., "2004 Voting-Age and Voting-Eligible Population Estimates and Voter Turnout." United States Elections Project. February 8, 2005. <http://elections.gmu.edu/Voter_Turnout_2004.htm>

Why is turnout so low? Many factors explain why voter turnout has declined in America. Among them are advance registration, lack of political efficacy, lack of party competition, voter fatigue, and, above all, lack of interest and information in political participation on the part of voters.

Many states require voters to register in advance of an election. States with election-day registration, Maine, Minnesota, Wisconsin, have higher voter turnout. (See Table 4.3.)

Lack of political efficacy means that voters feel the political system is not responsive to them. Studies have shown that those with a high sense of political efficacy almost always vote. Moreover, America has a two-party system, the Democratic Party and the Republican Party. Many voters think there are few fundamental differences between these two parties. Critics argue that the United States stands virtually alone in the democratic world in the lacking of a major left-wing socialist party.

Furthermore, Americans are asked to vote in a dozen or more separate elections in the space of four years. The frequency of elections in America may contribute to voter fatigue, thus causing low voter turnout. Finally, many Americans, by choice, do not want to seek political information. Some political scientists explain this in terms of "**rational ignorance**."[8] That is, when the cost of acquiring information is greater than the benefits derived from the information, it is rational to remain ignorant. Therefore, voters think that political participation has no impact on them, so they remain "rationally ignorant" of public affairs.

DETERMINANTS OF VOTING BEHAVIOR

Factors that influence voter turnout include age, education, income, and ethnicity. Voter turnout tends to be higher among middle-aged voters than among younger or older voters. Voters with a high level of education tend to vote more frequently than those with a low level of education. Furthermore, voters from high-income families tend to vote more often than low-income voters. Also, voter turnout is higher among white voters than it is among African-American and Hispanic voters. Finally, Protestants tend to vote Republican, whereas Catholics and Jews lean toward the Democratic party. (See Table 4.6.)

TABLE 4.6   TURNOUT IN 2004: PRESIDENTIAL VOTE BY SOCIAL GROUP

All Voters (%)		Kerry (%)	Bush (%)
All voters		48	51
Gender	Male	44	55
	Female	51	48
Race	White	41	58
	Black	88	11
	Hispanic	53	44
	Asian	59	41

TABLE 4.6 TURNOUT IN 2004: PRESIDENTIAL VOTE BY SOCIAL GROUP (CONT.)

ALL VOTERS (%)		KERRY (%)	BUSH (%)
Age	18–29	54	45
	30–44	46	53
	45–59	48	51
	60+	46	54
Income	Less than $15,000	63	36
	$16,000–$30,000	57	42
	$31,000–$50,000	50	49
	$51,000–$75,000	43	56
	$76,000–$100,000	45	55
	$101,000–$150,000	42	57
	$151,000–$200,000	42	58
	$201,000+	35	63
Education	No college degree	47	53
	College Graduate	40	59
Religion	Protestant	40	59
	Catholic	47	52
	Jewish	74	25
	None	67	31
Attended Religious Services			
	Weekly	39	60
	Occasionally	53	46
	Never	64	34
Party ID	Democrat	87	10
	Republican	7	93
First Time Voters		54	45
Region	Northeast	56	43
	Midwest	48	51
	South	42	58
	West	50	49
First Time Voter		54	45

Source: Simon, Roger. "Second Act." *U.S. News and World Report,* November 15, 2004, 17–30.

THE RESULTS OF THE 2004 PRESIDENTIAL ELECTION

In the 2004 presidential election, voter turnout was approximately 55 percent of the voting-age population compared to 51 percent in 2000, 55 percent in 1992, and 50 percent in 1988. (See Table 4.4.)

There were few surprises in the overall composition of the vote. (See Table 4.6.) The gender gap and the racial division in voting continued. More male voters, 55 percent, voted for George W. Bush than for John Kerry. More white voters voted for Bush than Kerry (58 percent versus 41 percent). Furthermore, Kerry received 88 percent of black votes and 53 percent of Hispanic votes. He dropped from the percentage of Hispanic and black votes Gore received in 2000. Over 93 percent of Republicans voted for Bush, and 87 percent of Democrats voted for Kerry. Kerry won first-time voters, by 54 percent to Bush's 45 percent—but there were not enough of them. Only 11 percent of the people went to the polls for the first time as opposed to 9 percent in 2000. Kerry also did equally well among young voters between ages 18–29, his most supportive age group. In the 2004 presidential election, 37 percent of the voters were Democrats and 37 percent Republicans. Kerry carried all of the Northeastern states, the West Coast states, and all but one, Ohio, of the Great Lake states. (See Table 8.2 on page 198–199.) Iowa and New Mexico voted for Gore in 2000, but Kerry lost in them in 2004. The only 2000 red state (Republican) that turned blue (Democrat) in 2004 was New Hampshire.[9]

REASON FOR INCREASE IN 2004 VOTER TURNOUT

Voter turnout was higher in the 2004 presidential election than in 2000. In the 2000 election, close to 51 percent of qualified voters voted, while in 2004 approximately 55 percent cast their ballots. The 2004 turnout increase can be attributed to several factors. The turnout was driven by strong feelings—pro and con—about President Bush and his administration's domestic and foreign policies. Those who supported President Bush favored his leadership quality, the war in Iraq and on Al-Qaeda; and above all, his stand on moral issues. According to the *Economist*, "Eight out of ten of these moralists voted for George W. Bush."[10] These voters did not want to change leadership in midstream, and to a person of unclear and shifting position, John Kerry, in the White House. (See Table 4.7.)

TABLE 4.7   MOST IMPORTANT QUALITY

Percentage Who Said:		Who They Voted For:	
		Bush (%)	Kerry (%)
25%	Will bring needed change	5	95
17%	Has clear stand on issues	78	21
17%	Strong leader	86	13
11%	Honest, trustworthy	70	29
9%	Cares about people like me	24	75
7%	Intelligent	8	91
8%	Strong religious faith	91	8

Source: *USAToday*. November 4, 2004.

John Kerry's support came mainly from those voters who accused President Bush of going to war against Iraq too soon without giving diplomacy a second chance, presidential lack of candor with respect to declaring war against Sadam Hussein, divisions in the nation due to Bush's divisive policies, lack of compassion, and his economic policies, which favored the rich, and a growing and dangerous national debt.

VOTER TURNOUT: THE UNITED STATES VERSUS OTHER DEMOCRACIES

The voter turnout rate in the United States is lower than that of other industrial democracies. (See Table 4.8.)

There are several reasons why the voter turnout rate is higher in these countries compared to the United States. The governments of other democracies make sure that all qualified voters are on the voter list. Some European countries, for example, Australia, Belgium, and Switzerland, have compulsory voting. Penalties for not voting range from fines to disenfranchisement for repeat offenders. With the exception of Switzerland, these countries hold less frequent elections than the United States. Furthermore, other democracies offer more party choices to their voters. This makes parties more competitive, disciplined, and able to mobilize the voters. The American party system lacks a major left-wing Socialist Party. Finally, unlike Europe's political culture, the political culture in the United States, which emphasizes self-reliance, does not encourage American voters to rely on government to solve problems.

TABLE 4.8 COMPARISON OF VOTER TURNOUT BETWEEN THE UNITED STATES AND OTHER DEMOCRACIES

Country	Approximate Voter Turnout (%)
Belgium	90
Germany	85
Sweden	85
Denmark	80
Italy	80
Austria	80
France	80
Great Britain	60
Canada	60
Japan	60
United States	55

Source: Thomas E. Patersnon, *We the People: A Concise Introduction to American Politics* (Boston: McGraw-Hill, 2005), p. 232.

ELECTIONS

Many types of elections are held in the United States. The most frequently held ones are: the primary, general, special, and recall elections.

Primary Elections

The primary election occurs before the candidates from different parties run against one another in a general election. It allows voters who identify themselves with a particular party to select nominees. It was adopted by most states at the turn of the century. Prior to the adoption of the primary, two other devices were used to nominate candidates. These were caucuses and conventions. A **caucus** was considered an undemocratic device because only party bosses took part in the selection process. The caucus was replaced in many states by **conventions** in the 1830s. This device was more democratic than the caucus because more people were allowed to participate. Yet the convention method was not fully democratic. To make the method of nomination fully democratic, state legislatures turned to the primary as a means of nominating party candidates at the beginning of the twentieth century. The Democrats and Republicans still use the convention method to select presidential candidates.

TYPES OF PRIMARIES

There are several types of primaries: the closed, open, closed caucus, open caucas, and the blanket dual primary. The **closed primary** requires individuals to register their party preference at the same time they register to vote. Thus, they may vote only in their own party primary. This type of primary election promotes party loyalty and partisan politics. It is the most popular type of primary among the states. (See Table 4.9.)

TABLE 4.9 PRIMARIES

STATES WITH OPEN PRIMARIES	STATES WITH CLOSED PRIMARIES	STATES WITH CAUCUS C = CLOSED/O = OPEN
Alabama	Arizona	Alaska (C)
Arkansas	California	Colorado (C)
Georgia	Connecticut	Hawaii (C)
Idaho	Delaware	Iowa (O)
Indiana	Florida	Kansas (C)
Mississippi	Kentucky	Maine (C)
Montana	Louisiana	Massachusetts (C)
Ohio	Maryland	Michigan (O)
S. Carolina	Nebraska	Minnesota (O)
Tennessee	New Jersey	Nevada (C)
Texas	New York	New Hampshire (C)
Vermont	Oklahoma	New Mexico (C)
Virginia	Oregon	North Carolina (C)
Wisconsin	Pennsylvania	North Dakota (O)
Illinois	Rhode Island	Utah (C)
Missouri	South Dakota	Washington (C)
	West Virginia	Wyoming (C)

Source: "2004 Presidential Primary Election Guidelines for Independent Voters." Independents Corner. <http://www.independentsforkerry.org/uploads/media/2004-primary-guidlines.html>

An **open primary** election does not require individuals to register their party preference in advance of an election. Thus, voters can vote for a party's candidates whether or not they belong to that party. An open primary promotes a nonpartisan election, where party loyalty is not stressed. A modified form of the open primary is called a blanket primary election. It is the least popular of the three types of primaries.

A **closed caucus** requires voters to be registered party members in order to be able to participate in that party's caucus. The **open caucus** is the opposite of the closed caucus.

One does not have to be a registered party member in order to attend the party caucus. A caucus is a gathering of voters to nominate presidential candidates.

In **blanket primaries**, voters could cast their votes for candidates of different parties. The only restriction was that a voter was limited to one party nomination per office. That is why independent voters preferred this type of primary. The blanket primary was used in Washington, Louisiana, Alaska, and recently California.

California adopted the blanket primary after 60 percent of state voters approved Proposition 198, a 1996 ballot initiative, and used it during the 2000 elections. Subsequently, the Supreme Court, in *California Democratic Party et al. v. Jones, et al.*, in a 7–2 ruling, declared California's blanket primary election unconstitutional. It ruled that political parties in California have a constitutional right to exclude nonparty members in primary elections and that the blanket primary law in California violates a political party's First Amendment right of association. This ruling was expected to boost the significance of political parties, whose influence with American voters has been eroding. The three other states that held blanket primaries had to revise their system.

The **dual primary** is prevalent only in most of the southern states. It requires a candidate to receive a majority of the votes, 50 percent plus one vote, in the primary to be nominated. If no one receives a majority, a runoff or second primary between two candidates with the most votes is held.

General Election

The names of the winners of the primaries appear on the ballot in general election in which all the voters choose the winners for each elected office. Unlike the primary election, the general election is held on the same day, the first Tuesday after the first Monday in November of even-numbered years. In addition, unlike the primary election, which is conducted by officials of the political parties, the general election is the responsibility of state officials. In Texas, the secretary of state is the chief election officer. The secretary of state is appointed by the governor and confirmed by the Texas senate. The office is responsible for distributing election supplies and receiving election results.

Special Election

Special elections are held to meet special or emergency needs, such as ratification of a constitutional amendment or filling and elected office in case a member dies, resigns, or is expelled. In some states, including Texas, special elections are nonpartisan, and winning candidates must secure a majority vote.

Recall Election

The purpose of convening a recall election is to force an elected official out of office. These officials are forced out of office because they have lost the confidence of the voters. Over a third of the states and many municipal governments permit their residents to resort to recall election. The recall election starts with a petition signed by the required number of voters, based on a specific percentage of votes cast for a particular office in the previous election. Once the signatures have been certified, the recall election takes place.

ELECTION CAMPAIGNS

The basic aim of any campaign is to defeat one's opponents in the election. To accomplish this goal, a campaign must be organized, carefully planned, and must have sufficient funds. Abraham Lincoln described his 1846 run for the House of Representatives as follows: "I made the canvass on my own horse; my entertainment, being at the houses of friends, cost me nothing; and my only outlay was 75 cents for a barrel of cider, which some farm-hands insisted that I treat them to."

Today, election campaigns are far more complex and expensive. They call for political consultants, professional fund-raisers, media consultants and pollsters, volunteer workers, and campaign strategies. Successful campaign strategies include compiling computerized mailing lists, selecting a campaign theme, adopting a candidate image, monitoring the campaign by continually polling the voters, producing television tapes, radio spots, signs, and bumper stickers. Modern campaigns also require big money. The 2004 federal election campaigns were the most expensive in history. The two major political parties, political action committees, and other political organizations spent a total of $3.9 billion.

In the 2004 presidential election, candidates and national conventions expenditures totaled more than $1 billion. According to the Federal Election Commission, the candidates in the primaries raised $673.9 million seeking the nomination. The two major party nominees received $74.6 million each in public funds to conduct their general election campaigns. for their nominating conventions, the two major parties received $14.9 million each from the U.S. Treasury, while the host committees from the two convention cities, Boston and New York City, raised a total of $142.5 million in support of the convention activities. In addition, parties and other groups spent $192.4 million independently advocating the election or defeat of presidential candidates during the 2004 campaign.[11] Median expenditure for a House race was $560,000, and for a Senate race it was $3.5 million in 1996.[12]

SOURCES OF CAMPAIGN FUNDS

The former Speaker of the House of Representatives, Thomas P. (Tip) O'Neill once said, "There are four parts to any campaign: The candidate, the issues,…the campaign organization, and the money. Without money you can forget other three." Although money does not guarantee a win, well-financed candidates tend to increase their chances of getting elected. Federal candidates have several sources of money.

Candidate's Own Money

One source is the candidates themselves. Wealthy candidates back their own campaigns. In 1976, in the case of *Buckley v. Valeo*,[13] the Supreme Court struck down a section of the 1974 law that kept presidential candidates or their families from giving more than $50,000 to their own campaigns. In this case, the Supreme Court argued that giving money to one's campaign is a form of free speech, which is protected by the First Amendment. In 2000, the New Jersey Democratic senatorial candidate, John Corzine, who retired as head of investment bank, Goldman Sachs, spent $63 million of his own money winning the race.

Individual Contributions

Contributions made by individuals to candidates constitute the second source of funds. Based on the **Bipartisan Campaign Reform Act** of 2002 (BCRA) (its provisions did not go into effect until after November 6, 2002, elections), an individual can give up to $2,000 per election to any federal candidate's campaign. The limit is indexed to inflation, so it would increase over time. The law also allows individual donations of $25,000 to a national party committee (e.g., the Democratic National Committee, the Republican National Committee) per year and $5,000 to political action committees per year. Each individual contributor is limited to $95,000 per each two-year election cycle. (See Table 4.10.) The two-year election cycle starts on January 1 of odd-numbered years and extends to December 31 of even-numbered years.

Political Action Committee (PAC)

The third source of contribution to federal candidates is **political action committees** (PACs). PACs are committees set up by representing corporations, labor unions, and special interest groups that raise and spend campaign contributions on behalf of candidates or causes. The first PAC, the Committee on Political Education (or COPE), was formed by the Congress of Industrial Organizations (CIO) in 1943 in response to a federal law that banned direct contributions from labor unions to federal candidates. Over the past years, as a result of the Federal Election Campaign Act of 1974, other labor unions (and later, corporations and business groups) formed PACs of their own. The law requires that funds that are distributed from PACs must not come from the organization but from voluntary contributions of the members. Federal laws limit PAC contribution to $5,000 to candidates, other PACs, or state parties per year, and $15,000 to national parties per year. Individuals can give $5,000 per year to a PAC. The new law leaves PAC contribution limits unchanged. The above sources of contributions are also known as **hard money**, because the law regulates them and must be used for any activity that directly advocates the election defeat of a federal candidate.

PACs have been subject to great discussion and criticism in recent years. This is partly because their numbers have proliferated from just a few hundred in the early 1970s to approximately 4,700 today. The amount of money they contributed to candidates from 1974 to 1992 increased from about $10 million to more than $189 million. Most of the money went to finance the campaigns of incumbent members of Congress.[14] (See Table 4.10.)

TABLE 4.10   CONTRIBUTION LIMITS

	TO A CANDIDATE PER ELECTION	TO NATIONAL PARTY PER CALENDAR YEAR	TO PAC PER CALENDAR YEAR	TOTAL PER TWO-YEAR ELECTION CYCLE
Individual may give:	$2,000	$25,000	$5,000	$95,000
Multi-candidate committee* (PAC) may give:	$5,000	$15,000	$5,000	No limit

*A multi-candidate committee is a political committee with more than 50 contributors, which has been registered for at least six months and, with the exception of state party committees, has made contributions to five or more candidates for federal office.

Soft Money

Another source of campaign contributions used to be **soft money**. It referred to unlimited and largely unregulated contributions from corporations, labor unions, and the wealthy to the national party committees. The money was supposed to be spent on get-out-the-vote campaigns, voter registration drives, and administrative expenses, but it was regularly used to finance advertising that promoted candidates without ever explicitly endorsing anyone. The new law bans soft-money contributions to national parties. It also caps contributions to state and local parties at $10,000 per individual and requires that soft money to state parties be used for voter registration drives and get-out-the-vote efforts.

527 Group

Although the new law bans soft-money contributions to national parties, the 527 committees have become a major channel for soft money during elections. They derived this name, the 527 Group, from the section of the tax code. A 527 group is a tax-exempt organization that is created primarily to raise and spend unlimited amounts of money to influence the outcome of elections, as long as they do not specifically call for the election or defeat of a particular candidate, and are totally independent from the political parties. The PACs are also created under Section 527 of the Internal Revenue Code, but the 527 Group is not regulated by the Federal Election Commission and is not subject to the same contribution limits as PACs. Thus, a 527 group is permitted to accept contributions in any amount from any source. They are exempt from federal income tax on contributions received, but they are required to report their funding and expenditures to the Internal Revenue Service.

In the 2004 election cycle, 527 groups spent nearly $400 million. In the 2004 presidential election, they produced the Swift Boat Veterans for Truth's advertisements against unsuccessful presidential candidate John Kerry, and another series of media campaigns by the Moveon.org Voter Fund that depicted George W. Bush's ties to the Saudi Arabian royal family. (See Table 4.11.)

George Soros of the Soros Fund Management, and Peter Lewis of the Progressive Group donated more than $20 million each to the 527 committees that support Democratic candidates and causes. In addition, three Texans were among the top contributors to 527 committees. Bob Perry, the Houston homebuilder, gave $4.5 million; T. Boone Pickens, the Dallas entrepreneur donated $4 million; and Harold Simmons, another Dallas entrepreneur, gave $3.8 million.[15]

TABLE 4.11 TOP TEN 527 GROUPS

Name	2004 Fundraising (in million $)	2004 Expenditures (in milliion $)
America Coming Together	79	76
Joint Victory Together	72	72
Media Fund	59	54
Progress for America	45	35
Service Employees International Union	43	44
American Federation of State, County, and Municipal Employees	25	25
Swift Boat Veterans for Truth	17	22
Club for Growth	13	17
MoveOn.org	13	21
New Democratic Network	12	12

Source: "Top Contributors to 527 Committees, 2004 Election Cycle" <http://www.opensecrets.org/527s/527cmtes.asp?level=C&cycle=2004>

The activities of 527s have raised concerns about the return of soft money that was banned with the passage of the BCRA in 2002. Senator John McCain (R-AZ) and others have introduced legislation in the 109th Congress to stop such spending before the 2006 Congressional elections get underway. The overriding goal of the bill is to require 527s to register with the Federal Election Commission and abide by the limits on fund-raising and spending.

PRESIDENTIAL CAMPAIGN FUNDS

In the wake of Watergate, Congress decided in 1974 to finance campaigns for the presidential nominations, presidential general elections, and nominating conventions with taxpayers' dollars. According to the Federal Election Campaign Act (FECA) of 1974, qualified presidential candidates receive money from the Presidential Election Campaign Fund, which is an account on the books of the U.S. Treasury. This fund is tied to the cost-of-living increase. These funds are distributed under several programs.

Primary Matching Payments

This funding is available during the nomination season to candidates who raise $5,000 in each state in at least 20 states in contributions of no more than $250. Once candidates meet this criterion, they receive public funds to match the first $250 of each private contribution they raise during the presidential primary election season up to a predetermined spending ceiling. Only contributions from individuals are matchable; contributions from PACs and party committees are not. In 1976, 15 Democratic and Republican candidates received a total of $25 million in federal funds to help pay for their primary campaigns. The overall primary spending limit is adjusted each presidential election year to reflect inflation. The Labor Department annually calculates the cost-of-living-adjustment (COLA) using 1974 as the base year. In 2004, the limit was $28.4 million.[13] (See Table 4.12.) President George W. Bush and two Democratic Party presidential candidates, John Kerry and Howard Dean, turned down the matching funds during the primaries to free themselves of federally mandated spending limits. Their decision helped to make the 2004 presidential election the most expensive in history.

General Election Funds

The two major parties presidential nominees are each eligible to receive public funding to be spent during the general presidential election. In return, they cannot raise or spend private funds after accepting their party's nomination. This does not mean that individuals and organizations cannot spend money independent of the two presidential campaigns. This law went into effect in the 1976 presidential election. President Gerald Ford and challenger Jimmy Carter each received $21.8 million in taxpayer money to spend on their fall campaigns. Each presidential election year, the general election spending is also adjusted to inflation. In 2004, the two major-party candidates each received $74.62 million in the form of public funding.[16] (See Table 14.12.)

Third-party presidential candidates may qualify for a lesser amount of public funding after the election if they receive at least 5 percent of the popular vote. They may receive public funds in an amount proportionate to the votes received by that party as compared with the major parties in the previous presidential election. Pat Buchanan, the Reform Party presidential candidate, received $12.6 million in public funds in 2000. He was qualified to this total amount because Ross Perot, the 1996 Reform Party presidential candidate, received approximately 8.5 percent of the popular vote. The first third party candidate to receive public funding was John Anderson. The poor showing by Pat Buchanan in the presidential election of 2000, less than 1 percent of the popular vote, disqualified the Reform Party nominee in 2004 from getting any federal funds.

Party Convention Funds

Each major party's presidential nominating convention is also financed by federal grant. The two major parties in 1976 each received $4 million. In 1996, they received $12.4 million each, adjusted to reflect inflation. Third-party presidential nominating conventions are entitled to this funding provided that their nominees receive at least 5 percent of the popular vote in the previous presidential election. (See Table 14.12.)

TABLE 4.12 PUBLIC FUNDS IN PRESIDENTIAL CAMPAIGNS

	PRIMARY MATCHING FUNDS (IN MILLION $)	CONVENTION (IN MILLION $)	GENERAL (IN MILLIION $)
1976	25	4	44
	*15	*2	*2
1980	31	9	63
	*10	*2	*3
1984	37	16	81
	*11	*2	*2
1988	68	18	92
	*15	*2	*2
1992	43	22	110
	*12	*2	*2
1996	59	25	153
	*11	*2	*3
2000	62	30	148
	*10	*3	*3
2004	28	30	149
	*8	*2	*2

* Number of candidates/parties that received funding.

Source: "Public Funds in Presidential Campaigns" Federal Election Commission <http://www.fec.gov/press2005/20050203pressum/fundhistory/pfd>

The Presidential Election Campaign Fund is financed mostly with public money. By checking a box on their income tax returns, taxpayers may direct $3 of their tax to the fund—the check-off amount was increased from $1 to $3 in 1994. The long-range future of the Presidential Campaign Fund is threatened due to decline in taxpayer participation. According to the *Congressional Quarterly*, "In 1993, only 14.5% of tax returns were checked off…down from 18.9% in 1992."[17]

WHO CANNOT CONTRIBUTE?

The following individuals and groups are prohibited from contributing to federal campaigns: individuals who have contracts with government, foreign citizens, corporations, labor unions, and national banks. In addition, cash contributions of more than $100 are prohibited. No candidate can accept an anonymous contribution that is more than $50. Finally, no one is allowed to make a contribution in another person's name.

THE FEDERAL ELECTION COMMISSION

As part of the Federal Election Campaign Act of 1974, Congress established the Federal Election Commission (FEC) as a regulatory agency charged with administering and enforcing federal campaign finance law. The FEC has jurisdiction over the financing of campaigns for the U.S. House, Senate, the presidency and vice presidency.

It has six members who serve staggered six-year terms. The commissioners are appointed by the president with the advice and consent of the U.S. Senate. No more than three commissioners may belong to the same political party. The commissioners elect two members each year to act as chairperson and vice chairperson. (For more information about the FEC see www.FEC.gov.)

CAMPAIGN EXPENDITURE

Modern campaigns are very expensive. In 2004, a record $3.9 billion was spent on presidential and congressional campaigns, up from $3 billion four years earlier.

Campaigning requires extensive travel arrangements, TV time, newspaper ads, posters, brochures, pamphlets, bumper stickers, polling costs, data processing, and staff salaries. (See Table 4.13 and Table 4.14.)

TABLE 4.13 CAMPAIGN FUNDING

Sources of Funds	Amount	Percentage
Individual Contributions	$2.5 billion%	64
Public Funds (presidential candidates and party conventions)	$207 million	5
The 527 Committees	$386 million	10
The Political Action Committee	$384 million	10
Candidate Self-funding	$144 million	4
Convention Host Spending	$139 million	4
Other Candidates' Revenues	$102 million	3
Total	$3.9 billion	100

Source: "The $Billion Campaign: Better, or Just Louder?" *Congressional Quarterly Weekly*, October 30, 2004, pp. 2546–2550.

TABLE 4.14 CAMPAIGN SPENDING

Sources of Expenditures	Percentage
Television and radio	40%
Staff salaries, consultant fees	20%
Office rent, equipment, travel	15%
Fund-raising expenses	10%
Legal and accounting fees, print media, polling	9%
Canvassing/get-out-the-vote efforts	6%

SUMMARY

America has come a long way toward making the political process more democratic and participatory. During the nineteenth century and a good part of the twentieth century, specific groups of voters were denied the right to participate in the political process. The Thirteenth, Fourteenth, Fifteenth, Nineteenth, Twenty-Fourth, and Twenty-Sixth Amendments to the Constitution were adopted to remedy the situation. Today it is easy to qualify to vote, but voter turnout in all elections has declined. For example, turnout for the 1996 presidential election was the lowest in the past 30 years. There is no one specific explanation for this trend. Students of voter behavior offer a combination of factors that may explain the decline in political participation.

One of these is the frequency of elections. America is one of the few Western democracies that hold frequent elections. These elections come in the form of primary elections, general elections, special elections, and recall elections. The Swiss have elections almost as frequently as Americans, and perhaps that is the reason why Switzerland has a comparable turnout rate.

According to an old adage, "money is the mother's milk of politics." Well-financed candidates have a better chance of winning elections than those who are poorly financed. In the 1970s, Congress passed a series of laws, the Federal Election Campaign Acts (FECA), to regulate campaign finance practices. Some of the provisions of those laws were recently amended by the so-called Bipartisan Campaign Reform Act of 2002 (BCRA). These laws cover campaign contribution disclosures, campaign contribution limits, and the prohibition of campaign contributions and expenditures by certain groups. Due to the existence of loopholes in the federal election campaign laws, the 527 groups became a major channel for soft money during the 2004 presidential election, and the total expenditures on elections have skyrocketed in recent years.

KEY TERMS

- **Blanket primary**
- **Caucus**
- **Closed primary**
- **Convention**
- **Dual primary**
- **Federal Election Campaign Act**
- **Federal Election Commission**
- **Franchisement**
- **General election**
- **Hard money**
- **Issue ads**
- **Jim Crow law**
- **Literacy test**
- **"Motor voter" Law**
- **Open primary**
- **Political action committee**
- **Poll tax**
- **Primary election**
- **Provisional ballot**
- **Rational ignorance**
- **Recall election**
- **Soft money**
- **Special election**
- **Universal suffrage**
- **White primary**

INTERNET SOURCES
1. Public Opinion Polls and Research
   a) http://ww.gallup.com/The-Poll/thepoll.htm
   This Gallup Organization's site provides information on public opinion on various historical and especially contemporary issues. It also contains the organization's newsletter discussing current events in the United States and globally.
   b) http://www.libuconn.edu/RoperCenter/gallupress.htm
   This site, maintained by the University of Connecticut Roper Center for Public Opinion Research, is similar to the Gallup Organization's.
   c) http://www.icpsr.umich.edu/index.html
   The University of Michigan's Inter-University Consortium provides this site for Political and Social Research (ICPSR)-Site for Social Science Data. It contains important research data on various issues from voting, Supreme Court decisions, foreign policy, etc.
2. Political Participation
   a) http://www.libertynet.org/~edcivic/iscvhome.html
   The Institute for the Study of Civic Values (ISCV) is responsible for maintaining this site. It contains information on First Amendment and civil rights. It's an excellent source for historical documents and especially major speeches by U.S. presidents and other national and international leaders. This site also provides education materials on voting, elections, and campaigns, etc.
   b) http://www.umich.edu/~nes/nesguide/nesguide.htm
   The Inter-University Consortium maintains this site for Political and Social Research (ICPSR) at the University of Michigan. This Center has national election data, especially that of presidential elections between 1952 and the present. Information on voter behavior and their views on various issues are also provided.
   c) http://www.auburn.edu/tann/cp/
   This site, entitled Citizen Power, contains information on democratic governments around the world: what they do, similarities and differences between them and that of the United States, voting, elections, etc.
3. Voting
   a) http://www.voter.cq.com/
   This site is provided by the Congressional Quarterly and entitled the American Voter. It provides information on legislation and policy issues on various issues as determined by the U.S. House of Representatives and Senate. Of importance are background data on elected officials to these chambers of the U.S. Congress.
   b) http://www.vote-smart.org
   Organized by Project Vote Smart, this site provides information on candidates vying for political office, especially to national positions in the U.S. Congress

and the White House. Their opinions and views on various issues are also included in this site.

4. Campaigns and Elections

a) http:www//voter.cq.com

(Same as entry for 3 (a) on voting)

b) http://www.geocities.com/CapitolHill/6228/elections.htm

This site contains data on presidential election returns from 1948 to the present: Who voted for what candidate and by what percentage; and performances of the presidential candidates in the Electoral College.

c) http://www.rollcall.com/election/turnoutchart.html/

This site is maintained by Roll Call and contains information on voter turnout and demographics on various national elections, especially that of the presidency.

5. Campaign Finance

a) http://www.fec.gov/

Maintained by the Federal Election Commission (FEC), this site provides important data information on various campaign-related issues: federal-state laws, limits on campaign-election contributions, candidates' spending limits, their itinerary, etc.

NOTES

[1] John Stuart Mill, *Considerations on Representative Government* (Chicago: Henry Regnery, Bateway, 1962), p. 144.

[2] M. Margaret Conway, *Political Participation in the United States* (Washington, D.C.: Congressional Quarterly, 1991), p. 32.

[3] Quoted in Harold J. Spaeth, *The Constitution of the United States* (New York: HarperPerennial, 1991), p. 155.

[4] *Guinn v. United States*, 238 U.S. 347 (1915).

[5] *Smith v. Allwright*, 321 U.S. 649 (1944).

[6] *Harper v. Virginia Board of Elections*, 383 U.S. 663 (1966).

[7] To learn more about HAVA refer to the Texas Secretary of State's Web page, http://www.sos.state.tx.U.S.

[8] For detailed discussion on this phrase see, Anthony Downs, An Economic Theory of Democracy (New York: Harper 1957).

[9] Simon, Roger. "Second Act." *U.S. News and World Report,* November 15, 2004: 17–30.

[10] "The Triumph of the Religious Right." *Economist,* November 11, 2004, <http://www.economist.com/world/na/PrintFriendly.cfm?Story_ID=3375543>

[11] "2004 Presidential Campaign Financial Activity Summarized." Election Commission, February 3, 2005. <http://www.fec.gov/press/press2005/20050203pressum/20050203pressum.html>

[12] Federal Election Commission.

[13] *Buckley v. Valeo*, 424 U.S. 1 (1976).

[14] Most of the information about federal campaign finance is based on "Campaign Finance Reform," *Congressional Digest*, October 1998.

[15] "Those Pesky 527s." *Start Telegram*, November 3, 2004, B-1 p. 13

[16] For detailed discussion of campaign contributions and expenditures in the 2004 presidential elections refer to the Federal Election Commission's website, www.fec.gov.

[17] J. D. Salant, "Presidential Campaign Fund," *Congressional Quarterly*, August 19, 1995.

Chapter 5

Collective Participation: Interest Groups, Movements and Political Parties

In no country of the world has the principle of association been more successfully used or applied to a greater multitude of objectives, than in America.

Alexis de Tocqueville

INTRODUCTION

Alexis de Tocqueville, a French aristocrat touring the United States in the early part of the nineteenth century, had noted that since the early stages of American society, associations have been a key element of democracy.[1] He stated that Americans' tendency to collectively participate could be attributed to the egalitarian attribute of American society. Students unfamiliar with the American democratic process could easily conclude that interest groups have corrupted the country's democracy; political parties polarize the nation every four years during the presidential elections; and movements are responsible for radical destructive activities—usually associated with developing countries. When carefully examined, these observations might be found to be misleading. Collective participation, in the form of interest groups or political parties, is the glue that holds the country's political system together. The groups are an important mechanism through which citizens make their ideas, needs, and views known to government officials. What these groups are, and their impact in shaping America's democratic terrain, will be examined in this section.

INTEREST GROUPS

An interest group can be defined as an organized body of individuals who share common political goals and try to influence public policy. While Alexis de Tocqueville, in *Democracy in America*, suggested that the ease with which Americans form organizations is a reflection of a strong democratic culture, James Madison, the fourth president and one of the authors of the **Federalist Papers**, considered all contending groups as factions and warned of their dangers. He used this term in *Federalist No. 10* to describe "a number of citizens, whether amounting to a majority or minority, who are united and actuated by some common impulse of passion or of interest, adverse to the rights of other citizens, or to the permanent and aggregate interests of the community."

While concerned that factions could destabilize a government, Madison suggested that we could not totally ignore them in democratic equation. He noted that the causes of political differences and creation of factions to be "sown in the nature of man" and it was a mistake to try to eliminate factions, because that would restrict liberty. Madison stated that "it could not be less folly to abolish liberty, which is essential to political life, because it nourishes faction, than it would be to wish the annihilation of air, which is essential to animal life, because it imparts to fire its destructive agency" (*Federalist No. 10*). However, relief from factions should come from controlling their activities. The establishment of a republic (representative democracy), with functional as well as territorial separation of powers, and not a democracy (direct or Athenian democracy), Madison suggested, would cure the "mischief of factions."

In contemporary America, far from when Madison wrote *Federalist No. 10*, factions are present in almost any group. American politics is called the politics of conflict within and without different groups. Sources of conflict may be different due to beliefs over social values; competition for scarce resources; different social priorities; diversity of population by race, wealth, religion, and occupation. The Democratic and Republican parties, for example, comprise different factions. These are the different groups of people who vote for them, but not necessarily share similar political views or principles. Jews, African-Americans and labor unions, for example, generally vote Democratic. However, they hold different views on divergent issues.

The same is true for the Republican Party with different factions that do not necessarily agree on all the issues for which the party stands. Most evangelical Christians, for instance, vote Republican. And this is because of the party's stance on moral Biblical values: abortion, homosexuality, same-sex/gay marriage, euthanasia, etc. But some Republicans, while not sharing similar values, may vote for the party simply for its conservative economic and fiscal stand.

From the foregoing, factions could either be analyzed as per James Madison's *Federalist No. 10* or in terms of contemporary American political groups and their internal structure and composition.

TYPES OF INTEREST GROUPS

George F. Will, columnist, in an opinion column titled, "Will's Rule of Informed Citizenship," stated that anyone who wants to learn about the U.S. government, should not begin by reading the Constitution or the Declaration of Independence. Such persons should instead read selected portions of the Washington, D.C.'s phone directory, which contains listings of interest groups with their headquarters in our nation's capital. One quickly realizes that American politics is that of conflict among more than ten thousand interest groups. Indeed, there are interest groups that represent almost every conceivable aspect of life. People can be members of interest groups and not be aware of it. Any group that organizes to garner benefits for its members, whether calling for regulation or seeking to end regulation, is an interest group.

Business and Occupational Groups

These are interest groups that represent the economic interests of their members. The main voice for big business in the United States is the National Association of Manufacturers (NAM). This organization was founded in the late nineteenth century. Another example of an interest group representing big business interest is the Business Roundtable. This interest group is open only to America's largest companies—180 of the Fortune 500 largest corporations were founding members. The Chamber of Commerce is another group established to promote the interest of small businesses. This interest group was formed in the early part of the twentieth century. Currently, it has close to four thousand local branches all over the United States. Many other businesses belong to different trade associations, including the Automobile Manufacturers Association, the American Electronic Association, and the Aerospace Industries Association. Various labor groups such as the United Steel Workers and the American Federation of Labor-Congress of Industrial Organization (AFL-CIO) also represent Labor. The AFL-CIO used to be made up of two separate groups: AFL represented skilled workers and CIO was the voice of unskilled and semiskilled workers. They did not merge until 1955. Currently, it has close to sixteen million members.

Civil Rights Groups

Minorities and women got organized to end political, economic, and social segregation and discrimination in America. They also have been involved in social welfare and immigration policies. Examples of civil rights groups include the National Association for the Advancement of Colored People (NAACP), the Urban League, the Southern Christian Leadership Conference (SCLC), the Native American Rights Fund (NARF), the League of United Latin American Citizens (LULAC), the Mexican-American Legal Defense and Educational Fund (MALDEF) and the National Organization for Women (NOW). They work to assure opportunities and fair treatment for members of their groups. For instance, NOW has sought to assure women's rights in society before the law and at the workplace.

Ideological Groups

These groups are formed to promote a particular ideology. For instance, Americans for Constitutional Action (ACA) promotes conservative issues and causes, while People for the American Way (PAW) represents liberal interests.[2] Ideological groups support or oppose issues such as taxes, foreign policy and federal expenditures based on their ideological disposition. Other ideologically oriented interest groups include Americans for Democratic Action (ADA), formed by Hubert Humphrey and Eleanor Roosevelt to oppose centrist policies of President Harry Truman; the American Civil Liberties Union (ACLU), put together to promote civil liberties issues; and the Concord Coalition, a conservative group concerned about tax and budget issues.

Religious Groups

A variant of the ideological group is the group that wishes to transform society along the lines of its religious beliefs. These groups take up issues such as supporting school prayer, opposing homosexual rights, securing government vouchers for students to attend religious schools, and banning abortion by a constitutional amendment. Protestants often try to influence government through an organization called the National Council of Churches (NCC), Catholics through the National Catholic

Welfare Council (NCWC), Jews through the American Jewish Committee (AJC) and the American Jewish Congress (AJC), Muslims through the Islamic Circle of North America (ICNA) and Islamic Society of North America (ISNA).

Single-Issue Groups

As the name implies, this category is made up of groups whose members promote one particular policy or social problem. Members of such groups are intensely and emotionally committed to promoting their goals. Thus the National Rifle Association (NRA) and the National Coalition to Ban Handguns are against or for gun control. Similarly, the National Right to Life Committee (NRLC) and the National Abortion Rights Action League (NARAL) stand on opposite sides of the single issue of abortion. Other single interest groups include the Sierra Club and the Environmental Defense Fund (EDF), both of which fight for the preservation of the environment.

Public Interest Groups

These groups are formed to promote and protect the interests of average citizens as consumers and holders of individual rights. Some of the best known public interest groups include the League of Women Voters (LWV), Common Cause (CC), Public Interest Research Groups (PIRG), the American Civil Liberties Union (ACLU), and Citizens for Tax Justice (CTJ). The LWV is a nonpartisan political organization that attempts to encourage participation in politics and works to increase understanding of public issues through education and advocacy. In the past, it sponsored presidential debates. The CC has been in existence since 1970. It attempts to strengthen American democracy by making certain that government is open, ethical and accountable. The PIRG is an alliance of state-based, citizen-funded organizations that protects the interest of consumers against big business. A well-known consumer advocate, Ralph Nader, challenged General Motors and its Corvair automobile, which he considered unsafe, in the 1960s. The ACLU is made up of attorneys who work in courts and legislatures to defend and preserve individual rights and liberties. Finally, the CTJ is a nonpartisan research and advocacy organization that promotes fair taxation in government.

Professional Associations

Another category of interest groups is the association of professionals. Groups such as the National Education Association, the Texas Community College Teachers Association, the American University Professors, the American Bar Association, and the American Medical Association, focus on the collective interests, values, and status of their profession. Other groups are organized to represent the interests of engineers, accountants, librarians, cosmetologists, pharmacists and many other professional groups.

SOURCES OF GROUP INFLUENCE

There are many interest groups on the American political scene. All interest groups are not equally powerful and successful. Their power and success depend on their size, the degree of their commitment, their unity and sense of purpose, their leadership, and the resources at their disposal.

Large interest groups such as the American Association of Retired Persons (AARP), with more than 33 million members, exercise influence by virtue of their members. Many of AARP's members are strongly committed to their cause of preserving the benefits they receive from government, including Social Security and Medicare. The AARP is feared by members of Congress because it has convinced legislators that its members will vote for or against them solely on specific issues. However, larger interest groups may face the problem of internal schism.

Because of this difficulty, it is not surprising that those smaller and cohesive groups with more intensity of feeling often exercise power and success far greater than their numbers might suggest. A single-issue group, devoted to such causes as pro-life, pro-environment, or gun control, is often most intense. Their members are emotionally attached to their causes and willing to get actively involved.

Money is another important ingredient and source of power and influence for interest groups. Considerable financial resources are not only necessary for maintaining headquarters and keeping members informed, but also lobbying and supporting candidates for office. Not all interest groups have equal amounts of money. Interest groups with a lot of financial resources will be able to use the money to hire reputable lobbyists and contribute money to sympathetic candidates in order to increase their chance of getting elected. One source of money is membership fees. Another source of money is political action committees (PACs). They are the financial arm of interest groups. By law, PACs are allowed to solicit money from their members on a voluntary basis. The money raised by PACs will be spent during elections to support specific candidates and causes. (See pages 91–92 for a detailed discussion of PACs.)

INTEREST GROUP STRATEGIES

Interest groups use a variety of techniques and strategies in order to promote their goals and affect government decisions in their favor. The most frequently used strategies are lobbying, litigation, grass-roots lobbying, electioneering, coalition building, protest, and demonstration.

Lobbying

Lobbying refers to a situation where individuals face their elected officials in the lobbies of government buildings to try to persuade them on how to take action on specific issues. Lobbyists are hired by interest groups to communicate with the appropriate governmental authorities about a group's needs and to influence government's decisions that affect its members. A lobbyist provides the interest group access to the government. Most lobbyists are former legislators who are well-connected to politics and politicians.

Lobbyists lobby all branches and levels of government. The key to being a successful lobbyist is having access to lawmakers. Lobbyists are considered the members of the "Third House"[3] in Congress. While the Senate and House are set up on a geographical bases, lobbyists represent people on the basis of their interests. In 1997 there were more than 11,500 **registered lobbyists** in Washington, D.C. That is more than 21 lobbyists for each of the 535 members of Congress. Why would a legislator listen to a lobbyist or an interest group, let alone help advance their cause by passing or defeating appropriate legislation? Lobbyists and interest groups provide the legislator with the essentials for being an effective politician: votes, information, and money. Members of an interest group can be used as tools of persuasion by lobbyists. If a legislator listens to the concerns of an interest group and acts in a manner that favors the group, they can broaden their voter and contribution pools.

Lobbyists can provide legislators with information. State and federal lawmakers must consider thousands of pieces of legislation each session. Lobbyists can provide research and expertise on pending legislation. The access to information becomes even more important to legislators on the state level. In Texas, for example, the state legislature meets every two years for 140 days and must consider between 4,000 and 6,000 bills. There is not enough time to become educated about thousands of issues, so a lobbyist, providing information, becomes almost a necessity. Lobbyists also provide experts to testify at congressional committee hearings.

Interest groups also target the executive branch with their lobbyists. Very often lobbyists want favorable interpretation of existing rules and regulations by government agencies and departments. For example, environmental groups seek a tighter definition of "clear air" and industry groups advocate a looser definition of "clean air." Furthermore, interest groups may lobby the executive branch to influence the presidential nominees who will serve in positions the interest groups regard as sensitive to their own interests. In addition, interest groups hire former government officials, especially senior members of the White House, as their lobbyists. They are also appointed to regulatory bodies that govern their industries. This practice is called "revolving door." Many critics argue that it may give private interests unfair influence over government decisions.

Litigations

In addition to lobbying Congress and the executive branch, interest groups also seek to realize their goals through lobbying the courts. This can be accomplished by the sponsoring of court cases or by filing *amicus curiae* briefs ("friend of the court" briefs) with the courts. Interest groups lobby the judicial branch by sponsoring court cases. The National Association for the Advancement of Colored People (NAACP) sponsored several such cases including *Brown v. Board of Education* (1954). The NAACP sued the school board in Topeka, Kansas, claiming that "separate but equal" was inherently unequal. To be successful the group needed a plaintiff who attended a segregated school whose facilities were equal to that of the white school. The NAACP "plaintiff shopped" until they found Linda Brown, a child attending school under such circumstances. In addition to providing injured parties or plaintiffs, interest groups may lobby the court through litigation they finance rather than one in which they participate.

Another method of lobbying the courts is to file an *amicus curiae* brief. These briefs inform the court of an interest group's views on the case. In the case of *Webster v. Reproductive Health Services* (1989), *amicus curiae* briefs were filed by 35 interest groups favoring the state's position, and 40 interest groups filed briefs in favor of the defense.[4] Interest groups will also send representatives to testify before the Senate Judiciary Committee's confirmations hearings. Several pro-choice abortion interest groups testified against Robert Bork and Anthony Kennedy because these nominees to the Supreme Court were perceived as pro-life.[5]

Grassroots Lobbying

Grassroots lobbying is an attempt by lobbyists to influence public officials indirectly through their constituents, the general public, or other groups. One example of grassroots lobbying is the use of constituents to achieve the group's goal. Interest groups mobilize large numbers of constituents to write, phone, or send e-mails to their legislators or the president and make their views known to them. Interest groups also resort to producing advertisements in national magazines and newspapers, mass mailings, and television commercials to build a positive image and support among the members of public for their causes. It has been stated that a group which has earned a positive reputation among people will have a much easier time convincing government officials to consider their demand.

Electioneering

Interest groups live by the following motto: "Elect your friends, defeat your enemies." Even though the ultimate goal of an interest group is to influence government decisions, they also want to influence the outcome of elections. One step in the process of electioneering is to make campaign contribution to candidates. Money is usually given to the candidates through political action committees. In an era where campaigning for office costs millions of dollars, candidates know that the key to winning is money. Interest groups know that candidates and legislators are more likely to take an interest in their cause if they receive a contribution to the campaign.

Interest groups form political action committees (PACs) to solicit and distribute campaign contributions. Corporations and labor unions are forbidden by law from giving direct contributions to candidates, so they create PACs to distribute money to candidates.

Incumbents generally receive more PAC money than challengers because PACs and interest groups prefer to maintain the relationship with a Congressperson they have already lobbied.

Coalition Building

Another strategy used by interest groups is to build a coalition with other like-minded interest groups who are concerned with the same issues. Coalition building is needed when an interest group realizes that it alone does not have the technical capability or financial resources to have a real impact on an issue. Another purpose of coalition building is to avoid duplicating one another's lobbying efforts.

Protest and Demonstration

Interest groups that lack financial resources may resort to nonviolent peaceful demonstrations as a way of publicizing and promoting their cause. Those who opposed nuclear power plants resorted to marching, picketing, and blocking entrances to a power plant to express their opposition to nuclear energy. Martin Luther King Jr. organized mass demonstrations during the civil rights movement of the 1950s and 1960s. King's source of inspiration was Mahatma Gandhi of India who resorted to nonviolent civil disobedience against British rule in India. The opponents of the Vietnam War also used this strategy effectively to stop the war.

POLITICAL/SOCIAL MOVEMENTS

Political or social movements are groups organized for the purpose of drawing government's attention to society's injustices. They are born out of the view that unless the oppressed exhibit radical actions against government, those in power would trample upon such persons' liberties.

This concept explains why social movements are generally associated with revolutionary or radical methods, and whose members reject regular channels of political influence in favor of direct action. Social movements, although not averse to freedom and liberty, believe that political leaders will not address certain societal problems unless they are forced to do so by radical means.

DIFFERENT TYPES OF MOVEMENTS

Movements are generally episodic groups that utilize revolutionary and radical methods in forcing government to address issues that might affect a cross-section of the society, and not just their members. Movements evolve from the spontaneous activities of certain radical individuals who galvanize a large segment of the population to join them in order to transform the status quo.

Typical movements base their argument against government on emotional issues such as life and death; fairness and unfairness; and war and peace. Movements generally believe that democratic governments exist solely for the benefit of the rich and wealthy, and consequently, that the laws, economic policies, and legal system have been put in place simply to perpetuate their rule at the expense of the rest of society.

Women's Movement

The history of social movements in America started with the clamor of women for equality of participation. Having been oppressed at the workplace and deprived of political participation they challenged the male domination of American society. Susan B. Anthony, for example, exemplified the genre of women who challenged male domination of politics and called for universal suffrage.

Susan B. Anthony and Elizabeth Cady Stanton, another leader of the women-suffrage movement, founded the National Women Suffrage Association. By 1869, securing the right to vote became the primary focus of this organization. For the next several decades, activists carried out a ceaseless and sustained campaign, from leaflets and massive petition drives to street-corner speeches, legislative lobbying and street parades, in order to realize their goal. Finally, on August 26, 1920, the Nineteenth Amendment to the U.S. Constitution was ratified. With the passage of this amendment, American women secured the most basic promise of democracy, the right to vote.

Civil Rights Movement

Although there were sporadic anti-slavery rebellions and riots against slave masters, none of these was as well organized and had as far-reaching an effect as the 1950s' and 1960s' civil rights marches. The American black population came of full political age and awareness when the Black Panthers, for instance, threatened the stability of American politics through destructive activities, including bombings of public places; assassinations; kidnappings and similar actions that, in contemporary times, would simply be considered terrorism.

On the opposing side of this radical political equation, although with shared causes, was Reverend Martin Luther King, Jr. (MLK) and his supporters. They were mostly preachers and respected blacks. Undeterred by police brutality, black protestors—supported by non-blacks who strongly believed in their cause—staged political marches, rallies, and peaceful demonstrations in defiance of government bans on such activities.

Borrowing from Mahatma Gandhi's passive resistance movement against British rule in India, MLK and his followers finally broke America's resolve against racial equality. Ultimately, the U.S. Congress passed the 1964 Civil Rights Act followed by the Voting Rights Act of 1965. Advocates of social movements would contend that without such radical actions, American blacks would still have been denied voting rights and deprived of their liberties.

Anti-War Movement

The Vietnam War and its attendant evils gave vent to the anti-war movement. This consisted of a number of independent interests, united only in opposition to the Vietnam War. Many young Americans were opposed to that war and considered American involvement in it unjust and unwarranted. They organized resistance movements to the war through huge marches, street battles with police, and destruction of private and public property. Some resisted the national draft and fled the country.

The antiwar movement achieved its goal when Richard Nixon ordered the withdrawal of American troops from Vietnam. The supporters of the anti-war movement would state categorically that without such radical activities, the Vietnam War would have continued. Their opponents, however, disagree and argue that the war came to an end at exactly the right time regardless of the anti-war opposition to it.

Echoes of the anti-Vietnam War movement once again resonated when opponents of the second U.S.-Iraq War gathered in major American cities to protest American action in Iraq. They accused the oil interest who wished to swap Iraq's oil for young America's blood. Numbering in the thousands, they challenged the Bush Administration to show evidence of a terrorism linkage between the September 11, 2001, attack on America and Saddam Hussein's government. These protestors wanted American troops withdrawn from Iraq.

Anti-Globalization Movement

Another example of social movement is anti-globalization or anti-capitalist group. The movement has mushroomed world-wide in recent years, with grassroots campaigners holding protests against globalization. Their major goal is to bring attention to the political and social inequalities between poor and rich nations. The major thrust of their argument is that wealthy nations, usually represented by the so-called G-8 (Canada, France, Germany, Japan, Italy, Russia, United Kingdom, and United States), control more than 90 percent of the world's wealth. And most of this is derived from poor nations. This income inequality and imbalance inflame members of the anti-capitalist movement.

They disrupt meetings of industrialized nations and multinational corporations such as the World Trade Organization (WTO), International Monetary Fund (IMF), World Bank, Exxon and others. Their goal is to publicize these organizations' unjust economic and social policies through radical and destructive actions. In 2003, for instance, due to security concerns that plagued recent international summits, the Canadian government was forced to relocate the venue of the G-8 summit meeting from Ottawa to a remote mountain resort of Kananaskis, far away from the disruptive activities of these groups.

Anti-Abortion Movement

The anti-abortion movement has left its mark on the American political landscape. These groups are comprised mainly of Christians who are vehemently opposed to government's legalization and liberalization of abortion rights. Their activities escalated after the U.S. Supreme Court's 1967 *Roe v. Wade* decision legalized abortion. Members and supports of this group have blocked entrances to various abortion clinics, picketed homes of physicians who perform abortions, firebombed abortion clinics, and even shot doctors.

Although the Supreme Court has allowed anti-abortion protests outside clinics where abortions are performed,[6] the Court has designated a "bubble zone" between protesters and anyone within 100 feet of a healthcare facility.[7]

Anti-abortion advocates support their actions by stating that life begins right at conception and not at birth. Consequently, just as life is precious to doctors who perform abortions, so it is to those unborn babies who are defenseless against the medical establishment and their backers in government.

Environmental Movement

By far the most noticeable of America's social movements are the environmentalist groups. They are the self-acclaimed protectors of the environment against government policies that endanger the eco-system. They argue that the rich nations, through their wealthy corporations and business activities, destroy marine life by polluting the world's waterways and atmosphere. Groups such as the Green Peace and People for the Ethical Treatment of Animals (PETA) stand out at the forefront of the environmentalist groups. Their argument is that animals are being used for various drug tests before they are exposed to humans, and that rivers are being polluted by crude oil explorations in poor countries. Consequently, their members invade science labs to free animals used in experiments. Sometimes, they confront oil tankers and warships as protest against their destruction of marine life.

Gay Rights Movement

American homosexuals have come out of the closet. This statement means that gays and lesbians no longer hide their activities. Prior to the 1980s, it was unheard of for individuals with an alternative sexual lifestyle to claim their rights in public.

Gays and lesbians in America argue that government and society at large discriminate against them. They claim that the U.S. Constitution's First Amendment rights grant them the same equality as everybody else. They argue that government refusal to grant them equal rights status is outright discrimination against American gays and lesbians. Their activities, in the form of Gay Awareness Day and demonstrations, have prompted more than 10 states to pass propositions declaring same-sex marriage unconstitutional. And in the 2004 Presidential Election, President George W. Bush vowed that he would support a constitutional amendment banning same-sex marriage.

In all, social movements have brought a new dimension to the character of the American democracy; an action supported by Madison in *Federalist No. 10* when he cautioned that instead of abolishing factions, they should be curtailed through laws, rules and regulations. And that is essentially what government has done by granting movements the right to express their views, but without depriving others of their due rights.

POLITICAL PARTIES

A **political party** is an organized group that seeks to influence the government through winning elections. The major political parties in the United States are the Democrats and the Republicans.

Political parties are not called for in the U.S. Constitution. Parties were viewed by the founders as **factions**—selfish groups that were destructive to the needs of the whole. Parties formed in spite of the founders' views, and were forged even though the U.S. Constitution never mentions their existence. The early political parties evolved over time.

The first parties formed due to differences of opinion on the function of a national government. The **Federalists** (ancestors of today's Republicans) supported ratification of the U.S. Constitution and a strong national government. They were generally supported by affluent citizens whose interests were business, industry, manufacturing, and trade.[8] The **Anti-Federalists** (ancestors of today's Democrats), a pejorative term used by the Federalists to identify the members of the Democratic-Republican Party, initially opposed ratification of the U.S. Constitution, opposed the creation of a strong national government and were supported by farmers and those working in agriculture.[9]

The tradition of two parties began with the Federalists and Anti-Federalists in the 1790s. The next evolution of the parties occurred in the early 1800s with the former Federalists, now named Whigs, and the former Anti-Federalists, the Jacksonian Democrats. The **Whigs** were still the party of industry and the **Jacksonian Democrats** were opposed to what they thought were government favors to business.[10] The Jacksonian Democrats were concerned that people be treated equally and claimed that the Whigs' business elite received government favors that harmed the people.[11]

The Whigs and Democrats remained the names of the parties until the Civil War era, when the Whigs gave way to the **Republican** party.[12] In this era the Republicans generally represented northern industry and the Democrats represented the southern agricultural communities.[13]

Illustration of Republican Symbol

© Bettmann/CORBIS

From the Civil War to the present day the parties have kept the names Democrat and Republican. The names have remained consistent, but each party's ideology has shifted over time. The Federalists, today's Republicans, favored a strong central government, while today's Republicans want the states to have more control. The Anti-Federalists, today's Democrats, were leery of a strong federal government, but the Democrats now favor such, stating that it is necessary to ensure equality. One factor has remained steady over the 200-year evolution of the parties: the Republicans have traditionally been associated with business and industry, while the Democrats have been aligned with the laboring class or middle class. Today's Democrats and Republicans are still split on issues of money, the economy, the role of the national government, and issues of equality. (See Table 5.1.)

TABLE 5.1   SELECTED ISSUES FROM DEMOCRATIC AND REPUBLICAN PLATFORMS

Democrats	Republicans
Economy	
A national economic strategy is required to invest in infrastructure, defense conversion and a national information network. Provide worker retraining and good jobs for all.	Oppose any attempt to increase taxes and advocate cutting them. Advocate a balanced budget amendment. Express confidence in the free market.
Health Care	
We will enact a uniquely American health-care system providing universal access to quality, affordable health care, with tough controls on costs. We will fight a united war on AIDS.	Government control of health care is irresponsible and ineffective. Health-care choices must remain the hands of the people. AIDS prevention is a personal and moral responsibility.
Environmental Protection	
We will protect natural resources, oppose environmentally harmful activities, and support energy efficiency, recycling and pollution prevention.	Environmental progress must continue in tandem with economic growth. Unemployment is also a form of pollution.
Social Values	
We support *Roe v. Wade* and a national law to protect every woman's right to choose. Handguns and assault weapons must be controlled. No American must suffer from the deprivation of any civil right, including sexual orientation.	The fetus has a right to life, and we therefore support a constitutional human life amendment. We stand for the constitutional right to bear arms. We oppose the inclusion of sexual preference as a protected civil right.
Cultural Values	
We support public support of the arts, free from political manipulation and rooted in freedom of expression.	Elements within the entertainment industry disparage traditional morality and family values.

Source: Copyright © University of Michigan.

WHY A TWO-PARTY DEMOCRACY

By and large, there are single-, two-, and multi-party systems. America's party structure is considered a two-party system. Overwhelmingly, a majority of the electorate casts its votes for candidates of the two major parties, Democratic and Republican. There are several reasons for the domination of the two-party system in American.

Historical Tradition

By the late 1850s, the Democrats and Republicans were fully established as the dominant groups in the United States. Between then and now, many families have been politically socialized to vote for either of these two parties. Many people would hardly vote for a third party. That is because they are accustomed to voting for either of the two parties in the country. As long as such behavior persists, third parties will not be able to command a plurality, much less a majority of voters in an election.

Absence of Religious and Left-Leaning Parties

Thomas R. Dye introduced the concept of political culture in the perpetuation of the two-party system in America. According to his analysis, unlike European countries with religious parties, the lack of religious groups with strong ideological attachment to specific beliefs encourages America's two majority parties, Democrats and Republicans, to support almost similar issues: free enterprise, individual liberty, religious freedom, separation of church and state, and equality of opportunity. "No party," according to Dye, "challenging these values has ever won."[14]

This is also true of left-leaning political parties. Unlike European political parties, the American party system lacks the presence of a left-leaning socialistic party. Working class voters disproportionately support socialist parties in Europe. In the absence of a left-leaning socialist party, most members of labor unions and workers tend to rally their support behind the Democratic Party.

Electoral Laws

Just as there are laws regulating various political activities, there are also those limiting political parties. These laws discriminate against third parties and prevent them from playing a dominant role in the mainstream of American politics. For example, a minor party's presidential candidate cannot automatically get on any state ballot without first obtaining a substantial number of signature petitions—a very challenging accomplishment for a candidate with modest financial backing. In order to be placed on New York's ballot in the 2004 presidential elections, Ralph Nader, the Green Party presidential candidate, had to secure 50,000 signatures.[15]

In addition, for third party presidential candidates to qualify for federal public funding during the presidential general election, they have to garner 5 percent of the popular vote. In the 1996 presidential election, the Reform Party candidate, Ross Perot, won 8 percent of the popular vote. In the 2000 White House race, Ralph Nader, the Green Party candidate, won less than 3 percent of the popular vote. And in the 2004 race, he obtained less than 1 percent of the popular vote.[16] With such stringent electoral laws, it becomes almost impossible for Third Party candidates to win major national elections.

Election System

Americans vote for candidates in elections, and not for the political parties associated with these candidates. In order to win, therefore, a candidate must collect a plurality, the most votes, and not a majority. This is the winner-take-all system based on single-member-district election procedure. This system of election works to the benefit of the two major parties in America, because one of them will most often come out first, and the other, second. As long as this procedure continues, third parties will hardly fall in the first place, thereby leaving the two major parties to win all elections. In Europe, voters cast their ballot for the party and not the candidate. Each party wins a proportion of seats in parliament relative to the percentage of votes it receives in an election. This system of election is known as the proportional representation system

ORGANIZATION OF POLITICAL PARTIES

American political parties are decentralized and pragmatic. They get engaged in conflict without principle. Fidelity to principle is less important than winning elections. Consequently, American parties are loose coalitions of interests organized at the national, state and local levels.

National Party Organization

There is no unified form of party organization. There are, rather, three distinct groups organized at the national level, and together described as the national party organization. These are: the national party convention, the national party committee, and the congressional party caucus.

National Party Convention

The national party convention is convened every four years. The delegates selected at state party conventions or primaries attend the national conventions. The delegates mainly consist of regular or voting delegates and alternate or non-voting delegates. They come together to nominate their respective party presidential candidates, finalize a party platform, and write rules and regulations that would govern their party's activities.

National Party Committee

The national party committee is made of members from all 50 states and territories of the United States. Compared to the national party convention, this party organization is more important and durable. It keeps the party alive at all times, especially the period between presidential elections. The members of each party's national party committee elect a chairperson who is responsible for the day-to-day activities of each party. The national party committee is involved in fund raising activities, planning campaign strategy for elections, and coordinating efforts to keep the party winning elections.

Congressional Party Caucus

Independent from the national party convention and the national party committee is each party's organization at the U.S. Congress. Members of each party in Congress organize themselves into a caucus. Their activities are focused mainly on themselves as elected members of Congress. These might include voting as a unit on pertinent issues to their party, assisting one another in reelection bids, especially on fundraising activities, and protecting their united interests as elected officials.

State Party Organization

The state party organization is similar to its national counterpart. The only difference is that its activities are solely organized at the state level. State party organizations are convened to select delegates to attend the national party convention, adopt a state party platform, and to select members of the Electoral College during the presidential election year. The state party committee is headed by the chairperson of the party and is responsible for coordinating statewide party activities, including elections, fundraising, and establishing contact with other levels of party organization.

Local Party Organization

The various local party organizations in America are considered the lifeline of each major party. They are closest to the grass root and thereby are relied upon by state and federal party organizations to deliver votes for their candidates. Depending on the state, the local party organization generally comprises the precinct and county or senatorial/congressional district. Each party has chairpersons at the precinct and county levels. Their main responsibilities are to keep party unity and generate votes for the party through phone calls, direct mailing, and advertisements.

ARE AMERICAN POLITICAL PARTIES IN DECLINE?

There are two alternative schools of thought on this question: advocates and opponents of party decline. Advocates of party decline argue that American political parties have lost their original influence and therefore are no longer capable of doing what made them prominent in the past. This assumption could be examined in several areas relative to party responsibility, loyalty, and activity. In recent years, scholars have generally stated that party identification has diminished considerably. Consequently, many voters from the two dominant parties now identify themselves as independents. They vote for candidates of different parties in an election. This trend is referred to as party dealignment.

Opponents of party decline point to the loose structure of party organization. They argue that the absence of a hierarchy of authority, present in the organization of the political party, limits the political potency of the American party system. They also argue that American parties might be experiencing general political amnesia in certain areas, but overall, they are waxing stronger in the winning of elections and keeping the organization alive from one election to the other. They state that what is masquerading as party decline is indeed party realignment. This occurs when members of one dominant party shift, temporarily, their allegiance to the other major party for some specific reasons. For example, many Democrats crossed over party lines and voted for the Republican Party candidates in the 1980s. The same is true for Republicans.

THIRD PARTIES

Despite the strong tradition of the two-party system, periodically a third party will develop, usually in response to some area that is not being addressed by the major parties. In addition to the history behind the two-party system, the electoral system hinders the viability of third parties. Third-party candidates must meet certain state requirements in order to even have their names on ballots while candidate names from the Democratic and Republican parties are automatically included.[17] In most elections the candidate with the majority of votes wins the race, which requires that the winner appeal to a broad base of people. Since third parties generally form in response to an area that is not being addressed by the Democratic or Republican party, their constituent bases are small and not adequate to gather the majority of the vote in a district or state.

Third parties are usually one of two types: issue parties (also called splinter or bolter parties) or ideological parties.[18] **Ideological parties**, such as the Socialist Party, offer a platform that is radically different from the two major parties. **Issue parties** form because the major parties are disregarding a specific issue. The Libertarian Party is an ideological third party, and the Reform Party an issue third party.

The **Libertarian Party** is an example of a third party that has managed to overcome the two-party bias in the electoral system. The party was founded in 1971 and their campaign literature states that as of 1996 they have "over 100 elected or appointed Libertarian officeholders in twenty-two states." The Libertarian party's platform includes "rolling back the size and cost of government, and eliminating laws that stifle the economy and control people's personal choices."[19]

The **Reform Party** is a fairly new third political party. Ross Perot was the party's presidential candidate in 1992 and 1996. The Reform Party's platform calls for a balanced budget amendment to the U.S. Constitution, campaign reform, and replacing the electoral college with a direct vote.[20]

In addition to famous third parties the public is familiar with, there are others that run candidates but rarely succeed in getting statewide or national exposure. Table 5.2 is a list of parties that had candidates on the general election ballots of the various states and the District of Columbia in the 2004 presidential race.[21]

TABLE 5.2 PARTIES REPRESENTED IN THE 2004 PRESIDENTIAL RACE

American Constitution Party	Liberty, Ecology and Community
America First Party	Liberty Union Party
American Independent Party	Mississippi Taxpayers Party
American Party	Natural Law Party
Arkansas Taxpayers Party	New Hampshire Taxpayers
Conservative Party	Prohibition Party
Concerned Citizens	Pacific Party
Colorado Prohibition Party	Patriot Party
Constitutional Party	Peace and Freedom Party
Democratic Farm Labor Party	Right to Life Party

TABLE 5.2 PARTIES REPRESENTED IN THE 2004 PRESIDENTIAL RACE (CONT.)

Freedom Party	Socialist Party of Arkansas
Green Coalition	Socialist Equality Party
Green Party Minnesota	Socialist Party, USA
Green Party of Colorado	Socialist Workers Campaign
Green Party	Socialist Workers Party
Grassroots Party	Taxpayers Party
Independent Party	Unaffiliated Independent Party
Independent American Party	U.S. Taxpayers Party
Independence Party	Virginia Reform Party
Independent Grassroots Party	Virginia Taxpayers Party
Liberal Party	Workers World Party
Looking Back Party	

POLITICAL PARTIES AND DEMOCRACY

Why do democracies have political parties? Political parties are essential ingredients to democratic governments because they are considered a democratic litmus test; they organize opposition to the government in power; present choice to voters in elections; manage political conflict; they are democracy's watchdog, and are responsible for educating voters.

Democratic Litmus Test

The difference between democratic and non-democratic systems is the presence of political parties. The existence of one political party, as in Communist societies, military juntas, and various authoritarian nations, is an indication of the lack of freedom and liberty, essential ingredients for the sustenance of democracies. For a nation to claim democratic status, it must show proof of, not just the presence of, one political party, but several parties engaged in free, fair, regular and competitive elections.

The former Soviet Union, for instance, was not regarded as operating a democratic system of government because it allowed only one party, the Communist Party. The same could be said of China, Cuba, Iraq under Saddam Hussein, North Korea, and many other dictatorships. Therefore, the presence of multi-parties in a society is a litmus test of democracy.

Organization of Opposition and Presentation of Choice

Without political parties, the struggle for political power would be left to individuals. These individuals, either through wealth, education, social status, or other means, could wield control and inordinate ambitions so much so that a majority of the people would be excluded from the decision-making process. But with the presence of political parties, no individual agenda is imposed on the entire society, except through consensus based on debate organized by the media and members of the society at large.

Organized opposition, in turn, will offer alternative candidates who enunciate different ideologies, programs of action, and issues upon which voters base their decisions during an election. Political parties provide voters a unique opportunity to express their voting rights based on issues presented by candidates representing different parties. Thus, organization of opposition and presentation of choices to the voters are important ingredients to democratic governments.

Democracy's Watchdog

Along with the mass media, political parties have become democracy's watchdog. Party leaders could be intoxicated by power, and therefore either sidetrack the nation's constitution or seek a vendetta against their political foes. However, with a party out of power constantly watching, it is difficult for a winning party to take laws into its own hands. The constant criticism and objection to certain policies of the party in power, by the opposition, would tame the abuses of power that could result without such strict supervision.

Education of Voters

Political parties help educate voters on specific issues during campaigns and elections. Media advertisements, direct mail, and other campaign materials help inform voters of the important issues they should focus on during an election. Such information is necessary to the voters, especially independent voters who otherwise might not be able to make up their minds on which political parties or candidates to vote for in a given election.

SUMMARY

Interest groups, political movements, and political parties are the building blocks of American democracy. They are an important mechanism through which citizens make their political views known to government officials

Interest groups are political organizations made up of like-minded individuals who band together in order to influence public policy. Any group that organizes to garner benefits for its members, whether calling for regulation or seeking to end regulation, is an interest group. There are many interest groups on the American political scene. All interest groups are not equally powerful and successful. Their success depends on their size, the degree of their commitment, their unity and sense of purpose, their leadership, and resources at their disposal. Interest grpoups use different strategies to affect government decisions. The most frequently used strategies are lobbying, litigation, grassroots lobbying, electioneering, coalition building, protest, and demonstration. Movements are generally episodic.

Groups that use extralegal means of getting government to address their grievances may also affect a cross-section of society. Some movements support the idea that governments exist solely for the benefit of the rich and wealthy, and therefore, they are the ones who disproportionately influence government decisions. In addition, they argue that laws are put in place to perpetuate their rule at the expese of the rest of society. Specific examples of movements are the women's movement, civil rights movement, anti-war movement, anti-globalization movement, and the gay rights movement.

Political parties are the last example of collective participation. They seek to influence government by winning elections. The U.S. has a two-party system. The two major parties, Democratic and Republican, have been in existence since the Civil War. Despite the strong tradition of the two-party system, many third parties have come into existence. These parties have rejuvenated the two major parties by making them adopt their issues.

KEY TERMS

Amicus curiae
Anti-federalists
Corporate PACs
Federal Election Commission
Federalists
Ideological parties
Interest groups

Jacksonian Democrats
Lobbying
Party dealignment
Party realignment
Third parties
Whigs

INTERNET SOURCES

1. **Business Interest Groups**
   a) http://www.uschamber.org/
   Maintained by the U.S. Chamber of Commerce, this site provides information on business links within the United States and various other nations. Access to public policy, laws, legislations, etc., are provided in this site.

2. Labor Groups
   a) http://www.aflcio.org/home.htm
   This official site of the American Federation of Labor-Congress of Industrial Organizations (AFL-CIO) provides information on workers' rights, laws, legislations, membership to local unions in all fifty states of the Union, and sociopolitical and economic issues that affect the American worker. Information on foreign labor unions is also provided.
3. Public Interest Groups
   a) http://www.commoncause.org/
   The Common Cause, like many other public interest groups, lobbies elected officials at all levels of government, on behalf of the generality of the public. One does not have to subscribe to membership of this organization to benefit from its political activities. This site provides information on the workings of government, especially on issues relative to waste of the taxpayers' money by elected officials.
4. Political Parties
   a) http://www.rnc.org/index.html
   This site, provided by the Republican Party National Committee, provides information on this party's activities relative to events at the national level of government. Activities of this party in the U.S. Congress and the presidency will be found in this site.
   b) http://www.democrats.org/
   This site is similar to 4a, but it relates to the Democratic Party National Committee.
   c) http://www.democrats.org/party/america/states/index.html
   Each state, as do various levels of local governments, organizes its own political party activities. This site therefore provides information on activities of the Democratic Party at the state level in all fifty states in the union. Information on laws, rules, regulations, finances, intra-party activities, etc., are provided in this site.
   d) http://www.rnc.org/hq/info/
   This site is similar to 4c, but it relates to the Republican Party.

NOTES

[1] Alexis de Tocqueville. *Democracy in America*. (New York: Menxor Books, 1956).

[2] Steven Kelman. *American Democracy and the Public Good*. (Fort Worth, Texas: Harcourt Brace, 1996), 278–280.

[3] Allan Rosenthal. *The Third House: Lobbyists and Lobbying in the States*, 2nd edition. (Washington, D.C.: C Q Press, 2001).

[4] Paul S. Herrnson, et al. *The Interest Group Connection: Electioneering, Lobbying, Policy Making in Washington*. (New York: Chatham House Publishers, 1998), 269–281.

[5] Ibid., pp. 279–280.
[6] *Scheidler v. New* (2003).
[7] *Hill v. Colorado* (2003).
[8] Steven Kelman. *American Democracy and the Public Good*. (Fort Worth, Texas: Harcourt Brace, 1996), 278–280.
[9] Ibid., pp. 278–280.
[10] Ibid., pp. 278–280.
[11] Ibid., pp. 278–280.
[12] Thomas R. Dye. *Politics in America*, 3rd edition. (Upper Saddler River, New Jersey: Prentice Hall, 1994), 216–218.
[13] Ibid., pp. 216–218.
[14] Ibid., p. 243.
[15] Tome Grace, "Election Cost Third Parties in Crucial States." *The Daily Star Online*. Friday 8 Nov., 2002.
[16] New York.com "2004 Election Results." 5 Nov. 2004. <http://www.nytimes.com/packages/html/politics/2004_ELECTIONRESULTS_GRAPHIC>
[17] Steven Kelman. *American Democracy and the Public Good*. (Fort Worth, Texas: Harcourt Brace, 1996), 246–247.
[18] Kenneth Janda, et al. *The Challenge of Democracy*. (New Jersey: Houghton Mifflin, 1997), 262-265. and Stephen J. Wayune, et al. *The Politics of American Government*. (New York: St. Martin's Press, 1995), 290-294.
[19] Information taken from 1996 campaign literature of the Reform Party.
[20] Information taken from a brochure entitled, *Ten Answers to Commonly Asked Questions about the Libertarian Party*.
[21] Information taken from the Federal Election Commission's web site, <hptt://www.fec.gov>.

Chapter 6

American Media in Politics

The people are the only censors of their governors.... The way to prevent...irregular interpositions of the people, is to give them full information of their affairs through the channel of the public papers...and were it left to me to decide whether we should have a government without newspapers, or newspapers without a government, I should not hesitate a moment to prefer the latter.[1]

—Thomas Jefferson's letter to a friend in 1787

INTRODUCTION

The September 11, 2001, terrorists' attack has changed America's political landscape and the role of the media in politics. Consequently, politicians, media moguls, and journalists now focus their attention on the war against global terrorism as much as they do on domestic and other foreign policy challenges.

The electronic media brought instant news footage of the events of 9-11 into every home, school, and workplace. The press subsequently followed with detailed analysis of the aftermath of the terrorists' assault. And when a U.S.-led force declared war on Afghanistan and Iraq, the media took Americans along with them to the battlefronts.

The media, long regarded as the **Fourth Estate**, have never left Americans in the dark concerning any worthy piece of news. Be it the war on terrorism; the massive federal deficit; Michael Jackson's child-molestation allegation; or even things as mundane as freeing "Willie" the whale, the American media are always there to inform and provide news to their customers, the public.

American journalists believe that it's their inherent right to bestride the political chasm between the people, as owners of power, and elected officials, as custodians of the people's power. Mass medians, supported by the First Amendment to the U.S. Constitution, ensure that they inform the people on how their power is being used; expose the abuse of such power; criticize inept public officials; and provide editorial suggestions to them where and when necessary.

This chapter will examine the historical and contemporary role of the American media, the constitutional basis of their power, and their influence in shaping this country's democracy.

ROOTS OF EARLY AMERICAN PRESS'S PARTISANSHIP

Although writing blossomed in England, the monarchy deprived journalists of the freedom to be democracy's watchdog: the right to criticize public officials, inform the public of how elected leaders were managing their power, and to correct societal ills. America's founders were not comfortable with such repressive measures, hence the need for a free press.

Eventually, when the idea of "taxation without representation" created a discord between England and American colonies, the pamphleteers were up in arms against the former. These writers wrote persuasive and convincing articles that incited the populace against the British. Although united against the British, after the War of Independence, journalists were factionalized under the first two major political groups: the Federalists and Anti-Federalists. Politicians, unfortunately, capitalized on this schism to further their personal political ambitions.

The controversy over whether or not to retain the *Articles of Confederation* further polarized journalists. This debate culminated at the 1787 Constitutional Convention in Philadelphia where delegates, rather than revise this document, wrote a constitution. Ratification of the U.S. Constitution further divided journalists. Three Federalists, James Madison, Alexander Hamilton, and John Jay's articles supporting ratification were serialized in the *New York Independent Journal*, and became known as the *Federalist Papers*.

With the Constitution eventually ratified, the Federalists, under James Madison, established their newspaper, *Gazette of the United States*, and Thomas Jefferson introduced that of the Anti-Federalists, the *National Gazette*. The establishment of these two party newspapers introduced the era of American partisan press. Later, the slavery controversy further drove a wedge between journalists, and this development lasted until after the Civil War.

The Penny Press

Prior to the 1930s, newspapers catered mainly to elites. Benjamin Day's *New York Sun* made the news available to everyone. Penny Press papers granted Americans, especially the poor, the opportunity to become active participants in the democratic process. Newspapers of this era sensationalized the news, especially political scandals, crime, and human-interest stories.

In later years, however, Horace Greeley's *New York Tribune* "took the press of the masses from the vulgar level of sensationalism to a position of promoting culture and stimulating ideas."[2]

Yellow Journalism Transforms American Press

The competition for newspaper circulation and readership was at its apogee in the late 1800s. Scintillating and bold headlines, pictures, cartoons and advertisements heralded the agenda journalists wanted readers to focus on. Two newspaper moguls dominated this era in American journalism: Randolph Hearst, owner of the *New York Journal,* and Joseph Pulitzer, proprietor of the *New York World*. The Yellow Kid, a cartoon character made to exemplify life on the streets, symbolized this newspaper warfare.

The news, during this time, was a direct carryover from the Penny Press days: sensationalization of sex, scandal, violence, human interest, crime, emotional issues, etc. The 1898 Spanish-American War is partly attributed to the evils of yellow journalism. Hearst's reporter in Cuba informed editors back home of inaction in the Spanish authority's intent to quell the Cuban insurrection. Hearst cabled back to the reporter: "You furnish the pictures, and I'll furnish the war."[3]

Muckrakers: Harbingers of Investigative Journalism

These late 19th century journalists were forerunners to contemporary investigative reporters such as Carl Bernstein and Bob Woodward of Watergate fame. These journalists, notably Ida M. Tarbell, Thomas Nast, and Lincoln Steffens, exposed corruption in government and business.

Tarbell, for instance, exposed John D. Rockefeller's Standard Oil Company's monopoly that prevented competitors from a fair share of the market. Steffens is famous for *The Shame of the Cities* series that exposed government corruption in various American cities. Thomas Nast enlivened and popularized America's press with his heart-throbbing cartoons.

President Theodore Roosevelt cynically referred to this cadre of journalists as **muckrakers** (a character in John Bunyan's *Pilgrim's Progress* so engrossed in raking muck that he hardly raised his head to enjoy nature's beauty).

EMERGENCE OF AMERICAN MASS MEDIA

Right from its inception, American journalists utilized services of pigeons, mules, donkeys, wagons and relay-runners to disseminate news. Gradually, however, technology began transforming the arduous task involved in the newspaper industry. Consequently, delivery of newspapers by animals was replaced by technology when the telegraph was invented in 1844. The transmission of news events from one location to another became easier and much faster after the telephone's invention in 1876. Newspapers intensified the correspondence system when reporters stationed in different parts of the world wired news events to their various headquarters.

Until the early 18th century, the press had complete dominance of the news business in America. Although the motion picture was invented in 1903, its impact on politics was not as crucial as that of radio and television, invented in the 1920s.

Politicians capitalized on the availability of radio broadcast and its appeal to the audience to campaign and canvass for votes during elections. President Franklin D. Roosevelt, for instance, utilized this medium to directly connect with Americans in his famous "Fireside Chats" during the Great Depression years.

When, in 1928, television transmission started beaming into some Americans' homes, newspaper readership took a further drastic plunge, and fewer people were attracted to the radio. The image of a talking head and actors on a tube box brought about a media revolution to the entire world, and not just America. Politicians were quick to utilize the benefits provided by television. The Nixon-Kennedy debate of the 1960 presidential election was the high-water mark of television broadcast in American politics. The rough and unshaven face that scores of Americans saw during the Nixon-Kennedy presidential debate swayed many voters away from supporting Republican candidate Nixon. The image of a youthful and energetic candidate Kennedy endeared him to most voters, and he eventually won that election to the White House.

The invention of the computer, fax machine, and the Internet has made Marshall McLuhan's prophecy of the world becoming a global village a reality.[4] The transfer of news events and pictures from one location to another for instant broadcast and publication has facilitated the journalists' job. Politics is no longer localized, but internationalized.

These changes have had tremendous effects on how America's elected officials and bureaucrats make foreign policy decisions. They are now more mindful of the media's ability to provide voters instant information. Compared to elected officials, viewers seem to rely more on ABC's Peter Jennings, Ted Koppel and other television network anchors and **spin doctors**, political analysts made available by journalists to interpret news events during national emergencies, campaigns and elections, especially after a president's address to the nation. Journalists no longer see themselves as news disseminators but active participants in the democratic process. They confront elected officials with embarrassing facts that demand immediate answers on live television or radio broadcast.

Presidential election results were prematurely broadcast to the world while those in the West Coast were queuing up to cast their ballots. The 2000 presidential election between candidates George W. Bush and Al Gore has re-ignited debates on the role of the electronic media, especially that of the television network anchors and electoral spin doctors, in predicting possible winners and losers of such crucial elections—an action that has aptly been described as horse-race elections.

WHO CONTROLS AMERICA'S MEDIA?

The American media are privately owned, and not government controlled. Consequently, they operate as any other business enterprise. Government does not censor the media except during war or national emergency. Although taxpayers' money supports some public television programs, the government still does not control the media. During the Gulf and Afghanistan Wars, for instance, journalists' movements were restricted and contents of their news censored.

Internal Censorship

However, editors do impose restrictions that could be interpreted as internal censorship, that is, an attempt to avoid public outcry against sensitive information that, if published or broadcast, could offend certain groups whose dollar power props up media organizations. On July 5, 2003, for example, MSNBC executives fired Michael Savage, a popular conservative radio talk show host, after he referred to an unidentified caller (suspected to be gay) to his show as a "sodomite [and told the caller to] get AIDS and die."[5]

During the second U.S.-Iraq war in 2003, NBC officials fired famous correspondent, Peter Arnett, for giving an interview to a state-run Iraqi television in which he criticized the U.S. government policy on the war, stating that "reports about civilian casualties are fueling opposition to the war back home...the first U.S. war plan failed because of Iraqi resistance."[6]

In May 2003, *The New York Times* officials fired Jayson Blair, a reporter, after discovering that he "fabricated comments...concocted scenes...stole materials from other newspapers and wire services...selected details from photographs to create the impression he had been somewhere or seen someone, when he had not."[7] Consequent to this embarrassment, some editors of *The Times*, Howell Raines and Gerald Boyd, Blair's immediate supervisors, resigned because they were "blamed for overlooking Mr. Blair's errors and warnings about the quality of his work by other editors."[8]

The same year, Rush Limbaugh, conservative radio talk-show host, informed millions of his astonished listeners nationwide that, "I am addicted to prescription pain medications...[and that] immediately following this broadcast, I am checking myself into a treatment center for the next 30 days....I look forward to resuming our excursion into broadcast excellence together."[9] Limbaugh didn't lose his job after the rehabilitation, and continues broadcasting.

Although he later resigned, he criticized Philadelphia Eagles quarterback, Donovan McNabb, during the 2003–04 football season "for receiving undeserved credit for the team's success that came from media outlets with 'social concern' and 'very desirous that a black quarterback do well, there is still more to this statement."[10]

In the aftermath of the Jackson-Timberlake 2004 Super Bowl breast-baring episode, the FCC started getting tough with purveyors of indecency, especially electronic media. The networks, in order to avoid stiff financial penalties, have begun streamlining sexually explicit shows. "NBC's post-Super Bowl safeguards included the blurring of an 80-year-old patient's briefly exposed breast on *ER* because it was deemed "too difficult for many of our affiliates to air."[11] Reacting to ABC's new guidelines, an *NYPD Blue* producer commented that, "in the current climate, every scene we do that has any kind of sexual content is being gone over with a fine-tooth comb."[12]

In February 2004, Clear Channel stopped broadcasting "Shock Jock" Howard Stern's program in six of its stations in the aftermath of the "fallout from Justin Timberlake's baring of Janet Jackson's breast."[13] It also fired radio DJ Bubba the Love Sponge, whose program is laden with overt sexual expressions.

"ABC-RV's announcement that the live 2004 Academy Awards will be broadcast on a five-second delay—the first time in the program's 76-year history—is just the lattest fallout from the singer's breast-baring Super Bowl performance....A five-minute delay was instituted on the Feb. 8 [2004] Grammys broadcast."[14]

Advertisers' Dollar Power

As business enterprises, the American media mostly depend on income from advertisement. It would be senseless, for example, to offend Coca-Cola, Pepsi, Dr. Pepper or Coors Beer knowing full well that their advertisement dollars help to sustain the news establishment.

In 2003, for instance, the CBS network ignited the anger of pro-Reagan viewers when it came out with a sweeps-week miniseries, *The Reagans*, which portrayed the former president negatively. A *Dallas Morning News* editorial entitled, "Reagan Miniseries: CBS right to pull the plug," states that "The project blew up in the network's face when conservatives, galvanized by talk radio and the Internet, mounted a campaign against it. A red-faced CBS yanked the miniseries last week."[15]

Commenting further on this miniseries, the editorial states, "When CBS pulled the miniseries, liberal commentators denounced the move as 'censorship.' That's absurd. The government had nothing to do with the network's decision; it was a matter of private corporation exercising its editorial judgment. If CBS put out an inaccurate and insulting dramatic interpretation of the life of Martin Luther King, the NAACP would organize the same kind of boycott, would prevail—and would deserve to."[16]

In a related article, Ed Bark informs his readers that the vice-president of the Media Research Center, a conservative organization, had urged major corporate advertisers to "refuse to associate your products with such a movie."[17]

The relationship between ad dollars and the pulling of the Reagan miniseries is obvious. If advertisers, willing to pay up to "$75,000 a second [or even]...$2.1 million"[18] per thirty-second ad (amount charged during the 2004 Super Bowl) are persuaded not to advertise their products on a particular television program, it would be worthless to air such a controversial show.

Interest Groups' Threats

Interest groups generally use threats as a ploy against media organizations that publish or broadcast what they consider distasteful information. Boycotts might succeed against some corporations but are ineffective when utilized against the media.[19]

Knowing the linkage between the advertisement dollars and media survival, interest groups have, at different times, threatened to stop buying products from huge companies that advertise in them. Religious leaders such as Jerry Falwell, Pat Robertson, Jesse Jackson and others, have unsuccessfully issued threats against the media through product boycotts.

Audience Power

There is a direct correlation between media entertainment, the audience, and advertisement revenues. Most Americans patronize television because of the non-news values they derive from viewing. Therefore, the more the infotainment,[20] that is, the blending of news, drama and entertainment, the greater the audience.

That's why the media will present news-cum-entertainment about Ben Affleck and Jennifer Lopez's on-and-off wedding plans; Madonna kissing Britney spears at the 2003 MTV Music Video Awards; and Michael Jackson's hoopla at his first court appearance in February 2004 to defend child-molestation allegations against him.

Increase in viewership translates into higher television rating which, in turn, drives up advertisement cost. That's why most television programs are directly tailored to dramatization and comic relief. The ratio between television news and entertainment has been shown to be in favor of the latter.[21] A program that fails to command high audience rating is cut.

A few years ago, it was inconceivable that a considerable number of Americans could flex their power against a particular television program. But after the "breast-baring" episode in the 2004 Super Bowl half-time show, it's becoming increasingly possible for the audience of regular television shows to flex their joint muscles against the networks. After this incident, it was widely reported that "Several members of Congress, the Parents Television Council and the Traditional Values Coalition expressed outrage"[22] over the Janet Jackson-Justin Timberlake breast-exposure extravaganza.

"…Parents and Grandparents Alliance [urged its members] to petition members of Congress to 'demand they act'…the Public Television Council, an 800-member watchdog group, welcomed the national outrage…on Capital Hill…Democrats and Republicans denounced her [Jackson's] behavior and embraced legislation to toughen FCC penalties against obscenity and indecent language on TV….At least 50 fellow House members…had co-signed the protest….The congressional outrage gave a hefty dose of momentum to bipartisan legislation proposing a tenfold increase in FCC fines against broadcasters airing obscenities or offensive language, from $27,500 per violation to $275,000. A maximum penalty of $3 million would be imposed for repeated violations."[23]

It was such outcry and condemnation that compelled FCC chairman, Michael Powell, to promise an immediate investigation into what Jackson and Timberlake referred to as a "wardrobe malfunction."[24] Summing up the effect of this indecent exposure, Miller, in a letter to the editor, tells readers that, "Let me give a 'high five' to all who wrote, called or e-mailed MTV, CBS or the FCC about the tawdry halftime during the recent Super Bowl. The Federal Communications Commission received over 200,000 complaints. After all the apologies, something concrete is happening. Look at these headlines: "MTV restricting racy videos to late-night spot" (Tuesday news story), "Sex scene in *NYPD Blue* may be censored by ABC" (Wednesday news story)."[25]

Corporate Ownership

Although government neither owns nor controls American media, a few corporations control more than ninety percent of the major mass media outlets. Just as political parties solely controlled early American newspapers, so also do a few corporate entities dominate the news industry in contemporary times. General Electric, Westinghouse, Disney World, and Time Warner have a firm control of almost all major media businesses, especially the television industry, in the country and a few overseas nations.[26]

In 2003, for example, the FCC voted to permit Rupert Murdoch, America's media top dog and News Corp., owner, to buy control of DirectTV, the nation's premier satellite broadcaster. It's reported that this organization, prior to this $6.6 billion purchase deal, owned "35 TV stations, reaching more than 44 percent of the U.S. population...a major broadcast network, Fox, eleven national and 22 regional cable and satellite channels (including Fox News, FX and national Geographic), *The New York Post, The Weekly Standard* and Harper Collins publishers. Production studios including Twentieth Century Fox. PanAmSat Corp., the satellite owner that most U.S. cable systems (DirectTV's competitors) rely on for the signals they relay to homes...."[27]

In 2004, television giant, Comcast Corp., made a move to purchase The Walt Disney Company. If successful, their combined assets would surpass Time Warner's, the world's largest media company. Presently, Disney independently owns the "ABC...network; cable networks, including ESPN and the Disney Channel; 10 theme parks...Walt Disney Pictures...Miramax Studios [and]...10 television studios."[28]

Conversely, Comcast "operates the nation's largest cable television company with more than 21 million subscribers...5.3 million high-speed Internet subscribers... extensive holdings in content providers, with majority stakes in Comcast-Spectator, owner of the Philadelphia Flyers and 76ers; Comcast SportsNet, E! Entertainment Television, the Style Network, the Gold Channel, Outdoor Life Network and G4."[29]

The danger inherent in this kind of development is that major television corporations that trade in non-media products also have ownership interests in the networks. For instance, Walt Disney has financial holdings in magazine publications, newspapers, cable television, theme parks and resorts, motion pictures, book publishing, music, etc.[30] And each of these businesses branches off in different ownership directions. It could be argued that since all these multi-faceted corporations have one ownership root, the possibility of protecting one another's economic turf can't be easily discounted.

Furthermore, media owners' profit motives are obvious when compared with the interests they express in news programs. And according to Krugman, "The handful of organizations that supply most people with their news have major commercial interests that inevitably tempt them to slant their coverage, and more generally to be deferential to the ruling party."[31] In their study, Herman and Chomsky[32] concluded that the American media are controlled by corporate entities that, in turn, determine the nature of news items they want seen and read about them on the air and in print.

Government Ownership

Although American media are privately owned, the federal government operates the *Voice of America* (VOA) that it uses in directly communicating with the world outside the United States.[33]

Other than the VOA, the government is also capable of establishing a radio station, especially during war, mainly for propaganda purposes. During World War II, for instance, the federal government directed its propaganda against Germany through Radio Free Europe. A similar medium, Radio Free Iraq, was utilized during the Gulf Wars against Saddam Hussein, and in Afghanistan against the Taliban. In February 2004, a U.S.-launched Arabic-language broadcast, *Alhurra* (The Free One) "began beaming news, talk shows and features to the Middle East...pledging to provide accurate and balanced news to viewers enabling them to make informed decisions."[34]

The U.S. Congress provides some financial support for public radio broadcast. This kind of fiscal assistance, however, does not mean that the federal government controls programming of the Public Broadcasting Service (PBS). This is the extent to which the American government would go in ownership of the media. Other than propaganda, Uncle Sam's radio is not put to domestic use against the American people, but directed at those it considers enemies abroad.

MEDIA REGULATION

The American media, as business enterprises, are regulated. Media regulation is different from censorship. The purpose of government regulation is to protect consumers from illegal practices by unscrupulous entrepreneurs. Media censorship, on the other hand, is the practice of telling mass medians what they can or cannot publish or broadcast, an activity that occurs during war or any other national emergency.

During the first Gulf and Afghanistan wars, for instance, military commanders censored the media by releasing only information they considered necessary to the public through the media. Journalists were not allowed to independently gather and report all aspects of the news the way they saw fit. But, during the second Gulf war, journalists were "embedded" among U.S. troops "in accordance with Pentagon ground rules allowing…journalists to join deployed troops. Among the rules accepted by all participating news organizations is an agreement not to disclose sensitive operational details."[35] Even then, Americans had a firsthand exposure to extensive military actions during these confrontations.

The **Federal Communications Commission** (FCC) is the government agency established by the U.S. Congress in 1934 for the purpose of regulating the American media, especially the electronic media. There are essentially two kinds of FCC-electronic media regulation: technical and content.

Technical Regulation

One form of regulation is related to the distribution of limited airwave frequencies among broadcasters in order to avoid chaos. If unregulated, it is most likely that one radio or television station owner could monopolize the entire airwaves. Another form of regulation is the ownership of different aspects of the media. In order to toughen violation of anti-trust laws, the FCC has been charged by the U.S. Congress to monitor and regulate ownership of the media. This regulatory agency therefore decides the number of media outlets an individual or organization can own at any particular time.

In 2003, for example, the FCC "voted to allow mergers of newspapers, television…and radio stations in most markets across the country, and to allow one company to own as many as three television stations in the nation's largest cities…to allow the four major television networks to buy local television stations reaching as much as 45 percent of the national audience, replacing the old cap of 35 percent. But they left in place a rule barring ABC, CBS, Fox and NBC from merging with one another."[36]

Content Regulation

Were contents of media outlets regulated, the listening audiences of Howard Stern, Rush Limbaugh, Dr. Laura Schlesinger, and many other broadcasters would be seriously disappointed. Anyone could just about say anything on radio or television or write about any views or opinions in print media without any form of censorship. However, libel, slander, and the fear of defaming one's character serve as a deterrent against an unlimited media freedom.

There are, however, certain undignified words and phrases that would not be permitted in any form of media purely for reasons of decency expected of a moral society. This view exempts specialized publications meant only for adults, *Playboy*, *Penthouse* and *Hustler* magazines being typical examples. Curse or fighting words, indecent speech, obscenity, "toilet jokes" and offensive language capable of inciting a riot or breaching the peace are not allowed in most America's media.

In a 1968 Supreme Court decision, a majority of the justices ruled against comedian George Carlin's monologue broadcast on a California radio station. Their reason was simply that the First Amendment does not protect such broadcast because people, some of whom are children tuning to the program, could be subjected to such language at home.[37]

During campaigns and elections, especially for national contests such as the presidency, the FCC requires that electronic media stations provide equal time to political candidates. This **equal time rule** requires that if one candidate is given broadcasting time by a radio or television station, the same must be made available to opponents seeking similar office, except, perhaps if a candidate rejects such an offer. Closely related to this is the **right-of-rebuttal rule** which grants anyone, especially political candidates, the opportunity to respond to criticism on the same radio or television station where it originated.

In 1969, the Supreme Court ruled in favor of advocates of the **fairness doctrine**, which required electronic media to present all sides of what is considered any controversial issue that directly affects the public. According to a majority of the justices, viewers and listeners' rights, and not those of broadcasters, is paramount. Consequently, the First Amendment does not grant any particular broadcaster monopoly rights to "the exclusion of his fellow citizens."[38] The FCC reversed itself and consequently abolished the fairness doctrine in 1987 because it violates the First Amendment rights of broadcasters.

The U.S. Congress also gets involved in electronic media content regulation. After the 2004 Super Bowl half-time breast-baring incident, for instance, the U.S. House voted overwhelmingly "to raise the maximum fine for a broadcast license-holder to $500,000 from $75,000. The penalty for a performer would also rise to $500,000 from $11,000."[39] On September 23, 2004, the FCC finally penalized CBS $550,000.[40]

THE SUPREME COURT AND MEDIA FREEDOM

The Supreme Court is responsible for interpreting the constitutionality of any argument, conflict or disagreement relative to one's right, liberty and freedom. Consequently, it protects the right of the media as provided for in the First Amendment to the U.S. Constitution.

The Supreme Court ruled that government "prior restraint" of the media violates tenets of the media's First Amendment rights.[41] However, during war and national emergencies, the Court stated that government has censorship power over the media.

In 1971, during Vietnam War, the federal government, basing its claim on national security, attempted to restrain the *New York Times* from continuing publication of the *Pentagon Papers* detailing its covert activities in Vietnam. But the Supreme Court disagreed with the government's argument and ruled that publication of its activities in Vietnam is of interest to the American public.[42]

High school authorities, according to a Supreme Court's ruling, have the right to exercise "editorial control" over the content of student speech, especially in a school-sponsored newspaper "so long as their actions are reasonably related to legitimate pedagogical concerns."[43]

The print media, unlike the electronic media (especially newspapers), are not required to provide "equal space" to political candidates seeking opportunity to reply to editorial criticism.[44] Such candidates, however, are not prevented from purchasing ad space for such purposes.

Prior to 1981, most U.S. courts barred television cameras from covering their proceedings. However, the Supreme Court ruled that the possibility that television cameras in court trials could sway jurors' judgment is remote.[45]

It's the prerogative of judges to control the ways and means by which television coverage is given to trials in their individual courts as was noticed during the sensational cases involving Michael Jackson, Kobe Bryant, Scott Peterson and Martha Stewart. Such a decision is summed up in Stanislaus County judge, Al Girolami's ruling disallowing courtroom television cameras in the 2003 Peterson preliminary murder trial, "To the extent that the television coverage would transform this very serious trial into 'reality' television show, the court is reluctant to allow it....The judge said the decision would help retain some privacy rights for witnesses 'who never asked to be involved' in the high-profile case."[46]

Some judges, however, circumvented the gag orders by barring reporters from their courtrooms during some controversial trials. In reaction, the Supreme Court, in another decision, ruled that the right of anybody, journalists included, to attend a court trial is guaranteed by the First Amendment.[47]

Although several states have instituted the **shield laws**, designed to protect journalists from revealing news sources, the Supreme Court is of the opinion that the First Amendment does not grant journalists the right to refuse to appear and testify before a judge or to reveal the source of their information, especially when it has to do with criminal offenses. When matched against journalists' right to protect their sources and the protection of the public from criminal tendencies, the judges ruled in favor of the latter.[48]

The First Amendment does not protect libel, slander or defamation of character. The Supreme Court, however, has made it difficult for public figures wronged by the media to sue and collect damages. Except when a statement by the media is made with "actual malice," that is, made with utter disregard as to whether or not the disputed statement is false, public figures can't easily sue and claim damages from journalists. In a Supreme Court ruling that produced the **Sullivan Principle**, the justices decided that journalists could castigate government officials because in America's democracy, "debate on public issues should be uninhibited, robust and wide-open."[49] This ruling was expanded in 1976 to include not only government officials, but also public figures.[50] These include political candidates, entertainment icons, sports stars, and others who willingly thrust themselves into the public arena or are directly involved in events of general public interests.

In recent years, the Court has placed limitations on its original definition of a public figure. Referring to a defense lawyer as a "communist-fronter," because a journalist considered him a public figure, was rejected as an argument by the Supreme Court justices.[51] Similarly, the Court ruled against *Time* magazine because it inaccurately stated in a published story that a woman the paper considered a public figure and who was involved in a bitter divorce dispute committed adultery.[52]

A private person, a non-public figure, according to a majority of the Supreme Court justices, can't be transformed instantly into a public figure status simply by getting involved in a matter that attracts public attention.[53] In the Supreme Court's opinion, journalists could be forced to produce information about themselves that could accurately determine their "state of mind" at the time they were writing a story considered libelous by a defendant where the Court is considering the issue of "actual malice."[54]

When the *Hustler* magazine, in 1988, published a parody that portrayed televangelist Jerry Falwell as a drunk who had sex with his mother in an outhouse, the Supreme Court ruled that a public figure was not protected against satire or political cartoons, no matter how outrageous or repugnant.[55] However, the justices in a different case held that the expression of opinion in a newspaper column might be deemed libelous if it's false and defamatory.[56]

THE MEDIA AND THE GOVERNMENT

In order for elected leaders to effectively carry out their responsibilities to the people, there must be accountability. Consequently, in fulfilling their *watchdog role*, mass medians become the intermediary between the people and elected officials. That's why government institutions must grant journalists the freedom they need to carry out that which the First Amendment guarantees.

In 1966, for instance, the U.S. Congress enacted the **Freedom of Information Act** requiring government to make information available to the public except when it has to do with national security, personal files, investigation records, and government agency secret documents.

In 1977, Congress passed the **Sunshine Act**. This law requires government bureaucracy to open its meetings to anyone who desires knowledge of what is going on at government agencies. To enhance coverage of its activities by the media, Congress opened its doors to live television. First, the House in 1979, and then the Senate, in 1986, allowed the C-SPAN cable television to give full coverage to its proceedings.

The presidency, just as any other branch of government or its agency, must ensure that Americans are granted the opportunity to gain knowledge of what it does with the people's power. That's why every president constantly holds press conferences with mass medians through whom they intimate the American people of governmental actions; except, again, where certain "secret" or "confidential" information might endanger national security.

Some presidents, however, have not felt very comfortable with the disclosure of what they consider sensitive government information. President Kennedy, for example, ordered the declassification of some categories of documents after a certain period, an action that President Reagan, in 1982, limited by issuing an executive order against automatic declassification of new documents. And in 1995, President Clinton reversed this order and reinstated automatic declassification of secret government documents. The Bush administration, during the Afghanistan war, issued an executive order reversing the 1978 Presidential Records Act that allowed presidential records to be declassified after twelve years. This new order would allow a president to withhold a former president's papers even if the former president wanted to make them public.[57]

Government officials, especially those attached to the president, would usually release information unofficially to the American people through the media without attribution. Two of such methods, **news leaks** and **trial balloons**, are provided to journalists either to test the popularity of a policy before it becomes official or get the public's reaction on whether or not the intended decision resonates positively with a majority of the people. This type of news is usually issued from "unofficial or anonymous sources," and sometimes from an "unnamed government official."

President F. D. Roosevelt, for example, used his Fireside Chats to effectively communicate directly with the public without media interference. His successors at the White House have also utilized various forms of media outlets to communicate with Americans, especially the president's weekly radio address carried live nationally by most radio stations.

The relationship between government officials and the media has aptly been described as *"symbiotic"* and *"adversarial."*[58] Although not limited to only government officials, the symbiotic relationship enables those who benefit from media exposure to utilize the services of journalists to fulfill their personal goals. Conversely, the media depend on such persons as sources for their much-needed information. On the other hand, however, the adversarial relationship between the media and their sources, especially elected officials, pits them against one another in a constant fighting mode.

This you-scratch-my-back-I'll-scratch-yours relationship encourages elected officials to make information readily available to journalists. In return, however, they expect favorable and positive media coverage to help boost their image. When this fails they get angry and accuse the media of being biased.

President Nixon, for example, did not have an amiable relationship with the media. His vice president, Spiro Agnew, in an angry tirade, referred to journalists as "nattering nabobs of negativism."[59]

SOURCES OF MEDIA POWER

The American media, unofficially, are described as the **fifth branch** of government[60] after Congress, the presidency, bureaucracy, and the Supreme Court. Officially, however, the First Amendment to the U.S. Constitution grants journalists the right to "press freedom."

Deciding What's News

This constitutional power therefore allows the media to decide the importance of the "who," and "what," of an event; "how" it gets reported; and the "when," "where" and "why" it gets reported at a particular time. The way it seems to most journalists, news isn't when "dog bites man" but when "man bites dog." The unusual, rather than the usual events, are what news is.

Angered by such uncontrolled power, Spiro Agnew, President Nixon's vice president, vented his spleen on the media, stating that "this little group of men [journalists]…wield a free hand in selecting, presenting and interpreting the great issues of our nation.…The American people would rightly not tolerate this kind of concentration of power…in the hands of a tiny and closed fraternity of privileged men, elected by no one, and enjoying a monopoly sanctioned and licensed by government."[61]

However, the inability to distinguish between news qua news and entertainment has embroiled the media in controversy. On December 28, 2003, for instance, the CBS News and its magazine show, *60 Minutes*, were reported to have paid entertainer Michael Jackson $5 million for an interview. And that's after he was accused of indecency with children. Jane Kirtley, the Silha Professor of Media Ethics and Law at the University of Minnesota referred to this financial arrangement as "checkbook journalism…covering people's expenses so they can come to your studios is one thing, but compensating anybody for telling their story is ethically problematic. It should raise the fundamental question in the minds of viewers or readers: Is this person motivated by a desire to tell the truth or to be paid? There's no doubt that what CBS and *60 Minutes* have done deviates from America's journalistic standards."[62]

The way it appears today, the argument could be made to the effect that "television's [read the media's] definition of news has become utterly corrupted by ratings wars that essentially are driven by entertainment stories."[63]

Influencing Public Opinion

The media also derive their power from influencing public opinion. Most Americans mold their views based on media information. As shown in Table 6.1, the public believes that the media are doing an excellent job in their coverage of terrorism. The public's response on this survey is directly based on information respondents obtained from reading newspapers, watching television, and listening to radio news broadcasts, without which it would be impossible to have a frame of reference on events that occur around them.

TABLE 6.1 PUBLIC'S VIEW ON WHETHER OR NOT THE MEDIA ARE DOING AN EXCELLENT JOB ON THEIR COVERAGE OF THE IRAQ WAR

IN GENERAL, HOW WOULD YOU RATE THE JOB THE MEDIA HAVE DONE IN COVERING THE IRAQ WAR?						
	EXCELLENT	GOOD	ONLY FAIR	POOR	DON'T KNOW	TOTAL
April 2–7, 2003	32	42	15	9	2	100
March 28–April 1, 2003	32	40	16	9	3	100
March 25–27, 2003	34	41	16	7	2	100
March 23–24, 2003	34	42	14	5	5	100
March 20–22, 2003	42	38	11	4	5	100

Survey conducted by the Pew Research Center For the People & the Press: http://www.people-press.org/reports/print.php3?PageID=699.

Setting the Agenda

Another means by which the media gain power is through **agenda setting**, a process whereby journalists decide what is important to be reported. Such information, perhaps printed on the front page of a newspaper or broadcast at the beginning of network news, becomes the focal point of discussion among most people for as long as the media keep the issue on the news front burner. Consequently, whatever the media fail to report, or bury in an obscure corner among other news items, is probably not important.

Politicians, knowing the role of the media in setting societal agenda, utilize and sometimes manipulate mass medians for their own selfish advantage. That's why journalists are able to boldly provide interpretation to certain news events either by editorializing or through specialized television programs such as CBS's *60 Minutes*, ABC's *Nightline, 20/20* and numerous others. These programs are so popular with viewers that the audience usually express opinions on issues based on what they obtain from the media.

Persuasive Influence

By editorializing on news events, journalists attempt to persuade the audience on a course of action they believe the government, for instance, should follow in preventing a depressed economy or international terrorism. This action has led some to compare the media's coverage of campaigns and elections to horse-race journalism: who's ahead in the polls, what message is resonating positively with the audience, and which of these is sending sour chords to certain groups, who might likely win or lose a particular election, and so forth.

Consequently, candidates who are not favored by the media most likely will not win an election. The media have thus crowned themselves kingmakers of America's elections, especially regarding the presidency. The media, for instance, in the 2004 presidential primary elections, initially crowned Democratic Party candidate Howard Dean "the frontrunner." But after he lost the Iowa caucus, journalists started distancing themselves from him. And when Dean made a post-Iowa caucus concession speech which, unfortunately, ended in a long and loud yell, the media started describing him as "intemperate," "temperamental," "ranting and raving," "unfit to be president," "ill-mannered," etc. This incident, now dubbed by the media as the "I-Have-a-Yell Speech," remained on the media's agenda-setting notice board for several hours the first day it was made.

Commenting on this incident, ABC's Diane Sawyer stated that "The media overplayed the Howard Dean famous yell—about 700 times the first few hours. Fox News and Cable Network News (CNN) editors agreed that the media overplayed the yell."[64]

Discussing the impact of the media in the 1990 Texas gubernatorial election, Gibson and Robison state that, "Fearful of being beaten by a competitor in what had become a virtual feeding frenzy, some news people threw basic journalistic standards of substantiation and fairness out of the window."[65]

The media are partly to blame for the 2000 presidential election fiasco between candidates Bush and Gore. "Four years ago, flawed data led the networks to declare Democrat Al Gore the winner in Florida. Later, they reversed themselves reporting that George W. Bush had won Florida and would be the next president. Finally, in the wee hours of the morning, the networks withdrew that and declared the race too close to call."[66]

Summing up the shameful manner by which the media handled the "vote calls" in this election, NBC anchor, Tom Brokaw stated, "We don't have egg on our face. We have an omelet."[67]

Education Process

Education of the public is one of the most powerful sources of media power. In reporting the news, journalists, deliberately or inadvertently, inform us about people, things, ideas, and concepts we know nothing about. Only a few Americans would ever have the opportunity to travel to Timbuktu, for example. But through a public television documentary, they get to know about the people and cultures of Timbuktu.

By giving coverage to news events, the media bring us directly to places far removed from our immediate environments. Consequently, we get to know about the drought and starvation in Ethiopia and North Korea; slavery in Sudan; and activities of the Mafia in New York. Through in-depth news coverage of several events, the media provide us adequate education.

The media influence fashion, trends and cultures. They also provide us entertainment through television sitcoms, sporting activities, and other forms of entertainment.

ARE AMERICA'S MEDIA BIASED?

Total media objectivity is a myth. Journalists are just everyday folks that live among us, and so they have their personal biases that naturally affect news presentation. Media bias, according to Goldberg,[68] occurs because the public interprets news events based on the subjective slant given each incident by journalists. That's why Democrats, for example, will characterize Republican-supporting newspapers and radio talk shows as biased, and vice versa.[69] In the 2004 presidential elections, for instance, "Bush won the backing of the *Chicago* (Illinois) *Tribune*; the *Rocky Mountain News* of Denver, Colorado; the (Carlsbad, New Mexico) *Current-Argus*; and the *Omaha* (Nebraska) *World-Herald*…Kerry racked up support from *The New York*

Times, the *Minneapolis* (Minnesota) *Star Tribune* and one of his hometown papers, the *Boston* (Massachusetts) *Globe*."[70]

An example of typical liberal media bias occurred in the 2004 presidential election. Dan Rather, CBS's anchor, obtained documents (later determined to be fake) on President Bush's service records in the National Guard proving that he used preferential treatment to avoid going to real combat in Vietnam. Document experts contacted by the CBS organization to verify the documents "warned CBS not to run the story, and certainly not to say that they (the experts) had verified that the documents were valid."[71] Davis observed that "There was one reason for CBS to press with this story amid warnings that would have stopped any ethical journalistic organization in its tracks: They seek to bring down a president."[72]

McGowan[73] reveals that journalists demonstrate bias in news coverage because of the need to achieve diversity. Consequently, in his view, issues that affect gays, lesbians, and abortion are given liberal news slant in view of the fact that most journalists consider themselves anti-establishment. This conclusion is given credence by evidence supporting media bias for "established institutions and values…particular candidates and policies [and] commercial bias"[74] within the ranks of American mass medians.

Financial limitation and competition for news scoops force journalists to be biased. Most media organizations, for instance, depend on news agencies for the news they disseminate. That's because they lack the financial resources and human capability needed to send reporters to cover important domestic and international news.

In order therefore to maximize their profit motive, the media provide the audience with **packaged news** laced with heavy dozes of entertainment and drama they believe will constantly satiate the public's information appetite. For the print media, the larger the circulation, the higher the amount charged for advertising space which, for the electronic media, advertising costs are determined by audience size.

Were the media objective, newspapers wouldn't endorse certain candidates over others, especially during presidential elections. In the 2004 presidential primaries, *The Des Moines Register*, for instance, endorsed John Edwards, referring to him as, "one of those rare, naturally gifted politicians who doesn't need a long record of public service to inspire confidence in his abilities."[75] Objectivity demands that the media present news facts exactly the way they occur, and then leave the interpretation to the voters to decide for themselves.

The American public can't be fooled to the contrary relative to media bias. The majority agrees that what they are presented as news by the media is not always accurate based on pure facts.[76] The profit motive of the media industry and the merger-mania that have characterized the news establishment make the presentation of news subjective.[77] To write an editorial or broadcast a documentary critical of a huge advertiser might prove counterproductive to the news organization concerned.

However, the fact that American media have stood up to the likes of Presidents Richard Nixon, during the Watergate scandal; Bill Clinton, in his extramarital affairs with several women, especially Monica Lewinsky; and several other powerful individuals, attest to the fact that the media are objective.

Media Irresponsibility vs. People's Right to Know

After September 11, most Americans are skeptical about the role of the media during national emergencies. There's no doubt that the media duly informed the public of what was going on subsequent to the terrorist attack. However, not knowing who and where the country's enemies were at such time, most Americans, as per Table 6.2, expected journalists to exercise utmost restraint relative to security news events.[78]

TABLE 6.2 PUBLIC'S ASSESSMENT OF MEDIA COVERAGE OF IRAQ AFTER THE INVASION

IN TRYING TO KEEP THE PUBLIC INFORMED, ARE NEWS REPORTS MAKING THE SITUATION IN IRAQ SEEM WORSE, BETTER, OR ABOUT RIGHT?

	WORSE THAN REALLY IS	BETTER THAN REALLY IS	ABOUT RIGHT	DON'T KNOW	TOTAL
RESPONSE	38	14	36	12	100

Survey conducted by the Pew Research Center For the People & the Press: http://www.people-press.org/112801que.htm

In October 2002, unknown serial killers whom the media referred to as tarot-card "or" sub-urban snipers terrorized Virginia and Washington-area residents. These unknown persons had shot eleven persons and killed nine of them. The last victim was a 47-year-old female FBI analyst. The law enforcement community was shocked. In order to catch these elusive criminals, the FBI and Pentagon sent a surveillance plane to monitor the area from which the suspects were operating. The District of Columbia police had warned the media to keep certain details off the news in order not to give the suspects vital information. However, newspapers not only gave details of the surveillance planes, but also followed their articles with detailed diagrams, maps, illustrations, and even sketches of the plane's capabilities and pinpoint accuracy of identifying the snipers.

On Sunday, October 20, 2002, the snipers, apparently after reading the newspapers' accounts of the surveillance planes, moved ninety miles away from their initial operation area to Ponderosa where they shot the 12th victim. On Monday, October 21, 2002, in an *ABC Nightly News With Peter Jennings*, Jennings stated that the theory behind the snipers' relocation is that the "media might have revealed too much about the Pentagon's surveillance plane's activities; that's why the snipers might have eluded the police."

On Tuesday, February 11, 2003, the Fox News Channel broadcast an English language translation of a 16-minute live audiotape of someone purporting to be Osama bin Laden. According to a newspaper column, "The network seemed to have forgotten that in October 2001, national security adviser Codoleezza Rice had asked TV executives to be careful with bin Laden videotapes because they could contain subtle signals for his operatives."[79]

During the second Gulf war, the Pentagon expelled correspondent Geraldo Rivera, reporting for CNN, from Iraq "for drawing a map in the sand revealing troop locations and movements….Although he is not officially 'embedded,' Rivera's map-drawing breaks one of the first and most commonsensical rules of reporting on wartime troops: Don't reveal troop locations."[80]

At the height of the second Iraq war, in 2003, the Bush Administration was criticized for using the false pretense of the presence of weapons of mass destruction (WMD) for launching the war. One critic was Joseph C. Wilson, a former U.S. ambassador who, after his investigation, reported that the Administration misled Americans on the allegation that Iraq attempted to purchase uranium from Niger, a West African country. Obviously, someone in the Bush Administration wasn't pleased with Wilson's revelation. Consequently, a White House official sought to get even with Wilson by leaking information to the media that his wife was a CIA operative.

Robert Novak, a popular conservative newspaper columnist, used this very sensitive revelation in his July 14, 2003, column.[81] What was the news value in this revelation to the American people?

The coalition forces successfully liberated Iraq. However, some Iraqis regarded it as an American-led invasion. They took up arms against the invaders. Back home,

U.S. Soldiers in Afghanistan

by Spc. Harold Fields

Americans were bombarded by news from Iraq. Protesters were criticizing the war. And displeased about the media's coverage, President Bush, on Monday, October 13, 2003, while addressing regional broadcasting companies, told them that, "I'm mindful of the filter through which some news travels, and somehow you just go over the heads of the filter and speak directly to the people."[82] If what the media were reporting to Americans were all about actions of the insurgents in Iraq, the number of troops killed, and how terrible things were over there, the question to be asked is: Are there any Iraqis who support the toppling of Sadaam Hussein at all?

WHO WATCHES DEMOCRACY'S WATCHDOGS?

Information is power. The control of it therefore gives unimaginable advantage to its holder. One with information could expose and embarrass others in whatever manner he desires—a ploy Joseph McCarthy capitalized on in his Communist scare accusations of the 1950s.

The media decide the frontrunner in most national elections, especially that of the president. They control the lens that snoops in the darkest corners of public figures' secrets. No wonder President Lyndon Johnson faulted the media for his failure to seek a second term at the White House.[83]

The role of the media in Princess Diana's death is well documented.[84] Was the public desirous of knowing everything the Princess did, including activities in her private life? The media stalked Democratic presidential candidate, Gary Hart, until they caught him in a sexual escapade with Donna Rice, an action that eventually forced him out of the 1988 White House race.

Unlike branches of the government, the media have unchecked powers. According to Pat Robertson, "Private citizens and public officials are slandered and convicted in the press by so-called investigative reporters who act as prosecutor, judge, and jury."[85] If the media are regarded as the fourth branch of government, and journalists mere mortals, wouldn't it be fair to subject them to the same checks and balances politicians are exposed to? Table 6.3 confirms the public's view that the media, at least during war or emergency, should be controlled. After all, it's a democracy and no one should have absolute power, not even the media.

TABLE 6.3 PUBLIC'S VIEW ON THE AMOUNT OF COVERAGE GIVEN BY THE MEDIA TO THE IRAQ WAR

DO YOU THINK THE MEDIA ARE GIVING TOO MUCH, TOO LITTLE, OR ABOUT THE RIGHT AMOUNT OF COVERAGE TO THE MILITARY SITUATION IN IRAQ?

	TOO MUCH COVERAGE	TOO LITTLE COVERAGE	ABOUT THE RIGHT AMOUNT
1. Allied troop casulties	15	20	63
2. Iraqi civillian casualties	17	28	61
3. Anti-war sentiment in the U.S.	40	18	38

Survey conducted by the Pew Research Center For the People & the Press: http://www.people-press.org/reports/print.php3?PageID=699

SUMMARY

The American media have been vigorously involved in politics right from the foundation of the republic. Journalists were partly instrumental in rallying and inciting the American public against the British invading army during the War of Independence. However, after the war, the press was factionalized along political lines. Politicians manipulated journalists for their selfish ends.

The influence of the muckrakers brought about drastic changes to the American press. The newspaper circulation competition between Randolph Hearst and Joseph Pulitzer resulted in yellow journalism and the start of the Spanish-American War.

Although the press continued to dominate early American politics, its influence increased tremendously in the 1920s with the invention of radio and television, bringing about the idea of "mass media" to the news profession. The invention of the fax machine, Internet, and related technologies has enabled the American media to have a tremendous influence on the nation's politics as never before.

KEY TERMS

Agenda setting
Democracy's watchdog
Equal time rule
Fairness doctrine
Fifth branch of government
Fourth estate
Freedom of Information Act
Horse-race journalism
Infotainment

Muckrakers
News leaks
Packaged news
Public figures
Right-of-rebuttal rule
Shield laws
Spin doctors
Sullivan Principle
Trial balloons

INTERNET SOURCES

a) http://www.yahoo.com/News/
This site provides information on major newspapers, radio and television stations in the United States.

b) http://www.naa.org
Provided by the Newspaper Association of America, this site provides information on most American newspapers: publication, circulation, statistical data, history and development of major elite newspapers, etc., can be found in this site.

c) http://www.asc.upenn.edu/APPC/
The Annenberg School of Communications at the University of Pennsylvania Media Research Center organizes this site. It provides useful research data on various media news coverage both within the United States and overseas.

d) http://www.people-press.org/11280lsl.htm
The Pew Research Center for the People and the Press is responsible for organizing this site. It provides information on the performances of the media in general: how journalists cover news items and events, the public's views and opinions of the coverage of specific events by the media, etc.

NOTES

[1] Michael Emery et al., *The Press and America: An Interpretive History of the Mass Media*, 9th ed. (Boston: Allyn and Bacon, 2000), 77.

[2] Emery et al., 107.

[3] Ibid., 200.
[4] Marshall McLuhan, *Understanding Media* (New York: Signet Paperback, 1964).
[5] The Miami Herald, "Entertainment: MSNBC fires Savage on anti-gay remarks." 7 July, 2003. The Miami Herald. Online. 7 July, 2003. http://www.miami.com/mld/miamiherald/entertainment/6251351.htm
[6] Robert Philpot, "When reporter is the story," *Star-Telegram* (1 April, 2003): 13B.
[7] David House, "Poisoning the archival wells," *Star-Telegram* (18 May, 2003): 3E.
[8] BBC News, "New York Times editors quit," BBC News. 5 June, 2003. BBC News. Online. 5 June, 2003. http://news.bbc.co.uk/2/hi/americas/2966588.stm
[9] John Austin, "Limbaugh checks into rehab clinic," *Star-Telegram* (11 Oct., 2003): 1.
[10] Michael Hiestand, "Limbaugh quits NFL show amid race flap," *USA Today*, 2 Feb., 2004. USA Today.com. Online. 2 Feb., 2004. http://www.usatoday.com/sports/football/nfl/2003-10-02-limbaugh-resigns_x.htm
[11] Ed Bark, "From Janet's affront to Howard's end," *The Dallas Morning News* (27 Feb., 2004): 1.
[12] Ibid., 2A.
[13] Ibid.
[14] Cary Darling, "Is pop culture cleaning up its act, or just taking cover?" *Star-Telegram* (28 Feb., 2004): 1.
[15] Reagan Miniseries: CBS right to pull plug." Editorial. *The Dallas Morning News* (8 Nov. 2003): 28A.
[16] Ibid., 28A.
[17] Ed Bark, "No Teflon here: As outcry rises, CBS drops 'Reagans,' *Dallas Morning News* (5 Nov., 2003): 1.
[18] Chris Isidore, "The $2.3m bargain," *CNN Money*, 30 Jan., 2004. CNN Money. Online. 1 Jan. 2004. http://money.cnn.com/2004/o1/29/commentary/column_spportsbiz/superbowl_sportsbiz/inde …2/2/2004. Jan. 30, 2004.
[19] See, for example, George McKenna. *The Drama of Democracy: American Government and Politic* (Guilford, Connecticut: The Dushkin Publishing Group, Inc., 1990), 387.
[20] William A. Henry III, "Requiem for TV's Gender Gap" (*Time*, August 22, 1983), 57.
[21] See, especially, Doris A. Graber, *Mass Media and American Politics* (Washington, D.C.: Congressional Quarterly Press, 1984), 78-9; W. Lance Bennett. *News: The Politics of Illusion*, 3rd ed. (White Plains, N.Y.: Longman, 1996), chapter 2.
[22] MSN Entertainment News, "Janet Jackson Apologizes for Bared Breast," *MSN News*, 3 Feb., 2004. MSN News. Online. 3 Feb., 2004. http://entertainment.msn.com/tv/article.aspx?news=148561
[23] Dave Montgomery, "Halftime escapade produces backlash," *Star-Telegram* (Sunday Feb. 8, 2004): 1.
[24] *MSN Entertainment News*, 3 Feb., 2004.
[25] Marjorie Miller, Letter to the editor. "Viewer complaints making a difference!" *The Dallas Morning News* (Sat. 14 Feb., 2004): 30A.
[26] Joseph Turow, *Media Today: An Introduction to Mass Communication* (Boston: Houghton Mifflin Co. 1999), 391.
[27] Edward Wasserman, "A new kind of mogul," *Star-Telegram* (4 Jan., 2004): 3E.
[28] Vikas Bajaj, "Megamergers: do they pay?" *The Dallas Morning News* (12 Feb., 2004): 1A.

29 Ibid., 2A
30 Ben Bagdikian, *The Media Monopoly* (Boston: Beacon Press, 1997).
31 Paul Krugman, "Malfeasance in the media," *Star-Telegram* (1 Dec., 2002): 5E.
32 Edward S. Herman and Noam Chomsky, *Manufacturing Consent: The Political Economy of the Mass Media* (New York:: Pantheon Books, 2002), 25.
33 Voice of America, *Voice of American Charter*, http.www.ibb.gov/pubatt/voacharter.html
34 Edmund Blair, "New U.S. TV channel faces sceptical Arab audience," *MSNBC Wire Services*, 16 Feb., 2004. MSNBC News. Online. 16 Feb., 2004. http://msnbc.msn.com/id/4272508/
35 Gary Tuchman, "Tuchman: Republican Guard is the main target," *CNN News*, 24 March, 2003. CNN News. Online. 24 March, 2003. hppt://www.cnn.com/2003/WORLD/meast/03/24/otsc.irq.tuchman/index.htm
36 Jim Landers, "FCC loosens rules on media control," *The Dallas Morning News* (Tuesday 3 June, 2003): 1A.
37 *FCC v. Pacifica Foundation*, 438 U.S. 726 (1968).
38 *Red Lion Broadcasting Co., Inc. v. Federal Communications Commission*, 395 U.S. 367 (1969).
39 David Stout, "House votes to raise fines for broadcast indecency," *Star-Telegram* (13 March, 2004): 6A.
40 The Associated Press, "'Wardrobe Malfunction' costly for CBS," *Star-Telegram* (Thursday Sept. 23, 2004), 1A.
41 *Near v. Minnesota*, 283 U.S. 697 (1931).
42 *New York Times v. United States*, 403 U.S. 713 (1971).
43 *Hazelwood School District v. Kuhlmeier*, 484 U.S. 260 (1988).
44 *Miami Herald Publishing Co. v. Tornillo*, 418 U.S. 241 (1974).
45 *Chandler and Granger v. Florida*, 449 U.S. 560 (1981).
46 Brian Skoloff, "Judge Bans Cameras From Peterson Hearing," *Burlington County Times*, 9 Feb., 2004. Burlington County Times. Online. 9 Feb., 2004. http://www.phillyburbs.com/ph-dyn/news/1-08192003-144105.html
47 *Richmond Newspapers, Inc. v. Virginia*, 448 U.S. 555 (1980).
48 *United States v. Caldwell; Branzburg v. Hayes*; In the Matter of Paul Pappas, all 408 U.S. 665 (1972)
49 *New York Times v. Sullivan*, 376 U.S. 254 (1964).
50 *Curtis Publishing Co. v. Butts and Associated Press v. Walker*, 388 U.S. 130 (1967); *Rosenbloom v. Metrodedia*, 403 U.S. 29 (1971).
51 *Gertz v. Robert Welch, Inc.* 418 U.S. 323 (1974).
52 *Time v. Firestone*, 424 U.S. 448 (1976).
53 *Wolston v. Reader's Digest*, 443 U.S. 157 (1979).
54 *Herbert v. Lando*, 441 U.S. 153 (1979).
55 *Hustler Magazine v. Falwell*, 485 U.S. 46 (1988).
56 *Milkovich v. Lorain Journal Co.*, 497 U.S. 1 (1990).
57 *The Dallas Morning News* (Friday, Nov. 2, 2001), A4.
58 Susan Welch et al., *American Government*, 5th ed. (Minneapolis, St. Paul: West Publishing Co.,1994), 233.

⁵⁹ Theodore J. Lowi and Benjamin Ginsberg, *American Government: Freedom and Power* (New York: W. W. Norton and Co., 1996), 572.

⁶⁰ D. Grier Stephenson, Jr. et al., *American Government*, 2nd ed. (New York: Harper Collins Pubs.1992), 379.

⁶¹ Quoted in *Democracy Under Pressure: An Introduction to the American Political System*, 8th ed. by Milton C. Cummings, Jr. and David Wise (Fort Worth: Harcourt Brace College Publishers, 1997), 273; from John Anthony Maltese's *Spin Doctors Control: The White House Office of Communications and the Management of Presidential News.*

⁶² Tim Rutten, "CBS smudges the journalistic line," *Star-Telegram* (4 Jan., 2004), 3E.

⁶³ Tim Rutten, "CBs smudges the journalistic line."

⁶⁴ *ABC World News Tonight With Peter Jennings*, Wednesday January 28, 2004.

⁶⁵ L. Tucker Gibson, Jr. and Clay Robison, *Government and Politics in the Lone Star State: Theory and Practice*, 4th ed. (Upper Saddle River, New Jersey: Prentice Hall), 134.

⁶⁶ Arnold Hamilton, *Dallas Morning News*, (Wed. January 27, 2004): 7A.

⁶⁷ Quoted in, Thomas Dye et al., *Politics in America*, 4th ed. (Upper Saddle River, New Jersey: Prentice Hall, 2001), 261.

⁶⁸ Bernard Goldberg, *Bias: A CBS Insider Exposes How the Media Distort the News* (Washington, D.C.: Regnery Publishing, Inc., 2001).

⁶⁹ Bagdikian, *The Media Monopoly*, 44-5.

⁷⁰ CNN.com., "Bush, Kerry win newspaper endorsements," *Inside Politics*, 18 Oct. 2004. CNN.com. Online. 18 Oct., 2004. http://www.cnn.com/2004/ALLPOLITICS/10/17/election.endorsements/index.html

⁷¹ Mark Davis, "Rather's Waterloo?" *Star-Telegram* (Sept. 19, 2004): 3E.

⁷² Ibid.

⁷³ William McGowan, *Coloring the News: How Crusading for Diversity Has Corrupted American Journalism* (San Francisco: Encounter Books, 2001).

⁷⁴ Welch et al., pp. 244-248.

⁷⁵ *The Dallas Morning News*, "Elections '04," (12 Jan., 2004): 5A.

⁷⁶ Time Mirror Center, *Time Mirror News Interest Index* (Jan. 16, 1972).

⁷⁷ Fred Smoller, "The Six O'clock Presidency: Patterns of Network News Coverage of the President," *Presidential Studies Quarterly* 26 (Winter 1986), 34.

⁷⁸ See Peter Jennings's Public Forum Special on: *Media Coverage on the Aftermath of September Eleven Terrorism Attack*. ABC, WFAA-TV (Channel 8), Dallas, Texas, November 18, 2001.

⁷⁹ David House, "Handling 16 minutes of air time to a terrorist," *Star-Telegram* (Feb. 16, 2003): 3E.

⁸⁰ Robert Philpot, "When reporter is the story," *Star-Telegram* (Tuesday April 1, 2003): 13B.

⁸¹ See G. Robert Hillman and Michael Mittelstadt's article, "Justice opens leak inquiry," *The Dallas Morning News* (1 Oct., 2003): 1A.

⁸² Dana Mildbank, "Bush bypasses media 'filter' to make case," *Star-Telegram*, 14 Oct. 2003. Star-Telegram. Online. 14 Oct., 2003. http://www.dfw.com/mld/dfw/news/nation/7009720.htm?Ic

⁸³ See Lyndon Johnson's interview in David Halberstam's *The Powers That Be* (New York: Dell Books, 1979), 15-6.

[84] Richards Jeffrey and Wilson Scott, *Diana: The Making of a Media Saint* (London: I.B. Tauris, 1999); Gerard Charles, *The Media of the Republic* (Grensborough: Steele Wilson Books, 1999).
[85] Pat Robertson, *The New World Order* (Dallas, TX: Word Publishing, 1991), 242.

Chapter 7

Congress

Congress may slip without the union perishing, for above Congress there is the electoral body which can change its spirit by changing its members.
　　　　　　　　　　　　　　　　　　　　　　—Alex de Tocqueville

INTRODUCTION

One of the three branches of the federal government is Congress. It is often called the federal branch closest to the people. This is because members of Congress are elected directly by the people, whereas the members of the Electoral College elect the president, and members of the judiciary branch are appointed by the president and confirmed by a majority vote of the Senate. The writers of the Constitution gave the members of Congress the power to translate public will into public policy—that is, to make the laws and represent the people. According to Article I of the Constitution, "all legislative powers herein granted shall be vested in a Congress of the United States, which shall consist of a Senate and House." The following sections provide essential information regarding the institution of Congress, its membership qualifications and characteristics, its powers and functions, the legislative process, and its organization.

THE INSTITUTION OF CONGRESS

The institution of Congress emerged as a result of the Connecticut or Great Compromise. This compromise established a bicameral or two-chambered legislature—the Senate and the House of Representatives. The Senate was to represent the states, and its members originally were appointed by state legislatures. This changed in 1913 with the adoption of the Seventeenth Amendment. Today, two members of the U.S. Senate are elected from each state at-large, that is, by the entire voting body of the state. According to Article I, Section 3 of the Constitution, the Senate "shall be composed of two senators from each state." Thus, each state is represented equally in the Senate. When the first Congress convened in 1789, the Senate had 26 members. Since the admission of Alaska and Hawaii in 1959, there have been 100 senators.

Representation in the House is based on population. Each state is guaranteed at least one representative. In the 109th Congress, seven states have one representative: Alaska, Delaware, Montana, North and South Dakota, Vermont, and Wyoming. The first Congress had 59 members in the House, and each represented 30,000 people. As new states were added and the population grew, the membership of the House increased to 435 members, and each currently represents approximately 647,000 people. The **Congressional Reapportionment Act of 1929** fixed the membership of the House at 435. In addition, the House has five additional nonvoting members who represent American Samoa, the District of Columbia, Guam, Puerto Rico, and the Virgin Islands. The title of representative from Puerto Rico is Resident Commissioner. He is elected to a four-year term of office. The rest are elected to a two-year term of office, and each is referred to as a Delegate.

REAPPORTIONMENT

Every 10 years, Congress reallocates the 435 congressional districts among the states in terms of gains or losses in population as determined by the publication of the national census. This process is called reapportionment. It is required in order to maintain equal representation. The House is reapportioned using a formula called the "method of equal proportions," which assigns every state one congressional seat and then divides the remaining 385 by population. The Commerce Department's Bureau of Census prepares the reapportionment plan for the president, who forwards it to Congress for action.[1] The latest reapportionment of the House seats was announced on December 28, 2000.

According to census data, from 1990 to 2000, the rate of population growth was 23.5 percent in Florida, 13.8 percent in California, and 28.8 percent in Texas. In contrast, there was hardly any population growth in the so-called Rust Belt states of New York, Michigan, and New Jersey. As a result, California, Florida, and Texas gained congressional districts, whereas Michigan, New Jersey, and New York lost districts in the 1990s. The biggest losers in 2000 were New York and Pennsylvania; each lost two congressional seats. As a result of the 2000 reapportionment, 8 states gained, 10 states lost, and the remaining 32 states' districts did not change. The most dynamic growth occurred in the mountainous states of the West: Nevada's population grew by 66.3 percent and Arizona's two-seat gain was a result of its 40 percent population increase. (See Table 7.1.)

TABLE 7.1 APPORTIONMENT OF THE U.S. HOUSE OF REPRESENTATIVES, 2000

STATE	NUMBER OF SEATS	CHANGE FROM 1990
Alabama	7	0
Alaska	1	0
Arizona	8	+2
Arkansas	4	0
California	53	+1
Colorado	7	+1
Connecticut	5	−1
Delaware	1	0
Florida	25	+2
Georgia	13	+2
Hawaii	2	0
Idaho	2	0
Illinois	19	−1
Indiana	9	−1
Iowa	5	0
Kansas	4	0
Kentucky	6	0
Louisiana	7	0
Maine	2	0
Maryland	10	0
Massachusetts	10	0

TABLE 7.1   APPORTIONMENT OF THE U.S. HOUSE OF REPRESENTATIVES, 2000 (CONT.)

State	Number of Seats	Change from 1990
Michigan	15	−1
Minnesota	8	0
Mississippi	4	−1
Missouri	9	0
Montana	1	0
Nebraska	3	0
Nevada	3	+1
New Hampshire	2	0
New Jersey	13	0
New Mexico	3	0
New York	29	−2
North Carolina	13	+1
North Dakota	1	0
Ohio	18	−1
Oklahoma	5	−1
Oregon	5	0
Pennsylvania	19	−2
Rhode Island	2	0
South Carolina	6	0
South Dakota	1	0
Tennessee	9	0
Texas	32	+2
Utah	3	0
Vermont	1	0
Virginia	11	0
Washington	9	0
West Virginia	3	0
Wisconsin	8	−1
Wyoming	1	0

Source: *Congressional Quarterly Weekly*, January 20, 2000.

REDISTRICTING

Following the reapportionment of congressional districts, state legislatures draw the boundary lines for each congressional district so that legislative districts are all

FIGURE 7.1   STATES' MEMBERSHIP TO THE HOUSE OF REPRESENTATIVES

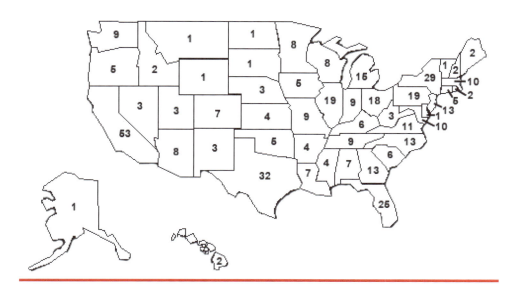

approximately equal in population. This process is call redistricting. Even though Congress requires that districts should consist of "contiguous territory," be "compact," and contain an "equal number of people," over the years some state legislatures have abused these legislated stipulations.

In the early 1960s, 21 states contained a district with twice the population of the smallest one. For example, the state of Tennessee had not redistricted since 1901. As a result, 42 percent of its population lived in four urban counties, but that group elected 8 percent of the state senators and only 20 percent of the state representatives. In other words, districts were malapportioned before they were redrawn. Prior to the 1960s, the Supreme Court refused to correct for population discrepancies that existed among districts. The Court felt that it should not get involved in partisan political disputes and that Congress should deal with such problems.

Redistricting and the Warren Court

But in a series of decisions made during the 1960s, the Supreme Court, led by liberal Chief Justice Earl Warren, declared malapportionment unconstitutional. In the landmark case of *Baker v. Carr* (1962),[2] the Supreme Court ruled that legislative reapportionment was not a "political question," and therefore the federal courts could rule on such cases. Furthermore, the Court invalidated a Tennessee legislative reapportionment that had remained unaltered for several decades despite the loss of population in many counties and large increases in others.

In the 1964 decision on *Wesberry v. Sanders*,[3] the Court invalidated unequal congressional districts in Georgia. In this case, Justice Hugo Black (associate justice of the Supreme Court from 1937 through 1971) argued that the Constitution clearly intended to have "equal representation for equal numbers of people"—in short to guarantee that "one man's vote in a congressional election is to be worth as much as another's." This statement by Hugo Black became an important democratic principle known as "one person, one vote." The case created the legal basis for ending the rural bias in congressional representation. In another 1964 decision, *Reynolds v. Sims*,[4] the Court extended the principles of "one person, one vote" to apply to the apportionment of seats in both houses of a state's legislature.[5]

GERRYMANDERING

Although the population issue of "one person, one vote" has been resolved, the problem of gerrymandering remains a roadblock on the path to equitable representation. Gerrymandering is a process of drawing district boundaries to help increase the chance that a candidate from a particular political party or a particular group will be elected. The former is called **partisan gerrymandering**, and the latter is called racial gerrymandering or majority-minority districts.

The term was first used in 1812 when the Democratic-Republican majority of the Massachusetts legislature split Essex County in order to dilute the strength of the Federalists. An artist added a head, wings, and claws to the awkwardly shaped Essex district, making it look like a salamander. A newspaper published the map as a cartoon and labeled it a gerrymander, after Governor Elbridge Gerry, who approved the new districting plan. (See Figure 7.2.)

The stakes in the redistricting process are very high. The way a district is redrawn determines an incumbent's chance of being reelected. Therefore, redistricting is an intensely partisan consideration, with each party trying to create districts that will maximize its control of state houses and the U.S. House of Representatives.

Gerrymandering Tactics

Legislatures use different tactics to gerrymander districts. The most frequently used are vote diffusing, vote concentrating, and pairing techniques. Vote diffusion is the act

FIGURE 7.2   GERRYMANDER

Source: *Congressional Quarterly Weekly*, 9 January 1999, 62–63.

of spreading blocs of opposition party voters across a number of districts so that the opposition will gain a majority in the district. Vote concentration is the opposite of vote diffusion. It is the act of concentrating blocs of opposition party voters in a single or small number of districts while creating safe majorities for one's own party in the remaining districts. The pairing technique is used in districting two or more incumbent legislators' residences or political bases so that both are in the same district. This will assure that one of the incumbents will lose the election.[6]

The Republicans benefited from the 2000 congressional redistricting. The Republican Party controls far more state legislatures and has many more governors than it did a decade ago. They are the key participants in the highly partisan district line-drawing process. In addition, the 2000 census shows a continuing population shift from the East and Midwest to the South and West—states that vote Republican.

But it is not clear whether the Republican Party will gain House seats over the next decade. Because redistricting is not simply a partisan exercise, incumbent House members will guard their existing districts if a slight alternation might help elect their challengers.

Racial Gerrymandering

In the early 1990s, the goal of redistricting changed from favoring one party over another to increasing the chances of electing minority candidates. This was the product of the 1982 amendment to the 1965 Voting Rights Act. This became known as racial gerrymandering or majority-minority districts. It was due to the creation of majority-minority districts that the ranks of African-Americans in the House swelled from 26 to 39, and that of Hispanics increased from 12 to 19 in 1992. These gains were particularly significant in the South where the congressional delegations of Alabama, North Carolina, South Carolina, and Virginia included blacks for the first time since the turn of the century.[7]

But the Supreme Court, led by a conservative Chief Justice William Rehnquist, has objected to race-based legislative districts, even when drawn to increase the power of racial minorities. The Supreme Court's 1993 ruling on a North Carolina district in *Shaw v. Reno*[8] held that districts created with race as the sole common interest could be found unconstitutional, and the case was returned to the lower court for further consideration. Finally, in the case of *Miller v. Johnson* (1995)[9] the Court argued that the Georgia legislature's decision to use race as the "predominant factor" for redrawing district lines violated the Constitution's guarantees of equal protection under the law. In 1996, in *Bush v. Vera*[10] and *Shaw v. Hunt*,[11] the Court voided three districts in Texas and one in North Carolina, respectively, on the grounds that race was used as the "predominating factor" in drawing these four districts. Finally, in the case of *Reno v. Bossier Parish School Board*[12] (1998), the Court limited the Justice Department's ability to force states to draw minority districts.

However, the Court's position recently has changed. In the case of *Hunt v. Cromartie*,[13] (2001) the Court ruled that state legislatures could create districts in which blacks or Hispanics formed the majority, so long as they do it for political reasons. That is, even though the Constitution forbids the government from making decisions based on race, there is no such legal ban on making decisions based on political or partisan grounds. Therefore, if African-American voters are shifted into a new district to create a majority Democratic district, the move could be justified as a political decision, not a racial one.[14] *Shaw v. Reno* upheld the much-disputed North Carolina district 12 in Congress. Justice Sandra Day O'Connor, who previously voted with the conservative majority to strike down *Shaw v. Reno*, switched sides and joined the liberal bloc to uphold it this time.

THE MEMBERS OF CONGRESS

There are 535 members of Congress—435 in the House, and 100 in the Senate. To run for Congress, an individual must fulfill the requirements listed in the Constitution. To serve in the House, one must be at least 25 years of age, must have been a U.S. citizen for seven years, and must be a resident of the state (but not necessarily the district) from which one is elected. A senator must be at least 30 years of age, must have been a U.S. citizen for nine years, and must reside in the state from which one is elected.

Although constitutional requirements can be easily fulfilled by most of the population of the country, the collective profile of the 109th Congress illustrates that members of Congress do not represent a cross section of the American population. A perfectly representative legislative body would be composed much like the general population in terms of race, sex, ethnicity, religion, and the like. But that is not the case. Members of Congress are predominantly white, male, and upper-class lawyers. (See Table 7.2.)

TABLE 7.2 COLLECTIVE PROFILES OF MEMBERS OF THE 109TH CONGRESS

	HOUSE	SENATE
Party		
Republicans	232	55
Democrats	202	45
Independents	1	1
Average age	55	60
Gender		
Men	370	86
Women	65	14
Race		
White	369	95
Black	40	1
Hispanic	23	2
Asian/Pacific Islander	2	2
Native American	1	0
Asian Indian	1	0
Prior occupation*		
Law	160	58
Business and banking	163	30
Public service/politics	164	32
Education	86	16

TABLE 7.2 COLLECTIVE PROFILES OF MEMBERS OF THE 109TH CONGRESS (CONT.)

	HOUSE	SENATE
Physician	16	4
Military Service	110	31
Religion		
Baptist	65	7
Episcopalian	32	10
Jewish	26	11
Lutheran	18	3
Methodist	51	12
Mormon	11	5
Presbyterian	36	14
Protestant-Unspecified	33	5
Roman Catholic	129	24

*Some members specify more than one occupation.

Source: "Minorities in the 109th Congress." *Congressional Quarterly*, 2004. <http://oncongress.cq.com/flatfiles/editorialFiles/temporaryItems/mon20041103minorities.pdf>

In the 109th Congress, 2005–2007, there are 7 new Republican and 2 Democratic Parties' Senators, and 24 new Republicans and 14 new Democrats as House members. There are more Republicans in the 109th than in the 108th Congress. The Republican Party has its biggest margin since 1928.[15] Congress includes two independents, both from Vermont: Senator James M. Jeffords and Representative Bernard Sanders. Both caucus with the Democrats. The House freshmen include 8 women, 4 blacks, 2 Hispanics, and Bobby Jindal (R-LA), the son of an Indian immigrant. Nine members of the 109th Congress were born outside the United States.

Minorities in the 109th Congress

Although Congress is still disproportionately dominated by white men with backgrounds in law and business, gains continue to be made in every successive election cycle by minorities. Together, minorities constitute about 13 percent of the 109th Congress. The House of Representatives has 40 African-Americans (9 percent, compared with 12.3 percent of the U.S. population) and 23 Hispanic members (5 percent, compared with 12.5 percent of the U.S. population). (See Table 7.3.)

TABLE 7.3 HOUSE BLACK MEMBERS IN THE 109TH CONGRESS

Name	House
Arthur Davis	Alabama
Barbara Lee; Juanita Millender-McDonald; Maxine Waters; Diane Watson	California
Corinne Brown; Alcee L. Hasings; Kendrick B. Meek	Florida
Sanford D. Bishop; John Lewis; Cynthia A. McKinney; David Scott	Georgia
Dany K. Davis; Jesse L. Jackson Jr.; Bovvy L. Rush	Illinois
Julia Carson	Indiana
William J. Jefferson	Louisiana
Elijah E. Cummings; Albert R. Wynn	Maryland
John Conyers Jr.; Carolyn Cheeks Kilpatrick	Michigan
Bennie Thompson	Mississippi
William Lacy Clay; Emanuel Cleaver II	Missouri
Donald M. Payne	New Jersey
Gregory W. Meeks; Major R. Owens; Charles B. Rangel; Edolphus Towns	New York
G. K. Butterfield; Melvin Watt	North Carolina
Stephanie Tubbs Jones	Ohio
Chaka Fattah	Pennsylvania
James E. Clyburn	South Carolina
Harold E. Ford Jr.	Tennessee
Al Green; Sheila Jackson-Lee; Eddie Bernice Johnson	Texas
Robert C. Scott	Virginia
Gwen Moore	Wisconsin

Source: *Congressional Quarterly Weekly,* January 31, 2005

The Senate has one African-American, two Hispanics, and two Asian/Pacific Islanders. There are 25 Hispanic members of the 109th Congress. Of this number, there are 23 in the House and 2 in the Senate, the largest number ever to have served in a single Congress. Of the 23 members of the House, 19 are Democrats and four are Republicans. (See Table 7.4.)

TABLE 7.4 HOUSE HISPANIC MEMBERS IN THE 109TH CONGRESS

Name	State	Party Affiliation
Raul M. Grijalva; Ed Pastor	Arizona	Both D
Joe Baca; Xavier Becerra; Grace F. Napolitno; Lucille Roybal-Allard; Linda T. Sanchez; Loretta Sanchez; Hilda L. Solis	California	All D
John Salazar	Colorado	D
Lincoln Diaz-Balart; Mario Diaz-Balart; Ileena Ros-Lehtinen	Florida	All R
Luis V. Gutierrez	Illinois	D
Robert Menendez	New Jersey	D
Jose E. Serrano; Nydia M. Velazquez	New York	Both D
Henry Bonilla	Texas	R
Henry Cuellar; Charlie Gonzalez; Ruben Hinojosa; Solomon P. Ortiz; Silvestre Reyes	Texas	All D

Source: *Congressional Quarterly Weekly*, January 31, 2005.

All 40 African-American members of the House are Democrats. Barak Obama (D-IL) is the fifth African-American ever elected to the Senate. He defeated his Republican opponent, Allen Keyes, by receiving 70 percent of the vote. There are two Hispanic senators, the first time two have ever been elected to the Senate. Mel Martinez (R-FL) is an immigrant from Cuba. Ken Salazar, the other Hispanic, is a Democrat from Colorado.[16]

There are two sets of Hispanic members who are brothers, and one set who are sisters. Mario and Lincoln Diaz-Balart, Republicans from Florida, serve in the House. Den Salazar serves in the Senate and his brother, John Salazar (D-CO), serves in the House. Linda and Loretta Sanchez, Democrats from California, serve in the House. Four House members of the 109th Congress, Dan Boren (D-OK), Dan Lipinski (D-IL), Connie Mack (R-FL), and Russ Carnahan (D-MO), had parents who served in Congress.[17]

Women in the 109th Congress

Women constitute 15 percent of the House and 14 percent of the Senate (as compared to 51 percent of the U.S. population) in the 109th Congress. There are 82 women in the 109th Congress—65 women in the House, plus the delegates from the District of Columbia, Guam and the Virgin Islands, and 14 in the Senate. (See Table 7.5.)

There are 42 women Democrats and 23 women Republicans in the House and nine women Democrats and five women Republicans in the Senate of the 109th Congress. That is an increase of five over the past Congress. Majority members of women in both houses of Congress are Democrats.

TABLE 7.5 WOMEN MEMBERS IN THE 109TH CONGRESS

NAME	STATE	PARTY AFFILIATION
SENATE		
Lisa Murkowski	Alaska	R
Blanche Lincoln	Arkansas	D
Barbara Boxer; Dianne Feinstein	California	Both D
Mary L. Landrieu	Louisiana	D
Susan Collins; Olympia Snowe	Maine	Both R
Barbara A. Mikulski	Maryland	D
Debbie Stabenow	Michigan	D
Hillary Rodham Clinton	New York	D
Elizabeth Dole	North Carolina	R
Kay Bailey Hutchison	Texas	R
Maria Cantwell; Patty Murray	Washington	Both D
HOUSE		
Marry Bono	California	R
Lois Capps; Susan A. Davis; Anna G. Eshoo; Jane Harman; Barbara Lee; Zoe Lofgren; Juanita Millender-McDonald; Grace F. Napolitano; Nancy Pelosi; Lucille Roybal-Allard; Linda T. Sanchez; Loretta Sanchez; Hilda L. Solis; Ellen O. Tauscher; Maxine Waters; Diane Watson; Lynn Woolsey	California	All D
Diana DeGette	Colorado	D
Marilyn Musgrave	Colorado	R
Rosa Delauro	Connecticut	D
Nancy L. Johnson	Connecticut	R
Ginny Brown-Waite; Katherine Harris; Ileana Ros-Lehtinen	Florida	All R
Corinne Brown; Debbie Wasserman-Schultz	Florida	Both D
Cynthia A. McKinney	Georgia	D

TABLE 7.5 WOMEN MEMBERS IN THE 109TH CONGRESS

Name	State	Party Affiliation
Melissa Bean; Jan Schakowsky	Illinois	Both D
Judy Biggert	Illinois	R
Julia Carson	Indiana	D
Anne M. Northup	Kentucky	R
Carolyn Cheeks Kilpatrick	Michigan	D
Candice S. Miller	Michigan	R
Betty McCollum	Minnesota	D
Jo Ann Emerson	Missouri	R
Shelley Berkley	Nevada	D
Heather A. Wilson	New Mexico	R
Sue W. Kelly	New York	R
Nita M. Lowery; Carolyn B. Maloney; Carolyn McCarthy; Louise M. Slaughter; Nydia M Velazquez	New York	All D
Virginia Foxx; Sue Myrick	North Carolina	Both R
Stephanie Tubbs Jones; Marcy Kaptur	Ohio	Both D
Deborah Pryce	Ohio	R
Darlene Hooley	Oregon	D
Melissa A. Hart	Pennsylvania	R
Allyson Y. Schwartz	Pennsylvania	D
Stephanie Herseth	South Dakota	D
Marsha Blackburn	Tennessee	R
Kay Granger	Texas	R
Sheila Jackson-Lee; Eddie Bernice Johnson	Texas	Both D
Jo Ann Davis; Thelma Drake	Virginia	Both R
Cathy McMorris	Washington	R
Shelley Moore Capito	West Virginia	R
Tammy Baldwin; Gwen Moore	Wisconsin	Both D
Barbara Cubin	Wyoming	R

Source: *Congressional Quarterly Weekly*, January 31, 2005

Dominant Age, Profession, Party and Religious Denomination

Congress has been getting steadily older. The average age of House members in the 109th Congress, is 55, and that of the Senate is 60. In the 109th Congress, the youngest senator, at age 40, is John Sununu, Jr. (R-NH). The oldest, 87, is Robert C. Byrd (D-WV). In the House, Patrick McHenry (R-NC) is the youngest at 29, while Ralph M. Hall (R-TX) is the oldest at 81. Of the 40 freshmen, 8 Republicans and 4 Democrats are at least 55 years old. The oldest is 67-year-old Republican Joe Schwartz of Michigan. The average length of service of the members of the House is 9.3 years. Representative John Dingell (D-MI) has the longest consecutive service of any member of the 109th Congress, 49 years. The average length of service in the Senate is 12.1 years. Senator Robert C. Byrd has served 46 years.

The majority of the 109th Congress has experience in the legal profession and business world or the public sector. Nearly 40 percent list "law" as occupation, 34 percent list "business," and 29 percent have been public servants. The 109th Congress has 20 physicians—16 House members and 4 senators. Finally, there are three Rhodes scholars in the Senate and five in the House.

As a result of 2004 elections, the Democrats lost seats in both the House and the Senate. There are 232 Republicans, 202 Democrats, and one independent in the 109th Congress. The independent member of the House is Bernard Sanders (I–VT). Senator James Jeffords of Vermont defected from the Republican Party in 2001, and became an independent member of the Senate.

Protestants (Episcopalians, Methodists, Baptists, Presbyterians, and others) collectively constitute the majority religious affiliation of members. However, Roman Catholics account for the largest single religious denomination.

CONGRESSIONAL ELECTIONS

Elections are held in November of even-numbered years, and members of Congress begin their term of office on January 3 following the November election. Each Congress lasts two years and is numbered; thus the First Congress convened in 1789, and the 109th convened in 2005. Members of the House of Representatives are elected every two years. Thus, in 2004, the entire membership of the House was up for reelection. Senators, on the other hand, serve six-year terms. The Senate terms are staggered so that only one-third of the senators come up for reelection every two years—in 2004, 34 members were up for reelection. Fourteen members of the House, 9 Republicans and 5 Democrats, retired at the end of the 107th Congress. In the

Senate of the 109th Congress, four Senators publicly announced that they were not going to seek reelection; all four were Republicans.

Incumbency Factor

For many politicians, the most important election is the first election. Those who run for reelection usually emerge winners—this is more the case for House members than for senators. This is so because the entire state is more diverse than districts represented by a House member. In addition, senators have less personal contact with the voters than do House members. Finally, senators receive more media coverage and are more likely to be held accountable on controversial issues.

In addition, several factors explain the electoral success of the incumbents. Among them are better name recognition, **franking privilege** (free mail service to the constituents), greater access to media, more ease in raising campaign money than challengers have, more campaign experience, and the credit for federal monies given to the incumbents' states or regions.

Concerns about the entrenched positions of incumbents, the high disapproval rate among voters of the job performance of members of Congress, and the influence of political action committees on congressional elections have led to calls for term limits. But these attempts have not produced any fruitful results. In addition, congressional attempts for a proposed constitutional amendment fell significantly short of the necessary two-thirds majority on the floor of the House in 1995. The Supreme Court, however, in *U.S. Term Limits v. Thornton*,[18] declared state-imposed congressional term limits unconstitutional in 1995.

PRIVILEGES AND REMOVAL OF MEMBERS

Based on Article I, Section 6, members of Congress cannot be arrested while attending sessions of Congress or while going to and returning from sessions except in case of treason, felony, and breach of peace. Furthermore, members of Congress cannot be questioned in any place for remarks made in Congress.

According to Article I, Section 5, each chamber, with the concurrence of two-thirds of its members, may expel a member. As of 2005, 15 senators and 5 representatives have been expelled. Representative Michael Myers (D-PA) was expelled in 1980 after being convicted on bribery and conspiracy charges resulting from the FBI's Abscam sting operation. The latest representative to be expelled was James Traficant (D-OH). He was expelled in 2002 for violations of the House Code of Conduct arising from his felony conviction.

The alternative to expulsion is reprimand or censure. **Censure** is a formal condemnation of a member's action or the action of any other high federal official, including the president. This formal condemnation is read aloud in the chamber with the accused standing before the assembled members.

Reprimand is a milder form of censure. The accused is not required to stand before the members while the condemnation is read. Former House Speaker Newt Gingrich was the first speaker to be reprimanded by the full House. He agreed to accept the House ethics investigative subcommittee's finding that he illegally used tax-deductible donations to fund two college courses that he taught. He also admitted to providing inaccurate information to the ethics committee on two instances. On January 21, 1997, the full House voted to approve the House Ethics Committee's recommendation to reprimand the Speaker and approved a $300,000 penalty against him.

In 2004, the House Ethics Committee admonished the House Majority Leader, Tom Delay (R-TX), for pressuring a congressman to vote for a Medicare bill by offering to help his son win a House seat. About the same time, three Delay associates were indicted on felony charges by the Travis County grand jury. They were accused of fund-raising abuses in their work with **Texas for Republican Majority**, a group Delay helped create to usher in GOP control of the House. All have denied wrongdoing.

Salaries and Benefits

The salary of rank-and-file members of 109th Congress is $158,100 per year. Leadership of Congress is paid more than the rest of its members. The annual salary of the Speaker of the House is $203,000. The majority and minority leaders of both chambers of Congress each receive an annual salary of $175,000 per year. Member salaries are indexed to the cost of living adjustment (COLA). It takes effect annually unless Congress votes not to accept it.

In addition, members of Congress are entitled to retirement and health benefits under the same plans available for other federal employees. A member is qualified after five years of service. Members elected since 1984 are covered by the Federal Employees' Retirement System (FERS). Those elected prior to 1984 were covered by the Civil Service Retirement System (CSRS). In 1984, all members were given the option of remaining with CSRS or switching to FERS.

Members are not eligible for a pension until they reach the age of 50, provided that they have completed 20 years of service. The amount of a member's pension depends on the years of service, and the average of the highest three years of his or her salary. By law, the starting amount of a member's retirement annuity may not exceed 80% of his or her final salary.[19]

POWERS AND FUNCTIONS OF CONGRESS

Article I, Section 8, of the Constitution grants Congress the power to take the following actions: coin money, conduct foreign relations, regulate interstate commerce, levy and collect taxes, declare war, raise and support the military, establish a post office, establish courts inferior to the Supreme Court, establish naturalization and bankruptcy laws, punish counterfeiters of federal money and securities, grant patents and copyrights, punish piracies and felonies on the high seas, and punish offenses against the law of nations.

The Constitution also grants certain powers to each chamber of Congress. The Senate approves presidential appointments by majority vote and ratifies treaties signed by the president by a two-thirds vote. On the other hand, the House of Representatives has the power of originating all bills for raising of revenue. Another power vested in the Congress by the Constitution is the right to propose amendments to the Constitution. Also, should two-thirds of the state legislatures demand changes in the Constitution, it is the duty of Congress to call a constitutional convention.

In addition, Article I, Sections 2 and 3, give both chambers of Congress the right to act in the impeachment proceedings. **Impeachment** is the process of bringing formal charges against a federal official in the House. It is the first step in the process for removing the president, vice president, or other government official from office upon conviction of "treason, bribery, or other high crimes and misdemeanors." The House of Representatives has "the sole power of impeachment"—that is, the power to bring charges. A simple majority is needed to pass articles of impeachment on the floor of the House. The Senate has "the sole power to try all impeachments." A two-thirds vote is required in the Senate for conviction. When the president is to be tried, the chief justice of the Supreme Court presides. A conviction in an impeachment proceeding results only in removal from office and disqualification to hold "any office of honor, trust, or profit under the United States." A person convicted in an impeachment, however, is subject to further "indictment, trial, judgment, and punishment according to law." (For a discussion of President Clinton's impeachment hearings, see Chapter 8.)

Furthermore, Article IV gives Congress the power to admit new states into the union. In order for a territory to become a state, the territory must petition Congress and draft a constitution with a republican form of government. Congress has to approve statehood by a simple majority, and the president must concur with its decision. Puerto Rico is a case in point. It used to be a Spanish colony until the United States defeated Spain and occupied it in the Spanish-American War of 1898. In 1998, a referendum was held in Puerto Rico to allow its citizens to vote to become the 51st state; to become an independent country; to remain a commonwealth; or "none of the above." Although 2.5 percent of those who participated in the referendum opted for independence, the majority voters, 50.1 percent, voted for "none of the above."

Finally, according to the Twelfth Amendment, if no candidate receives a majority of votes in the Electoral College, the House selects a president (by a majority of the state delegations) and the Senate chooses a vice president. While the House has selected two presidents, Thomas Jefferson and John Quincy Adams, the Senate has selected one vice president, Richard M. Johnson, who served under President Martin Van Buren in 1837. Congress also has the power to approve the selection of a new vice president when a vacancy occurs in that office, according to the Twenty-Fifth Amendment. (See Table 7.6.)

HOW A BILL BECOMES A LAW

Among the most important responsibilities of Congress is its law-making function, detailed in Article I, Section 7, of the Constitution. Proposed laws are introduced in the form of bills to both the House and Senate. For a bill to become a law, it has to go through several stages.

Committee Action

The presiding officers of each chamber assign a bill to an appropriate committee or subcommittee. The subject of legislation usually determines its committee. If a committee considers a bill to have little merit, it is discarded or pigeonholed. Bills with merit are assigned to a subcommittee for further work. Public hearings are held on bills, which serve to inform both the public and subcommittee members about their merits and problems. After public hearings, the subcommittee members convene a **mark-up session**, where a bill is subject to further review by committee members. Suggestions for changes in the wording may be made, and then the bill is sent to the full committee. More hearings may be held on the bill at the committee level. After another mark-up session, the bill is reported out of the committee to the floor of each chamber.

TABLE 7.6   THE CONSTITUTION'S DISTRIBUTION OF POWERS TO CONGRESS

Powers of Both Houses	Powers to Each Chamber of Congress	
	Senate	House
To coin money	Senate approves presidential appointment	Originates bills for raising of revenues
To conduct foreign policy		
To regulate commerce		
To provide an army and a navy	Ratifies treaties	Brings impeachment charges
To declare war		
To establish courts inferior to the Supreme Court	Holds a trial of an impeached official	Chooses a president if no candidate emerges with a majority vote in the Electoral College
To establish post offices		
To establish naturalization and bankruptcy laws	Chooses a vice president if no candidate emerges with a majority vote in the Electoral College	
To grant patents and copyrights		
To propose amendments to the Constitution		
To admit new states		
To confirm selection of new vice president due to vacancy in that office		

Rules Committee

In the House, the bill must first pass through the Rules Committee before it is introduced to the floor. This committee grants each bill a rule. An open rule permits unlimited amendments to a bill on the floor. A closed rule means no amendments may be offered on a specific bill. The entire House must approve the rule given a bill by the Rules Committee before action on the bill can continue. Often, amendments are considered by a "committee of the whole" procedure, which allows the House to function with fewer members (at least 100 members) in attendance than allowed under regular House rule. The entire House must approve decisions made by the "committee of the whole."

Senate Action

A bill follows a similar route through the Senate. The bill is assigned to a committee by the leadership of the Senate. In contrast to the House procedure, the bill may be filibustered in the Senate. It is the ultimate, but not an insurmountable weapon of a senatorial minority. To filibuster means to keep talking until a majority of the Senate either abandons the bill or agrees to modify its most controversial provisions. To conduct a filibuster, the presiding officer must recognize the first senator seeking to speak. Once recognized, a senator may hold the floor as long as desired—the record is 24 hours and 18 minutes, set by Strom Thurmond, (R–SC) in opposition to 1957 civil rights legislation. The senator holding the floor may yield to like-minded colleagues, as long as those senators' comments are made in the form of questions. After a senator yields the floor, the presiding officer may put the pending question to a vote only when no other senator seeks recognition. A filibuster can be stopped when three-fifths of the Senate (60 members) vote for a cloture motion, also called a cloture petition. Cloture is a procedure that allows senators to debate and no senator may speak for more than one hour unless other senators yield him or her their time.

Conference Committee

The conference committee must resolve any differences between the House and Senate before the president considers a bill. The conference committee is composed of several members of both chambers, known informally as "conferees," usually those members who worked on the bill. After resolving the differences between the House and Senate forms of a bill, the conference committee then reports this compromise bill back to the floor of each chamber. After approval by members of both the Speaker of the House and the president pro tempore (temporary president of the Senate) will sign the bill. Finally, the bill is sent to the president's desk for consideration. (See Figure 7.3.)

Presidential Action

If the president does not sign a bill within 10 days while Congress is in session, it automatically becomes law. A bill will not become law if the president fails to sign within 10 days while Congress is not in session. This is called a **pocket veto**. Sometimes the president vetoes a bill and sends it back to Congress with his written objections. A presidential veto kills a bill unless a two-thirds majority in each chamber votes in favor of the bill and overrides the president's veto, making the bill become a law in spite of the president's opposition. During the 103rd through 106th Congress, President Clinton vetoed a total of 37 bills, pocket-vetoed one bill, and Congress overrode two of his vetoed bills.

RESOLUTIONS

Besides passing bills, members of Congress pass resolutions, including joint resolutions, simple resolutions, and concurrent resolutions. **Joint resolutions** are used

FIGURE 7.3 HOW A BILL BECOMES A LAW

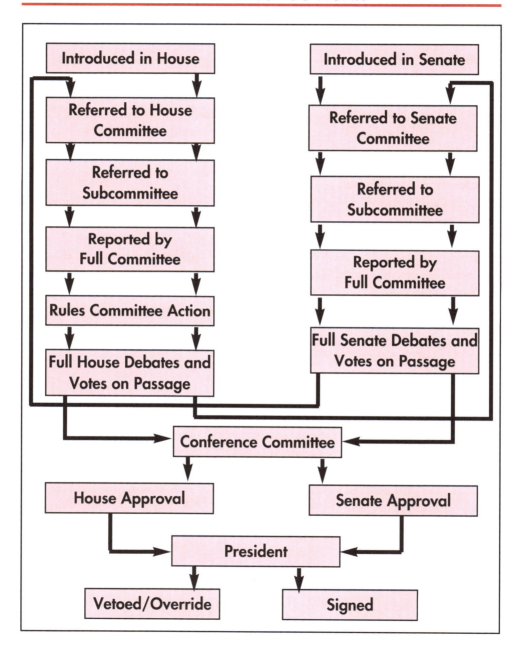

for purposes other than legislation, like making a continuing appropriation or establishing a permanent joint committee. A joint resolution annexed Texas to the United States on March 1, 1845. Like bills, joint resolutions must be signed by the president in order to become laws. Simple resolutions and concurrent resolutions do not require the president's approval. **Simple resolutions** are passed by only one chamber and usually deal with routine housekeeping matters. For example, the House passed a simple resolution honoring the women who served the United States in different military capacities during World War II. Both chambers must pass **concurrent resolutions**. For example, Congress uses a concurrent resolution to fix the time of adjournment.

OVERSIGHT

Congress does more than write laws. Another important function of Congress is the oversight. Congress ensures that the administration is carrying out its laws the way Congress intended. The primary purpose of oversight is to determine what happens after a law is passed. Oversight has many other purposes: to make sure programs conform to congressional intent; to ferret out "waste, fraud, and abuse"; to determine whether programs may have outlived their usefulness; and to ensure that programs and agencies are administered in a cost-effective and efficient manner. Oversight is based on the constitutional powers given to Congress to pass laws, to create agencies and programs, to provide funding for these agencies and programs, and to investigate the executive branch.

Congress has established the Government Accountability Office (GAO; previously, the General Accounting Office) to help with its oversight function. The GAO audits and evaluates government programs and activities to ensure effective receipt and disbursement of public funds. As the investigative arm of Congress, the GAO performs reviews requested by committee chairs and ranking minority members, as well as those required by law or initiated by the GAO itself. For example, in February 2002, the GAO filed a lawsuit, known as *Walker v. Cheney*,[20] against the Bush Administration in the U.S. District Court in Washington, D.C. The plaintiff, David Walker, is the U.S. Comptroller General and the head of the GAO. The defendant, Dick Cheney, is the vice president, and head of the Administration's energy task force, the focus of the litigation. Some in Congress wanted to know whether Bush campaign donors had a disproportionate influence over the task force. The White House, which used the task force to draft its national energy policy, said the GAO was not entitled to the information. The GAO filed this lawsuit when Cheney refused to share names, notes, and minutes of the task force meetings with people outside of government.

CONSTITUENT SERVICE

Members of Congress also provide services for those constituents who have problems with the bureaucracy. They act as liaisons between federal and state agencies and constituents when difficulties are encountered. Examples include helping the elderly to secure Social Security benefits or helping veterans to obtain medical assistance. Members of Congress also stay in touch with their constituents by using franking privilege to find out where they stand on particular public issues of concern to both members and constituents.

ORGANIZATION OF CONGRESS

Congress consists of a complex network of party organizations, committees, subcommittees, personal and committee staffers, and support agencies.

Party Leadership: The House

The presiding officer of the House of Representatives is the Speaker. The position of Speaker is established in Article I, Section 2 of the U.S. Constitution. The post combines the duties of presiding officer with those of majority party leader. Although the Speaker is formally elected by a vote of the entire House at the beginning of each Congress, on January 3 of odd-numbered years, the actual election of the Speaker takes place at the majority party's organizational meeting prior to the regular convening of Congress. The Speaker refers bills to different committees, recognizes members who wish to speak on the floor, interprets the rules of the House, and appoints the chair of the powerful Rules Committee and of Select and Conference committees. Finally, the Speaker is next in the line of succession to become president after the vice president.

    The second-ranking leadership position is the House **majority leader**. The majority party elects its majority leader. He is the party leader on the floor of the House. The majority leader assists the Speaker in scheduling legislation and deciding party strategy and floor debates. The minority party elects a **minority leader.** He or she acts as the minority party's principal spokesperson and strategist. Assisting the floor leaders of both parties is the whip organization, composed of the leaders, deputy whips, at-large whips, and regional whips. The **whips** inform members about upcoming key votes, attempt to "whip up" support for the party position on important roll-call votes, and work to maintain party unity. (See Table 7.7.)

TABLE 7.7 OFFICERS OF THE 109TH CONGRESS

SENATE	HOUSE
President, Dick Cheney	Speaker of the House, Dennis Hastert, (R–IL)
President Pro Tempore, Ted Stevens (R–AK)	
DEMOCRATS	DEMOCRATS
Minority Leader, Harry Reid (NV)	Minority Leader, Nancy Pelosi (CA)
Minority Whip, Dick Durbin (IL)	Minority Whip, Steny Hoyer (MD)
Secretary of Conference, Debbie Stabenow (MI)	Chairman of Caucus, Robert Menendez (NJ)
REPUBLICANS	REPUBLICANS
Majority Leader, Bill Frist (TN)	Majority Leader, Tom Delay (TX)
Majority Whip, Mitch McConnell (KY)	Majority Whip, Roy Blunt (MO)
Chairman of Conference, Rick Santorum (PA)	Chairperson of Conference, Deborah Pryce (OH)

Source: "Leadership of the 109th Congress." *The CapitolNet.* <http://thecapitol.net/FAQ/cong_leadership.html.>

Party Leadership: The Senate

The Senate leadership is composed of president, president *pro tempore,* majority and minority leaders, and their whips. According to Article I, Section 3 of the Constitution, the vice president is the chief presiding officer of the Senate, but the role is entirely ceremonial. In practice, he presides on ceremonial occasions and when Senate leaders expect a close vote. The vice president can only vote in order to break a tie vote, which happens infrequently. For example, during his eight years as the vice president, Al Gore cast four tie-breaking votes. On most other occasions, senators take turns as presiding officer.

The Senate also elects a president *pro tempore* ("for the time being") from the majority party. The Senate tradition is to elect the majority party senator with the longest continuous service to the post. This position is set forth in Article I, Section 3 of the U.S. Constitution. The president *pro tempore* presides over the Senate in the absence of the president of the Senate. Even the president *pro tempore* does not often actually preside. Most often the task is given to junior members of the majority party. The president *pro tempore* is also named in statute, the Presidential Succession

Act of 1947, as third in the line of succession to the presidency, right after the vice president and the Speaker of the House.

The leadership of parties exercises the actual power of the Senate. The leadership is elected by party members on secret ballot at the beginning of each new Congress—every two years. They collectively prepare the Senate's agenda, influence committee assignments, and assign legislation to the committees of the Senate. But leadership power is exercised by the majority leader. The majority leader has the exclusive right to schedule bills for floor consideration. Whatever legislation the majority leader schedules, however, can be filibustered, and therefore can be delayed or stopped. Like the House of Representatives, both parties in the Senate have whips whose major function is to line up voting support on issues.

THE COMMITTEE SYSTEM

The actual work of Congress is mainly conducted by committees. Therefore, committees are considered little legislatures. These committees determine the fates of thousands of bills introduced to Congress. The committees divide labor, develop expertise, and ensure task specialization. The different types of committees include standing committees, subcommittees, select committees, and joint committees. **Standing committees** are permanent committees. (See Table 7.8.) They are specialized in particular areas and deal with bills related to those areas. Most standing committees are divided into **subcommittees** that deal with specialized areas of the parent committee's jurisdiction.

Another type of committee is the **select committee**. These are temporary committees established for a particular purpose—to research a problem or to conduct an investigation. After conducting an investigation, they are required to make recommendations to their respective chambers in Congress. The last type of committee is the **joint committee**, whose membership is drawn from both chambers of Congress. Some of them, called standing joint committees, are permanent but have no authority to initiate legislation. The permanent joint committees in the current Congress include Joint Economic, Joint Library, Joint Printing, and Joint Taxation.

In both chambers of Congress, each party's special committee has the task of assigning party members to different committees. Committee assignments are subject to the approval of all party members. A chairperson heads each committee. The chairs of committees are members of the majority party. They make decisions about the work of their committees, including meeting times, bills to be considered, when hearings will be held, and which witnesses will be called to testify for or against a bill. Since 1971, committee chairs have been selected by secret ballot. This has reduced the importance of seniority, which is an important factor in the selection of committee chairs. In addition, when the Republicans took control of the House in 1995, under the leadership of Gingrich, they limited a committee and subcommittee chairperson's tenure to three terms or six years, and the Speaker's term to four terms or eight years.

TABLE 7.8   COMMITTEES OF THE 109TH CONGRESS, 2005

SENATE (ALL REPUBLICANS)	CHAIRPERSON	HOUSE (ALL REPUBLICANS)	CHAIRPERSON
Agriculture, Nutrition and Forestry	Saxby Chambliss (GA)	Agriculture	Bob Goodlatee (VA)
		Appropriations	Jerry Lewis (CA)
Appropriations	Thad Cochran (MI)	Armed Services	Duncan Hunter (CA)
Armed Services	John Warner (VA)	Budget	Tim Nussle (IO)
Banking, Housing & Urban Affairs	Richard C. Shelby (AL)	Homeland Security	Christopher Cox (CA)
		Energy & Commerce	Joe Barton (TX)
Budget	Judd Greg (NH)	Education & Workforce	John A. Boehner (OH)
Commerce, Science & Transportation	Ted Stevens (AK)		
		Government Reform	Tom Davis (VA)
Energy & Natural Resources	Pete V. Domenici (NM)	House Administration	Robert W. Ney (OH)
Environment & Public Works	James M. Inhofe (OK)	International Relations	Henry J. Hyde (IL)
		Judiciary	F. James Sensenbrenner (WI)
Finance	Chuck Grassley (IA)		
Foreign Relations	Richard G. Lugar (IN)	Resources	Richard W. Pombo (CA)
Health, Education, Labor & Pensions	Mike Enzi (WY)	Rules	Phil Gingrey (GA)
		Science	Sherwood Boehlert (NY)
Judiciary	Arlen Specter (PA)	Small Business	Donald Manzullo (IL)
Rules & Administration	Trent Lott (MS)	Standards of Official Conduct	Doc Hastings (WA)
Small Business and Entrepreneurship	Olympia Snowe (ME)		
		Veterans' Affairs	Steve Buyer (IN)
Veterans' Affairs	Larry Craig (ID)	Transportation & Infrastructure	Don Young (AK)
Homeland Security and Governmental Affairs	Susan M. Collins (ME)		
		Ways & Means	William M. Thomas (CA)

TABLE 7.8   COMMITTEES OF THE 109TH CONGRESS, 2005

SENATE (ALL REPUBLICANS)	CHAIRPERSON	HOUSE (ALL REPUBLICANS)	CHAIRPERSON
Special and Select Committees		Select Committee	
Indian Affairs	Daniel Inoye (HI)	Intelligence	Peter Hoekstria (MI)
Ethics	Harry Reid (NV)		
Intelligence	Bob Graham (FL)		
Aging	John Breaux (LA)		
JOINT COMMITTEES			
Economic Committee	Senator Robert F. Bennett (UT)		
Printing	Representative Robert W. Ney (OH)		
Taxation	Senator Charles E. Grassley (IA)		
Library	Senator Ted Stevens (AK)		

Source: "Leadership of the 109th Congress." The CapitolNet. <http://thecapitol.net/FAQ/cong_leadership.html.

Staff and Support Services

Along with the 535 members of the House and Senate, more than 30,000 other individuals are part of Congress. Some of these individuals provide specialized advice and information to the members of Congress.

Personal and Committee Staff

Every senator, representative, and congressional committee hires staff members to help them with their legislative functions. Staff work involves answering correspondence, doing casework, handling press relations, scheduling committee hearings, writing bills and amendments, recruiting witnesses during committee hearings, and developing questions that members ask from witnesses.

Each representative has a staff of about 20. The size of a senator's staff depends on the population of the state he or she represents. The average size of a Senate staff is 70. As many as 30 professional and clerical staffers work for most House committees, whereas Senate committees may employ 40 or more.

Congressional Budget Office

The Congressional Budget and Impoundment Control Act of 1974 created the Congressional Budget Office (CBO). It provides Congress with the objective, timely, nonpartisan analyses needed for economic and budget decisions and with the information and estimates required for the congressional budget process.

Congressional Research Service

The Congressional Research Service (CRS) is a unit of the Library of Congress, the national library of the United States, with the world's most extensive collections in many areas. The CRS provides research and information to the members of Congress. It provides timely, objective information and analysis in response to congressional inquiries at every stage of the legislative process concerning subject areas relevant to policy issues under study by members of Congress.

Government Accountability Office

The Government Accountability Office (GAO) was established in 1921. The Comptroller General of the United States, who is appointed by the president with Senate approval for a term of 15 years, heads this office. The GAO audits, evaluates, and investigates government agencies and programs. Members of Congress, through their committee chairpersons, make the majority of these reviews in response to specific requests.

Government Printing Office

The Public Printer, who is nominated by the president and confirmed by the Senate, heads the Government Printing Office (GPO). Although the office was created primarily to satisfy the printing needs of Congress, today the GPO prints, binds, and disseminates information for the entire federal government. Congressional documents, census forms, federal regulations and reports, IRS tax forms, and U.S. passports are produced by or through the GPO.

Office of Technology Assessment

In 1972, Congress established the Office of Technology Assessment (OTA) to provide congressional committees with analyses of emerging, difficult, and often highly technical issues. Services include major assessment reports, background papers, briefings, and testimony before congressional committees. Among its many projects, the OTA has conducted studies on the long-term effects of chemical tests and the reliability of lie detector tests.

Summary

The most representative branch of the government is Congress. The institution of Congress emerged as a result of the Connecticut Compromise on the floor of the Philadelphia Convention. This compromise established a bicameral legislature, the House and the Senate. Each state is represented equally in the Senate—two senators from each state. Representation in the House is based on population. There are 435 members in the House of Representatives. The 435 members of the House are redistributed among the states every 10 years following the publication of the new national census. Following the redistribution of 435 districts, state legislatures must redraw district lines to ensure population equality. An important issue with redistricting is gerrymandering—a process of drawing district boundaries to help increase the chance of a candidate from a political party or a particular group to be elected.

Other problems are associated with Congress. First, members of Congress do not represent a cross section of the American population. They are predominantly male, white, Anglo-Saxon, Protestant, and they are usually businesspersons or lawyers. The creation of majority-minority districts by the state legislatures helped increase minority representation in the House in the early 1990s. The Supreme Court stated that race cannot be used as the dominant factor to redraw district lines. However, the Court ruled that districts can be gerrymandered for political reasons. In addition, the issue of abortion and the high-profile sex scandals of the 1980s and 1990s caused more women to run for election in the 1990s. As a result, the membership of women in both chambers of Congress has increased since 1992. Another problem is low turnover among the members of Congress. Most of those who run for reelection are elected. Challengers lose to incumbents due to lack of money, weaker name recognition, and less campaign experience. Finally, most members of Congress are more responsive to organized interest groups than to the voters who elected them.

KEY TERMS

- At-large election
- Bicameral legislature
- Censure
- Cloture
- Committee of the whole
- Concurrent resolution
- Conference committee
- Filibuster
- Franking privilege
- Gerrymandering
- Impeachment
- Incumbent
- Joint committee
- Joint resolution
- Majority leader
- Malapportionment
- Mark-up session
- Minority leader
- Pairing technique
- Partisan gerrymandering
- Pocket veto
- President pro tempore
- Racial gerrymandering
- Reapportionment
- Redistricting
- Reprimand
- Rules Committee
- Select committee
- Seventeenth Amendment
- Simple resolution
- Subcommittee
- Vote concentration
- Vote diffusion
- Whip

INTERNET SOURCES

a) http://www.house.gov
Information on the U.S. House of Representatives is provided in this site. This includes, but is not limited to movement and passage of bills, legislation, committee actions, campaign activities and itinerary of individual House members, etc.

b) http://www.senate.gov
Information on this site is similar to that of a) but relative to the U.S. Senate.

c) http://thomas.loc.gov
This is the official site of the Library of Congress. It contains original copies of historical documents of the United States as well as state and foreign governments. Information on contemporary political, economic, and social governmental and nongovernmental activities can also be found in this site.

d) http://www.opensecrets.org
This is the Center for Responsive Politics' web site. It provides information about how much political candidates raised and who contributed to their campaigns.

e) http://www.vote-smart.org
This site lets us find out who represents you by entering your zip code
f) http://www.rollcall.com, http://www.hillnews.com, and http://library.cqpress.com
These sites are newspapers and magazines that specialize in reporting on Congress.

NOTES

[1] For an excellent discussion of reapportionment, see Mark E. Rush, *Does Redistricting Make a Difference?: Partisan Representation and Electoral Behavior* (Baltimore: The Johns Hopkins University Press, 1993).

[2] *Baker v. Carr*, 369 U.S. 186 (1962).

[3] *Wesberry v. Sanders*, 377 U.S. 1 (1964).

[4] *Reynolds v. Sims*, 377 U.S. 533 (1964).

[5] Theo Herrington, "The Texas Legislature and Redistricting," in *Texas Politics Today*, William Maxwell and Ernest Crain (New York: West Publishing Company, 1995).

[6] Ibid., 132–133.

[7] Juliana Gruenwald, "Court Ruling Expected to Spark More Suits," *Congressional Quarterly* (July 1, 1995), 1947–1948.

[8] *Shaw v. Reno*, 113 /s. Ct. 2816 (1993).

[9] *Miller v. Johnson*, 515 U.S. 900 (1995).

[10] *Bush v. Vera*, 517 U.S. 952 (1996).

[11] *Shaw v. Hunt*, 116 S. Ct. 1894, 135 L. Ed. 2nd 207 (1996).

[12] *Reno v. Bossier*, Parish School Board 520 U.S. 471 (1998).

[13] *Hunt v. Cromartie*, 526 U.S. 541 (2001).

[14] Davis G. Savage, "High Court Flexible on Redistricting," *State Legislatures*.

[15] Kathy Keily. "New Congress Reflects Nation's Division of Diveristy." 2005. *USA Today*. <http://usatoday.com/news/Washington/2005-01-02-congressx.htm.>

[16] L. Mildred Amer. "Memberhsip of th 109th Congress." *CRS Report for Congress*. <http://www.senate.gov/reference/resources/pdf/R22007.pdf>

[17] Ibid.

[18] *U.S. Term Limits v. Thornton*, 514 U.S. 776 (1995).

[19] "Salaries and Benefits of U.S. Congress Members." *U.S.Government Information/Resource*. http://usgoverninfo.about.com/library/weekly/aa031200a.htm>

[20] David M. Walker, the plaintiff, filed the case in the U.S. District Court for the District of Columbia.rules charges renamed three committees. Government Reform and Oversight became Government Reform; House Oversight became House Administration; and National Security reverted to its name of Armed Services.

Chapter 8

Office of the President of the United States

The Vice President of the United States is nothing. But tomorrow it may be everything.
   —(An anecdote attributed to one of the early vice presidents contemplating the possible ascendancy to the presidency.)

INTRODUCTION

This chapter on the presidency will present the structure and functions of what many regard as the most powerful office in the world. Yet, it is an office which still must yield to the demands of a democratic society.

We have no royalty in the United States, but the presidency is the closest we have to a position that inspires reverence. The presidency has been changed and molded by the times and by the men who have held the office. This chapter will attempt to portray the constitutional and political outlines of the president of the United States.

The office of the president of the United States is regarded as the most powerful in the world. In many ways it is. The United States of America, at the start of a new century, stands unchallenged as the greatest world power. The office of the president of this powerhouse of a country naturally is imbued with respect and significance.

As this chapter will relate, this commanding office has military, economic, political, and other leadership assignments. The occupant of this office is regarded as an extremely important figure worldwide.

In spite of all this, the occupant of this office of the president is also a rather vulnerable figure. In a democracy such as ours, the media, political opponents, and even foreign governments can wreak havoc on the president.

It is ironic that while the president of the United States has at his fingertips the command of a mighty military, he still must answer for his decisions and actions while in office. The Watergate episode of President Nixon, the Iran-Contra scandal which occurred during the presidency of Ronald Reagan, and the Whitewater/Monica Lewinsky controversies of President Clinton are widely known examples.

This chapter will attempt to acquaint the student with the office of the presidency.

THE CONSTITUTION AND THE PRESIDENCY

According to Article II of the United States Constitution, "The executive power shall be vested in a President of the United States of America. He shall hold the office during the term of four years, and together with the Vice President, chosen for the same term, be elected as follows…." This Article also details how the president and vice president shall be elected to office. The Twelfth, Twentieth, Twenty-Second, and Twenty-Fifth Amendments refined this process.

Article II also lists the qualifications one must possess to be elected president. One must be a natural born citizen, attain thirty-five years of age, "and been fourteen years a resident within the United States."

Article II lists the responsibilities of this office:

> The President shall be Commander in chief of the Army and Navy of the United States, and of the militia of the several states, when called into the actual service of the United States; he may require the opinion in writing of the principal officer in each of the executive departments, upon any subject relating to the duties of their respective offices, and he shall have power to grant reprieves and pardons for offences against the United States, except in cases of impeachment.

Readers may recall the controversial pardon which President Ford accorded to former President Richard Nixon during the Watergate episode. The same Article goes on to award the president the power to make treaties with the **advice and consent** of the Senate, and appoint ambassadors, judges, and other public officials as provided by law.

The president is commanded to present a **State of the Union address** and to make sure that all laws of the country are faithfully executed. The president is given the responsibilities to receive ambassadors and other public ministers. In this role, he is **chief of state**.

Finally, the Article ends by stating the ominous words, "The President, Vice President, and all civil officers of the United States, shall be removed from Office on Impeachment for, and Conviction of, Treason, Bribery, or other high Crimes and Misdemeanors."

In addition to these formal powers, the president is regarded by tradition as the leader of his or her political party. Many functions are inherent in the office, both formal and informal.

The United States has no king or queen. This is no monarchy. The president is awarded mighty powers and responsibilities, but is also limited by other branches of the federal government. Additionally, public opinion and the media have influence over the president and the direction of the presidency.

The importance of the public and the media can be illustrated by President Nixon's troubles with Watergate. The book *All the President's Men* by Bob Woodward and Carl Bernstein, and the movie of the same name, featuring Robert Redford and Dustin Hoffman, are both entertaining and informative on this issue.

President Clinton's troubles with what have been labeled "Filegate," "Travelgate," and his relations with women are also illustrative. For months, the media commented on, interpreted, and focused on his problems. The focus of media is never to be underestimated in these days of instant communication and increased media competitiveness.

WHO CAN BECOME PRESIDENT?

According to Article II of the Constitution, a candidate for president must be: A natural-born citizen (can be born abroad of parents who are American citizens), thirty-five years of age, and a resident of the United States for at least fourteen years. Aside from these constitutional qualifications, there are informal, traditional, and political features that make for a serious presidential profile. It helps for a serious contender to come from a large state. There is, of course, no legal requirement, but it is helpful politically. Voters from a state where a future president resides will most likely vote for him or her. This is important, especially if it is a state rich with electoral votes like the large population states of California, New York, and Texas.

However, it must be noted that several modern era presidents have come from less than large populated states. President Harry Truman came from Missouri, President Kennedy from Massachusetts, and President Clinton from Arkansas.

A serious contender must also have great physical and emotional stamina. Campaigning for the presidency requires a constant and strenuous agenda. Lack of sleep, media scrutiny, criticism, handshaking, and incessant speech making can take a toll on a presidential candidate.

Candidates must also have families and personal backgrounds that will not be embarrassing under examination. These standards may change over time, but still the public and other candidates will demand some sort of personal and family standards consistent with broader societal demands.

Although there is no religious test required for public office, only persons of the Christian faith have been successful. Until 1960, all American presidents have been Protestants. In 1960, and amid some controversy (especially in the southern states), John Kennedy became the first person of the Catholic faith to become president.

Now, at the beginning of the twenty-first century, there have not been serious presidential contenders who were of the Buddhist, Hindu, Jewish, Muslim or other non-Christian faiths.

It is also helpful if the presidential candidate is happily married, likes sports, and otherwise has a traditional personal lifestyle. The former governor of California, Jerry Brown—a bachelor—made a serious, though unsuccessful, run for the presidency in 1992. His bachelorhood never became an issue, but it might have if he had gained his party's nomination.

An earlier former Republican governor was hindered in his attempt at the Republican presidential nomination because of his divorce. Nelson Rockefeller, a popular governor of New York, had divorced his wife of many years and married a younger woman. This episode was one factor that ended his presidential ambitions.

However, social mores change as they impact running for high political office. In 1980, Ronald Reagan, a former California governor, ran successfully for the presidency. He, too, was a divorced man. His divorce never became a campaign issue.

HOW TO BECOME A PRESIDENT

There is no special time period set aside for running for the presidency of the United States. Immediately after one presidential election, the political commentators begin their search for what may happen in the next election.

Often, four years prior to the next election, serious presidential contenders visit every part of the country making speeches, meeting media personnel, raising money, and speaking to important local and state leaders. They do this to keep their name recognition high and to prepare for a possible presidential campaign. Unsuccessful contenders in one presidential race may prepare themselves for another. Richard Nixon lost to John Kennedy in the 1960 presidential election. He then went back to California and unsuccessfully campaigned for governor of that state. Later, he began to campaign nationwide for Republican candidates to keep his name recognition high. In 1968, his many years of campaigning for local Republicans, meeting with local party Republican leaders, and keeping his name prominent paid off. He was nominated by the Republican Party and later won the presidency, although in a close election, over Hubert Humphrey—Lyndon B. Johnson's vice president.

There are a variety of factors that can influence the public toward or against a presidential contender. All America's presidents have been white males. Hopefully, this trend will change at some point in the twenty-first century. General Colin Powell, a hero of the Gulf War and the Secretary of State in the Bush Administration, was seriously considered as a contender in 1996, although he declined to formally announce his candidacy.

A former United States member of Congress, Geraldine Ferraro of New York, was the first woman chosen as a vice presidential candidate by a major party in 1984. Another female member of Congress, Pat Schroeder of Colorado, formally announced her candidacy for the presidency in 1992, but later dropped out of the campaign.

There are, of course, more formal and regular paths to the White House. First and foremost, a candidate must gain his party's nomination. To do so, a candidate has to go through a series of presidential primaries and caucuses.

Contemporary American politics have been characterized by a two-party rule. Only the Democrats and the Republicans have been able to successfully gain the White House. It has been increasingly difficult for other political parties to run successful candidates. Part of the reason for this is that minor parties have a very hard time gaining access to state ballots. Various states have rigid qualifications for political parties to gain ballot access in running for president. (See Table 8.1.)

TABLE 8.1   SOME PROMINENT THIRD-PARTY CANDIDATES

Party	Candidate	Year	% of Vote	Winner	Party	% of Vote
Anti-Masonic	William Wirt	1832	7.8	Andrew Jackson	Democrat	54.2
Liberty	James G. Birney	1844	2.3	James K. Polk	Democrat	49.5
Free Soil	Martin Van Buren	1844	10.1	Zachary Taylor	Whig	47.3
American (Know-Nothing)	Millard Fillmore	1856	21.5	James Buchanan	Democrat	45.3
Greenback	Peter Cooper	1876	0.9	Rutherford B. Hayes	Republican	47.9
Greenback	James B. Weaver	1880	3.3	James A. Garfield	Republican	48.3
Prohibition	John P. St. John	1884	1.5	Grover Cleveland	Democrat	48.5
Populist	James B. Weaver	1892	8.5	Grover Cleveland	Democrat	46.1
Socialist	Eugene V. Debs	1900	0.6	William McKinley	Republican	51.7
Socialist	Eugene V. Debs	1904	3.0	Theodore Roosevelt	Republican	56.4
Socialist	Eugene V. Debs	1908	2.8	William H. Taft	Republican	51.6
Progressive (Bull Moose)	Theodore Roosevelt	1912	27.4	Woodrow Wilson	Democrat	41.8
Socialist	Eugene V. Debs	1912	6.0	Woodrow Wilson	Democrat	41.8
Progressive	Robert M. La Follete	1924	16.6	Calvin Coolidge	Republican	54.1
Socialist	Norman Thomas	1928	0.7	Herbert Hoover	Republican	58.2
Union	William Lemke	1936	2.0	Franklin D. Roosevelt	Democrat	60.8
States' Rights (Dixiecrats)	Strom Thurmond	1948	2.4	Harry S. Truman	Democrat	49.5
American Independent	George C. Wallace	1968	13.5	Richard M. Nixon	Republican	43.4
None (Independent)	John Anderson	1980	6.6	Ronald Reagan	Republican	50.7
Libertarian	Ron Paul	1988	0.5	George Bush	Republican	53.4
New Alliance	Lenora Fulana	1988	0.2	George Bush	Republican	53.4
The Green Party	Ralph Nader	2000	2.5	George W. Bush	Republican	48.0

Source: *Congressional Quarterly's Desk Reference on American Government*

 In 1992, Ross Perot, an independently wealthy resident of Dallas, Texas, made a highly publicized run for the presidency. He founded and led a political party named the Reform Party. This party did gain access to many state ballots and Perot was able to play an important role in the presidential election. Though unsuccessful in becoming president, Perot managed to gather enough votes to play what is called a "spoiler" role. Although he denied turning the election away from President George Bush and to Bill Clinton, he did direct media attention to budgets and tax issues. Perot's candidacy worked to the disadvantage of the incumbent, President Bush.

Ralph Nader, the founder of Public Citizen, a consumer advocate interest group, was a presidential candidate of the Green Party in 1996, 2000, and 2004. In his latest run for the presidency, he received about 456,356 or 0.38 percent of the votes—not enough to ensure federal funding for the next time around.[1] Many voters are also reluctant to vote for any except major party candidates for fear of "throwing away" their votes. Although this position is highly debatable, it does play a role in keeping the Democratic and Republican parties dominant.

Candidates are governed both by state and federal laws, and by political party regulation in their quests for the presidency. Candidates must decide whether or not they wish to receive federal matching money. If they wish to, they are limited on their total expenditures. If they do not, as did George W. Bush and John Kerry in 2004, they can spend as much as they wish on their campaigns. Most candidates, even very wealthy ones, opt to receive the federal money. (For a detailed discussion of this topic refer to chapter 4.)

THE NOMINATION PROCESS

Various state laws dictate the routes a candidate must take to win his or her party's nomination. One route is called the **Caucus-Convention** method. This method pivots on various meetings at the precinct, district, and state levels to select delegates that will attend the national nominating conventions. A caucus is a meeting at which members from each party get together to publicly discuss the presidential candidates they support. Unlike a primary, which uses a secret ballot, voters participating in a caucus openly declare which candidate they support.

The national party conventions are held in the summer preceding the fall election every four years. Delegates are selected in various states to attend the national convention to vote for their party preferences. (See Table 8.2.) The political party, through its own mechanism, determines the number of delegates from each state.

The political party also determines whether or not the respective delegations reflect the nation's population. This has been an especially contentious issue for the Democrats from the mid-1960s to the end of the twentieth century.

The most popular route to gain delegates for a candidate is the **presidential preference primary**. This system is used in most states. All party members can vote in

TABLE 8.2   DELEGATE APPORTIONMENT/ELECTORAL VOTES 2004

State	Electoral Votes	Democrats	Republicans
Alabama	9	62	48
Alaska	3	18	29
American Samoa	0	6	9
Arizona	10	64	52
Arkansas	6	47	35
California*	55	441	173
Colorado	9	63	50
Connecticut*	7	62	30
Delaware*	3	23	18
District of Columbia*	3	39	19
Florida	27	201	112
Georgia	15	101	69
Guam	0	5	9
Hawaii*	4	29	20
Idaho	4	23	32
Illinois*	21	186	73
Indiana	11	81	55
Iowa*	7	57	32
Kansas	6	41	39
Kentucky	8	57	46
Louisiana	9	72	45
Maine*	4	35	21
Maryland*	10	99	39
Massachusetts*	12	121	44
Michigan*	17	155	61
Minnesota*	10	86	41
Mississippi	6	41	38
Missouri	11	88	57
Montana	3	21	28
Nebraska	5	31	35
Nevada	5	32	33
New Hampshire*	4	27	32
New Jersey*	15	128	52
New Mexico	5	37	24

* States won by John Kerry

TABLE 8.2 (CONTINUED)

STATE	ELECTORAL VOTES	DEMOCRATS	REPUBLICANS
New York*	31	284	102
North Carolina	15	107	67
North Dakota	3	22	26
Ohio	20	157	91
Oklahoma	7	47	41
Oregon*	7	59	31
Pennsylvania*	21	178	75
Puerto Rico	0	57	23
Rhode Island*	4	32	21
South Carolina	8	55	46
South Dakota	3	22	27
Tennessee	11	85	55
Texas	34	232	138
Utah	5	29	36
Vermont*	3	22	18
Virgin Islands	0	6	9
Virginia	13	98	64
Washington*	11	95	41
West Virginia	5	39	30
Wisconsin*	10	87	40
Wyoming	3	19	28
Democrats Abroad	0	9	0
American Samoa	0	6	4
Guam	0	6	4
Virgin Islands	0	6	4
Totals	538	4,370	1,981

Source: "Democratic Convention." The Green Papers. <http://www.thegreenpapers.com/P04/d.phtml> and Republican Convention." The Green Papers. <http://www.thegreenpapers.com/P04/R.html>

a primary for a candidate they wish to see as their national party nominee. Only members of each party can vote in their respective primaries. The candidate who wins the most votes receives the most delegates to the national convention.

Iowa has been awarded the privilege of holding the first presidential choice caucus, and New Hampshire, the first presidential preference primary. Very early in the election cycle, aspiring candidates are seen visiting both Iowa and New Hampshire to meet party leaders and acquaint themselves with the public. It has been suggested that these two states, small in population and generally homogeneous in population profile, have enormous media clout in defining issues and influencing candidate selection. The more populous states like California, New York, and Texas come a bit later in the delegate selection process, but their power is not to be overlooked.

The various nominees are selected at the respective **national conventions**. Traditionally, the presidential nominees are allowed to choose who they want as vice presidential nominees or their running mates. The presidential nominee could, if they wish, allow the entire convention to choose the vice presidential nominee, but most choose not to.

The Democrats held their 44th national convention in Boston, Massachusetts July 26–29 in 2004. A total of 4,353 regular delegates (voting delegates) and 611 alternates (non-voting delegates) attended the convention. The superdelegates constituted 802 out of 4,353 delegates. They are party and elected officials such as Democratic members of Congress, Democratic governors, and members of the National Democratic Committee. Republicans do not reserve delegate seats for party and elected officials. California had the largest delegation with 441 delegates. Guam, American Samoa, and Virgin Islands had the smallest with five and six respectively.

The Republicans held their 38th national convention in Madison Square Garden, New York City, from August 30 to September 2, 2004. A total of 2,509 delegates and 2,344 alternates participated in the convention. California had the largest delegation with 173 delegates and 170 alternates. Guam, American Samoa, and Virgin Islands had the smallest nine and six alternates each.

PRESIDENTIAL CAMPAIGN AND ELECTION

The national campaign begins after the political parties choose their nominees for president and vice president. Each political party writes a platform where their goals, issues, and positions are outlined. The **platform** can be a very controversial document, but rarely do candidates commit themselves to every detail of it.

Each presidential candidate chooses his or her own way to campaign. Some choose to visit every state in the Union. Others only visit states most likely to vote for them in the fall. It is a time for strategy and political polling.

Somewhere near the end of the campaign, usually in October of the election year, a national debate is held between the major party candidates. The national debate, which is a major media event, began in the modern era with the 1960 Kennedy-Nixon debates. This series of debates was televised and has become the model for all subsequent nationally televised presidential debates.

During the national campaign season, which begins in earnest after Labor Day, the presidential candidates travel extensively across the nation. The media travel with the major candidates, scrutinizing and analyzing every speech and action. The nation's major newspapers write editorials supporting or challenging various contenders for the White House.

The presidential campaign is a major democratic event. People and media worldwide follow the campaign. For the major candidates, it is often the culmination of years of preparation, fund raising, and political challenge.

The popular election is conducted in November. Eventually, the **popular votes** are translated into **electoral votes**. If Texas, for example, votes by a majority or even a simple plurality for one candidate over another, the entire state's electoral vote goes to the winner. The total numbers of members of Congress each state possesses determines each state's electoral vote. As a result of reapportionment at the beginning of this century, Texas has 32 members in the House and 2 in the Senate. This gives Texas 34 electoral votes. (See Table 8.2.)

The winning party electors of fifty states and the District of Columbia go to their respective state capitals on the first Monday after the second Wednesday in December and vote for the president and vice president, respectively. Their votes are tallied and placed in a sealed envelope addressed to the president of the U.S. Senate. The president of the Senate will call for a joint session of Congress on January 6 where he will open the sealed envelopes and count the presidential and vice presidential electoral votes. Each has to receive at least 270 electoral votes in order to be the next president and vice president. If top presidential and vice presidential candidates receive less than 270 electoral votes, the U.S. House of Representatives will decide who should be the next president, and the U.S. Senate the next vice president. (See Figure 8.1.)

Twenty-six states and the District of Columbia require electors to cast their ballot according to the popular vote and the remaining twenty-four states' electors are not bound by state law to cast their vote for a specific candidate. Texas belongs to the latter category of states. (See Table 8.3.) In addition, all states but Maine and Nebraska use the **winner-take-all system** to cast their electoral vote. For example, all of Texas's 34

FIGURE 8.1 HOW PRESIDENTS AND VICE PRESIDENTS ARE CHOSEN

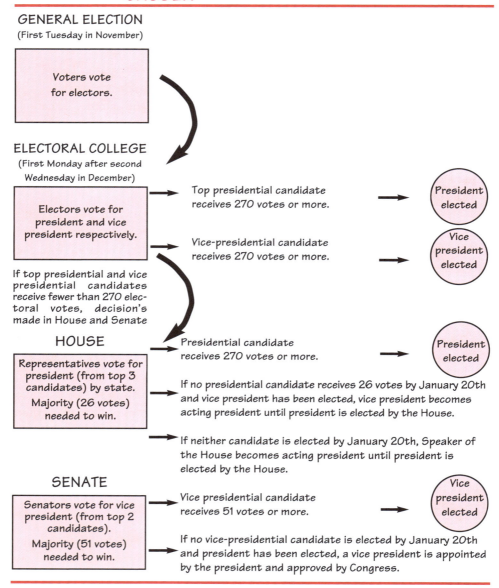

Source: "How Presidents and Vice Presidents are Chosen" from *When No Majority Rules: The Electoral College and Presidential Succession*, by Michael J. Glennon, CQ Inc., 1992, p. 20.

electoral votes went to the winner of the 2004 presidential election, in this case George W. Bush. The legislatures in Maine and Nebraska decided that electors would be apportioned based on who wins each congressional district in the state. For example, Nebraska has five electoral votes because it has three House and two Senate seats. Since the Senate seats are elected statewide, the state's two electoral votes are cast for the presidential candidate who won the popular vote in Nebraska. The remaining three electoral votes are distributed to each presidential candidate based on their electoral performance in each of these three congressional districts.

The Constitution provides for how electors are to be chosen by the various states. Because of the Electoral College, it is possible for a candidate to actually lose the popular vote and nevertheless be elected president. This has happened in four presidential elections: 1824, 1876, 1888, and 2000. (See Table 8.4.)

In the 1824 election, no candidate won the necessary majority of 131 votes in the Electoral College; the House then selected John Quincy Adams as president. Even though Hayes barely won the majority of the electoral votes, the Florida, Louisiana, Oregon, and South Carolina election returns were disputed. Congress, in joint session, declared Hayes as the winner in 1876. In the 1888 presidential election, Cleveland had more popular votes than Harrison, but the 233 electoral votes of Harrison against 168 cast for Cleveland elected Harrison president. Finally, in the 2000 presidential election, Al Gore won the popular vote but the electoral vote went to George W. Bush.

These elections are considered anomalies. In the twentieth century, the Electoral College has ensured that the presidents have both sufficient popular support and electoral support to govern. Proposals to abolish the Electoral College have failed, perhaps because of this reason.

TABLE 8.3   ELECTORS BOUND BY STATE LAW

STATE	STATE	STATE
Alabama	Maryland	Ohio
Alaska	Massachusetts	Oklahoma
California	Michigan	Oregon
Colorado	Mississippi	South Carolina
Connecticut	Montana	Vermont
District of Columbia	Nebraska	Virginia
Florida	Nevada	Washington
Hawaii	New Mexico	Wisconsin
Maine	North Carolina	Wyoming

TABLE 8.4   PRESIDENTIAL ELECTIONS

Election Year	Candidates	Popular Vote	Electoral Vote
1824	John Quincy Adams	105,321	84
	Andrew Jackson	155,872	99
	Henry Clay	46,587	37
	William Crawford	44,282	41
1876	Rutherford Hayes	4,033,950	185
	Samuel Tilden	4,284,757	184
1888	Benjamin Harrison	5,444,337	233
	Grover Cleveland	5,540,050	168
2000	George W. Bush	50,456,160	271
	Al Gore	50,996,110	266*
2004	George W. Bush	60,693,281	286
	John Kerry	57,355,978	251+

*In the Electoral College vote on December 18, 2000, one Gore elector from the District of Columbia left her ballot blank to protest the city's lack of representation in Congress.

+In the Electoral College vote on December 13, 2004, one Kerry elector from Minnesota voted for John Edwards.

"Faithless Elector"

An unknown Minnesota Democrat earned a footnote in history by casting one of the state's 10 Electoral College votes for John Edwards, John Kerry's presidential running mate. The Edwards' vote gives Minnesota its first "faithless elector," the dubious name for Electoral College members who snub the candidate who won the state's popular vote in the general election. John Kerry, who defeated President George W. Bush in Minnesota but lost overall, wound up with 9 of the state's electors.

This was not the first time this has occurred. In the 2000 presidential election, an elector from the District of Columbia left her Electoral College ballot blank and did not cast her vote for Al Gore, who won the popular vote in the District of Columbia. This was her way of protesting the city's lack of representation in Congress. Washington, D.C., is the seat of the federal government with no representation in Congress. The civic and political leaders in the District of Columbia have been unsuccessful in convincing members of Congress to treat the area as a state and allot a House member and two Senators in Congress.

THE 2004 PRESIDENTIAL ELECTION

The campaign for the President of the United States never really concludes. It is a continuous process from one election cycle to the next. To paraphrase a famous quotation, "Old candidates never die, they just fade away, only to run for the presidency another day."

Candidates for public office are recycled. Governors run for the U.S. Senate; senators run for governor; and both governors and senators campaign for the presidency. And so it was in the election for president in 2004. The Republican Party effectively had no primary contest since the incumbent president, George W. Bush, was willing to run for the office again. So, the public's attention turned primarily to the individual who would win the nomination of the Democratic Party for the President of the United States.

Bush Portrait on Caucus Day in Iowa

© Reuters NewMedia Inc./CORBIS

Like all presidential contests, there were more entrants in the presidential field than simply the main Democratic and Republican contenders. Ralph Nader, the Green Party candidate in the 2000 election year, was back again, running as an Independent with Green Party support, but seemingly without the strong backing he was able to muster in previous years.

The Libertarian Party nominated a computer programmer from Texas, Michael Badnarik. These candidates and others, carrying the banners of minor parties, or simply representing themselves, may have some effect on the major candidates in a variety of states. It is widely assumed that Ralph Nader did affect the outcome in the 2000 presidential contest, especially in the tight race that unfolded in Florida in that year.

The primary contests for the presidential nomination among the Democrats began early in 2004 with primaries in Iowa and New Hampshire, the traditional early primary contests. The declared would-be nominees were: John Kerry, Senator from Massachusetts; Bob Graham, Senator from Florida; Dennis Kucinich, a House member from Ohio; John Edwards, Senator from North Carolina; Howard Dean, a former Governor of Vermont; Carole Mosley Braun, a former Senator from Illinois;

Joe Lieberman, Senator from Connecticut and former vice-presidential nominee; General Wesley Clark, a retired four-star general; Dick Gephardt, a House member from Missouri; and Al Sharpton, a civil rights leader from New York.

Initially, it was former Vermont governor, Howard Dean, who captured public attention and media focus. Governor Dean became the early front-runner, without ever winning a primary contest state, by strongly criticizing the ongoing war in Iraq. He also proposed a series of domestic policies pivoting upon the elimination of the Republican tax-cut programs and expansion of health care. He was able to raise large sums of campaign contributions through early use of the Internet.

As the campaign in the primary states heated up, there were a series of debates in many of the states holding primary elections. The debates gave the viewers a chance to see and hear the Democratic contenders. Perhaps the most sensational and catching statements came from Al Sharpton, but he was not able to win many delegates to the Democratic National Convention, held in Boston in the summer of 2004.

Though Governor Howard Dean was the early front-runner, and some media pundits declared that he would win the nomination, surprisingly, it was Senator John Kerry who was able to win the Iowa and New Hampshire primaries. These wins catapulted the Massachusetts Senator into the front-runner position, and gave him the lead in amassing a sizeable number of delegates to the Democratic Convention. The other Democratic presidential contenders each left the race at various times, mostly throwing their support behind Kerry.

In the immediate months after the Democratic primary, the presidential contest between incumbent President George W. Bush and Democratic nominee John Kerry began to intensify. They started running political advertisements on media outlets, while fundraising for both continued at full steam. Both candidates were able to raise unlimited amounts of money before the nominating conventions because they had chosen not to receive federal matching funds at this point.

The presidential contest between Bush and Kerry was conducted against the backdrop of an ongoing war in Iraq, and the fight against international terrorism. Political pollsters predicted a very close election, perhaps reminding some of the close contest in 2000.

Earlier, President Bush indicated that he would choose the current Vice-President, Dick Cheney, to run with him on the Republican ticket. Kerry, in the months leading up to the Democratic Convention, had yet to select a running mate, though speculation remained as to whom he would choose. Eventually, he chose fellow

Senator and Democratic primary contender, John Edwards of North Carolina as his Vice-Presidential choice.

The war in Iraq added a spark to the race, as not seen perhaps since the Vietnam War era. Kerry was critical of the conduct of the war and the president's unilateral posture. He argued also that if elected, he would focus more on domestic security than attempts at democratizing the world. His criticism of the Republican administration would pivot upon a better health program for citizens and protection of American jobs against "outsourcing."

The President responded by arguing that several dictatorial regimes, as in Afghanistan and Iraq, had been overthrown during his administration, international terrorism seriously confronted, and democracy expanded globally. Domestically, the President contended that the economy had improved, jobs had been created, and tax cuts and a new medicare prescription drug bill had been enacted.

Apart from the presidential election on November 2, 2004, voters elected one-third of the U.S. Senate and all 435 members of the House. These individual state elections, in some instances, affected the outcome of the presidential contest as voters were drawn to either President Bush or Senator Kerry via a Senate or House race.

TABLE 8.5 OUTCOME OF PRESIDENTIAL ELECTION OF 2004

Candidate	Party	Electoral Vote	Popular Vote	% of Popular Vote	Ballot Access
George W. Bush	Republican	286	62 million	51	50+DC
John F. Kerry	Democrat	251	59 million	48	50+DC
Ralph Nader	Independent, Reform	0	456,356	0.38	34+DC
Michael Badnarik	Libertarian	0	396,888	0.32	48+DC
David Cobb	Green	0	119,465	0.10	27+DC

Source: "U.S. Presidential Election, 2004." Wikipedia, the Free Encyclopedia. <http://en.wikipedia.org/wiki/U.S._presidential_election_2004#Election_results>

The outcome of the 2004 presidential contest was not as dramatic nor as close as that of 2000 in which the president won by one electoral vote over his Democratic rival, Vice-President Al Gore. The State of Florida re-checking the popular vote kept the nation on the edge of their political seats for some time. Finally, the Florida vote narrowly went to President Bush enabling him to win the presidency.

In 2004, the electoral vote was decided in favor of President Bush over John Kerry by 286 to 251. (See Table 8.5.) There was neither the drama nor the uncertainty that clouded the 2000 presidential contest. President Bush carried both Florida and Ohio, states considered pivotal to a presidential victory.

The Center for the Study of the American Electorate reported that 122.3 million people voted in the November 3 presidential election. The voter turnout was 60.7 percent of eligible voters as reported by the same study.[2] This was the highest turnout in many years for a presidential election. Further, the Republicans solidified their control of both the House of Representatives and the Senate. Interestingly, on the same day as the presidential election, 11 states passed ballot measures that banned same-sex marriages.

All told, the 2004 presidential election was a win for the Republican Party. The Democratic Party would quickly regroup and engage in political introspection with hopes for more successful elections ahead.

THE DRAMA OF THE 2000 PRESIDENTIAL ELECTION

The year 2000 was a presidential election year. The election results that year were filled with more drama than any in recent years. The presidential primaries preceding the general election were of great interest to the public because there was no incumbent president seeking the office. The election was expected to be very close. But hardly any media pundit could have foreseen how close and dramatic the outcome would be.

The principle Democratic Party contenders were former United States Senator Bill Bradley of New Jersey and the then-Vice President Al Gore. The two met in a series of nationally televised debates. The political clout of the vice president eventually overwhelmed the senator and gained Al Gore the Democratic Party presidential nomination.

The principle Republican presidential contenders were Senator John McCain of Arizona, a Vietnam-era war hero, and the then-Governor of Texas, George W. Bush, the son of the former president. Other Republican presidential candidates were Steve Forbes, a multi-millionaire magazine publisher championing federal tax reform (flat tax); Gary Bauer, a spokesperson for a conservative group; Orrin Hatch, a United States Senator from Utah; and Alan Keyes, a conservative spokesman.

The Republic primaries were highly contentious, especially that of South Carolina. Governor George W. Bush was considered the front-runner to gain the Republican nomination. However, Senator McCain, advocating campaign finance reform, gave the governor a very good and competitive race for the nomination. At the conclusion of the primaries, however, Governor George W. Bush had enough delegates to gain the Republican nod as their candidate for the presidency.

But the real drama of the 2000 presidential election was still to come. Al Gore, the Democratic nominee, and George W. Bush, the Republican nominee, were locked in a presidential race so close and debated that it took a U.S. Supreme Court decision to conclude the election. Only one electoral vote gave George W. Bush the presidency, although Al Gore had more popular votes than George W. Bush. (See Table 8.4.)

The election returns from the State of Florida were so controversial that the formal declaration of a victor was postponed for weeks after the general election. The reliability of Florida voting returns was challenged as thousands of ballots were thrown out because some voters' intent was difficult to decipher. Both Florida and federal courts were called upon to settle the issue of counting and re-counting the ballots. Finally, George W. Bush, through the U.S. Supreme Court decision, became the new president of the United States on January 20, 2001, after one of the closest, most contentious, and litigated elections in recent memory.

THE PRESIDENT'S CABINET AND ADVISORS

After the election of a president, the **cabinet** and other top officials and advisors to the president are chosen. The new president is empowered by the Constitution to choose top officials of the new administration. The president's choice could be very crucial to the success or failure of his presidency.

Cabinet officers and other top officials, once selected by the president, in most cases, need approval by the U.S. Senate. Presidential choices are usually given swift approval by the Senate. Occasionally, there are controversial appointments that are not routinely ratified. This happens not only with executive, but some judicial appointments as well.

Cabinet appointments include the Secretary of Defense, Secretary of State, Secretary of the Treasury, Attorney General, and Secretary for Health and Human Services. Others are Energy, Housing and Urban Affairs, Interior, Transportation, Labor, Commerce, Agriculture, Education, and Veterans Affairs. (See Figure 9.2 on page 227 for a complete list of departments.)

Over the years, various cabinet offices have had their names changed and their functions transferred. There was once a department of Health Education and Welfare. It was later changed to Health and Human Services. The education functions were transferred to a separate cabinet post—that of the Secretary of Education. There used to be a cabinet level office called the War Department. Its name was changed and some of its functions transferred to a new Department of Defense. After the 2001 terrorist attack on America, Congress created the Homeland Security Department.

The president needs congressional approval for appointment of members of cabinet but not for their removal. Each cabinet secretary serves at the pleasure of the president, and could be removed at any time. Each department has a deputy and a number of assistants who exercise important powers over specific activities. Those who are selected as cabinet heads are often friends of the president or persons who helped him during the campaign. Cabinet heads often exercise enormous powers and responsibilities. Presidential style and delegation of authority often define the powers of cabinet heads.

In addition to cabinet secretaries, the president selects a number of top staff positions. (See Figure 8.2.) The most important are the Chief of Staff, National Security, Chief Economic, and Domestic Advisors. The Office of Press Secretary has also become important in an era of media political clout. The president also has a number of legal advisors who advise him on matters pending before Congress and often on more personal legal affairs.

FIGURE 8.2   EXECUTIVE OFFICE OF THE PRESIDENT

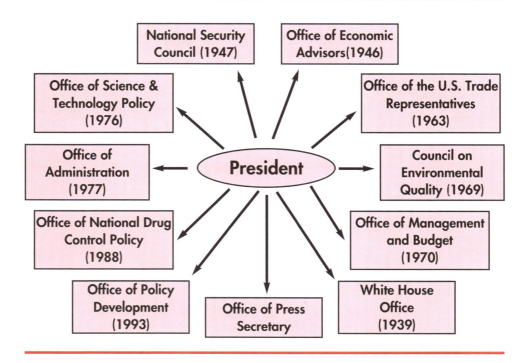

These top appointees are cruical, if not more important, than the cabinet secretaries. This again depends on presidential style and delegation of authority. The modern day arrangement of presidential advisors and staff originated in the 1950s with the election of former General Dwight Eisenhower as president. He was used to a military style of command which he brought to the White House. However, presidents have had close staff and advisors throughout the history of the office. Recently, however, with the need for quick decisions and an expanding government, the number of advisors and their powers have increased.

THE MANY ROLES OF THE PRESIDENT

Chief Executive

The Constitution states that the president must faithfully execute the laws. This makes the president the chief executive official. In this capacity, the president and his executive staff must carry out congressional and judicial rulings whether they approve of them personally or not.

Commander in Chief

Presidents have deployed federal troops to execute and defend judicial rulings of which they personally may not have approved. And the executive departments must always put into action and continue to administer any laws passed by Congress in accordance with constitutional directive.

Perhaps the most dramatic of the presidential duties and responsibilities is that of Commander in Chief of the Armed Forces. This is a constitutional directive. The president directs the armed forces into action when necessary and appropriate. Occasionally, there is tension between the president and Congress over the direction of foreign policy and in situations where American forces can be dispatched. The most dramatic example of this conflict was during the Vietnam War. The Constitution gives Congress the prerogative to declare war.

However, the president's authority over the armed forces often makes for a warlike situation. These two authorities often come into conflict. During the Vietnam War, Congress never declared war. It did, however, pass a declaration empowering the president in his conduct of the war. This support was embodied in the **"Gulf of Tonkin Resolution,"** named after a naval incident involving American forces.

After the war continued for many years, Congress began to hold hearings on the conduct of the engagement. The American public grew increasingly polarized over the war. Eventually, Congress passed the **War Powers Ac**t, which allows the president to commit troops for a period of time. If the country is attacked, the president needs no congressional approval.

The War Powers Act has never been challenged as being unconstitutional. The federal courts have never ruled upon it. Many American troops have been deployed around the world for combat and peacekeeping purposes without the declaration of war. In the twentieth century, Congress only formally declared World Wars I and II. Many other "wars" were operations entered into by the Commander in Chief. Examples are the Korean, Vietnam, and the Gulf wars.

In order to head off controversy, the president usually consults with Congress on a prolonged conflict or dangerous situation overseas. Modern examples have been the Gulf War in 1991 and the sending of troops to Bosnia later in the decade. The president, as a matter of courtesy and to gain support, will consult with congressional leaders regarding situations demanding quick decisions. In 1998, President Clinton and his advisors gave information and briefings to the Speaker of the House and the Majority Leader of the Senate before initiating cruise missile strikes against terrorists in Afghanistan and the Sudan.

Chief Diplomat

A corollary to the role of Commander in Chief is that of chief foreign policy maker. This also is a constitutional stipulation. The president is empowered to make treaties, though Senate ratification is needed for them to be effective.

The Congress will periodically give powers to the president. The feeling is that the president is uniquely situated and developed to make quick decisions and negotiations with foreign governments.

Manager of the Economy

Throughout the years, Congress has given the president various economic powers involving tariffs and trade. The federal courts have allowed Congress to give up some of its special prerogatives within certain limitations. For example, Congress has passed laws restricting various economic dealings with foreign governments. It then allows the president, at his discretion, to make exceptions to the sanctions.

Chief of State

The president of the United States is also accorded the privilege of being Chief of State. This is a duty whereby the president represents the United States of America on formal occasions. We have all heard the stirring music "Hail to the Chief."

Whenever foreign leaders arrive in this country for official visits, the president, in a formal setting, greets them. The greeting by the president to foreign leaders is an important function. It signals to them that they are welcome to this country and, have the attention of the president of the United States.

Chief Legislator

The president is also given constitutional directive to present a State of the Union address to Congress and to the nation. This annual event provides the president the opportunity to outline his ideas and plans for the coming year. Congress makes the laws, but the president is a powerful molder of public opinion and can influence Congress toward his plans. The State of the Union address also enables the president to give a great inspiring speech. The reactions of Congress and the nation indicates the president's popularity and influence.

Party Leader

Another crucial role of the president, though one developed by tradition, is that of the head of the political party. If the president is a Democrat, he is accorded the privilege of being his party's leader. The president is listened to and accorded special privilege on party policy, though there is no formal enforcement mechanism. The president also is able to raise money for the party.

THE GROWTH OF PRESIDENTIAL POWER

Congress, not the executive, is generally regarded as the most powerful branch of government. However, the office of president has grown more powerful over the years. It is accurate to state that the president is the most powerful leader on earth. The president as Commander in Chief is allowed to respond to foreign attack. The president has the authority to respond with nuclear weapons in a major crisis.

These are powers not ever understood or imagined by the early writers of Article II of the Constitution. While the president is the most powerful leader on earth, it is an office very vulnerable to public scrutiny and opinion in America's democracy. It is paradoxical that a president who could easily destroy the world also had to worry about his relationship with a young woman named Monica Lewinsky.

Presidential power has greatly expanded in the twentieth century. The presidency has increased in power and prestige commensurate with the growth and expansion of the United States as world power. The major world wars ended with the world spotlight on this country. The last decade saw the collapse of the Soviet Union and

Soviet Empire. As the Soviet Empire disintegrated, international terrorism became the major issue following the September 11, 2001, disaster. The world is watching the United States and its presidential leader's actions concerning major political and economic issues.

A Case of Presidential Impeachment

Regrettably, many people are acquainted with the office of the president due to scandals. Although various scandals have plagued this office throughout history, the modern era has been through Watergate, Iran-Contra, and Whitewater.

In 1998, the U.S. House voted to impeach President Clinton on two charges: obstruction of justice and perjury. Under federal law, a special prosecutor, Kenneth Starr, was appointed to investigate the president's role in a failed Arkansas savings and loan company—the Whitewater.

Background to Impeachment

The investigation of the president went back to his days as Arkansas governor. The investigation covered campaign donations and other financial transactions dating back to the 1980s. President Clinton and his wife were implicated. The special prosecutor, Kenneth Starr, investigated all the charges for several years. His final report found nothing on which to formally indict President Clinton. This investigation was publicly known as **Whitewater**. This is the name of a failed land development financed by a federally insured savings and loan association in Arkansas. Several individuals associated with the Whitewater investigation were indicted and convicted, but not the president.

Just when President Clinton's problems seemed to be over, another issue struck his administration. This was the **Monica Lewinsky scandal**, which captivated the country, and indeed much of the world for over one year. This scandal led to the impeachment of the president. Ms. Monica Lewinsky was a young intern at the White House. She and the president soon developed a sexual relationship, culminating in an embarrassing situation.

Some years earlier, another woman, Paula Jones of Arkansas, had filed a lawsuit against the president. She alleged that the president had sexually harassed her while he was the governor of Arkansas. The president's lawyers contended that the Jones lawsuit could not go forward as long as the president was in office. The contention was that it would be too distracting and capable of impeding his presidential duties and responsibilities.

The legal question of whether the president could avoid a private lawsuit while in office made its way to the United States Supreme Court. In the case of *Jones v. Clinton* (1998), the Court unanimously ruled that the lawsuit could indeed be tried while the president was still in office. The Supreme Court ruling paved the way for the case to proceed. In the course of the lawsuit, Jones' attorneys took depositions from the president and Ms. Lewinsky.

Also, they both testified before a federal grand jury. It was in the course of this grand jury testimony that the obstruction of justice and perjury charges were made. At various times, both the president and Ms. Lewinsky tried to hide their relationship from the public. However, in a "soap opera" setting, their secret relationship became public. The president's detractors contended that it was not the intimacy between him and an intern that troubled them but their attempt to conceal it.

The House Takes Action

The Special Prosecutor, Kenneth Starr, eventually reported his findings to the House of Representatives. The report was publicly known as the "Starr Report." The House authorized the House Judiciary Committee to begin hearings on the possible **impeachment** of the president. The committee's finding was sent to the entire House of Representatives for consideration.

The Judiciary Committee voted along party lines to send impeachment charges to the full House. Their hearings and scrutiny of the Starr Report convinced a majority of the committee to vote for the president's impeachment.

Shortly thereafter, the full House convened to consider the impeachment charges. The Constitution directs that the House has the sole authority to consider impeachment. The United States Senate is responsible for trying an impeached federal official. The House voted to impeach the president on two charges. The House Judiciary Committee had voted favorably on four charges of impeachment, but the full House only passed two of them. Again, the impeachment was mostly along party lines. Most Republicans voted for impeachment and Democrats, overwhelmingly, voted against.

The Senate Trial

In 1999, the United States Senate voted not to convict the president on either of the two impeachment charges. The Senate votes on both charges were short of the two-thirds vote needed for conviction. The atmosphere in the Senate was partly jury trial and political conversation. The House Judiciary Committee selected a group of

Republican representatives to present their case to the Senate. They were labeled "managers" because they were to manage the case for the presidential conviction and removal. President Clinton was allowed to present his case against conviction as well. The president sent a team of lawyers to argue on his behalf before the Senate, which was presided by the U. S. Supreme Court Chief Justice, William H. Rehnquist. It was an important historical and political event.

Even though the Senate did not vote to convict, the dishonor on the president was great. His defenders in the Senate made it clear that they believed the president committed perjury. However, they contended that the two charges arising out of a series of intimate encounters did not reach the level of conviction and removal. The president was not convicted and removed from office. However, the Constitution states that he could still be charged with offenses after leaving office.

Reaction to Clinton's Impeachment

The reverberations from the impeachment of President Clinton have been far-reaching. The **Special Prosecutor Act,** which gave force and impetus to the charges against the president expired in the summer of 1999, and was not renewed.

A national debate ensued in the media and among citizens. The questions ranged from purely legal debates to that of trust and marital commitment. Among the most important questions was whether what the president did was a private matter or one of public concern.

Out of this impeachment and trial, it is likely that future aspirants for this office will be subjected to more media and public scrutiny. The private life of contenders to the White House and their public record will be increasingly examined. Will the microscopic examination keep some qualified people from seeking this high office?

What Americans want from a president has always been debated. Should the president, in addition to the roles and responsibilities outlined earlier, be a moral leader as well? How could the president, as world leader, keep some part of his or her life private? Must a president be a good speaker in the age of instant communication and television? How can a president find knowledgeable and experienced people to fill cabinet roles and other high staff offices?

SUMMARY

The president of the United States is an official widely known to the public. However, the many roles and responsibilities surrounding the office often make it hard to grasp. This chapter has attempted to define the office, its duties, responsibilities, and how one is elected to this position.

The U.S. presidency is always at the center of debate and controversy. It is an office which the world looks to for explanations and definitions of our nation's actions and goals. The president of the United States of America evokes a kind of majesty and aura lacking in most other public offices.

KEY TERMS

Advice and consent
Cabinet
Caucus-Convention
Chief of State
Electoral vote
"Faithless elector"
Gulf of Tonkin Resolution
Impeachment
Monica Lewinsky scandal
National convention

Platform
Popular vote
Presidential preference primary
Reform Party
Starr Report
State of the Union Address
War Powers Act
Whitewater
Winner-take-all

INTERNET SOURCES

a) http://www.whitehouse.gov/
This is the official site of the White House. It includes information on the various sections that comprise this office. Activities of the U.S. president: bills initiated, executive orders, itinerary, foreign policy decisions, tours of the White House, etc., can be found in this site.

b) http://www.fedworld.gov
This site provides information on the various agencies that are controlled directly and indirectly by the president. Information on each of the departments within the executive, regulatory and independent agencies are provided for in this site.

NOTES

[1] "U.S. Presidential Election, 2004." *Wikipedia, the Free Encyclopedia.* <http://wikipedia.org/wiki/U.S.presidential election,_2004#Election_results>

[2] See Committee for the Study of the American Electorate: http://www.gspm.org/csae/

Chapter 9

The Federal Bureaucracy

History, in general, only informs us what bad government is.
—*Thomas Jefferson to John Norvell, 1807*

INTRODUCTION

Bureaucracy is of the executive branch that carries out policies and laws made by the legislative branch. Frequently, these policies are unclear and sometimes difficult to interpret. When a public policy is unpopular, people tend to blame the government agencies that are supposed to carry them out and enforce them rather than blaming the lawmakers who actually wrote the laws. The Internal Revenue Service (IRS) serves as a prime example. Not many Americans love this government agency, which is responsible for interpreting, administering and enforcing tax laws. It has become fashionable to distrust and even hate the IRS because of its role in collecting income taxes, auditing citizens, and penalizing those who violate the tax code. Most people would rather undergo a root canal surgery than endure an IRS audit. Many Americans wrongly assume that the IRS enacts tax laws. Blaming the IRS for tax laws is like blaming meteorologists for rainy weather.

This chapter will examine the nature and functions of the federal bureaucracy. Questions such as "How does the bureaucracy fit within the overall scheme of government?" and "How has the bureaucracy grown?" are considered. The various types of bureaucracies, also known as government agencies, are identified. It will be realized that bureaucracy is an essential agent of the government, and though some of the criticism directed at these agencies and their employees is well deserved, the agencies more often than not perform exemplary jobs.

GOVERNMENT IN ACTION

On your drive to school or work, do you wonder aloud why the roads are so smooth? Do you marvel at the efficiency with which the signal lights work to relieve congestion at intersections? Do you take notice of the fact that all the posted signs make traffic flow safer and more efficiently? Probably not. You are not alone. Most of the work done by government agencies, which carry out public policies, better known as the bureaucracies, goes unnoticed. This is government in action.

However, when things go wrong people begin to take notice or even complain. When your tax refund does not arrive on time, or when the check you mailed last week hasn't arrived at the auto insurance company, you blame the government agencies responsible for carrying out these tasks—the IRS and the United States Postal Service (USPS). This is government inaction.

The Fourth Branch?

As illustrated above, the role of the bureaucracy is largely taken for granted. We do not notice the efficiency with which the National Weather Service operates any more than we think about how the water we shower with gets to our homes. Yet, these essential functions, and literally hundreds of others, are all made possible by the work of millions of government employees responsible for carrying out the laws and policies made by the legislative branch of government.

Bureaucracy has often been described as "the fourth branch" of government. Technically speaking, bureaucratic functions fall under the executive branch, which, as you will recall from the previous chapter, is responsible for carrying out and enforcing laws. Bureaucracy is not addressed in the Constitution, yet every American encounters its activities every day. People complain when they cannot get immediate results from government. They accuse government employees of being lazy or incompetent. Meaner people have been known to call bureaucrats greedy and corrupt. To be sure, hardly anyone ever holds government workers in high esteem.

The Nature of Bureaucracies

By their very nature, bureaucracies are ever-expanding and often complicated. Imagine how challenging it is to the Postal Service, for example, to deal with the tremendous volume of mail it processes—some 600 million pieces daily.[1] Max Weber recognized that overall government efficiency depends on the structure of the agencies charged with performing the function.[2] Bureaucracies are created to carry out the programs devised by law makers. For example, the Social Security Administration was created to implement and manage the Social Security system. The Internal Revenue Service came into being in order to collect taxes. If there were no such programs, there would be no Social Security Administration nor would there be an IRS. Moreover, as Congress modifies programs, bureaucracies must be poised to adapt to the changes. Oftentimes it is left to the bureaucracies to determine the best course of action to take in administering these programs, and this leads to policy-making by the officials who are charged with implementation.

> The German sociologist Max Weber (1864–1920) was the first to use and to define the term "bureaucracy." According to Weber, the ideal bureaucracy contains the following characteristics:
>
> <u>Hierarchy:</u> Employees are ranked in a hierarchical order, with a rigidly adhered to chain of command, and with information flowing up and down that chain in a systematic manner.
>
> <u>Impersonality:</u> The organizations are characterized by impersonal rules that specifically describe everyone's stated duties.
>
> <u>Written rules of conduct:</u> Everyone within the organization understands what his or her job performance expectations are.
>
> <u>Promotion based on achievement:</u> Maximum efficiency calls for appointments and promotions to be based on ability and merit, not on personal preferences.
>
> <u>Specialized division of labor:</u> Individuals are specialists in their fields and undergo extensive training.
>
> <u>Efficiency:</u> The goal of the organization and all its activities are directed to promoting the maximum efficiency using the least resources.
>
> Weber believed that advanced societies could be evaluated in terms of their bureaucratic efficiency. He never claimed to favor large bureaucracies, but maintained that they were necessary for sound government. His work is still highly regarded today and applied in both the business and government sectors. It is doubtful that many government agencies have attained Weber's lofty ideal.

One consequence that complexity brings is **overspecialization**, a condition that occurs when government rules are so complicated that only those who actually perform the tasks understand them. The IRS is a case in point. Tax laws are so specialized that it takes IRS workers years to understand them. As a result of this highly specialized knowledge, some of these workers must make decisions on how these laws must be carried out. This practice has come to be known as **legislative rule**, whereby the policies enacted by a government agency take the same effect as a law passed by Congress.

Once a bureaucracy is created it almost never fades into the sunset. The National Aeronautics and Space Administration (NASA) was created in 1958 for the purpose of examining the feasibility of manned space missions. That goal was accomplished by the early 1960s, and as everyone knows, NASA today is larger than ever. It is involved in joint ventures with other nations, in partnerships with privatized endeavors into space, in the military, and even in weather-related science. NASA is typical of federal bureaucracies in that it is an ever-expanding and complex agency that many have come to rely upon.

Talk about downsizing the scope of the bureaucracy is popular among politicians running for national office, but it has proven a difficult feat to accomplish. The latest "big government" downsizing program, called "Reinventing Government" was launched by President Clinton and managed by Vice President Al Gore. Although the program did very little in the way of actually reducing the number of stale and archaic programs and agencies, it was a resounding success in educating Americans about just how big government has become. Watch the presidential debates and you'll take notice that all the candidates will outline their plans to reduce the size and scope of the government. They will target the bureaucracies, as if they are the root of the growth and waste.

The reality is that it is the lawmakers who are principally responsible for creating programs that require bureaucracies to carry them out. So while it is very popular to talk about reducing the size of government, most politicians are more than just a little hesitant to cut certain programs.

WHO ARE THE BUREAUCRATS?

George Washington's staff consisted of a part-time secretary he paid with his own money. The entire federal workforce consisted of fewer than 50 employees, most of them clerks and secretarial aides. Today, the federal government employs about 2.5 million full-time civilian (non-military) personnel.[3] More than 80 percent of these employees work outside the Washington, D.C., area. The employment opportunities span virtually all professions, from teachers to engineers, scientists, historians and medical professionals. (See Table 9.1.)

There have been significant gains made by women and minorities in the federal workforce. The percentage of women employed by the federal government has grown to almost 45 percent, a sharp rise from the 1960s when women represented only 25 percent of the total employees. African-Americans currently comprise nearly 18 percent of all federal workers, up from 11 percent in the 1960s.

Work force participation rates vary considerably by agency. The data show wide differences in the participation rates of certain groups among executive departments and independent agencies with 500 or more employees.

- The Department of Justice is the largest employer of Hispanics. Its 13,315 Hispanic employees represent 14.19% of the Department's permanent work force. The Department of Veterans Affairs (VA) is the largest employer of Blacks. The 48,689 Blacks in the VA represent 24.21% of the permanent VA work force. The VA employs 115,724 women, which is 57.55% of the VA's permanent work force.[4]

Each of the states and most local governments have their own bureaucracies for providing government services at the other levels of government. Over the years, the number of government workers has increased tremendously. Today, nearly 20 million Americans are employed by the government at the federal, state or local level. This represents one out of every six wage earners who is employed full-time. While the number of federal employees has remained generally constant over the past 20 years, the number of state employees has risen slightly and the number of local government employees has nearly doubled.

TABLE 9.1   THE DIVERSITY OF THE FEDERAL WORKFORCE

Male	55%
Female	45%
College Degree	39%
Non-college graduate	61%
Black	16.7%
Hispanic	6.1%
Asian/Pacific Islander	4.3%
Native American	2.0%

Source: Office of Personnel Management, 2005

THE STRUCTURE OF AMERICAN BUREAUCRACY
Cabinet Departments

The fifteen cabinet departments are responsible for the majority of activities associated with the executive department's mission of carrying out and enforcing public policy. Collectively, these departments comprise the president's cabinet. In the federal government system, the term "department" usually implies a political entity having a wide span of control. Most of the cabinet departments oversee a number of "agencies," which are smaller units of government with a more narrow or specific area of control.

Each of the top cabinet officials is appointed by the president and confirmed by the Senate. The department heads carry the title of **secretary** (except in the case of the Justice Department, which is headed by the Attorney General). The number of cabinet posts has varied over the years. Originally, there were only three: the Department of State, which oversees foreign affairs; the War Department (re-named the Department of Defense), which is responsible for national defense matters; and the Treasury Department which among other tasks, oversees the printing of currency and the collection of taxes. As the nation's population and span of control grew, so did the number of cabinet-level departments.

The most recent cabinet-level department, Homeland Security, was created in 2003 largely in response to the terrorist attacks that took place on American soil on September 11, 2001. Although for the most part the Department of Homeland Security was a restructuring of existing government agencies, the fact remains that the lawmakers consider cabinet-level departments the most important. Tracing the creation of cabinet positions is like a history lesson in American government because one can see when the nation's leaders thought a policy arena important enough to make it a top-level position. A list of the cabinet positions also reveals the breadth of the president's reach in terms of power and span of control. Many foreign observers find it astonishing that the United States can change administrations so often through a smooth and seemless transition of power. (See Table 9.2.)

Since the president delegates a great deal of his administrative duties to his cabinet members, his appointees must possess two important characteristics: ability to perform the job and the absolute confidence of the president. Cabinet members are expected to speak candidly to the president about matters of national, and sometimes international, importance. For this reason, presidents have frequently appointed people they have known for years or those who have demonstrated a high degree of knowledge in the specific area the post calls for. Cabinet members are among the very few who have regular access to the president and with whom the president is on a first-name basis.

TABLE 9.2   THE CABINET DEPARTMENTS

Department	Secretary	Year Established	Employees (1994)
Agriculture	Mike Jonanns	1889	63,000
Commerce	Carlos Gutierrez	1903	3,000
Defense	Donald Rumsfeld	1789	310,000
Education	Margaret Spellings	1979	30,000
Energy	Samuel Bodman	1977	17,000
Heath/Human Services	Michael Leavitt	1953	283,000
Homeland Security	Michael Chertoff	2003	180,000
Housing/Urban Development	Alfonso Jackson	1965	25,000
Interior	Gale Norton	1870	10,000
Justice	Alberto Gonzales	1849	7,000
Labor	Elaine Chao	1913	45,000
State	Condoleezza Rice	1789	5000
Transportation	Norman Mineta	1966	34,000
Treasury	John Snow	1789	300,000
Veteran's Affairs	Jim Nicholson	1989	35,000

A good example of this relationship can be found in President Kennedy's administration. Kennedy appointed his brother, Robert, to the post of Attorney General. Because everything the cabinet members do reflects directly on the president, he conducts regular cabinet meetings and confers with members privately. Cabinet members possess a level of accessibility to the president that few others enjoy. Conversely, these powers come at a cost. There is absolutely no job security in being a member of the president's cabinet, as the president can remove any of them at any time.

Moreover, since each president gets to select his own cabinet, those who are in the cabinet know they can start packing when a new president moves into the White House, especially if the president is of a different party. A new president, especially of a different party, means that there will be an entirely new cabinet. (Cabinet members who have been fired or have resigned are eligible for executive-level government positions, but nearly all former members take high-paying and often high-profile positions in the private sector.)

The turnover rate within the cabinet is generally high, especially when the president is re-elected. President George W. Bush's first Secretary of State, Colin Powell, resigned shortly after the president won reelection, citing as his primary reason the desire to return to a less hectic life. Condeleezza Rice, the first African-American woman to hold a cabinet-level position, replaced Powell in Bush's second-term cabinet. Rice's biography is remarkable, if not incredible. She graduated from the University of Denver at age 19 with a degree in—and we're very proud of this—political science. She went on to earn her Ph.D. in the same discipline, but what she experienced in the meantime remains legendary. While attending college she met, and was much impressed by Josef Korbel, a Czech refugee who happened to be Madeleine Albright's father. You may recall that Albright was appointed by President Clinton to be the first woman to serve as the Secretary of State. Besides being fluent in several languages and an accomplished concert pianist, Dr. Rice's knowledge of foreign policy earned her a position as President Bush's National Security Advisor. Dr. Rice exemplifies the type of resume required to become a member of the president's cabinet.

While Dr. Rice's accomplishments and credentials reveal how much of a role competency plays at this level of the federal bureaucracy, the story of Attorney General Alberto Gonzalez exemplifies the level of trust a president has in his choice of members of his inner circle of advisors. Alberto Gonzalez grew up poor in south Houston. After graduating from Rice University, he earned his law degree from Harvard University and taught law at the University of Houston Law Center. He began his relationship with then-Governor George W. Bush when Bush appointed him as Texas Secretary of State. When a vacancy in the Texas Supreme Court became available, Governor Bush appointed him to that court. When he was elected president, he persuaded Gonzalez to leave the Texas Supreme Court to serve as his White House general counsel. Gonzalez was elevated to the position of Attorney General shortly after Bush won re-election in 2004.

There is a fascinating story behind each cabinet member who has ever served. The common thread, at least in recent history, has been an impressive resume, a high level of experience in the field, and a close, personal relationship with the president they serve.

Since cabinet members possess such an awesome degree of power and make decisions that affect millions of people, they must be approved, or "confirmed" by the United States Senate. Upon naming a cabinet nominee, the Senate conducts investigations that include public hearings aimed at learning more about the nominee, much as it does for judicial nominees. The entire Senate votes to either confirm or deny the appointment.

Each of the cabinet departments is responsible for the operation of a number of related entities, which may be called bureaus, agencies, services or offices. For example, the Treasury Department oversees the United States Marshal Service, the Secret Service and the Bureau of Alcohol, Tobacco, and Firearms. The Department of Commerce oversees the Census Bureau, NASA, the Patent and Trademark Office, and the Minority Business Development Agency.

Independent Agencies

Independent agencies exist to regulate an industry or major government program that does not fall under any of the cabinet departments, such as the Interstate Commerce Commission (ICC) and the Environmental Protection Agency (EPA) and about 200 more. Unlike the cabinet-level positions which are generalized, these agencies generally carry out a very specific function of purpose. For example, the Central Intelligence Agency, formed in 1947 largely as a result of the attack on Pearl Harbor, was created for the purpose of gathering and analyzing intelligence from sources worldwide.

These specialized agencies must be created by agreement between the president and Congress. They are called "independent" agencies because they are, ostensibly at least, supposed to be free of partisanship or loyalty to a popular cause.

The leadership of these agencies vary. Most of them are managed by a board of commissioners, appointed by the president and confirmed by the Senate. Unlike cabinet members, these appointees cannot be removed.

Although these independent agencies employ less than thirty percent of the federal workforce, and are accountable for less than ten percent of total government expenditures, their influence is highly felt. Consider the area of control some of these agencies have, and you'll get a feel for the remarkable power they wield. The **ICC**, for instance, sets the safety and performance standards for the entire interstate trucking industry. Everyone knows that the environment is of tremendous importance and concern, so we rely on the **EPA** to balance the rights and privileges of many large corporations with the people's expectation of a safe and clean environment. There are literally trillions of dollars at stake in the arena regulated by the **Securities and**

Exchange Commission (SEC), which ensures that the stock and commodities trading takes place above board. And, speaking of money, the Federal Reserve Board has the awesome responsibility of controlling the supply of the United States currency.

The regulatory roles of some of these agencies have come under increased scrutiny because of the relatively large degree of discretion the top managers have. Unlike the secretaries who oversee the cabinet-level agencies, the president has relatively little control over independent agency leaders. While he can dismiss a cabinet member for any flimsy reason, he cannot fire the head or a board member of an independent agency. Moreover, the appointments to the boards must contain members of both parties. On the one hand, the leaders must have a high level of expertise due to the complexity or the technical nature of the agencies they head.

On the other hand, some maintain that the combination of expertise and discretion allow these agencies too much independence. And since they are somewhat removed from the direct control of the president and Congress, it makes them potentially less-than-democratic institutions. This is not to say that there are no checks and balances in the realm of independent agencies. After all, the president and Senate are provided the opportunity to interview and investigate potential leaders. Congress controls all agency funding, and is not likely to finance programs that are not on the congressional agenda. Furthermore, the courts will have the final say when the constitutionality of agency activity is in question.

Director of National Intelligence

In 2005, President George W. Bush signed into law the broadest restructuring of the U.S. intelligence services in more than half a century. Creating the Director of National Intelligence (DNI) was a key recommendation of the national commission that investigated the September 11, 2001, attacks on America. The underlying purpose of reorganization of the intelligence services is to prevent a repetition of the intelligence failures that preceded September 11, and led to overstatements about Saddam Hussein's weapons programs. The creation of the DNI will ensure that the intelligence agencies work as a single, unified enterprise.

The DNI is headed by John Negroponte who replaced the Central Intelligence Agency director as the nation's top intelligence official. He oversees the government's 15 military and civilian agencies, including the Central Intelligence Agency (CIA), the Federal Bureau of Investigation (FBI), Defense Intelligence Agency (DIA), National

Security Agency (NSA) and the Department of Homeland Security. In addition, John Negroponte delivers the President's daily intelligence briefing and has ultimate authority over the nation's sprawling intelligence apparatus, including an estimated $40 billion annual budget.

Government Corporations

At first glance, the term "government corporation" appears to be a contradiction in terms. In fact, the term is very descriptive of the nature and role of such entities. These are government entities that are set up, for the most part, to be run as corporations. We say "for the most part" because no two government corporations are exactly alike. A characteristic that they do share, however, is that they charge for the services they provide.

The **United States Postal Service** (USPS) is by far the largest of these government corporations. True to its role, it charges customers for the products and services it provides. Another example is the **Public Broadcasting Service** (PBS), which relies on private-sector grants and "viewers like you" for part of their operating budget. In the case of the Postal Service, private sector corporations such as United Parcel Service and others actually compete for the government's business. The **Tennessee Valley Authority** (TVA) is a federal corporation, the nation's largest electric-power producer, a regional economic-development agency, and a national center for environmental research.[5] The TVA was established because no private enterprise would bear the expense of providing electrification to the area.

AMTRAK, the government-owned transcontinental passenger rail service, gets most of its operating funds from passenger fares. Unlike the USPS, which has been self-sufficient since 1984, AMTRAK currently loses money. However, recent changes in management and administration have led AMTRAK officials to predict that the service will be self-sufficient by 2007.[6]

THE EXPANDING BUREAUCRACY

As pointed out earlier, the number of federal employees working under George Washington's administration could fit into a minivan—if, indeed, minivans had been around back then. It wasn't long until other cabinet posts were added. The scope and responsibility of the cabinet posts grew rapidly, as did the nation.

The Formative Years

By the mid-1800s, the federal government was employing many people. Most of the new government positions were filled under the system of patronage, which meant that jobs were awarded to those close to or those who supported the president or other high government officials. Under the patronage system, sometimes called the spoils system, it was *who* you knew—not *what* you knew—that got someone the job. Before the system was reformed, it was common for newly-elected presidents to fire entire staffs and replace them with their own friends and political supporters.

Change came about largely as the result of the assassination of President **James A. Garfield**, who was elected in 1880. Upon winning the presidency, thousands of people sought government jobs. One man who was refused a job assassinated President Garfield, prompting Congress to pass the Civil Service Reform Act of 1883, which later became known as the **Pendleton Act**. The Act greatly reduced the use of patronage by creating a commission to grant government jobs on the basis of qualifications. Positions such as the presidential cabinet posts and a few other high-profile positions are still chosen by the president, but a great majority of the federal jobs now fall under clear guidelines. The Pendleton Act also affected promotions and transfers within government agencies. Most agencies use competitive exams, seniority and past performance records to determine which employees receive promotions. As a result, most government employees don't worry about a newly-elected president firing them, since it wasn't the outgoing president who hired them.

Bureaucratic Growth

The Progressive Era marked a period of unprecedented industrial growth in the United States. Up to this time, the government intervened little, if at all, in the manner in which business and industry conducted themselves. Some corporations regularly engaged in price-fixing and other unfair practices to punish their competitors. The exploitation of workers, especially the newly-arrived immigrants in the sprawling cities, was common practice. There were no laws against child labor and no occupational safety guidelines. As a result, thousands of workers were abused, injured and sometimes killed. The general public was horrified as these transgressions came to their attention, and they demanded government intervention. In response, the federal government created dozens of new agencies to oversee and regulate certain segments of the private sector. The passage of the Sixteenth Amendment (1913), which authorized a federal income tax, provided the government with ample funding for these agencies.

Franklin Roosevelt's **New Deal** marked another major era of growth in federal bureaucracy. In an effort to restart the nation's economy, literally hundreds of new federal programs were implemented, creating a veritable alphabet soup of agencies. Many of these agencies, such as the Federal Deposit Insurance Corporation (FDIC) are still in business today. Others were more temporary in nature, such as the National Industrial Economy Act (NIRA), which was created for the purpose of overseeing major industries and their business practices. The newly-created bureaucracies mushroomed in both number and size. This increase necessitated additional rules regulating the employees' conduct. Critics of this unprecedented growth in government employment complained that the employees could easily affect the congressional and even presidential elections by virtue of their positions in government. In response to these concerns, Congress passed the **Hatch Act** in 1939, which prohibits federal employees from engaging in political activity while on duty or while acting under the color of office.

The most recent era of considerable growth in the size of government occurred during the 1960s, reflecting new technologies and major events. America's plan to send manned missions into space and to the moon necessitated a host of new programs and agencies. President Lyndon Johnson's plan to eliminate poverty and illiteracy caused a new wave of growth in the federal bureaucracy.

Johnson called his comprehensive plan the **Great Society**. Besides declaring "war" on poverty in America, his vision included expansion of government programs intended to improve the quality of life for millions. In 1965, he proposed 115 recommendations to Congress, more than 90 of which were passed. The Great Society targeted those most perceived to be in need. One of the novel programs was the Appalachian Development Act which pledged nearly $1 billion to improve the infrastructure of the region. A lasting program called Head Start provided nourishment and expanded educational opportunities for the pre-school children of low-income families. The Great Society introduced America to programs such as Medicare and Medicaid, and it strengthened the rights of immigrants who legally entered and became employed in this country.

The Bureaucracy Today

There is no question that modern American bureaucracy is large and complex. Nearly 2.5 million employees perform some 1,500 specific tasks. Legislation, as discussed in the previous section, has professionalized bureaucrats and resulted in a more responsive system. Some observers are critical of the overspecialization that naturally occurs in all large and complicated systems. These, and the administrative rules that the highest-ranking bureaucrats must make are the principal criticisms of the system. One of the more recent areas of discussion centering on federal employment has been the treatment of **whistle-blowers**, employees who make public accounts of waste or fraud. There was a time when workers who "blew the whistle," that is, called attention to mismanagement, were sanctioned for their efforts. The sanctions included transfers, demotions, and other punishments. In 1978 legislation was enacted to protect and encourage the practice of whistle-blowing, legislation that was strengthened in 1989 by President George Bush.

This is not to say that all is well in the modern bureaucracy. Despite legislation and much good faith on the part of the top echelon, there are some very real problems in making a system so large run smoothly and in the same direction. With so many agencies, it seems obvious that there will be contradictory policies and unneeded duplication of effort. Presidents have recognized this. Every president since John F. Kennedy has proposed some type of bureaucratic reform. The latest was Bill Clinton's **Reinventing Government** program, in which he and Vice President Al Gore commissioned a comprehensive overview of the bureaucracy. The result of the study, released in a report entitled **The National Performance Review**, contains hundreds of proposed reforms.

Other measures that tend to modernize, and thus ensure a more responsive government, include the passage of **sunshine** and **sunset review** laws. Sunshine laws mandate that an increasing number of government agency meetings take place in the open, thus allowing the press and citizens to attend and see first hand what goes on. Of course, not all government agencies are required to conduct their meetings in the open. Agencies dealing with national security and personnel matters are some of the exceptions. Sunset review laws call for a periodic review of each and every government agency and program to determine if it is still necessary. There is no such provision for sunset review in the federal government, although many states have adopted this important measure. In most states, a sunset review panel composed of legislators and citizens review agencies' roles and then recommends continuation, abolishment, or the merging of two or more agencies.

THE IRON TRIANGLE

Bureaucracies are created to carry out the policies made by elected officials and are expected to be apolitical. But the nature of bureaucracy is to be ever-expanding, which means that these agencies nearly always display a certain degree of self-concern. They tend to protect their own interests while attempting to broaden their scope and importance. One does not have to look hard to see political influence in the methods used to maintain their prominence.

The most potent example of such bureaucratic self-perseverance is the **iron triangle**, a three-way alliance between government agencies, interest groups, and legislative groups, particularly committees. These coalitions account for much of the policy making in the United States. Although not mentioned in the Constitution, political scientists have identified them and marveled at their growth.

One of the primary tactics used by interest groups is to provide campaign contributions. Legislators require money to run for and keep their elected offices. The money from interest groups and their political action committees is a welcome lifeblood for them. Another primary tool of the interest group is providing much-needed information, both technical and practical, to elected officials. Anything that makes a legislator's political fortunes makes that legislator more likely to be sympathetic to the interest group's point of view. In return for these favors, interest groups expect favorable action by the legislators they support.

In its interaction with government departments, legislators expect to receive staff services. The staff of a government agency will help legislators gather data on that agency. In return for this assistance, the agency expects funding from the legislators. It is, after all, the legislators' responsibility to fund the agency. Without funding, the agency goes away. The more funding, the larger the agency becomes.

Interest groups that have vested interests in what a certain government agency does or how the agency implements policy provide valuable data and testimony to legislative committees that determine the amount of appropriations the agency receives. Favorable data and favorable testimony can be helpful to the agency. Agencies realize this and work to keep interest groups on their side as they implement legislation. In a sense, many agencies regard interest groups as their clients.

SUMMARY

Perhaps the most remarkable aspect of the bureaucracy has been its sheer growth. As government grows in scope and size, so do the number of bureaucracies. This fact is most apparent at the very top of the government hierarchy, the presidential cabinet. There are now fourteen cabinet positions compared to only three when the nation was in its infancy. President Washington's bureaucracy consisted of a few part-time workers, and now there are over three million individuals who work at carrying out the nation's laws and policies. Bureaucracies, by their very nature, are hierarchical and highly structured.

We can classify government agencies by identifying how close their ties are with the executive branch. At the very top are fourteen members of the presidential cabinet, men and women who are hand picked by the president and responsible for broad policy arenas. Independent agencies exist to carry out less essential, but nonetheless important, government functions. These agencies are essential to the day-to-day operations of the federal government. Government corporations are operated somewhat like businesses, in that they generally charge user fees and in some cases are self-sufficient.

Growth in bureaucracy has not come without problems. Over time, many of these issues have been resolved, or at least addressed, by reform measures ranging from civil service to laws like the Hatch Act, which serve to take "politics" out of the bureaucratic arena.

KEY TERMS

- Agency
- Bureaucracy
- Government corporation
- Great Society
- Hatch Act
- Head Start
- Independent agency
- Iron triangle
- Legislative rule
- National Performance Review
- New Deal
- Overspecialization
- Patronage
- Pendleton Act
- President's cabinet
- Reinventing Government
- Secretary
- Spoils system
- Sunset law
- Sunshine law
- Whistle-blower

INTERNET SOURCES

a) http://www.cweb.loc.gov/global.executive/fed.html
Information about this site is similar to what is provided in Chapter 8, subsection b).

NOTES

[1] United State Postal Service.
[2] For detailed discussion see Max Weber. *The Prtestant Ethics ad the Spirit of Capitalism.* (New York: Scriber's Press, 1958).
[3] U.S. Office of Personnel Management.
[4] U.S. Equal Oportunity Employment Commission Report, 2005.
[5] Tennessee Valley Authority Mission Statement, Septermber 1998.
[6] Amtrack Corporate Communications, June 1998.

Chapter 10

The Judiciary

The Constitution of the United States was made not merely for the generation that then existed, but for posterity—unlimited, undefined, endless, perpetual posterity.

—Henry Clay

INTRODUCTION

Article III of the U.S. Constitution establishes the federal judiciary headed by the Supreme Court. The judges and justices of the federal courts are appointed by the President and confirmed by the Senate. According to Article III, judges and justices serve for life "during good behavior."

This feature of our Constitution allows for an independent judiciary which is not encumbered by a need to run for election by popular vote. It also guarantees that judges shall not be removed except by impeachment.

This fact does not mean that the federal judiciary is apolitical. Politics are often central to being appointed by the president and gaining approval by the Senate. In fact, in recent years, the two-part process of appointment by the president and confirmation by the Senate has become very divisive. Presidents Clinton and Bush had such difficulty getting confirmation hearings for their appointees that both resorted to interim appointments (a process by which a president may appoint a federal judge during a recess of the Senate for one year).

An important power of the federal courts is the power of judicial interpretation. The fact that the Supreme Court is the final interpreter of the Constitution places it at the center of the nation's governmental system. Article III, Section 1, states that "The judicial Power of the United States shall be vested in One Supreme Court, and such inferior courts as the Congress shall from time to time ordain and establish." And Section 2 of the same article states that "The judicial Power shall extend to all Cases in Law and Equity, arising under this Constitution, the Laws of the United States, and Treaties made, or which shall be made under their Authority." In short, if there is a question about the Constitution, or the laws or treaties of the United States, the Supreme Court is the final arbiter.

Some federal courts' interpretation of the Constitution and laws become controversial when they require us to do something we do not want, protect someone we detest, support some principle we do not agree with, or comply with rules that cause us discomfort.

This chapter begins with a discussion of the sources of American law. It then focuses on the structure and jurisdiction of federal courts, which includes district courts, courts of appeal, specialized courts, and the Supreme Court. It also explores the constitutional basis for judicial review in which the courts review the acts of states and national governments in order to determine their constitutionality. In addition, the policy-making role of the federal courts is examined. The chapter ends with a brief discussion of two dominant judicial philosophies; judicial activism and judicial restraint.

INTERPRETIVE POWER

The federal courts are an inactive branch of government. This means that they cannot go out and look for problems to solve. They must wait on citizens to bring problems to the courts. Do not, however, mistake this inactivity for weakness. The courts do not make statutes, constitutional provisions, amendments, or regulations. Courts do, however, have great interpretive power. This interpretive power is exercised by rendering decisions in cases construing what the law means. The interpretations in these cases can be binding on lower courts in cases relating to the same laws.

Decisions of the courts also form a body of law called the common law or case law as opposed to legislative/statutory law. The decisions in such cases are binding as precedent and provide guidance to lower courts on deciding cases with similar facts in the future. We depend on the courts to make law in areas that do not lend themselves to statutory construction. One example of this would be an area of tort law known as negligence. For obvious reasons, it would be impossible to determine the number of ways that persons could be negligent under even one set of circumstances.

To attempt drafting a statute that lists all activities or behavior that could constitute negligence would be impossible. For this reason, courts have enunciated the **reasonable person standard**. This standard allows the jury in each case to compare the care exercised by a defendant in a negligence case to that which would have been exercised by a reasonable and prudent person in the same or similar circumstances. In essence, the jury interprets the standard and applies it to each case based up the jury's collective opinion of what a reasonable person would have done under the same circumstances.

This sort of tailored justice in non-statutory areas of law gives our system a tremendous amount of flexibility for fair interpretation under unlimited circumstances. Stability, however, is required for citizens to tailor their conduct to the required standards. This is accomplished by a concept called **stare decisis**, also called precedent, which, loosely translated, means "let the decision stand." The fundamental basis of this concept is that unless the courts determine that there is a good reason to change what has occurred in previous cases with similar facts, the courts should follow the precedents set by previous courts in similar cases. To do so allows citizens to tailor their conduct to what is expected by the courts rather than be forced to guess what conduct is expected.

Citizens are expected to base their present conduct on standards set in previous cases. Let's test this theory to see if it works. Ask yourself this question, "Would a doctor have a legal problem if he were to accidentally forget to remove a sponge left in a person's abdomen during surgery?" If you knew that this would constitute negligence on the part of a doctor without going to law school or studying the law, then *stare decisis* must be how you know, and it must be working to some extent. Just by living in America over the years, hearing and reading about cases, you have determined that doctors have a duty not to leave sponges in patients. You know this just by living here and hearing about previous cases.

CATEGORIES OF LAW

Laws may be defined as principles and regulations established and enforced by a government in order to control the behavior and actions of people. There are several sources of American law. Law can emanate from constitutions which set up frameworks for government, statutes which are legislative enactments, rules and regulations which are promulgated by agencies of the governmental bureaucracy, and case law which comes from court decisions. First, in order of authority and power, is federal constitutional law, which forms the basis for all law. By virtue of the supremacy clause, Article VI, all laws which contradict the Constitution of the United States are void.

The weight given to the various sources of law flows in this order: the Constitution of the United States, federal statutes, federal rules and regulations, federal case law, state constitutions, state statutes, state regulations and state case law, etc. When they conflict each must yield to the authority of the one that precedes it. In other words, if there is a federal constitutional provision, federal statutes which conflict with it are void. Federal regulations which conflict with federal statutes must yield; where a federal regulation on a matter is involved, those regulations, not case law, govern.

We also have two broad categories of American law: criminal law and civil law. **Criminal law**, almost all of which is statutory, sets forth the conduct which a state determines not to tolerate, and for which a fine or imprisonment or both will be imposed. In short, if you can get time or a fine, it's a crime. Everything else falls into the vast category of civil law.

Criminal offenses are divided into levels of seriousness. The statutory schemes for defining the level for each offense differs from state to state. There are, however, three broad categories of offences:

- **Capital crimes**, where the penalty range includes death,
- **Felonies**, where the penalty is usually served in the penitentiary and can extend in the most serious felonies to life (in some cases without the possibility of parole), and
- **Misdemeanors**, where the penalty is usually served in a county or local jail and not for extensive amounts of time. In some cases misdemeanors are punishable by fines only (for example, most speeding violations).

The simplest way to define **civil law** is that it is everything that is not criminal law. It includes innumerable types of law, including contracts, property, torts, constitutional law, real estate, wills, probate, bankruptcy, family law, and many others.

THE FEDERAL COURTS: STRUCTURE AND JURISDICTION

The Constitution requires only one Supreme Court in Article III. Inferior courts may be ordained and established by Congress. (See Figure 10.1.) As mentioned earlier, judges serve lifetime tenures and cannot be removed but by impeachment,

FIGURE 10.1   UNITED STATES FEDERAL COURT SYSTEM

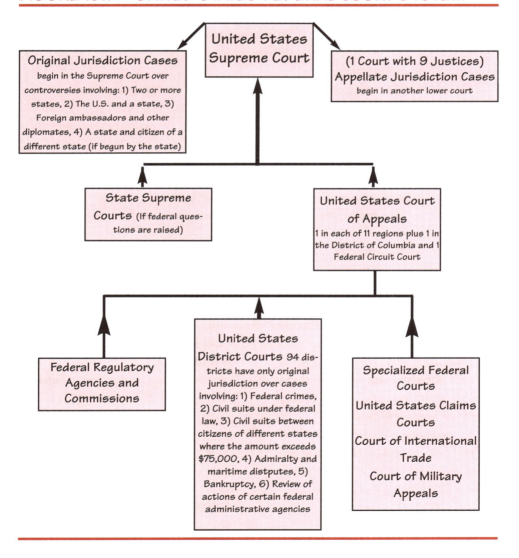

nor may their salaries be reduced. This does not apply to all federal judges, however. Some statutory or legislative courts have been created by Congress, and these judges serve for fixed terms.

Federal District Courts

The workhorse of the federal system is the Federal District Court. In total, there are 94 U.S. district courts. There are 89 district courts in 50 states. District courts also exist in Puerto Rico, the Virgin Islands, the District of Columbia, Guam, and the Northern Mariana Island. Federal District Courts are the basic trial courts of the federal system. They have original jurisdiction (the authority to hear and decide cases) in both civil and criminal cases.

A trial court is the forum in which the facts of a case are determined by a jury and the legal issues by a judge. This is also the court which would appear most familiar to most Americans because most movie or television portrayals of courts are of a trial. In this forum there is a judge, often a jury, lawyers for the two sides (plaintiff and defendant or government and defendant), and witnesses. Evidence is presented in three types: testimonial, demonstrative, and documentary.

The judge's role is to make rulings on the scope of issues which will be tried (usually in a pre-trial order) and on a schedule for discovery, before the trial, and at the trial, what is or is not admissible, and what instructions should be given to the jury. The jury is to determine the credibility of the witnesses, consider the exhibits, and make decisions on what the facts of the case are.

The two primary areas of federal jurisdiction are: **Federal Question Jurisdiction**, where the constitution, treaties and/or laws of the United States of America are involved and, **Diversity of Citizenship Jurisdiction**, where parties on each side of the case are citizens of different states (no plaintiff can be a citizen of the same state as any defendant) and various other listed situations such as controversies between states, between states and citizens of another state, between states and foreign states, between citizens or subjects and others listed in Article III, Section 2. (Diversity cases must involve at least $75,000.)

Once a case is filed in federal court, there is no guarantee that it will stay there. Federal courts have certain requirements which must be adhered to in order to be heard in federal court. These requirements include:

> **STANDING:** In order to have standing a party must be a real party in interest. One must have a stake in the outcome of the litigation. For instance a

plaintiff who has suffered real losses from unlawful activities of the defendant would have standing.

CASE OR CONTROVERSY: There must be a genuine cause of action or conflict between the parties for a party to pursue litigation in federal courts. The federal court does not entertain friendly lawsuits.

HYPOTHETICAL QUESTIONS: The federal courts do not answer hypothetical questions. For instance, one may not sue Santa Clause in an effort to prove or disprove his existence.

ADVISORY OPINIONS: Federal courts do not give advisory opinions. For instance, a state can not send questions to a court about whether a statute will be unconstitutional before passing it.

POLITICAL QUESTIONS: The federal courts have traditionally not heard cases involving political questions. They have generally left such questions to the legislative and executive branches of government.

MOOTNESS: The case or controversy must be continuing. If the issues upon which a party sues has ended and leaving nothing to be resolved, the case is moot and will not be heard. An example would be a suit involving illegal hiring discrimination in which the plaintiff had been hired and given back-pay to the date of the application for employment. Unless some other issues are unresolved, this case would be moot.

Courts of Appeal

The United States Courts of Appeals serve eleven geographic circuits, the District of Columbia Circuit, and the United States Court of Appeals for the Federal Circuit also known as the Federal Circuit. (See Figure 10.2.) The geographic circuit courts are intermediate appellate level courts, which decide cases appealed to them from federal district courts. Most persons would not be familiar with the proceedings in an appellate court. The presiding parties are called justices not judges. There are no witnesses, no jury, and usually a panel of three justices will hear oral arguments from attorneys for both sides of an appeal. Facts determined by a jury in the trial court are not reconsidered on appeal. Only legal matters are considered: whether a particular ruling on admissibility of evidence was correct, whether an instruction given to the jury was correct, or whether the lower court properly interpreted the law.

The Federal Circuit was established by Congress in 1982. It was formed by the merger of the United States Court of Customs and Patent Appeals and the appellate division of the United States Court of Claims. The Federal Circuit is unique among the

FIGURE 10.2   GEOGRAPHIC BOUNDARIES OF THE FEDERAL COURTS OF APPEALS

thirteen circuit courts of appeal. It has nationwide jurisdiction in disputes concerning trademarks, patents, copyrights, and claims against the government. Appeals to the court come from all federal district courts, the U.S. Court of Federal Claims, the U.S. Court of International Trade, and the U.S. Court of Veterans Appeals.

The Court of Appeals for the District of Columbia Circuit has geographic responsibility for appeals arising from cases heard in the capital and has special jurisdiction over appeals from decisions of federal agencies. Most cases are heard by panels of three justices. When decisions across the circuit are not uniform and in extremely important cases an **en banc** hearing may be had. This means that all the judges in the circuit will hear the case in all except the Ninth Circuit. Due to its size and the number of judges, the Ninth Circuit uses 11 randomly drawn judges.[1]

Specialized Courts

The Court of International Trade and the United States Court of Federal Claims are two specialized trial courts that have nationwide jurisdiction. The former deals with cases involving international trade and customs issues and the latter has jurisdiction over most claims for money damages against the U.S., disputes over federal contracts and other claims against the United States.

The Federal Circuit, and the Court of International Trade, for example, have judges who serve lifetime tenures, as would other judges. On the other hand, some specialized courts are legislative courts and the judges do not serve lifetime tenures. Examples would include the U.S. Court of Military Appeals, the Court of Claims, the Tax Court, and others.[2]

Supreme Court

The final arbiter, and ultimate authority in the United States court system, is the Supreme Court. It has nine justices, one chief justice and eight associated justices. (See Table 10.1.) It is the only federal court with both original and appellate jurisdictions. According to Article III, Section 2 of the U.S. Constitution, the Supreme Court has original jurisdiction "in all cases affecting Ambassadors, other Public Ministers and Consuls, in those in which a state shall be a Part." In all other cases the Supreme Court has appellate jurisdiction. The Court does not have to hear any appeal it does not want to.[3] In other words, the Supreme Court determines its own appellate jurisdiction.

TABLE 10.1 MEMBERS OF THE UNITED STATES SUPREME COURT

Name	Date of Birth	Year of Appointment	President Who Appointed
William H. Rehnquist (Chief Justice)	1924	1986	Ronald Reagan
John Paul Stevens	1920	1975	Gerald Ford
*Sandra Day O'Conner	1930	1981	Ronald Reagan
Antonin Scalia	1936	1986	Ronald Reagan
Anthony M. Kennedy	1936	1988	Ronald Reagan
David H. Souter	1939	1990	George Bush
Clarence Thomas	1948	1991	George Bush
Ruth Bader Ginsburg	1933	1993	Bill Clinton
Stephen G. Breyer	1938	1994	Bill Clinton

*Announced her retirement in July 2005. President George W. Bush nominated John G. Roberts to replace her.

The Court will accept cases involving substantial constitutional questions; where the federal government is a party in the dispute; two or more federal courts of appeals have decided the same issue in different ways; and the highest court in a state has held a federal or state law to be in violation of the U.S. Constitution, or has upheld a state law against the claim that it is in violation of the Constitution.

THE SUPREME COURT AT WORK

The term of the Court begins the first Monday in October each year and lasts until June. The Court determines its own appellate jurisdiction by issuing a **writ of certiorari**, also known as "**cert petition**," a Latin term neaning "made more certain."

In a typical year, the Court may receive seven thousand cert petitions asking it to review decisions of lower or state courts. The Court, in recent years on the average, has accepted about one hundred of them for full review. It therefore rejected about 96 percent of the applications for certiorari it received.

Cases on appeal to the Supreme Court emanate from circuits, the highest courts of various states, or court of appeals for the armed forces and other legislative courts. (See Figure 10.3.)

FIGURE 10.3   HOW CASES GET TO THE SUPREME COURT

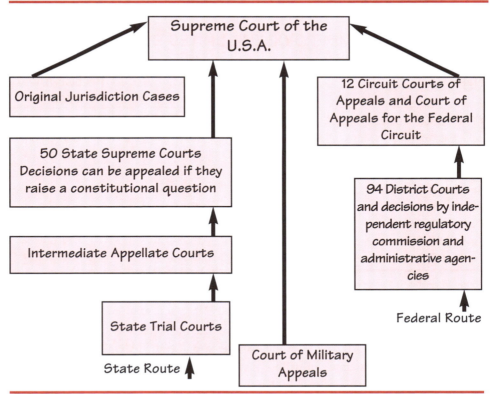

The Court will not issue a writ of certiorari unless at least four justices approve of it. This is called the **rule of four**. The rule of four implies that the Court's agenda is determined by minority of its members. A denial is not a decision on the merits of a case, nor does it indicate agreement with lower court's opinion. However, the judgment of the lower court prevails in cases that are not accepted by the Court on appeal.

Deciding Cases

Once the Supreme Court grants a writ of certiorari in a particular case, the attorneys for the parties are required to submit written briefs, detailed arguments of the case so that the justices can become familiar with facts and issues of the dispute. A brief summarizes decisions and discusses other cases the Court has decided that may have an impact on a pending case.

After all procedural steps have been taken, cases are scheduled for **oral arguments**: when lawyers on both sides of the issue appear before the justices to argue the merits of their cases. The period for oral arguments usually ends in April to allow for the writing of opinions. During oral arguments, the attorneys will be questioned and even challenged by the justices.

Following oral arguments, the court will issue its opinion. The senior justice on the majority gets to decide who will write the opinion if the chief justice is not in the majority. Obviously, a unanimous opinion is less likely to lead to further litigation in lower courts than a 5–4 decision.

Often, several opinions are published. The possibilities include:

- **Majority opinion**—the opinion of the majority of the justices,
- **Dissenting or minority opinion**—disagrees with the majority opinion as to result and legal reasoning,
- **Concurring opinion**—agrees with the result but disagrees with the legal reasoning,
- **Per curiam opinion**—by the court without identifying an author.

THE POWER TO MAKE PUBLIC POLICY

According to Alexis de Tocqueville, "There is hardly a political question in the United States which does not sooner or later turn into a judicial one."[4] This comment made by this French commentator on American society in the nineteenth century is even more accurate today. According to Dye, "It is the Supreme Court and the federal judiciary, rather than the President or Congress that has taken the lead in deciding many of the most heated issues of American politics."[5]

Although the main function of judges is to interpret and apply the law to specific cases, inevitably judges make policy when carrying out the task. The major policy-making tools of the federal courts are the power of judicial review, interpretation of the constitutional provisions, interpretation of statutes, and judicial independence.

Judicial Review

The power of judicial review allows courts the right to declare actions of the executive and legislative branch of both federal and state governments unconstitutional. This power is not mentioned in the Constitution. However, the Constitution was used to establish this power to be exercised by the federal judiciary. It is based on the supremacy clauses of Articles III and VI where it states that the Supreme Court has jurisdiction over all cases arising under the Constitution and laws of the United States.

The defining moment for judicial review was enunciated by Chief Justice John Marshall's opinion in *Marbury v. Madison* (1803).[6] In this case, the Court declared that Section 13 of Judiciary Act of 1789, the *writ of mandamus*, contradicts Article III, Section 2 of the U.S. Constitution, and was therefore null and void. The **Writ of Mandamus** is a court order to a public official to perform an act that is legally required. A contemporary example of the power of judicial review is the case of *U.S. v. Lopez* in 1995. The Court struck down the **Gun-Free School Zones Act** of 1990, which made it illegal to possess a firearm within 1,000 feet of a public or private school. The power of judicial review is exercised far more frequently against state laws and practices than federal ones.

Constitutional and Statutory Interpretations

Other major policy-making tools of the federal courts are constitutional and statutory interpretations. Some provisions of the Constitution such as "due process of law" or "interstate commerce" are general. The courts will determine the meaning of these provisions of the Constitution. The courts also make policy in their interpretation of **statutory laws**. Statutory laws are passed by Congress. Statutory interpretation involves determining the meaning of vague phrases in the statute like "fairness," "equitableness," and "good faith" enacted by Congress.

Judicial Independence

The final policy-making tool of the federal courts, as one of the three branches of government, is independence of the judiciary. According to Article III of the Constitution, a federal judge who sits on a constitutional court serves for life and his or her salary cannot be reduced. Because of judicial independence, it is only in America that judges play a crucial role in making public policy. In Britain, by contrast, Parliament is supreme, and the court cannot strike down its laws.

Construction of the Constitution

A controversial argument concerning the federal courts is on the interpretation of the U.S. Constitution. The two opposing positions on this debate are **strict construction** and **loose construction**. A strict constructionist argues that the court is bound by the words of the Constitution and by interpretations which can clearly be found or implied by it. Advocates of this position argue that we are bound by the "original intent" of the document. Loose constructionists point out that one original intent was that the Constitution would change and, that one of the greatest features of the Constitution is its "majestic vagueness." This allows the Constitution to be interpreted differently from generation to generation based upon the world in which the current generation lives, not life in the eighteenth century. Therefore, they suggest that the courts are bound, not by words, but by the principles stated in the Constitution.

Judicial Activism vs. Judicial Restraint

Another controversy is on the adequacy of the use of the interpretive power of the court to make policy changes, often called judicial activism. This argument is between those who believe that the court should leave matters of policy to the legislative branch and those opposed to this view. Judges who support the former position embrace the judicial philosophy of judicial restraint, and their opponents are known as judicial activists. Whether one supports judicial activism or restraint may depend on an individual's position on some of the decisions made by the court.

A CHANGING ROLE OF THE COURT

In his study, Christopher E. Smith of the Michigan State University denotes changes in the focus of the Supreme Court over time.[7] The main period includes that of institutional definition from 1790–1865. During this period, John Marshall, as chief justice, became a major influence in shaping the Court as an authoritative entity in

American government. The Court clarified the extent of judicial power, enunciated judicial review, and handed down decisions like *Marbury v. Madison*,[8] a unanimous opinion written by Marshall. At the end of this era, however, the *Dred Scott v. Sanford*[9] decision, rendered by the Roger Taney Court, is perhaps as infamous as the Marshall court is famous for its decisions.

The next period, 1865 to 1937, saw America change from an agrarian to an industrial society. This period of the Supreme Court was more protective of business interests than of to social rights. Examples include decisions favoring business against attempts to regulate child labor in factories and mines,[10] and state regulation of the number of work hours.[11]

The third period, 1937 to the 1990s, focused on civil rights and liberties. During this era, especially under the Warren Court, the rights of individuals and minority groups were generally expanded and protected until such declarations of rights generated opposition. The resulting swing to the right, and the elections of Republican presidents Nixon, Reagan, and Bush led to appointments on the Supreme Court that have produced justices with different views from the Warren Court, namely, the very conservative Rehnquist Court.

SUMMARY

The federal court system in the United States, theoretically, functions outside the scope of popular opinion. This is due to the protections afforded federal judges in Article III of the Constitution, most notably lifetime tenure. This makes the judicial branch the protector of groups or persons who have causes that are right, yet unpopular. The federal courts gained the reputation for being protectors of the weak between the late 1940s and the late 1960s. For this reason, federal judges are often unpopular.

The power of the federal courts is limited by the fact that it is an inactive branch, unable to go out and give opinions unless sought out by a litigant. Once the court is called, however, it has great interpretive power. A great body of our law comes from case law. This is especially true in areas without a large body of statutory or regulatory law. The two broad categories of law are criminal and civil law. We have a multilevel system of federal courts with limited jurisdiction, and certain standards which must be met in order to confer jurisdiction to hear cases.

The power of the federal courts was solidified by the Supreme Court's decision in *Marbury v. Madison* and *McCulloch v. Maryland*. The former case cemented the power of judicial review, and the latter, the Court's role in settling disputes between the states and federal government concerning their respective powers.

Today, the power of the federal courts to help shape the relationship between governments at different levels, and all governments and citizens, is largely accepted as a valuable feature of our pluralist democracy and our ability to work toward an open and fair society.

KEY TERMS

- Amicus curiae
- Appellate jurisdiction
- Capital crime
- Civil law
- Concurring opinion
- Criminal law
- Dissenting opinion
- Diversity of Citizenship
- En banc
- Federal question
- Felonies
- Judicial activism
- Judicial restraint
- Jurisdiction
- Loose constructionist
- Misdemeanors
- Oral argument
- Original jurisdiction
- Per curiam opinion
- Recess appointment
- Rule of four
- Stare decisis
- Statutory law
- Strict constructionist
- Writ of certiorari
- Written briefs

INTERNET SOURCES

a) http://www.uscourts.gov/
Information on U.S. Federal Courts is provided in this site. It includes historical and contemporary decisions, profiles of justices of federal district and appellate courts, and the status of controversial cases before some of the justices, etc.

b) http://www.oyez.at.nwu.edu/
This is the official site of the U.S. Supreme Court. Information in this site includes historical and contemporary cases handled by this Court, profiles of justices who have served, major decisions, history of the court, tour information, activities during its session, etc.

c) http://www.ncsc.dni.us/
Information on state-level courts in the fifty states of the Union can be found in this site organized by the National Center for State Courts. Pending decisions on some controversial cases, history of each court, profile of justices, etc., are provided.

NOTES

[1] Christopher E. Smith, *Courts, Politics, and the Judicial Process* (Chicago: Nelson-Hall 1997), 246–250, 289–292, 315.
[2] Ibid.
[3] Ibid.
[4] Alexis de Tocqueville, *Democracy in America* (NY: Mentor Books, 1835) p. 75.
[5] Thomas Dye, et al., *Politics in America* (NJ: Prentice Hall, 1999) p. 465.
[6] *Marbury v. Madison*, 5 U.S. 137, 1 Cranch 137, 2 L. Ed 60 (1803).
[7] Christopher E. Smith, *Courts, Politics, and the Judicial Process* (Chicago: 1997), 246–250, 289–292, 315.
[8] Marbury v. Madison, 5 U.S. 137, 1 Cranch 137, 2 L. Ed 60 (1803).
[9] *Dred Scott v. Sanford* 60 U.S. 393 (1857).
[10] *Hammer v. Dagenhart* 247 U.S. 251 (1918).
[11] *Lochner v. New York* 198 U.S. 45 (1905).

Chapter 11

Civil Liberties in America

If the Constitution means anything, it means the right to be left alone.
—Justice Louis Brandeis,
Associate Justice, U.S. Supreme Court

INTRODUCTION

Civil liberty is an issue of immense importance to every person. It holds that the individual should not be left at the mercy of the state with all its power. The state does need power and the right to exercise it; however, it should be kept in check.

The dilemma of civil liberties is to give power to government without having this power abused. The individual must be protected: by law, tradition, and custom in the possession of basic rights and liberties. This is what civil liberties is all about. What are these rights and liberties? How are they to be interpreted, defined, and applied? These issues will be discussed in this chapter.

CIVIL LIBERTIES EXAMINED

This chapter will examine the most important ethic of American life—the basic freedoms, liberties, and rights that distinguish this nation from others. America takes pride in itself as a nation founded on basic freedoms. We trumpet these to the world. Every American school child has heard the ringing words of the Revolutionary War cry, "Give me liberty or give me death."

The preamble to the United States Constitution states that:

> We the People of the United States, in Order to form a more perfect Union, establish Justice, insure domestic Tranquility, provide for the common defense, promote the general Welfare, and secure the Blessings of Liberty to ourselves and our Posterity, do ordain and establish this Constitution for the United States of America.

In this chapter, the words **liberty, right**, and **freedom** will be used synonymously as is done in many of our governmental documents. This chapter will wrap all of them up in the general academic heading of civil liberties.

The Declaration of American Independence states:

> We hold these Truths to be self-evident, that all men are created equal, that they are endowed by their Creator with certain unalienable Rights, that among these are Life, Liberty, and the Pursuit of Happiness—That to secure these Rights, Governments are instituted among men, deriving their just powers from the Consent of the Governed....

Civil liberties, for our purposes, are those individual rights clearly outlined in the U.S. Constitution. These can be found in various parts of the Constitution, but those most commonly referred to are in the Bill of Rights.

This chapter will not explore the laws—though they are of much importance—commonly referred to as civil rights laws, passed by Congress.[1] Again, it will limit its scope to freedoms, rights, and liberties specifically mentioned in the Constitution.

Civil liberty in our country is a very precious, but often misunderstood, concept. It is a very important aspect of our daily lives that lies at the very heart of what we are as a people and stand for as a nation.

INDIVIDUAL RIGHTS VS. MAJORITY RULE

We are a nation of approximately 293 million people. We have a government that operates under a political system of majority rule. However, civil liberty controversies arise very often because of the erroneous belief that the majority is pitted against the minority. The Bill of Rights was passed to protect the individual from the tyranny of the majority.

Civil liberties hold the view that even if everyone in America has passed a law and believes in it, still one individual alone may be protected against it. The **Bill of Rights** to the United States Constitution, which is the core of civil liberties, was adopted on December 15, 1791. The government cannot, no matter how many people support it, take away these individually protected rights.

So, we are a nation of a majority rule, yet we honor and protect the fundamental rights of individuals. This is a very unique notion. Many people feel comfortable about overriding certain rights until it touches them. This is a very human reaction.

CIVIL LIBERTIES AND GOVERNMENT

If we believe the government has intruded in our lives we often hear the phrase, "I have my rights!" Some of you may have used that phrase at some time in your life. As a teenager, you may have worn long hair or colored it green. If a town passes an ordinance prohibiting teens from wearing earrings or baggy pants, your reply might have been, "I have my rights, you can't do that to me. I can wear what I want to. It's in the U.S. Constitution." Most likely your reply would have been correct. The courts, however, have established what and how individual rights are upheld against a government.

On the other hand, assume you work for a private company that has a dress code. They do not allow their employees to wear baggy pants, long hair, or males to wear earrings. However, you do wear baggy pants and long hair. The boss tells you how to dress for business. Your reply is the same as you gave in high school, "I have my rights. I can wear what I want to. It's in the U.S. Constitution."

Can you utilize the Constitution in both examples to protect you from this intrusion on your personal dress code? Is there any difference between a public town and a private company in their demands upon you?

In one example, a public entity is making demands, and in the other, it is a private company. Civil liberties' protections pivot upon what a public entity, or perhaps more fundamentally, what the government, is doing to you.

Private demands by your boss may seem unreasonable, but if not forbidden by some local, state, or federal law, they are usually allowed. On the other hand, those actions by a governmental entity may be challenged if believed to be in conflict with the U.S. Constitution.

In 2004, an interesting issue occurred at Kennedale, Texas, that drew national attention. A citizen and minister, Jim Norwood, was concerned about persons frequenting adult video stores in or near Kennedale. He took photos of those entering the adult establishments and sent them to those pictured. Some considered his actions as privacy violations or certainly not of his responsibility. He contended that he was really trying to help those customers refrain from bad conduct and become more responsible citizens.

The photographs by Norwood may indeed be intrusive, but they don't reach the standard of being a civil liberties violation since no governmental entity or penalty was involved. Interestingly, Jim Norwood was elected Mayor of Kennedale in May 2004.

Civil liberties protections in America are primarily against the wrongs done to individuals by government. They do not extend to perceived wrongs done to you by your spouse or boss, for example. These private actions may have some redress in the courts, of course, but they are not in the category of civil liberties.

On January 15, 1998, a high school senior in New Braunfels, Texas, was arrested in a grocery store because another customer had complained about a shirt he was wearing. The shirt had an image of rock star, Marilyn Manson, and what the customer believed was an obscene expression on its back.

The high school student was arrested under a state law prohibiting obscene displays. The American Civil Liberties Union (ACLU) declared that actions of the New Braunfels police amounted to censorship in violation of the First Amendment. An ACLU spokesman was reported to have said, "It's an outrageous violation of free speech and we have to take a very hard look at it."[2]

Others in the New Braunfels community had a different perspective. One resident was quoted as saying, "This is a bastion of conservatism and the little [----] should have known better. And so should his mama. If they want to live here, they have to accept the community mores. If he wants to be a jerk and wear dirty words on his back, let him go to Austin."[3]

This is a good example of the community pitted against what one individual believes are his First Amendment free speech protections. Classic disputes like this arise periodically and are decided on a case-by-case basis by the courts using well-defined judicial concepts for constitutional interpretation.

OPRAH WINFREY V. TEXAS CATTLE FEEDER

In early 1998, in a federal court in Amarillo, Texas, a cattle feeder decided to sue Oprah Winfrey under a 1995 Texas law passed to protect okra, tomatoes, and other foods from unwarranted criticism. The media labeled the law the "veggie libel law."

This case was filed in a federal court because the First Amendment to the U.S. Constitution was at issue, and the parties to the dispute from different states.[4] Texas is a governmental entity, and in the eyes of some cattlemen, Oprah had violated the state's law.

The First Amendment to the U.S. Constitution is about protections from governmental intrusion. It states that, "Congress shall make no law...abridging the freedom of speech...." The courts have ruled that the First Amendment to the U.S. Constitution applies to states (Incorporation Doctrine) in many instances. This means that if Texas or any other state abridges protected freedoms, it, too, is accountable under the law just as the federal government.

In Oprah's television show on April 16, 1996, she allowed a man to make remarks about the "mad cow" disease. His remarks talked about this disease becoming a possible epidemic. In response, Oprah stated that she was not too enthusiastic about eating any more burgers. The cattlemen contended that her remark and those of her guest, at the time, contributed to a fall in beef prices. They stated that this was precisely what the Texas law was meant to prevent.

LIMITATIONS ON CIVIL LIBERTIES

Does Oprah not have the right to free speech as established in the First Amendment of the United States Constitution? Or does free speech have certain limitations? Some judicial scholars argue that the First Amendment's free speech protections are absolute. This means that no matter what a person says or writes, there should be no recourse. No state or federal entity can make any law infringing on free speech, even if beef prices go down or someone's reputation is hurt. They believe in a completely unfettered marketplace of ideas.

However, other scholars recognize limitations on free speech protections as well as other rights guaranteed by the First Amendment. The courts try to balance the freedoms in the Constitution with other factors such as the political and social climate of the times.

Perhaps the best known of these **"balancing" decisions** occurs in times of national crisis. In other words, does an individual have the right to yell "Fire!" in a crowded theater? The court answered "no" in a famous United States Supreme Court decision.[5]

However, the same or nearly identical words uttered in the **Schenck case** by the defendant could, in other circumstances, be less inciteful. Civil liberty is very often a question of one right being pitted against another right; for example, the right of citizens to be secure against the right of an individual to say certain things that may be disturbing or even harmful to the corporate political body.

Disputes arise almost every day that can be labeled as civil liberties issues. These disputes run the gamut and challenge the imagination.

For example, in Boca Raton, Florida, in July, 1998, the city council voted to enforce a ban on cemetery displays. In other words, no more statues of Jesus or Mary, no flag poles, no stand-up crosses or stars of David—no more grave decorations at Boca Raton Municipal Cemetery.[6]

The cemetery is a municipal nondenominational site. However, some of those who have loved ones buried there protested the ban. Do they have any constitutional protection if they wish to challenge the issue in court? Have their rights to free speech and religion been violated? Or is the city council correct in trying to keep the cemetery neat tidy and respectful, in their opinions?

In early 1998, the north Texas school district of Birdville suspended a fifteen-year-old honor student for three days for handing out leaflets at a high school. School officials said that the student needed permission for such action protesting a prison sentence handed out to a former student who had attended Birdville schools.[7]

A school administrator was quoted as saying that the schools have "the power to control leaflet distribution by students."[8] However, a Texas Christian University constitutional law professor responded that the school district's policy most likely violated the student's constitutional rights to free speech. "The broad rule," the professor contended, "is that students can communicate, unless there is a likelihood that what they are doing will disrupt the educational process."[9]

Schools do have the right to make and enforce rules and regulations to protect the educational process. They can control what goes into teachers' mailboxes or the use of school bulletin boards or what can be handed out in classrooms. The suspended student violated school policy by placing leaflets in teachers' mailboxes.[10] The law professor, however, replied that "Schools are adopting zero-tolerance policies in a lot of areas, and this seems to be zero tolerance of constitutionally guaranteed personal freedoms."[11]

The federal courts have tried to balance the rights of public school students with those in parochial educational institutions. Disputes and arguments covering a variety of subjects arise on school campuses throughout the nation on an almost daily basis.[12] Perhaps you have witnessed or even participated in one or more of such controversies!

Very often the courts must decide between competing rights—the rights of a group versus those of a lone individual. Or what about the religious freedom protections versus the obligation of the government not to establish religion?

In 1997, in the state of Alabama, a highly publicized dispute arose when a state judge displayed the Ten Commandments behind his judicial bench. He also conducted prayers before the court.[13] Is the judge correct in his contention that he is merely exercising his religious freedom? Or are his critics correct in contending that the judge violated the Establishment Clause of the Constitution?

Perhaps a week does not pass without some story focusing on civil liberties issues. Some of these never reach a state or federal court for adjudication, but simply are a matter for public debate and discussion. Those issues reaching judicial level can be of high importance to the entire country or stretch the imagination as to what some consider a free speech issue.

In 2003, the United States Supreme Court decided cases of high importance involving campaign finance and sodomy laws. But not all cases are of the same high order and significance. The year 2003 had various lower state and federal courts issuing rulings on whether or not it is within free speech guarantees to display various obscene hand signals to others as a sign of displeasure; or in another case to flash car headlights to warn oncoming traffic of police monitoring. The lower courts ruled in favor of the hand signals as well as the flashing of car headlights.

FREEDOM OF SPEECH AND PRESS

An individual or group right to freely express thoughts or beliefs by speech or in writing without government coercion has been one of our civilizing hallmarks. However, what exactly does free speech mean? What does a free press mean? The First Amendment states, "Congress shall make no law...abridging the freedom of speech, or of the press...."

What exactly does it mean to speak or write freely? And what exactly is considered speech? State and federal courts have devoted many years and important cases to these questions. They have ruled that there is no such thing as absolute free speech or press. Words are more protected than actions. And some kinds of speech and writing are more protected than others.

For example, political speech is given more protection than what is considered commercial speech. Obscenity and pornography are given little or no protection. But the courts have grappled over the years with what obscenity is, how it can be determined, and where it can be curtailed. Political speech and writing are given wide protective coverage because they are at the core democracy. Political ideas are considered so important that curtailing them is distasteful to the courts and legal scholars. However, there have been times in our country's history when even political discourse has been limited or curtailed. This is true especially in times of great emergency or danger.

Some critics contend that the Supreme Court, in a 2003 decision, *McConnell vs. FEC*, severely limited political speech, at least in one area, that of money in political campaigns. Congress passed the **McCain-Feingold Act** curtailing the use of "soft money."

The Act also prohibited the purchase, by interest groups, of various campaign advertisements in the media on a certain number of days before election. Some critics contended that both the monetary limits imposed and the curtailment of groups purchasing campaign ads at various times was a First Amendment violation. The Supreme Court disagreed holding the Act in compliance with the First Amendment free speech protections. Do you believe that money is a basic free speech right?

Some of the most significant landmark cases in civil liberties have pivoted around national security and First Amendment freedoms. For example, *Schenck v. United States* (1919), involved a man who was encouraging draftees to defy the draft. This occurred during the First World War, a time of danger and security concerns.

Justice Holmes delivered the majority opinion of the Unites States Supreme Court when he wrote about the **"clear and present danger"** test. This means that the speech or writing is tested against a variety of circumstances. The same words, written or spoken, may be taken or understood differently in one time period or situation than another. The "clear and present danger" test is still used today as a standard. It has been expanded to include another test, **"clear and probable danger."**

The Supreme Court has upheld state laws that punish advocating the forceful overthrowing of the United States government. This was illustrated after the Russian Revolution and the fear of a Communist Revolution spreading to the industrialized nations of the world, including America.

In 1925, the Supreme Court upheld a New York law punishing the advocacy of overthrowing the government by force. This was not, the court decided, an unconstitutional denial of free speech and press. This was the case of *Gitlow v. New York*. The Bill of Rights was considered a barrier against actions of the federal government only. But what if a state, like New York or Texas, passes a law that violates basic freedoms? Are the states responsible to its citizens under the Bill of Rights?

In the Gitlow case, the Supreme Court ruled that First Amendment guarantees are applicable to states. In subsequent years, by examining many cases, the Supreme

Court made most of the Bill of Rights applicable to the states. It is now understood that a state must live up to the same standards as the United States government in terms of basic rights and freedoms. Either a state court or a federal court can hear cases involving the Bill of Rights.

After the tragedy of September 11, 2001, and the prospect of future occurrences, Congress passed the Patriot Act. This Act facilitates the sharing of information between various governmental agencies. It also contains some parts that allow better monitoring of possible terrorist links. The Act was decried by some, yet hailed by others. It is an excellent example of one of the most basic dilemmas of civil liberties. The security of the nation must be sustained, but not at the expense of basic civil liberties. Without security, our daily lives are compromised, as is the life of the nation. Yet, we must continue to protect the rights of the individual. In past Supreme Court cases involving other national emergency eras, the justices have allowed a greater curtailment of basic rights when national security was at risk. The Patriot Act will come up for review and possible extension in 2005.

Commercial Speech

In terms of commercial speech, it is permissible for governments to limit signs, banners, and advertisements. Cities often limit the size and placement of billboards. Municipalities pass ordinances restricting the size of banners advertising various products and businesses. Various states limit what kind of signs can be placed alongside roadsides. Governments cannot ban commercial speech altogether, but they can limit it. Beauty, environmental concerns, and safety are balanced against absolute free speech advocacy.

Pornography and Obscenity

The issues of pornography and obscenity have always been of concern to the general public. The problem here is in knowing and defining what exactly is pornographic or obscene. This may seem ridiculous, but it has been a troubling issue before the courts. One jurist, Potter Stewart, stated that "I know it when I see it." This statement at first drew laughter. However, later it was taken more seriously to mean that a body of experiences can inform one as to what is obscene.

In *California v. Miller* (1973) the court attempted to define standards to judge obscene or pornographic materials. According to the Supreme Court, "The average person, applying contemporary community standards, would find the work as a whole appeals to prurient interests. Also, that the work as a whole lacks serious literary, artistic, political, or scientific value." It is very difficult to prove, even in very traditional communities, all parts of this test. Furthermore, the courts look unfavorably upon laws that are overly broad and loosely worded.

In a related area, the courts have ruled that cities may place "adult entertainment" in certain areas. According to the Supreme Court, adult entertainment cannot be totally excluded from a community, but can be limited to a specific part of town by zoning or other proper ordinances. Occasionally, private citizens, apart from the government, try to force "adult entertainment" venues out of their community or to another location.

In 2003, in Dallas, Texas, citizens in the Bachman Lake area were successful in forcing adult entertainment establishments to move to another part of the community with assistance from the city. In the same year, a small community church in Kennedale, Texas, attempted to curtail activity at a local adult entertainment location by photographing those entering the establishment. In these cases, not involving direct government intervention, there can be a clash of competing rights. The concern here is whether people have the right to partake in adult entertainment without private harassment.

There is no end to issues pivoting upon free speech and press. As our society and economy change, so do the questions. In 1997, the Supreme Court ruled that an act of Congress to regulate decency on the Internet was unconstitutional. The writer of the First Amendment likely never could have contemplated the Internet. Yet, in our own time the Internet has become a First Amendment issue.

In 2004, the Supreme Court, in another Internet-related case, ruled that Child On-Line Protection Act was a First Amendment violation. The Court ruled that the attempt to shield children from Internet pornography, while admirable, could also restrict legal adult access at the same time. The Court decision, *Ashcroft v. American Civil Liberties Union* (2004), was also sent back to lower federal courts to see if the Act could be implemented in a way not obstructive of First Amendment protections.

In 2003, the Supreme Court overturned a Texas law that made sodomy a punishable offense. This Supreme Court ruling, *Lawrence vs. Texas* (2003), overturned a prior decision by the Court, *Bowers vs. Hardwick* (1986), declaring Georgia's sodomy law constitutional. The 2003 decision set off a wide public debate on the subject of gay civil unions, legal in Vermont, and even the prospect of legalized gay marriages.

Interestingly, on May 17, 2004, the State of Massachusetts became the first in the country to legalize gay marriages.

The courts have ruled that free speech and press have more latitude when directed at a public personality than a private person. This does not mean that public people, sports stars, movie idols, and politicians have no recourse on what is said or written about them. They have to prove, however, the writer and speaker knew that the material is patently false and malicious. Private people do not have to prove all these things before contesting a potential libel or slander issue. Generally, **libel** (written defamation) and **slander** (spoken defamation) are often difficult to prove both by public and private persons.

> ### Hypothetical Case
>
> A public high school student writes a leaflet that is critical of his high school English teacher. The student writes the leaflet at home on his own computer and distributes it through the public mail at his own expense to all enrolled students and their parents. The leaflet is well composed and simply lists grievances about the teacher's grading. The public high school immediately suspends the student. The school administrators contend that this leaflet and mailing are disruptive to the educational process and that the student should have gone through established grievance procedures before resorting to his action.
> How would you rule?

Where does speech end and action begin? At the 1984 Republican National Convention in Dallas, a man burned an American flag in public. He was charged for this act under a state law and prosecuted. The Supreme Court ruled, however, that his flag burning was protected as free speech under the Constitution however reprehensible his act may have been.

FREEDOM OF RELIGION AND NON-ESTABLISHMENT OF RELIGION

The First Amendment to the U.S. Constitution states in part that, "Congress shall make no law respecting an establishment of religion, or prohibiting the free exercise thereof."

In 1943, a Pennsylvania town passed a license tax on the handing out of religious literature. Jehovah's Witnesses were taxed on such distributions. They challenged the constitutionality of this tax as abridgement to their religious freedom. The United States Supreme Court struck down the tax as an unconstitutional infringement on religious freedom.

The courts have allowed great leeway on the practice of religion. Governmental entities are allowed to waive property taxes on religious properties. This is not considered establishment of religion. Some public schools have allowed their students to leave school premises during school hours for religious purposes. This "released time" has been held to be constitutional in *Zorach v. Clauson* (1952). The Supreme Court has allowed religious practices of Santeria, a Caribbean religion now practiced in the United States, which involves animal sacrifices, to be held. The Court has allowed those whose religious practices forbid warfare to be declared "conscientious objectors."

Most American towns and cities have a great number and variety of religious institutions. The United States Tax Code allows for donations to legitimate religious institutions to be tax-deductible contributions. Throughout the country there are religious television shows, radio programs, and newspaper sections devoted to religious themes, practices, and announcements. Religious practices as guaranteed in the First Amendment have been given wide latitude.

On the other hand, however, the courts have held certain practices by governments as establishments of religion. The phrase "under God" in the Pledge of Allegiance has been challenged in recent years as constituting an establishment of religion. In 2004, the United States Supreme Court heard a case involving whether "under God" in the Pledge is an unconstitutional infringement on the Establishment Clause in the First Amendment.

The case, *Elk Grove Unified School District v. Newdow* (2004), was decided by the Supreme Court in June, 2004. The Court decided that Michael Newdow, who filed the original court case did not have "standing" to file the case. He did not have legal custody over his daughter in whose name the case was filed. This Supreme Court decision still left the main issue pivoting upon the Establishment Clause of the First Amendment undecided. It is likely that further cases will make their way to the Supreme Court based on "under God" in the Pledge. It will always be an important and controversial issue. But perhaps the most controversial and least understood of possible establishment practices is the subject of prayer in the public schools.

In a series of decisions dating back to the early 1960s, the Supreme Court declared that state-mandated prayer is unconstitutional. The federal courts have never said that prayer in public schools is unlawful. They have held that voluntary student-inspired prayer or practices that do not disrupt school activities are allowed under the Constitution.

Controversies arise almost yearly over the placing of religious displays on public property. If the display is purely religious as defined by the courts and supported entirely by public funds and on public property, it is likely to be declared unconstitutional. However, if the object is more secular than religious in nature, such as a Santa Claus and reindeer display, a Christmas tree, or a Hanukah menorah, and is supported and maintained by private funds, the courts most likely will allow it to be displayed.

Student Case Study

In 2004, an issue arose in Alabama that merits your scrutiny and discussion. The Chief Justice of the Alabama Supreme Court had placed a large granite monument with the Ten Commandments inscribed in front of the court chambers in a public courts building. The monument was challenged by some as violation of the Establishment Clause of the First Amendment. The Chief Justice stood his ground, rallied his supporters, and in the face of a federal court edict ordering removal of the monument, refused to give way.

A state judicial panel in Alabama eventually removed the Chief Justice from his position. In very dramatic fashion, the monument was moved out of the public courts building. This incident drew much media attention, but eventually lost its intensity. How do you view this case? Was the lower federal court decision correct or do you feel that the former Chief Justice of Alabama was correct in his steadfastness?

UNREASONABLE SEARCHES AND SEIZURES

The Fourth Amendment to the Constitution states in part that, "The right of the people to be secure in their persons, houses, papers, and effects, against unreasonable searches and seizures, shall not be violated, and no Warrants shall issue, but upon probable cause…." Like many other constitutional issues, search and seizure protections have changed over the years. For example, at the time of the writing of this important amendment, there was no communication via telephone, wireless devices, and computers.

If the state wiretaps a suspect and tries to use that conversation as evidence in a courtroom, would that be allowed? At first, such material was entered as evidence. Later, state and federal laws prohibited such wiretapping without proper judicial warrants.

Other questions arose involving evidence seized during searches. Foremost of these was finding evidence without a warrant. Could evidence seized this way be entered in a court proceeding? Such evidence was admitted both in state and federal courts. Evidence seized during an illegal search was called the **"fruit from a poisonous tree" doctrine**.

At the early part of the twentieth century, the U.S. Supreme Court, for the first time, disallowed evidence seized during an illegal (without a warrant) search. This landmark ruling, *Weeks v. United States* (1914), applied only to federal courts. In 1961, the Supreme Court, in *Mapp v. Ohio*, made the evidence seized during illegal searches non-admissible in state courts as well. The non-admissibility of illegally seized evidence in state or federal court is called the **exclusionary rule** and is an important part of our law.

In the latter case, the Supreme Court made the Fourth Amendment applicable to the states through the "Due Process" clause of the Fourteenth Amendment. Today, requirements of the Fourth Amendment, as most of the Bill of Rights, are applicable to states as well as the federal government.

Fourth Amendment cases are at the top of the most interesting and challenging to the federal courts. When a warrant is necessary, the issue of probable cause and the subject of the search have all become questions before the Supreme Court. The police search for drugs inspires a host of important policy and constitutional questions. For example, can police use drug-sniffing dogs, without a warrant, in drug searches? Is a dog trained to sniff out drugs and alerting police to drugs enough to constitute probable cause for an arrest?

Public school intrusions on student privacy have always been of great interest. Generally, the courts have ruled that student privacy is secondary to the health, safety, and order of a public school. In accordance with these rulings, the Supreme Court, in the case of *Board of Education of Pottawatomie v. Earls* (2002), ruled 5–4 in 2002 that public schools may require random drug tests of students engaged in competitive extracurricular activities.

> ### Hypothetical Case
>
> A young man is alone in his apartment listening to rock music. Suddenly, the police knock on the door and ask to enter. They announce they have a warrant to search the apartment. The student objects, stating that this is private property and they cannot enter. They then force their way through the door and search the home, seizing some evidence specifically mentioned in the warrant. The student contends that the police should not have forcibly entered his apartment, and that the evidence was thus seized illegally.
>
> You are a judge on the Supreme Court. Write a decision in this case.

DUE PROCESS OF LAW, SELF-INCRIMINATION, AND RIGHT TO COUNSEL PROVISIONS
Fifth and Sixth Amendment Rights

The public is acquainted with portions of the Fifth Amendment more than any other, with the possible exception of the First Amendment. "I'm taking the Fifth" is a well-known expression. This comes from the prohibition of being compelled to be a witness against oneself.

However, there are other important parts of this amendment. Among other rights it says, "...nor [shall any person] be deprived of life, liberty, or property, without due process of law...." The great phrase "due process of law" is found not only in the Fifth Amendment, which was originally applicable to the federal government, but also in the Fourteenth Amendment, which pertains to states as well.

Due process has come to mean those basic and fundamental rights, liberties, and privileges that have been part of our laws and traditions. In 1966, the Supreme Court, in a landmark decision, decided that arrested persons must be told their basic rights. In *Miranda v. Arizona* (1966), the Supreme Court ruled that the Fifth Amendment right, not to be compelled to be a witness against oneself, was fundamental. Therefore, the Court stated that interrogators must inform accused persons of their right to remain silent, that anything they say can be used against them, and that one has the right to counsel even if the accused cannot afford one. The public knows these rights as the **Miranda rights**. The last clause of the Fifth Amendment is called **eminent domain.** It gives government the power to take one's private property for publich use with adequate compensation. In 2005, the Supreme Court, in *Kelo v. New London*, ruled that local governments may seize people's homes and business—even against their own will—for private economic development. The Court argued that private economic development may provide benefits to the community, including new jobs and increased tax revenue. In its ruling, the Court noted that states are free to ban that practice.

The **Sixth Amendment** states that, "...to have compulsory process for obtaining witnesses in his favor, and to have the Assistance of Counsel for his defense."

In 1963, the Supreme Court, in *Gideon v. Wainwright*, ruled that the right to counsel must be available to the indigent in a state court, and that this right is pertinent to non-capital as well as capital offenses. The importance of this decision cannot be overstated. Long before this case, the right to counsel was afforded indigents in federal courts but not in states. The effort to make counsel available to indigents in state courts was a long and arduous process. The right to counsel in state courts by the poor had its beginnings in the 1930s.

In *Powell v. Alabama* (1932), the Court applied the right to counsel in capital cases by indigent defendants to states. This case was part of a series of court rulings emanating from what was known as the Scottsboro Cases that galvanized the nation in the early 1930s. The Scottsboro decisions of *Powell vs. Alabama* and *Norris vs. Alabama* triggered a larger series of debates about segregation and civil rights, especially in Southern States.

Today, by virtue of Court rulings, the right to counsel by those unable to afford one applies to capital and non-capital cases in state and federal courts. Until these important decisions, there was no inherent right to counsel in state courts. And many did not even know about this and other rights due them.

Until 1932, an accused person could be arrested, tried, and convicted in a state court of capital offenses, and executed without the right to counsel. Until 1963, an accused person could be arrested, tried, convicted, and sentenced to a long prison term without the right to counsel. We have come a long way in guaranteeing basic rights to those accused of crimes.

After the rise of international terrorism and the war in Afghanistan, issues arose that usually do not come to the judicial front unless in times of national emergency. Various prisoners, especially those captured in Afghanistan during the war, were transferred to Guantanamo, Cuba, a United States garrison. The questions arising pivoted upon the right to counsel, reading of various rights, and the right to a speedy and public trial.

The Guantanamo detainees were mostly of foreign origin, but others taken prisoner in the war against terrorism were American citizens. They too were held in various detention facilities, other than Guantanamo. Critics contend that they were deprived of basic Fifth and Sixth Amendment rights. Others contend that these accused terrorists were really enemy combatants and should be tried outside the normal civilian judicial procedures and court system. Various Federal District and Circuit Courts have held hearings on these detainees, with different rulings.

In mid-2004, the Supreme Court handed down important but complicated rulings on these matters. The cases involved two U.S. citizens: Yaser Hamdi and Jose Padilla. They were fighting against their own country and declared enemy combatants. The Supreme Court ruled that the United States Government has the right to hold enemy combatants as such, but they must be granted access to counsel and to the court system. The Supreme Court decisions were generally considered a blow against unlimited executive authority that wished to bar enemy combatants from access to counsels and courts. More accurately, it can be said that the Court still allows the government strong authority over enemy combatants, but allows those detainees some review of their status by our court system.

An important Sixth Amendment case, *United States v. Booker,* on the right to a jury trial was brought before the Supreme Court in 2004. It involves the question of whether a judge can increase a sentence in a criminal trial. It is contended that only a jury can increase sentences, thereby taking away the power of a judge. This case could render strict federal sentencing guidelines, now in place, unconstitutional.

Hypothetical Case

A young adult, completely without monetary resources, had been arrested on a felony charge by the local police and charged by a magistrate. The person was questioned quickly while in jail, but was not allowed an attorney, nor told one could have been provided. The police said that they did not have the time to tell the accused of his or her rights. The accused now wants anything said while in custody to be excluded from evidence.

You are the judge. Write the decision in this case.

CRUEL AND UNUSUAL PUNISHMENT
The Eighth Amendment

The Eighth Amendment has been the subject of much interpretation by the courts over the years. It states that, "Excessive bail shall not be required, nor excessive fines imposed, nor cruel and unusual punishment inflicted."

Perhaps the most crucial aspect of this amendment is the prohibition of cruel and unusual punishment. What exactly does this mean? What kind of punishments were cruel and unusual 200 years ago when this amendment was ratified? What kind of punishments would be cruel and unusual today?

The most dramatic subject to come before the Supreme Court in recent years was over the question of whether the death penalty constituted cruel and unusual punishment. In *Furman v. Georgia*, the Supreme Court temporarily halted all executions in the United States.

The issue presented was whether the death penalty could be meted out for non-capital crimes. For many years several state courts issued the death penalty for such crimes. The Court decided, however, that the death penalty should be reserved only for murder cases. Other death penalty cases would be considered as cruel and unusual punishment. The Court halted all executions until states conformed to their ruling. The Court was particularly concerned with the procedures involved in handing out the death sentence. The death sentence itself, the Court declared, did not violate the Eighth Amendment's cruel and unusual punishment.

In *Gregg v. Georgia* (1976), the Court ruled that the death penalty in states could commence again. However, two justices, William Brennan and Thurgood Marshall, dissented, stating that the death penalty did amount to a violation of the Eighth Amendment and should be ended. The debate over the death penalty and what constitutes cruel and unusual punishment continues today.

In 2004, various federal courts were asked to rule on the method of execution itself. Most states have done away with hanging, electrocution or firing squads, which have been traditionally used over the past two centuries. Today, most states use lethal injection of toxic chemicals to induce death, believing this method to be more humane. However, some lawsuits contend that this method may seem humane, but actually mask a great deal of pain and suffering, which could constitute a denial of Eighth Amendment protections.

In the case of *Roper v. Simmons* (2005), the Court ruled that juvenile death penalty was unconstitutional. The 5–4 decision tossed out the death sentences of some 70 death row inmates. Writing for the Court, Justice Anthony Kennedy stated that "When a juvenile commits a heinous crime, that State can exact forfeiture of some of the most basic liberties, but the State cannot extinguish his life and his potential to attain a mature understanding of his own humanity."[14] This ruling means that the states will not be allowed to seek the death penalty for minors.

Life and Death Politics

In March, 2005, a major controversy arose over a woman named Terri Schiavo in the state of Florida. Terri Schiavo had been kept alive by a feeding tube for over 15 years. Her desperate medical condition was caused by an eating disorder, which led to a heart attack in this young woman. Given authority under the Florida law, her husband, Michael Schiavo, removed her feeding tube. He argued that his wife was in a persistent vegetative state and would want to die. Bu her parents rejected that diagnosis and said she would want to live. They demanded that the feeding tube not be disconnected. Thus, the battle lines were drawn based on some central civil liberties issues.

Just three days after the feeding tube was removed on orders from a Florida judge, Congress passed legislation crafted just for Schiavo, and President Bush interrupted his vacation and flew from his ranch in Texas to Washington to sign it in the wee hours of the morning. The law placed the issue with the federal courts. Furthermore, religious conservatives embraced the case as part of a broader movement to protect what they call the "sanctity of life." They argue that all human life is of value, regardless of the human's stage of development, level of health, or ability.

This emotional matter was eventually concluded when neither the Florida nor federal courts intervened. Terri Schiavo's feeding tube remained disconnected and she died 10 days later. The controversy did not end, but merely raised a new dimension in civil liberties discussions. Furthermore, the Schiavo case has raised concerns for many about federal government encroachment on states' rights, the judiciary, and the role religion should play in politics and legal system.

> **Hypothetical Case**
>
> A woman is to be executed for the first time in a state's history. She admitted murdering two people with a pick-ax. However, after spending fourteen years in prison awaiting appeals, her execution date was set. During her incarceration she became a model prisoner, married, turned to religion, and drew global sympathy.
>
> On the date of her execution she fainted, became seriously ill, and her execution was postponed for two days. At her eventual execution the injection was incorrectly inserted, burning her arm and causing much pain and misery. The viewing crowd gulped and gasped at the episode. Eventually, another injection was inserted into her arm, killing her.
>
> Her attorney protested, contending that her execution constituted cruel and unusual punishment, and he demanded that all future executions be halted. The contention was that executions can and have been mishandled. Therefore, they can constitute an Eighth Amendment violation.
>
> You are the judge. Write the decision.

NON-ENUMERATED RIGHTS
Ninth Amendment

This amendment is one of the most important, yet is often overlooked by the public. Like the Eighth Amendment, it is simple and precise in its wording, yet leaves room for much interpretation. It reads, "The enumeration in the Constitution of certain rights, shall not be construed to deny or disparage others retained by the people." What are these rights retained by the people? All rights not specifically mentioned in other parts of the Constitution? The courts have not utilized this amendment in many cases over the years. Some believe that it is because the number of rights retained by the people is so numerous that it becomes rather amorphous and counterproductive to a stable and orderly society.

Perhaps the most well known decision utilizing this Amendment and the controversy swirling around it is *Roe v. Wade*, decided by the Supreme Court in 1973.

This controversial decision utilized the Ninth and the Fourteenth Amendments for its ruling. The Fourteenth Amendment contains an important word, "liberty." The Court's majority ruled that the right to abortion was pertinent to a woman's "liberty."

Also, the Ninth Amendment came into play for its reservation of rights to people. One of these rights is the "right to privacy." The Supreme Court, in earlier decisions, ruled that one of the most precious protections in the Constitution is the "right to be left alone." However, is the right to an abortion part of the "right to be left alone"? Nowhere in the Constitution is the "right to privacy" ever specifically mentioned. Where is it found? The Ninth Amendment is often used to encompass the right to be left alone and the right to privacy.

In another landmark decision, *Griswold v. Connecticut* (1965), the U.S. Supreme Court ruled again on the issue of privacy. This decision came out of a Connecticut law which prohibited the distribution, information, and medical advice dealing with birth control. A Planned Parenthood director and medical personnel were arrested and convicted for violating this law. The Court overturned the Connecticut law and perhaps paved the way for *Roe v. Wade* later. The Court ruled that there are implied rights to privacy in several of the Bill of Rights, especially the Ninth Amendment. The Court also wrote about liberty, which is protected in the Fifth and Fourteenth Amendments.

However, in a dissenting opinion, Justice Hugo Black argued that there is no constitutional right to privacy. Where can the right to privacy be breached and where are people to be left alone? There is no absolute right to privacy. The Court, in these landmark cases, states that the right to privacy is to be respected as a fundamental right to our lives. However, in an organized state, the government very often intrudes on our privacy. The major question is, "Where and when can the government invade our privacy?"

In a controversial case from Georgia in 1986, the United States Supreme Court ruled that the right to privacy is not protected when the subject involves homosexual behavior. In *Bowers v. Hardwick*, the court ruled that this type of behavior could be outlawed. The dissenting opinion in this case cited the "right to be left alone" as implied in the Constitution and Bill of Rights. In 2003, *Bowers v. Hardwick* was overturned by *Lawrence v. Texas*.

In 2004, the Supreme Court ruled in a case that involved privacy and civil liberties groups. The Court stated that the police have a right to ask for a person's name in the course of a routine investigation. A Nevada rancher who was stopped by police refused to reveal his identity, citing privacy rights. Privacy rights have been implied, though not specifically enumerated, in the Ninth Amendment. Here, however, the Court said that the police can arrest suspects who refuse to identify themselves in the course of an investigation.

> ### Hypothetical Case
>
> Three young people are inhaling prohibited drugs in the privacy of their apartment. The police obtain a valid warrant to search and seize the evidence and arrest them. The three contend that their right to privacy has been violated as well as their right to be left alone.
>
> Write the decision in this case. You are the judge.

EQUAL PROTECTION AND DUE PROCESS
Fourteenth Amendment

The Fourteenth Amendment is one of the most utilized of all amendments in the U.S. Constitution. It reads in part:

"No State shall make or enforce any law which shall abridge the privileges and immunities of citizens of the United States; nor shall any State deprive any person of life, liberty, or property, without due process of law; nor deny to any person within its jurisdiction the equal protection of the laws."

The provisions in this amendment have been used to unify this country. It brings all the fifty states into alignment with fundamental tenets of our nation. It speaks to the states. Its origins come out of the Civil War and were designed to bring states into compliance with national law.

The due process wording in this amendment has been used to make many parts of the Bill of Rights applicable to the states. The courts have interpreted what "due process of law" means—it means most of the provisions in the Bill of Rights. This alone illustrates the importance of this amendment.

Furthermore, the "equal protection" phrase in this amendment has been used to provide all Americans equal treatment by state and federal governmental entities. The landmark case of *Brown v. Topeka Board of Education* (1954), is one of many examples utilizing this important constitutional wording. Desegregation was accomplished by the Court, which ruled that every person must be treated the same under the law.

The controversial issue of affirmative action in university admissions and the granting of contracts by public entities is a Fourteenth Amendment issue. What exactly is meant by equal protection of the law? Ultimately, it is up to the courts to decide.

In 2003, the United States Supreme Court ruled that an affirmative action program utilized by the University of Michigan in undergraduate admissions was not unconstitutional. The Court ruled that race can be one factor, among others, that could be considered in admissions. Race alone cannot be the sole factor in admissions, however. This would constitute a quota system that was overturned by the Supreme Court in the *Regents of the University of California v. Bakke* (1978) involving admissions to a medical school in the University of California System.

> ### Hypothetical Case
>
> There is a state law providing that women cannot be admitted to an all-male state-supported school. The women contend that they are being deprived of their rights under the Fourteenth Amendment. The state contends that it has the right to separate men and women for educational purposes—that they can obtain a better education if not distracted by the opposite sex.
>
> Write an opinion in this case. You are the judge.

THE DOCTRINE OF INCORPORATION

The Bill of Rights did not automatically provide for protection from state violations of due process. Rather, the individual amendments were made to apply to the states in a piecemeal manner called the doctrine of incorporation. Over time, and through lawsuits brought by individuals and criminal cases, most provisions of the Bill of Rights have been made applicable to the states. For example, the Sixth Amendment states that the accused in criminal cases is to "have the assistance of counsel for his defense." This right applied only in federal court and state capital cases until 1963. In that year, the right was incorporated and made to apply to the states in *Gideon v. Wainwright* (1963).

Today, almost all parts of the Bill of Rights have been incorporated except the right to keep and bear arms (Second Amendment); the provision against quartering of troops in private homes (Third Amendment); the right to indictment by a grand jury (Fifth Amendment); the right to a jury trial in civil cases (Seventh Amendment); and the prohibition of excessive bail or fines (Eighth Amendment).[15]

THE FUTURE

In the future, there will be more questions and challenges to civil liberties in ways the writers of our Constitution never contemplated. In an effort to combat domestic crime and international terrorism in public places, surveillance cameras have been placed to monitor parking lots, sports stadia, and airports. Travelers coming and going to airports are now routinely subjected to searches of their persons and belongings. Do these practices violate civil liberties as defined in this chapter? Most likely, none of these exercises or programs would be held in violation of the Constitution.

Additionally, the advances of science will bring forth questions not known in earlier times. There will be more debates and dilemmas about when death occurs. What is life itself and how should it be defined? The science of genetics will pose questions. Can insurance companies, employers, and others discriminate on the basis of genetics? Can or should an employer fire or refuse to hire an employee who has some rare disease that may cost the company monetarily and cause other hardships?

What about stem cell research that shows so much promise in medicine? Should the government sponsor such research or ban it altogether? Is stem cell research a civil liberties issue at all? It is easy to predict that science will continue to pose all sorts of questions that will border or be at the center of the continuing civil liberties debate.

SUMMARY

Civil liberties in this country pivot on how the government and various state institutions impact persons. However, in an increasingly technologically determined and impacted society, our lives may be affected and intruded upon by nongovernmental bodies. Furthermore, the need for security impacts our lives as well. What should be our proper response to these private intrusions?

What about your neighbors who may be using a video camera for surveillance of the neighborhood? What about airline corporations that, for security purposes, demand extra surveillance and searches? What about random drug tests of athletes? What about corporations that can monitor customers' buying habits? What about your telephone calls being secretly taped by those you call? What about caller identification numbers?

The beginning of this chapter illustrated but a few of the many questions and controversies common to civil liberties. Hardly a day passes without another civil liberties question arising. Many people do not fully appreciate what civil liberties are about until they are personally affected. For example, in the widely reported Diane Zamora case that involved murder, an innocent man was arrested and held by police before the real perpetrator was found. Who would want to be an innocent person arrested for a heinous crime? Strict adherence to civil liberties protects us all.

> **Student As Judge**
>
> You are an Associate Justice on the United States Supreme Court. This case is before you to decide along with the other eight justices on the Court. You have made a movie called "Centigrade 9/11." In this movie, you have made some spectacular, but controversial statements about American policy and the president. The government has moved to curtail its distribution. Is this a constitutional issue? Would it be a constitutional issue if no private distributor could be found to market this controversial movie?

KEY TERMS

Balancing decision
Civil liberties
Clear and present danger
Due process
Eminent domain
Exclusionary rule
Fruit and poisonous tree doctrine
Libel
McCain-Feingold Act
Miranda rights

INTERNET SOURCES

a) http://w3.trib.com/FACT/
This site involves First Amendment rights issues: What are these rights? How can they be abused by the government, seeking redress, legal assistance, and various information that could help those who lack knowledge on these fundamental rights?

b) http://www.aclu.org/
The American Civil Liberties Union (ACLU) maintains this site. This organization prides itself on being the primary protector of the First Amendment rights as enshrined in the U.S. Constitution. Membership information is provided, as is information on the abuse and deprivation of these rights by government and its agents or agencies. Ways to contact legal services in the various states and local governments of the fifty states of the Union are given.

c) http://www.cc.org/publications/rights.html
This site, maintained by the Christian Coalition, provides information on religious freedom specific to Christians. Information on membership, court rulings on religious freedom, pending U.S. Supreme Court decisions, etc., are provided on this site.

NOTES

[1] Civil rights laws have been passed by Congress at various times. They have been amended and challenged in the courts. Most notably they were passed at the end of the Civil War and during the Great Society of President Lyndon Baines Johnson. They have covered a variety of subjects, but most notably have guaranteed public accommodations, housing, employment, schools, and voting rights to all Americans.

[2] *Dallas Morning News*, (2 February 1998), 1.

[3] Ibid.

[4] Article III, Section 2, United States Constitution.

[5] *Schenck v. United States* 249 U.S. 47 (1919), Justice Oliver Wendell Holmes.

[6] *Fort Worth Star-Telegram*, (14 January 1998), 7.

[7] *Fort Worth Star-Telegram*, (5 February 1998), 9B.

[8] Ibid.

[9] Ibid.

[10] Ibid.

[11] Ibid.

[12] Some of the most volatile and high profile disputes in public schools have been about religious practices. The courts have ruled that students have various religious rights to prayer and other ceremonies as long as they are student-inspired, are voluntary, and have no official backing. In a 1968 landmark ruling of *Tinker v. Des Moines* (1968), the Supreme Court ruled that students

could wear armbands to protest the Vietnam War. Students do not lose their constitutional rights, the court said, just because they are students.

[13] See the First Amendment of the United States Constitution: "Congress shall make no law respecting an establishment of religion, or prohibiting the free exercise thereof."

[14] Bill Mears, "High Court: Juvenile Death Penalty Unconstitutional," *CNN Washingto Bureau*, (1 March 2005). <http://www.cnn.com/2005/LAW/03/01/scotus.death.penalty>

[15] Lieberman, Jethro K., *The Evolving Constitution: How the Supreme Court Has Ruled on Issues from Abortion to Zoning,* (New York: Random House, 1992), p. 259.

Chapter 12

Civil Rights: Journey to Full Participation

The Fourteenth Amendment...was adopted with a view to the protection of the colored race, but has been found to be equally important in its application to the rights of all...."

—Oliver Wendell Holmes

INTRODUCTION

Government has often made distinctions between classes of people dating back to the earliest days of the Constitution. This has been done in many areas of the country historically and is done today as well. For instance:

- Politically astute seventeen-year-olds are not allowed to vote and yet even the most politically ignorant persons over the age of eighteen are allowed to vote.
- Males are involved in all phases of military activity in the armed forces, and women are not.
- Out-of-state parents, whose children score well on tests whose validity has been disputed, see those children admitted to the flagship universities of various states, while in-state taxpayers, whose children do poorly on those tests, see their children turned away from schools paid for with their own tax dollars.

It is not that states cannot discriminate against citizens; it is that such distinctions in law must not be arbitrary and capricious. The state action involved must be based on a legitimate, compelling state interest (such as education, public safety, etc.) and must be reasonable. Certain types of class distinctions, for instance, those based upon sex or race, are presumed to be unreasonable by the courts that look at them with suspicion.

These types of distinctions are often referred to as suspect criteria or suspect classifications. The courts will subject them to close scrutiny, meaning that they will look closely at the legitimate state interest which the policy is designed to accomplish and balance it against the rights of any persons affected by it. In other words, historically, the courts have presumed the constitutionality of laws or policies directed toward a legitimate state interest unless they use suspect criteria.

When suspect (suspicious) criteria like race, sex, etc., are used by the policies or laws, the courts will presume them to be unconstitutional, unless the state can show a compelling need to accomplish some legitimate state interest which requires that the use of the suspect criteria be a part of the policy. In recent years, the courts have required these classifications to be narrowly tailored to meet a specific and proper objective.

This approach has led many to question the federal courts' role in areas such as affirmative action since sex and race are used as criteria. Will the judicial branch change the extent to which states may remedy past discrimination?

The role of the courts will be examined in this chapter as well as their role in moving us toward a democracy, which has full and complete opportunities for all its citizens. In so doing, we will examine several movements for civil rights. We will focus on the civil rights movement of African-Americans and then examine that of Mexican-Americans in the Southwest. Finally, we will analyze the women's movement before discussing affirmative action as it affects all three groups.

ROLE OF THE SUPREME COURT

When did Americans begin to look at the Supreme Court as a champion of civil rights? Most would point to a dramatic series of cases filed by the National Association for the Advancement of Colored People (NAACP) Legal Defense Fund in the 1940s and 1950s, and the receptive Warren Supreme Court as two keys to this reputation. Prior to that time, the federal courts were, at best, not receptive to the rights of minorities.[1]

Prior to the second half of the twentieth century, the court endorsed discrimination against racial minorities and women. The Court favored slavery in the 1850s against congressional attempts to legislate against it in *Dred Scott v. Sanford*,[2] and allowed the incarceration of Japanese-Americans in concentration camps during World War II. The U.S. government, without much controversy, would later apologize and offer compensation to the survivors of the concentration camps.

But attempts at compensation for historical discrimination against African-Americans, including discriminatory laws on indentured servitude, slavery, and segregation from 1619 to the late 1960s, have been far more controversial. This issue has drawn such hostility and controversy that it lends credence to the statement by noted Harvard University professor Cornel West, "As a nation, we do not want the specter of our racist past. Yet, we cannot get away from it either."[3]

Though the early period of our history indicates an inability or reluctance to deal with controversial rights, the well-planned and hard-fought gains by the NAACP or Legal Defense Fund in the courts, and the Southern Christian Leadership Conference (SCLC) under the leadership of the Reverend Dr. Martin Luther King, Jr., demonstrate American democracy's ability to change injustice at perhaps its finest hour. Let's begin our journey down the road to civil rights through the eyes of groups of people denied these rights.

AFRICAN-AMERICAN CIVIL RIGHTS MOVEMENT

African-Americans arrived as indentured servants—not slaves—in Jamestown, Virginia, in August, 1619. By 1624, William, the son of Antoney and Isabella, was the first recorded black child born in the English settlements. Africans had traveled here with the Spanish and Portuguese earlier as explorers, servants, slaves, and free men. Blacks sailed with Pizarro, Cortes, Menendez, and Balboa. The best known black explorer, Estevanico, was one of those who found New Mexico and Arizona for the Spanish.[4]

Unfortunately, one of the great failures of our democracy is that black children born more than 300 years later, in 1954, were born in a segregated south, and without nearly the same opportunities that even newly arriving immigrants could take for granted. Denied to these Americans were rights and privileges such as eating in public restaurants, attending white schools, swimming in white city pools, or using the white-only bathrooms in the public facilities including courthouses across the South. Integration of the school systems in most of the South really began in the mid-1960s and was often only in small school districts unable to afford the costs of losing federal funds or challenging integration in court. In 1986, prosecutors were prohibited from systematically excluding black jurors from serving on juries, which was a common practice in cases involving black defendants nationwide.[5]

One of the great successes of the American democracy is that the most visible vestiges of segregation in the South have been erased. Even though covert discrimination against African-Americans is far from eliminated, southern cities have elected African-American mayors, judges, congressional representatives, county commissioners, and city councilmen. Some cities in the South have an African-American city manager.

Several school districts, including Dallas and Houston, had at least one African-American general school superintendent by the end of the 1990s. Changes of this magnitude would have been beyond the comprehension of people in cities like Dallas even in the 1960s when the Progressive Voters' League of Dallas had its work cut out for it, attempting to overcome years of intimidation in even getting African-Americans to exercise their right to vote in the city.

A Long Journey

The Constitution was not completely silent about slavery, or at least the slave trade. The U.S. Constitution, in Article I, Section 9, bars Congress from prohibiting the slave trade before 1808.[6] Interestingly, this section refers to the importation of such persons when referring to slaves. In 1865, ratification of the Thirteenth Amendment abolished slavery and involuntary servitude in the United States.

This did not end discrimination. For example, between 1899 and 1924, more than 1,400 African Americans were lynched. Many were harassed or killed, until the 1960s, for exercising rights taken for granted by other American citizens. In 1998, an African-American man was dragged behind a truck in Texas until he was decapitated. An article on hate crimes has been placed in the appendix for the statistics and information regarding hate crimes. (See Appendix B.)

Why the Courts?

African-Americans have consistently comprised about 12 percent of the total U.S. population. In addition to this numerical problem, African-Americans in the South were denied the right to vote by law prior to the Fifteenth Amendment, and thereafter by various legislative schemes. Barriers to the vote included grandfather clauses, literacy tests, understanding tests, poll taxes, white primaries, lynching, and other forms of intimidation such as being fired. This presents a great problem for doing things in our federal system for minorities. Only the federal courts, among government branches and levels, exist outside the control of the majority for most of the country.

This allows minorities to be at the mercy of the majority unless they could go to federal courts for protection under the Constitution. In other words, the president, who heads the executive branch, gets there by popular election; the Congress is selected by popular election; the governor, the state legislature, and in most instances, a majority of the state judges are selected by popular election. The only safe haven in our system from the whim and caprice of the majority is in the federal courts.

This is because federal judges have lifetime tenures, cannot have their salaries reduced, and cannot be removed unless impeached. In short, a courageous federal judge has no boss but the Constitution. Going to the president or the Congress with 12 percent of the population, many of whom cannot vote and most of whom have little money, is comparable to a really deserving but penniless football fan showing up at the Super Bowl without a ticket. Political power is the currency of the executive and legislative branches. The inability to vote is to be without political currency. The courts were the only place African-Americans could go, and the current makeup of federal courts causes many civil rights lawyers to consider that option illusory.

The Fourteenth Amendment

It could easily be argued that had the Fourteenth Amendment been enforced vigorously, there would not have been a need for the civil rights movement, or the Fifteenth, Nineteenth, Twenty-Third, Twenty-Fourth, and maybe the Twenty-Sixth Amendments. Its language would have allowed all these rights to be protected, had it been so interpreted. This was, however, not the case—political courage was not in great supply in the opinions rendered by our early Supreme Court justices.

The Supreme Court initially was far better at excusing and explaining away the misapplication of the Fourteenth Amendment than it was at applying it to protect the politically weak. Nearly 100 years later, the Warren Court showed the courage to lead Americans on issues of race rather than follow popular public opinion or excuse oppressive acts of the powerful. African-Americans had more success with the Congress than the courts in the 1860s. States, however, were a different matter.

In 1865, the Black Codes were enacted in southern states. It was illegal in Mississippi for African-Americans to own farmlands. In 1866, the U.S. Congress wrote the Civil Rights bill, which conferred citizenship on African-Americans and theoretically gave them the same rights in every state and territory as white citizens.

Overriding President Andrew Johnson's veto passed the act. Reality, however, outside the theoretical world was quite a different story. In July 1866, white Democrats, led by police, attacked a convention of black and white Republicans in New Orleans. Forty people were killed and 150 wounded. Meanwhile, in the northern state of Massachusetts, in July 1866, Edward G. Walker, the African-American son of abolitionist David Walker, was elected to the Massachusetts Assembly.[7]

Congress, with the passage of the Reconstruction Acts, which began in 1867, created rights and fostered progress for African-Americans. These rights included enfranchisement, holding political offices including the House of Representatives, participating in state constitutional conventions, and serving as civil servants, including policemen. All of these rights would soon evaporate before the eyes of black citizens in southern states after the Civil Rights Act of 1875—which had given African-Americans the right to equal treatment in inns, public conveyances, theaters, and other places of public amusement—was declared unconstitutional by the Supreme Court in 1883.[8]

It is little wonder that African-Americans today see the Supreme Court's rollback on civil rights positions of the 1980s and 1990s as suspiciously similar to the Supreme Court's position in the 1880s.

Modern Civil Rights Movement

African-Americans' journey to civil rights in this century has been two-pronged. It has been fought in the Courts most prominently by the NAACP and in the society at large by way of demonstrations, sit-ins, marches, and voter registration drives. The SCLC and Student Nonviolent Coordinating Committee (SNCC) were preeminent forces of these battles. Also important as factors were the roles of television and other mass media and the eloquent and determined leadership in the 1950s and 1960s of the Reverend Dr. Martin Luther King, Jr. The battle was fought in the minds of Americans and on the battlefield of public opinion. Its premier general was a young minister and Morehouse College graduate who had earned a Ph.D. from Boston University, Dr. King. He led a movement, which was informed by his studies of Ghandi's philosophy of nonviolent resistance, fueled by his eloquent oratory, and inspired by his unwavering courage.

We will not discuss details of the history of segregation. Rather, we will focus on a few of the most important cases that led to desegregation of schools. The architect of this strategy of using test cases was Charles Hamilton Houston who designed the well-planned series of cases filed by the NAACP beginning in the 1930s. Thurgood

The Supreme Court under Chief Justice Earl Warren Was Instrumental in the Brown vs. Board of Education Decision.

© Bettmann/CORBIS

Marshall and his brilliant NAACP Legal Defense and Education Fund team argued many of these cases before the Supreme Court. A brief list of a few of those cases and what they involved is as follows:

- *Missouri ex rel Gaines*—held that a state must provide equal educational facilities within the states in 1938.[9]
- *Sipuel v. Oklahoma State Board of Regents*—held that black students had the right to study law in the same state and at the same time as other citizens in 1948.[10]
- *Sweatt v. Painter* and *McLaurin v. Oklahoma State Regents*—held that there were intangible effects to segregation and that prevented the law school built for Sweatt from being equal to the University of Texas; and that McLaurin could not be segregated within a white school in 1950.[11]

Dr. Martin Luther King, Jr., on the Date of His "I Have a Dream" speech, August 28, 1963.

© Bettmann/CORBIS

- *Brown v. Board of Education of Topeka, Kansas*—held that segregation placed a badge of inferiority in the minds and hearts of black children, that in education, separate but equal has no place, and that "separate educational facilities are inherently unequal" in 1954.[12]

Outside the courts, great impetus was given to the push for first-class citizenship when Rosa Parks, a black seamstress, refused to give her seat on a bus to a white male passenger. She was arrested in Montgomery, Alabama. She is often called the "mother of the civil rights movement."

These battles outside the courts are also well documented but far too numerous to cover extensively here. However, we will discuss some key events from one brief period: 1957–1963.

As can be seen from this brief period in history, the gains of the civil rights movement for African-Americans have been costly and controversial. These gains were

Key Events of the Civil Rights Movement

February, 1957	SCLC organized at New Orleans naming the Rev. Dr. Martin Luther King, Jr., president.
1957	Tuskegee Boycott—Black citizens boycott stores.
1957	President Eisenhower had to use federal troops to integrate Central High School in Little Rock, Arkansas.
September, 1958	The Rev. Dr. Martin Luther King, Jr., was stabbed in the chest by a deranged black woman.
October, 1958	Jackie Robinson, Harry Belafonte, and A. Phillip Randolph lead 10,000 students in a march to integrate Washington, D.C., schools.
1959	Prince Edward County, Virginia, Board of Supervisors closed school system to avoid integration.
1960	Four students from North Carolina A & T start sit-in movement in a Greensboro, North Carolina, five-and-dime store.
1960	Pope John elevates Bishop Laurian Rugambwa of Tanganyika to the College of Cardinals, the first black cardinal of the modern era.
1960	San Antonio, Texas, becomes the first major southern city to integrate lunch counters.
1960	Dr. King was arrested in Atlanta. Democratic candidate for President, John F. Kennedy, calls Mrs. King to express concern.
1961	A bus with the first group of Freedom Riders was bombed outside Anniston, Alabama. The group was attacked in Anniston and Birmingham. Freedom Riders were later attacked by a mob in Montgomery, prompting Attorney General Robert Kennedy to send U.S. Marshals.
September, 1961	The Interstate Commerce Commission issued a regulation prohibiting segregation on interstate buses and in terminal facilities.
1961	Freedom Riders arrested in Jackson, Mississippi.
1962	A bus boycott started in Macon, Georgia.
July, 1962	Dr. King was arrested in Albany, Georgia, for a second consecutive year.
1962	Two churches burned near Sasser, Georgia.

September, 1962	Two youths in voter registration drive are wounded by shotgun blasts fired from a home in Rudeville, Mississippi.
Sept. 10, 1962	Black Air Force veteran, James H. Meredith, ordered admitted to the University of Mississippi by the Supreme Court.
Sept. 13, 1962	Governor Ross Barnett defied the federal government claiming interposition of state authority between federal judges and state university. President John F. Kennedy denounces the burning of churches in Georgia and supports voter registration drives.
Sept. 25, 1962	Governor Ross Barnett personally denies James Meredith's admission and the eighth black church in two months is burned in Georgia.
Sept. 26, 1962	Lt. Gov. Paul Johnson and state patrolman deny Meredith admission to campus.
Sept. 27-28, 1962	Gov. Barnett and Lt. Gov. Johnson found guilty of contempt by U.S. Court of Appeals.
Sept. 30, 1962	A large force of federal marshals escort Meredith to campus.
Oct. 1, 1962	12,000 federal soldiers restore order at the University of Mississippi.
November, 1962	Five blacks elected to the U.S. Congress.
April, 1963	Dr. King is arrested in anti-segregation demonstration in Birmingham, Alabama.
June, 1963	Medgar Evers, field secretary of the NAACP, is assassinated in front of his home in Jackson, Mississippi.
June, 1963	President Kennedy tells the nation that segregation is morally wrong.
Aug., 1963	More than 250,000 people participate in the March on Washington, where Dr. King gives his "I Have a Dream" speech.
November. 22, 1963	President John F. Kennedy is assassinated in Dallas, Texas.[13]

opposed by powerful majorities in states, and as illustrated in the 1883 decision, can never be considered permanent nor taken for granted.

Frustration with working within the system for slow and costly gains led to a disenchantment among young African-Americans in the late 1960s. This era, punctuated by the Watts Riot of 1965 and the assassination of Dr. King, ushered in the Black Power movement and more aggressive leaders such as Malcolm X, Stokely Carmichael, H. Rap Brown, and the Black Panther Party, led by Huey Newton and Bobby Seale. No group, however, was able to unify the African-American Community as effectively as Dr. Martin Luther King, Jr., or plan strategy as effectively as the NAACP. This movement also lost the battle of public opinion, always a mistake for a movement which is dependent upon legislative enactment. Coalition politics is a must for any minority group to be effective in the legislative branch.

The more recent struggle for economic equality has involved controversy concerning affirmative action. We will discuss this in a later section of this chapter as it impacts minority groups and women.

MEXICAN-AMERICANS IN THE SOUTHWEST
Early Texas

The history of Mexican-Americans in the southwestern United States has been one of displacement and exploitation as a result of military conquests. When Mexico, two years before independence from Spain, opened Texas to settlement by foreigners in 1819, it opened the door to Anglo settlers from the southern states. In 1827, Mexico outlawed slavery.

The abolition of slavery combined with already simmering stress, seasoned with Anglo feelings of superiority and anger over the requirement to pledge allegiance to Mexico and adopt Catholicism, fueled the Texas revolt of 1835–1836. The Republic of Texas was never recognized by Mexico. The U.S., however, did recognize the Republic of Texas. When in 1845, Texas joined the U.S., the stage was set for a war within Mexico which lasted from 1846–1848. At the end of this war, Mexico had lost over half of its territory. The U.S. added one-third to its territory including the present states of Arizona, California, Colorado, New Mexico, Texas, Nevada, Utah, and portions of Kansas, Oklahoma, and Wyoming.

In store for Mexican-Americans was a status change from citizens of Mexico to a colonized people. Through various mechanisms, including robbery, litigation, intimidation, fraud, and force, much of the economic wealth of the Mexican-American landowners was acquired by Anglo settlers.[14] By the end of the 1800s, Mexican-Americans were increasingly relegated to the lower echelon of society. The merger of ethnicity and social class made them a mobile labor force in many areas.

Push for Acceptance

The battle of Mexican-Americans was, however, more than an economic one. In this century, the battle has centered on being accepted as first-class citizens. The League of United Latin American Citizens (LULAC) was formed in 1929 with this as one goal. A vivid illustration occurred in 1948 when an attempt to bury a Mexican-American war hero in a local whites-only cemetery was refused by local officials in Corpus Christi, Texas.

This was the catalyst for the creation of the American G.I. Forum. In 1959, the Mexican-American Political Association was formed with the goal of "the social, economic, cultural and civic betterment of Mexican-Americans and all other Spanish-speaking Americans through political action." Organizations such as LULAC and the G.I. Forum proceeded through the 1950s and 1960s with political activism based on assimilation and working within the system.

The 1960s saw the emergence of a new Hispanic leader with the charisma to achieve national attention. Cesar Chavez, a labor union organizer and spokesman for the poor, became a nationally recognized advocate for justice after organizing California grape pickers in 1962, forming the National Farm Workers Association (NFWA). He led many protests including celebrated ones against California table-grape growers and lettuce growers to oppose the working conditions and wages of farm workers. The organization he founded merged with others, eventually becoming the United Farm Workers of America (UFWA) in 1973. Chavez stressed nonviolence and became an icon of the 1960s methods of protests, including hunger strikes, as tools to focus attention to his cause.

By the 1970s, a more activist group of young people beginning the "Chicano" movement began to emerge. More radical and activist than their predecessors, these groups often emphasized the distinctiveness of their culture rather than assimilating. These groups and movements include:

- El Partido de La Raza Unida, a political party founded in Texas by Jose Angel Gutierrez and others which was successful in taking over several south Texas county and city governments
- The Mexican-American Youth Organization, which was the beginning for Gutierrez
- The United Mexican-American Students
- Chicano Youth Organization

- El Movimiento Estudiantil Chicano de Aztlan, a campus-based movement active in the Farm Workers Movement

On the professional front, organizations starting to gain influence in the 1970s included Southwest Council de la Raza and the Mexican-American Legal Defense and Educational Fund. In recent years, the battle has been fought in the areas of affirmative action. As in the case of African-Americans, Mexican-Americans have also experienced persistent covert discrimination.

One uplifting outlook, however, for Mexican-Americans is that Hispanics now constitute the largest minority group in the United States and over 60 percent are likely to be Mexican-Americans. Also, due to the population density of Hispanics in states with fast-growing populations such as Arizona, California, Florida, and Texas, Hispanics will likely gain political power in the national arena, including seats in the U.S. Congress, electoral votes, and increased power in state legislatures. This opens a variety of possibilities for political empowerment of Hispanics in general and Mexican-Americans in particular in the southwestern United States. The result may be increased political power in the legislative and executive branches of these states and in the U.S. Congress.

The political parties have made efforts to openly court this population in recent years. In the courts, affirmative action has been under continual attack at a time when educational and professional opportunities for Mexican-Americans in the southwest have been increasing. An ironic turn of events found former Texas Attorney General Dan Morales interpreting a 1996 affirmative action ruling as requiring the dismantling of affirmative action programs at all Texas state colleges and universities. His opinion was later determined to be erroneous. This highlights the potential power of Mexican-Americans in Texas and at the same time the vulnerability of the gains made in the 1970s (a reduction in the number of Mexican-American students at the state's flagship universities).[15]

THE STRUGGLE OF WOMEN

Women in the 1830s organized around the issue of moral reform, concentrating efforts on anti-prostitution politics. The American Female Moral Reform Society grew throughout New York, New England, and the mid-Atlantic states in the 1830s and 1840s. Its goal was to reform sexual morality and to regulate sexual behavior in their communities. They sought to expose licentious men and protect seduced women and reformed prostitutes.

They also attacked the double standard applied to men and prostitutes. In the 1830s and 1840s, the number of chapters of the national reform association grew to more than 400. However, these groups perpetuated the female stereotypes of innate purity, domestic virtue, and maternal priorities.[16]

The Abolitionists' Movement and Women

In 1840, at the World Anti-Slavery Convention, Lucretia Mott, and Elizabeth Cady Stanton devised a plan for a woman's rights convention. In 1848, Elizabeth Cady Stanton helped organize the first woman's rights convention in Seneca Falls, New York. It convened that July. Approximately one-fourth of the signers of the Declaration of Sentiments, which would be drafted at the meeting, were members of the Society of Friends. Among the signers was Frederick Douglass.

Also prominent in the organization of the meeting were leading Quaker spokeswoman Lucretia Mott's fellow Quakers Mary Ann McClintock, Jane Hunt, and Martha Wright. Quakers were at the forefront of both the abolitionist and the early feminist movements, proclaiming equality before God and rejecting separate spheres of activity for females. Instead, their minimalist lifestyles and work on family farms emphasized visible female participation. Participants at the Seneca Falls Convention also included Amy Post, Mary Hallowell, Sarah Fish, and Sarah C. Owen. Amy Post and Sarah C. Owen later organized a Working Woman's Protective Union.[17]

On August 2, 1848, the Rochester Woman's Rights Convention, presided over by Abigail Bush, convened. Elizabeth Cady Stanton and Lucretia Mott thought it dangerous to have a female president and spoke out against it. After the Rochester Convention, the Working Woman's Protective Union proclaimed women's right to equal products of their labor or its equivalent (equal pay). This was considered a great departure from the separate-sphere ideology concerning a woman's role in society. The Rochester Convention demanded a broad spectrum of rights, including the right to vote and familial and economic rights.

Suffrage

In May, 1869, at the third annual meeting of the American Equal Rights Association (AERA), Elizabeth Cady Stanton, Susan B. Anthony, and Virginia Minor refused to support the endorsement of the Fifteenth Amendment. Lucy Stone, who later organized the American Woman's Suffrage Association, supported the endorsement, though she did not yield in her drive for woman's suffrage.[18]

The National Woman Suffrage Association (NWSA), which was aligned with Stanton, Anthony and AWSA, would later differ on several issues, including how to obtain the right to vote. For example, the NWSA sought litigation as a means; the AWSA thought this method foolhardy. The AWSA also focused on suffrage and not on broader issues. The NWSA, in the summer of 1869, took steps, after being unsuccessful in the legislative branch, at changing the law regarding the ballot, and used the courts to obtain suffrage rights. A call for action was made in *The Revolution*, a woman's rights publication by Susan B. Anthony and Elizabeth Cady Stanton to seek to obtain, through litigation, a single case construing the parameters of the Fourteenth Amendment so that the issue of woman's suffrage could be placed at the forefront of the political arena. Though it failed, this attempt energized the NWSA. The strategy of NWSA was based on Francis Minor's (Virginia's husband) interpretation of the Fourteenth Amendment that it had in fact enfranchised women.

The NWSA pursued litigation from 1869–1875. After the Supreme Court interpreted Minor's argument unfavorably in three civil rights cases, litigation was dropped as a strategy. Again, even though unsuccessful, it charged the interest of woman's suffragists. In 1890, NWSA merged with AWSA and formed the National American Woman Suffrage Association (NAWSA). The pursuit of the right to vote would continue until 1920 when the ratification of the 19th Amendment granted women the right to vote. The potential of women to use the executive and legislative branches changed forever. Today, only the most inept of politicians would ignore the enormous voting power of women.

Women and Labor

During and after the Great Depression, women witnessed the enactment of the 1933 National Industrial Recovery Act, which sanctioned lower pay for women and excluded domestic and agricultural jobs (both heavily women and ethnic minority). Section 213 of the Economy Act of 1932 allowed the government to fire one spouse if the other worked for the government. This reflected the unanimously accepted myth that working married women were responsible for unemployment. Of the 1,500 persons fired the following year, nearly all were women.[19]

The president of the California Institute of Technology proposed that 75 percent of jobs be reserved for men during this era. New England Telephone and Telegraph fired all its married women workers in 1931. The general view of women was that they would work until married and then go home. By definition, they were young "working girls" and by definition unmarried.

Over the years of the Industrial Revolution, especially from the 1890s to the 1930s, women's attempts to organize were stifled not only by corporate America and public opinion but by the unions themselves. Union leaders had sexist views and were suspicious that women would take jobs from men. In the 1930s, the Congress of Industrial Organization (CIO) was more receptive to women than the American Federation of Labor (AFL). Women, however, usually joined only in industries with large numbers of women or when they organized themselves. Four hundred black women stemmers in Richmond, Virginia, tobacco factories who walked out in a 1937 spontaneous strike, employed self-organization.

These women were told by the AFL that black workers could not be organized. The Southern Negro Youth Congress and the National Negro Congress stepped in to help form the Tobacco Stemmers and Laborers Union. This and other examples led to a view of the early unions as a mixed blessing for women. They, on the one hand, brought higher wages, but on the other, often excluded women and sought to maintain separate sexual roles in the workforce.

The Courts in Women's Struggles

In recent years we have seen a replay of women's early struggles. Like earlier attempts at litigation in attempts to obtain the right to vote which followed unsuccessful legislative attempts, modern women's rights leaders turned to litigation following defeats in the legislative branch. The defeats included the failure to ratify the Equal Rights Amendment. In 1966, the National Organization for Women (NOW) founded by Betty Freidan, began to move toward litigation. In 1971, the NOW formally incorporated its legal arm, modeled after the NAACP Legal Defense and Education Fund.

A big difference, however, was that the NAACP Legal Defense and Education Fund was a functioning law office with salaried attorneys who used volunteers for assistance in cases but directed much of the litigation internally.[20] The NOW had to rely upon volunteers. This proved to be problematic. Much of the NOW's participation in the legal fight consisted of preparing *amicus curiae* briefs in cases before federal courts. Unlike the Supreme Court of the 1800s, however, the courts did provide a few victories for women this time.

Some examples of litigated cases involving women's rights include:

- *Roe v. Wade* 410 U S 113 (1973), holding illegal Texas and Georgia laws prohibiting abortion during the first two trimesters.

- *Frontiero v. Richardson* 441 U S 677 (1973), holding it unconstitutional to require married female service people to prove their husband's dependency.

The battle since the 1980s for women as well as ethnic minorities, however, has focused on affirmative action and attempts to maintain prior gains in the area of protection from discrimination. This area was targeted by the Reagan Administration for dismantling in a sweeping effort including selection of federal judges for appointment, legislation, and a barrage of interest group sponsored lawsuits attacking affirmative action programs. The Clinton Administration attempted to preserve some of these programs with its "mend it but don't end it" policies.

PERILS OF PROGRESS

In our more recent history the attempts to attack discrimination based on race, religion, national origin, sex, and disability have become more difficult and controversial for a number of reasons. First, discrimination is more latent than patent today. A camera would have been all that was needed to show discrimination in the 1950s and the 1960s. Signs abounded with phrases such as "whites only" and "colored only"; state laws and municipal ordinances showed open and notorious discrimination and segregation. Today, almost no one would admit discriminatory intent in their actions.

Second, rather than a tight focus on specific types of discrimination, we have tried "one size fits all" legislation, seeking to eliminate all types of discrimination against all persons. In other words, we are not focusing on registering black voters in the South or on suffrage for women. Today's laws are attempts at outlawing discrimination against everyone.

Third, progress is far more visible today than ever before. Many white male executives, for instance, work with female, African-American, Hispanic, and Asian-American executives who make roughly the same amount of money and have the same education. These are often the only persons of minority groups these white males come in contact with on a regular basis. It is easy to see why they begin to feel that we have done enough. In this limited view of the minority world, we have seen great progress. Many do not come into contact with the majority of persons from these groups who do not fully participate in the "American Dream." Perhaps even some minorities in this group do not come into contact with them. Unfortunately, in the world of the vast majority of those in the under-classes of these minority groups, affirmative action has yet to arrive and fair treatment and equal opportunity are mere pipe dreams.

AFFIRMATIVE ACTION

One of the more interesting and controversial areas of modern civil rights involves the broad category called affirmative action. In this approach, government has tried to remedy a history of past discrimination and the lingering and present effects thereof by the use of various programs to increase the participation of women and minority groups in various activities. Since the 1978 *Bakke* decision, the attack against these programs has been relentless. This has resulted in the erosion of many of the gains for which these programs were a catalyst.

Many ask the question, "How long must these programs be used?" in view of the fact that we have attempted these remedies since the late 1960s. This however, fails to recognize that these programs have not been allowed to operate freely or in a

A Segregated Drinking Fountain.

© Hulton-Deutsch Collection/CORBIS

vacuum. Instead, they have been involved in defending their provisions in litigation dating back to a decade after the birth of these programs. Fairness also demands that one consider what those who reside in our cities' most blighted areas think when such questions are asked.

These persons have yet to see any meaningful effects of affirmative action on deprived street corners in the hearts of many inner cities. Many look at school districts, which have once again been segregated. When they hear people ask "Haven't we done enough?" they could very legitimately ask: "What have you done in my community?" Even though gains have continued to be made by the informed and educated upper-middle class minority communities in many areas, those in the blighted inner city areas have seen conditions worsen.

Two key types of affirmative action cases dominate litigation in the area. The two types of cases are in the areas of commercial/business and education.

COMMERCIAL/BUSINESS

A key case involving commercial/business affirmative action is in *Adarand v. Pena* (1995). This case involves a claim that the governmental practice of giving general contractors a financial incentive to hire "socially and economically disadvantaged individuals" as subcontractors, and the use of race-based presumptions to determine disadvantage, violates the Fifth Amendment's due process clause. Adarand was a Colorado-based company submitting the low bid on a guardrail portion of a contract granted to Mountain Gravel and Construction Company.

In spite of the low bid, Mountain Gravel awarded the contract to Gonzales Construction Company. Mountain Gravel's chief estimator submitted an affidavit stating that had it not been for an additional payment received because of hiring Gonzales, a "socially and economically disadvantaged" company, that Adarand would have been hired. At issue was whether disadvantaged business rules which have a presumption that Black, Native, Asian, Pacific American, and Hispanics and others are "socially and economically disadvantaged," violate the Fifth Amendment's due process clause. Individuals who were not in certain classes had to show, by clear and convincing evidence, that they were economically and socially disadvantaged, based upon certain criteria.

The contract involved in this case was impacted by separate provision—adding women presumptively to the "socially and economically" disadvantaged definition. In that provision, others also had to prove their disadvantage. The Gonzales Company was "certified" as a Disadvantaged Business Enterprise while Adarand was not.

The court ruled in favor of Adarand, holding that all racial classifications imposed by whatever federal, state, or local governmental action must be analyzed by a reviewing court under strict scrutiny. In other words, such classifications are constitutional only if they are narrowly tailored measures that further compel governmental interests. In the opinion, the court also traced a long line of cases regarding classification based on race. It relied on these precedents in reaching its decision. Included in that discussion were historical cases on race, such as:

- *Gibson v. Mississippi* 162 U. S. 565, 591 (1896) in which the Supreme Court held that the federal government and states, where civil or political rights are concerned, are not allowed to discriminate against a citizen because of his race.
- *Koramatsu v. U.S.* 323 U. S. 214 (1944) in which the Court approved violations of the rights of Japanese citizens in wartime based upon a theory of compelling governmental interest. In *Adarand*, the Court pointed to paranoia, prejudice, and racism as the real reasons for the decision in this case.

The Court also discussed the more modern history of its holdings regarding affirmative action as a remedy, including:

- *Regents of University of California v. Bakke* 438 U. S. 265 (1978) discussed later under educational cases.
- *Fullilove v. Klutznick* 448 U. S. (1980) which set up a two-part test for racial classification:
    1) Are the objectives within the power of Congress?
    2) Whether limited use of racial and ethnic criteria as used are constitutionally permissible. In other words, is a compelling governmental interest involved?
- *Wygant v. Jackson* 476 U. S. 267 (1986) involving race used in layoff determinations by a school board which held that providing minority students with role models was not sufficient to justify use of racial classifications.
- *Richmond v. J. A. Croson Co.* 488 U. S. 469 (1989) which held that there should be a single standard of review for racial classifications—one of strict scrutiny. States or local governments using racial classifications have the

authority to eradicate the effects of private discrimination within their legislative jurisdiction, but must have a strong basis as evidence for their conclusion that remedial action is necessary. The Court added that the remedy must be narrowly tailored to remedy the effects of prior discrimination.

From recent decisions, it appears that an ever-increasing standard is required for legislative attempts at remedies which attempt to overcome past discrimination. It seems clear from these decisions that any remedy must be related to documented past or present effects of discrimination and must be narrowly tailored to meet a specific and proper governmental purpose.

EDUCATION CASES

Perhaps the most durable case in the educational area, prior to the Supreme Court's ruling in *Grutter v. Bollinger et. al.* (which was decided June 23, 2003), has been the *Regents of Univ. of Cal. v. Bakke*, case 438 U.S. 265 in (1978). In this case, the Supreme Court reviewed a medical school's set-aside program that reserved 16 out of 100 seats for members of certain minority groups. The six separate opinions in this case led to a plethora of litigation in subsequent years. Increased litigation often follows when a decision is not by a clear majority but involves controversial issues. Justice Powell, the fifth vote, announced the judgment, which invalidated the program, but also reversed a state court's injunction against any use of race whatsoever.

In Justice Powell's view, the only interest asserted by the university that survived scrutiny was the interest in attaining a diverse student body. He stated that academic freedom has long been viewed as a special concern of the First Amendment; and that states' interest is not an interest in simple ethnic diversity. Rather, "the diversity in which the state has a compelling interest encompasses a far broader array of qualifications and characteristics of which racial or ethnic origin is but a single though important element."

Thereafter, universities across the country modeled their affirmative action programs after the Bakke standard. The barrage of litigation centered on whether Powell's diversity rationale was binding as precedent.

One of many cases challenging admissions policies appeared to end affirmative action in Texas' state universities and in the jurisdiction of the Court of Appeals for the Fifth Circuit (Texas, Louisiana, and Mississippi). The case was *Hopwood, et. al. v. State of Texas*, 78 F 3d 932 (5th Cir. 1996) cert. den. 518 U.S. 1033, 116 S. Ct.

2581.[21] At issue was the University of Texas Law School. In the Hopwood case, non-minority applicants challenged the admissions policy of the law school, which used race as one of its factors.

They asserted that such a policy violated the Fourteenth Amendment. The U.T. Law School is very competitive, ranked seventeenth nationally at that time by *U.S. News and World Report*, March 20 1995. The use of the affirmative action program produced the following statistics for the class of 1992 regarding overall grade point average and L.S.A.T. (a standardized law school admissions test) results.

	MEDIAN GPA/LSAT	
	RESIDENT STUDENTS	NON RESIDENT STUDENTS
White	3.56/164	3.72/166
Black	3.30/158	3.30/156
Mexican-American	3.24/157	3.38/174

Source: *Hopwood et al. v. State of Texas*, 1996.

In this case, the school admitted that the admissions process for Mexican-American and African-American students differed from the process for other students.

The U.S. Court of Appeals for the Fifth Circuit ruling left us with these rules:

- That the admissions policy did violate the Fourteenth Amendment;
- That discrimination based upon race is highly suspect under the equal protection clause;
- Courts are to employ strict scrutiny when evaluation all racial classifications.
- To justify an affirmative action program, a state must show present effects of past discrimination.

Using the strict-scrutiny analysis under the equal protection clause, a court asks whether the racial classification serves a compelling governmental interest, and whether it is narrowly tailored to the achievement of that goal.

Texas Attorney General Dan Morales interpreted *Hopwood* to prohibit affirmative action at all institutions, which also extended to grants. The next Texas Attorney General, John Cornyn, did not maintain this interpretation.

This case left us with the question: How much of a difference must there be in the performance of minorities in order for the state to have a compelling interest in maintaining an affirmative action admissions policy?

In 2003, the Supreme Court heard two cases decided on the same date involving the University of Michigan. One case *Gratz v. Bollinger* (02-516) Rev. in Part and Remanded,[22] involved the undergraduate freshman admissions program which automatically awarded 20 points of 100 needed to guarantee admission to persons in underrepresented minority groups. This program was held to be in violation of the Equal Protection Clause, Title VI and 42 USC Section 1981.

The Court, in referring to *Bakke* principles, called for particularized review of individual applications. Though it is not unconstitutional for race or ethnic background to be used as a plus factor in a particular applicants file, in this case, the program was not narrowly tailored to achieve a compelling interest in diversity and was a virtual quota system. It was therefore held unconstitutional.

The other case involved the University of Michigan Law School: *Grutter v. Bollinger et al.* 288 F. 3d 732, (affirmed, June 23, 2003).[23] In this case, the Supreme Court held that in the context of university admission, student body diversity is a compelling state interest opinion.

Thus, the Court endorsed Justice Powell's view on this issue from the *Bakke* decision. The Court noted that the law school's claim was bolstered by numerous expert studies and reports showing that such diversity promotes learning outcomes and better prepares students for an increasingly diverse workforce. The Court also cited assertions by major American businesses that today's marketplace requires exposure to widely diverse people, cultures, ideas and viewpoints. The Court also pointed out that high ranking retired officers and civilian military leaders had asserted that a highly qualified, racially diverse officer corps was essential to national security.

Perhaps most significant in informing future decisions was the holding that the law school's admissions program was narrowly tailored, and "flexible enough to consider all pertinent elements of diversity in light of particular qualifications of each applicant. The indication that per *Bakke* this program provided for a highly individualized, holistic review of each applicants file was instructive." The Court also pointed out that it is necessary that the school not make race or ethnicity the defining feature of the application. The Court, to this end, pointed out that this law school frequently accepts non-minority applicants with grades and test scores lower than underrepresented minority applicants (and other non-minority applicants) who are rejected.

The Supreme Court leaves us with the following rules for now:

- Narrow tailoring does not require the exhaustion of every conceivable race-neutral alternative.
- Race-conscious admissions policies must be limited in time. In her opinion, Justice O'Connor noted that 25 years from now, the use of racial preferences will no longer be necessary.
- The law school's use of race in admission decisions in this case was not prohibited by the equal protection Clause, Title VI or Section 1981.

SUMMARY

Classifications of groups of people by government for disparate treatment must be reasonable and based upon legitimate and sufficient governmental interests. Classifications based upon race, gender, religion, national origin, etc., are subjected to close or strict judicial scrutiny by the federal courts.

The Supreme Court has played a changing role over the years. The role has varied from protecting the powerful to protecting the oppressed or the weak. Much depends upon who sits on the Supreme Court at the time.

African-Americans have had a long, controversial, and intensely opposed fight for civil rights. This struggle dates back to 1619. Most of the victories of this group have been costly and many have been temporary. The major victories of the modern civil rights movement for African-Americans came during the convergence of several factors: The NAACP Legal Defense and Education Fund litigation strategy, the Warren Supreme Court, the civil rights movement, and the emergence of Dr. Martin Luther King, Jr., as the voice of the civil rights movement.

Mexican-Americans in the Southwest have been subjects of military conquests and various forms of exploitation since the 1800s. The battle for acceptance was led by LULAC and the American G. I. Forum for the first two-thirds of the 20th century. The 1970s brought a new approach among groups which emphasized the uniqueness of the culture of "Chicanos." This more aggressive approach led to the formation of a political party and campus based movements. The outlook for Hispanics, especially Mexican-Americans, is one of increased political power. As the largest minority group in the country, Hispanics have become a focus of both political parties.

Women began to question their role in American society in the 1830s. By 1848, the Woman's Rights Convention was held in Seneca Falls, New York. The woman's movement of the 1860s was focused upon the right to vote. Early tactics included attempts at legislation and litigation. Early courts were not protective of women's rights. In modern times, women have had a few legal victories and increased political power. Today, women have held most offices from the Senate down to city councilpersons.

The new civil rights debate centers around affirmative action. The progress of some minorities and women has fueled a feeling among many that the government has done enough. The more conservative climate of the 1980s brought numerous appointments of conservative jurists to the federal courts including the Supreme Court. This situation has operated to cause a chilling effect upon the willingness of minorities to seek help from the federal courts in civil rights cases. In light of the recent Michigan cases, we for now have a better map for designing affirmative action measures.

KEY TERMS

- Affirmative action
- American Equal Rights Association
- American Female Moral Reform Society
- Black codes
- League of United Latin American Citizens
- National Association for the Advancement of Colored People
- National Farm Workers Association
- National Organization for Women
- National Women Suffrage Association
- Progressive Voters' League
- Reconstruction acts
- Southern Christian Leadership Conference
- Student NonViolent Coordinating Committee
- Suffrage
- Suspect classification
- Suspect criteria
- United Farm Workers of America

INTERNET SOURCES

1. African-American Civil Rights Struggles
   a) http://www.lcweb.loc.gov/exhibits/african/intro.html
   This site is maintained by the Library of Congress and provides historical and contemporary documentation, and other pertinent information on African-American civil rights struggles.
   b) http://www.afroam.org/history/history.html
   Maintained by the Afro-America's Black History Museum, this site provides documents on the history of civil rights from the past to contemporary times.
2. Women's Equal Rights Struggles
   a) http://frank.mtsu.edu/~kmiddlet/history/women.html
   The history of women's struggles for equal rights is documented in this site. Information is given on voting rights, important names associated with women's political movement, legal assistance, office locations in different parts of the country, legislation, laws, etc.
3. Ethnic Groups Equal Rights Struggles
   a) http://www.chci.org
   Hispanic civil rights struggles are the main focus of this site. It gives historical information on the nature of this struggle, legal assistance to undocumented aliens, immigration education, voting rights, court cases, etc.
   b) http://www.lib.uconn.edu/NativeTech/links/general.html
   This site is similar to 3a) but caters mainly to the issues of civil rights relative to Native Americans.

NOTES

[1] Christopher E. Smith, *Courts Politics and the Judicial Process* (Nelson Hall Publishers, 1997).
[2] *Dred Scott v. Sandford*, 19 Howard 393 (1857).
[3] Ira J. Hadnot, Interview Cornell West, *Dallas Morning News*, 11 October 1998, 1.
[4] Lerone Bennett Jr., *Before the Mayflower* (New York: Penguin Books), 29–35.
[5] *Batson v. Kentucky*, 475 U.S. 79 (1986).
[6] United States Constitution, Article I, Section 9.
[7] Bennett, 34.
[8] Civil Rights Cases, 109 U.S. 3 (1883).
[9] Missouri ex rel Gaines, 305 U.S. 337 (1938).
[10] *Sipuel v. Oklahoma State Board of Regents* 332 U.S. 631 (1948).
[11] *Sweatt v. Painter and McLaurin v. Oklahoma State Regents* 339 U.S. 629 (1950).
[12] *Brown v. Board of Topeka, Kansas* 349 U.S.294 (1954).
[13] Bennett, 553–570.

[14] *Chicanos in the United States: A History of Exploitation and Resistance; Leobardo F. Estrada et al., Latinos and the Political System*, ed. F. Chris Garcia (Notre Dame, Indiana: University of Notre Dame Press, 1988).

[15] Jayne Noble Suhler, "College Minority Enrollment Rises," *Dallas Morning News*, 23 October 1998, 1.

[16] Mary P. Ryan, "The Power of Women's Networks," *U.S. Women in Struggle, A Feminist Studies Antholoogy*, ed. Claire Goldberg Moses and Heidi Hartmann (Chicago: University of Illinois Press, 1995) [this article was reprinted with changes and originally published in *Feminist Studies* 5 no. 1, Spring 1979, 66–85].

[17] Nancy A. Hewitt, "Feminist Friends," *U.S. Women in Strugle, A Feminist Anthology*, ed. Claire Goldberg Moses and Heidi Hartmann (Chicago: University of Illinois Press, 1995) [this article was reprinted with changes and originally published in *Feminist Studies* 12 no. 1, Spring 1986, 27–49].

[18] Karen O'Connor, *Women's Organizations' Use of the Courts*, (Lexington, MA: D. C. Heath and Company).

[19] Sharon Hartman Strom, "Challenging 'Women's Place': Feminism, the Left and Industrial Unionism in the 1930's," *U.S. Women in Struggle, A Feminist Studies Anthology*, ed. Claire Goldberg Moses and Heidi Hartmann (Chicago: University of Illinois Press, 1995) [this article was reprinted with changes from *Feminist Studies* 9 no. 2, Summer 1983, 359–386].

[20] O'Connor.

[21] *Hopwood et al. v. State of Texas et al.* 78 F 3d 932 (5th Cir. 1996) cert. den. 518 U.S. 1033, 116 S. Ct. 2581.

[22] *Gratz v. Bollinger et. al.* (02-516) (on cert. from 6th Cir. 2003) rev. in part and remanded.

[23] *Grutter v. Bolinger et. al.*(02-241) 288 F.3d 732 (affirmed June 23, 2003) .

Chapter 13
Public Policy

However beautiful the strategy, you should occasionally look at the results.

—*Winston Churchill*

INTRODUCTION

The study of public policy entails an understanding of the processes and institutions of government. As a separate field of study within the discipline of political science, public policy analysis examines the dynamics and forces that create our complex system of laws and rules. If we are to fully understand the "how" and "why" of government, we must expand our scope of study beyond the institutions that comprise our system. Public policy analysis does just that—it examines how and why our political behavior is the way it is. The study of policy requires a scientific approach (polls, surveys, measurements, etc.) that marries a pragmatic approach (defining the issues and resolving conflict). The result of good science and sound reasoning is what policy analysts seek.

Our laws and policies do not simply "happen." Rather, they evolve from ideas and notions to practice. Political scientists have devised several models to help explain the workings of public policy in the United States. The most widely held model asserts that public policy goes through five stages: agenda setting, formulation, adoption, implementation, and evaluation. Policies evolve and take form at each stage of the process. Moreover, we see the dynamics that exist in each of these stages, among competing groups, benefactors, and even among the government institutions that shape and implement these policies.

There are dozens of policy arenas found within the framework of government, some of which we will visit in the second part of this chapter. Within each policy arena, policy analysts seek to answer questions such as: How do problems and issues attract the attention of law makers? Why are some issues addressed while others seem to be ignored? How and when are policy alternatives considered? How do we measure the effect of public policies and by what process do we modify them?

PUBLIC POLICY

Public policy can be described as any course of action taken by the government that affects any segment of the public. It takes its form in laws, statutes, regulation, rules, and legislation. Although it is the legislative branch that is formally charged with "making the laws," public policy is created by all three branches of government. The executive branch, through executive orders and policy initiatives, creates public policy, often without the input—or the approval—of the legislative branch. The courts, through judicial review and precedence, establish policies that affect all Americans.

Public policy reflects the very essence of government because it is made at all levels of government. The federal government regulates foreign trade and domestic spending. State governments create public policies such as speed limits and motorcycle helmet laws. Local government, county commissioners' courts, city councils, and school districts make public policy by determining how land will be used, what hours public libraries will operate, and how many students will be allowed to enroll in a particular class.

The study of public policy analysis represents an entire sub-field of political science. Rather than placing the emphasis of their focus on particular institutions of government, public policy analysts probe the dynamics of interaction among the institutions and between the institutions and the public. Like politics, policy analysis is the study of power, distribution and outcome. Public policy often involves taking into consideration various choices available to solve a problem or issue, and the final product—the policy—represents a compromise among competing interests.

STAGES OF PUBLIC POLICY

Political scientists have established that public policy is a five-step process before an idea becomes an actual public policy. They have labeled each of these stages in order to better understand and analyze public policy. Moreover, an understanding of public policy is necessary in order to fully appreciate the nature of fiscal policy. Public policies evolve through these five stages: agenda setting, formulation, adoption, implementation, and evaluation.

Agenda Setting

Before any government agency initiates action, the need for such action must be recognized. During the agenda setting stage, the matter is brought to the attention of the government and a resolution is sought. Questions such as what makes the issue a public one are examined. The acquired immune deficiency syndrome (AIDS) crisis created public awareness and concern, especially when celebrities spoke out for the need of increased awareness and government-funded research. These actions resulted in greater government participation in the fight against AIDS. Sometimes, a single event can place an issue on the government's agenda. For example, in 1995, the Texas Legislature passed a series of bills known as the "Ashley Laws," which made it tougher for criminals convicted of sex crimes to be released on early parole. The Ashley Laws were a direct response to the 1994 abduction, sexual assault, and murder of a Plano, Texas, girl named Ashley Estelle by a parolee. Texans became outraged upon learning of this horrific crime, and many of them called, wrote, faxed and sent e-mail to their state legislators demanding that government implement safeguards in order to prevent recurrence of event. The result was the Ashley Laws and other public policies that deal more severely with child abductors.

The agenda setting stage is important not only to those who wish to create new policies. It is during this stage that opponents of governmental action become involved as well. If an individual, corporation or interest group opposes governmental intervention in a particular area, it will attempt to abort the policy process at this stage. Sometimes, these groups are successful, at least in the short-term. For example, the Texas Legislature, for years, had been considering adopting a right-to-carry (handgun) law, and although public opinion polls indicated that many Texans were in favor of such legislation, various law enforcement and other groups managed to keep the issue off the agenda. Many proponents of the handgun bill echoed the sentiment: "Doing nothing is a policy in itself."

Further evidence of the dynamics in the agenda setting stage occurred in 2005 when the U.S. Supreme Court ruled against the execution of minors who committed capital crimes while under 18 years of age. Prior to this ruling, about 20 states defined "juvenile" as a person younger than 17 years of age, meaning that as far as the criminal justice system is concerned, a 17-year-old was considered an adult and subject to the same punishments as a 40-year-old. Oklahoma, Virginia, and Texas, allowed 17-year-olds to be sentenced to death. Anti-capital punishment groups fought hard to get this issue on the public agenda, and their cause was struck down year after year in the legislative process. It became increasingly clear that the state lawmakers were not inclined to support raising the age when one becomes eligible for execution. The United States Supreme Court, in a 5–4 decision, declared in essence that juveniles could not be executed and defined juvenile as persons younger than 18 years of age. For many observers, this was regarded as an unlikely outcome because 16 years earlier, the same court upheld the execution of 17-year-olds.

Formulation

After a problem has been recognized and defined, the next step is deciding what will be done about it and who will do it. In the formulation stage, options are explored. Policy makers in this stage may decide that a new public policy is needed or that an existing one can be modified to address the issue in question. The level and degree to which the government will become involved is also established during this stage. For example, after the legislature passed the right-to-carry bill, the Texas Department of Public Safety was charged with formulating a policy to ensure that each of the bill's provisions (training, licensing, etc.) was met.

Formulation of public policy is made in all three branches of government. Most often, a legislative body such as Congress or city councils determines it. Most bills introduced in Congress contain specific formulation guidelines. The bills spell out which governmental agencies will carry out the laws. Occasionally, new agencies are created for the purpose, as in the case of the creation of the Tennessee Valley Authority. At other times, bureaucrats in government agencies make public policy decisions. Another possibility involves major restructuring of existing government agencies, such as when the Department of Homeland Security was created. In this example, the government merged, reassigned, and in some cases, eliminated certain long-standing agencies, such as the Immigration and Naturalization Services, and created ones with more defined roles. The courts may also become involved in the formulation of public policy. For example, the Supreme Court intervened in the redistricting plans of the Georgia and North Carolina state legislatures in declaring their racially-gerrymandered districts unconstitutional.

Adoption

At this stage, a government response to an issue is legitimized. Requirements are examined. Conflicts with existing policies are considered, as are specifics regarding costs and funding. The roles of the government agency or agencies that will be responsible for carrying out the policy are defined.

During this stage of the process, the government agency or agencies responsible for the public policy look back at past policy adoptions made by other states or countries. Chances are that other governments have already adopted similar policies and we can learn from their successes and failures. As one policy analyst once noted, "There is no need to reinvent the wheel every time a new policy comes down the pike."

Local governments provide us with an excellent example of "going to school" on other governments. Thousands of municipalities throughout the United States have adopted teen-curfew ordinances. Statistical data indicating that the crimes committed against teenagers after late hours were disproportionably high, and this research propelled the need for such legislation. Most city councils, warned by the city attorneys, were apprehensive of adopting a curfew because they knew the constitutionality would be challenged and they wanted to avoid lawsuits. Dallas, Texas, and some other trailblazing cities pioneered the first teen curfews in the nation, and sure enough, the challenges ensued. After the challenges were met, nearly all the other cities surrounding these pioneer cities adopted the exact language for their own teen-curfew ordinances, and these have remained in effect for decades.

Implementation

During this stage, the policy is carried out. Timing, public education and opinion regarding the policies usually have an impact upon the success of this phase. Policy and perceived fairness are among the issues addressed during this stage of the process. It is important that the agencies responsible for implementing a public policy thoroughly understand and adhere to the letter and spirit of the law, or inconsistencies will surely develop.

The media are often involved here. When the federal or a state government implements a major new public policy, such as the lottery, most newspapers and television stations provide the public with a rundown of the rules and regulations. The heads of the state agencies often generate press releases and conduct interviews with members of the media to clarify the policy.

Sometimes, there is a "grace period" in which the public is given notice in the form of "friendly reminders" rather than formal government sanctions. For example, Maryland's "Move Over" law requiring motorists to move over one lane when an emergency vehicle is on the shoulder, was adopted virtually word-for-word by several other states.

Evaluation

In theory, all public policies are evaluated periodically to determine whether they have the desired effect on the problems they are intended to address. Problems will arise if the desired effect of a policy is not clear or the method for making these measurements is ill-conceived. Policy makers may discover that during the evaluation process the policy is in need of some change in order to be more effective, and this may necessitate going back to the first or second stage of the process.

There is often disagreement on the effectiveness of public policies. For example, both opponents and proponents of affirmative action programs cite statistics to justify their position. While one side advocates abolishing the programs, the other indicates a need for expansion.

Most often, evaluation is carried out in a superficial manner. Government tends to evaluate what is easy rather than those factors that show the effectiveness of a program. It is easier, for instance, to count the number of people with claims a government agency processes than to determine the effect that a policy has actually had. Many states have a built-in evaluation process known as the **Sunset Advisory Committees**. These committees are comprised of legislators and citizens who are responsible for evaluating the need for all existing government programs. They report their findings to the legislature for action. Although the committee does not review the specific policies that are carried out by the agencies, it does conduct a comprehensive review of the agencies themselves. The federal government does not utilize the sunset system.

PUBLIC POLICY ARENAS

Perhaps the most controversial policy arena, at least on the domestic front, is that of public assistance. Other important and controversial policy issues and debates arise from educational and environmental concerns. In this section, we will explore the complexity and implications surrounding these policy issues.

Social Security

One of the most contentious domestic issues facing government today is Social Security. It has been in the agenda stage for at least a decade, as well as a featured topic of all recent presidential debates and congressional campaigns. Many Americans, under 40 and particularly those under 30, cannot understand why the discussion on this issue is so important. They believe Social Security is not important to them because they have been told all their lives that it will not be around when they reach retirement age. Ironically, however, the younger you are the more Social Security matters to you. It is America's working class that foots the bill, and younger generations will be footing it for much longer.

In their views, President Bush and some congressional leaders maintain that nothing will change for Americans age 50 and older. Each of the policy options being discussed, including a rise in the retirement age, a reduction in benefits, a hike in payroll contributions, and means testing, affect the younger employees much more than any other group.

Today, many Americans spend as many years in retirement as they spent working. Enjoying our longevity requires a larger retirement income, and today's youngest workers are paying benefits to those who retired before these workers were even born. One in six Americans currently collects some form of Social Security benefits, and that number is constantly on the rise. From 1940, when slightly more than 222,000 people received monthly Social Security benefits, until 2005, when almost 45 million people receive such benefits, Social Security has grown steadily. Social Security benefits provide income security not just to the elderly. Nearly 1 in 3 beneficiaries is not a retiree. The program provides needed income support to over 6 million recipients, 31 percent of whom are aged individuals; 56 percent disabled adults; and 13 percent disabled children.

Social Security's financing problems are long term and will not affect today's retirees and near-retirees. However, these groups of Americans are very large and serious. People are living longer; the first baby boomers are five years from retirement; and the birth rate is low. The result is that the worker-to-beneficiary ratio has fallen from 16-to-1 in 1950 to 3.3-to-1 in 2005. According to the Social Security Administration, within 40 years it will be 2-to-1. At this ratio, there will not be enough workers to pay scheduled benefits at current tax rates.

One of the policy options under consideration is a rise in payroll taxes. But economists regard this as only a short term solution, putting off the inevitable system collapse for another generation. Another possible solution is to impose a benefit cut for those younger than 40. This is a very real possibility in light of the fact that younger people have less tendency to become active in the agenda setting and formulation stages of the process. Oftentimes, people become involved in the policy adoption stage, but it is too late. The Social Security Chief Actuary has stated that if benefits were reduced to meet the shortfall in revenue for the combined program, the reduction would be 27 percent starting with the exhaustion of the Trust Fund in 2042; and would rise to 32 percent for 2078.

Another proposal currently on the table is to establish a **"means test"** for eligibility. Under this plan, Social Security payments would be reduced for those Americans who are deemed not to need it. For example, a responsible person who saves a percentage of his income, invests wisely, and accumulates a healthy nest egg would get a reduced Social Security benefit, or maybe even none at all. Those benefits would be re-directed to individuals who have had the same opportunities to save but may not have planned for the future or who have made poor choices. To many, this proposal seems unfair.

Many Republicans wish to allow individuals the choice to privatize a portion of their Social Security taxes by allowing them to place the funds in the stock market and other investment vehicles. Generally, Democrats do not regard this as a good idea because they say such practice could lead to over-speculation. If there ever were an issue that divides Americans, it is Social Security and what to do about it.

Public Assistance

Most people would agree that government ought to provide some degree of relief to individuals and families whose access to food, shelter, health care, and other essential commodities is limited. At issue, of course, is to whom this public assistance should go and to what degree and for how long. The debate has raged for decades and indeed has intensified as the competing demands for government resources become more competitive. Some political scientists refer to these government assistance programs as "redistributive policies," while much of the public lumps these under the general heading of "welfare." One of the major sources of the controversy over public assistance policies is rooted in the actual complexity of this arena. There are dozens of separate programs, each with its own rules, formulation and sets of issues.

To further complicate matters, the scope, nature and even the names of these programs change over time. For example, in 1996, Congress eliminated Aid to Families with Dependent Children (AFDC), a program, which had been around since the New Deal era, and replaced it with a program entitled Temporary Assistance for Needy Families (TANF). The type of relief offered by the agencies remains similar, except that under the new TANF program, the states are given greater autonomy in determining eligibility requirements and maximum lifetime benefit limits.

By giving the states greater discretion in redistributing these public assistance funds, the federal government has opened up a whole new proverbial can of worms. Proponents of states' rights claim that local control is better for the taxpayers and for the recipients of the programs for two reasons. First, it allows for local control, meaning that citizens of states have a greater voice in how their tax dollars are spent by means of state and local elections. Governors and state legislatures are more closely monitored and controlled by the citizenry, and are therefore more accountable to the people. Second, the practice of the federal government providing direct payment to recipients of these programs creates a more fertile ground for mismanagement, waste, and fraud to develop. On the other hand, opponents of the new policy claim that states tend to set the eligibility requirements unreasonably high and offer benefits that are unrealistically low. They argue that state government officials, desiring to appear "tough" on welfare programs, may be more concerned with getting reelected than they are in providing fair, reasonable relief to those in need.

Similar, but no less intense, policy debates continue in virtually all other aspects of the redistributive policy arena. The **food stamp program** provides an excellent example of the controversy. Soon after the program's implementation in the 1970s, it was discovered that a very small but highly visible number of recipients were "trading" their stamps for pennies on the dollar in order to purchase alcoholic beverages or illicit drugs. To counter this fraud, some states began replacing food stamps with "credit cards," which could not be sold, traded or otherwise compromised. In Texas, the program is called the **Lone Star Card** and contains a line of "credit" which is electronically deducted from the recipient's "account" at authorized retail stores and only for authorized food products. Problems with the Lone Star Card program became apparent when the state discovered that hundreds of recipients had been trading their food stamps to purchase child care services and bus fare so they could get to their jobs. Although such "trading" is illegal, it is a far cry from the type of activity the Lone Star Card was intended to prevent.

Education

All levels of American government are deeply involved in the issue of education, a controversial policy area. In 1785, the federal government appropriated land in what is now West Virginia, Kentucky, and Tennessee for the purpose of building and maintaining public schools in the future. The greatest debate over public education, especially from grades kindergarten through high school, centers around equality of opportunity. Some of the most hard-fought court cases of the twentieth century involved segregation and desegregation, busing, school funding, and prayer in public schools.

Each of these issues gives rise to enormous policy implications. Compounding the problems is the fact that most public schools are administered at the local level and highly regulated by the various state governments. In fact, the federal government typically provides less than 10 percent of grade school funding. This is only one reason why attempts by the federal government to establish nationwide policy is so often met with fierce resistance by local school boards.

During the eighteenth and nineteenth centuries, American public schools played a vital part in making the nation politically and economically powerful. The same system of education also fostered prejudice and racism during that time frame. Some European immigrants on the east coast, Asians on the west coast, and blacks throughout the country were often denied equal access to publicly supported education. Many political scientists and sociologists say this discrepancy resulted in these minority and ethnic groups not being able to obtain prominent roles in the private and public sectors. Ironically, the lion's share of the credit for making public schools equally accessible goes to the federal government, which is the level of government least directly involved in education policy.

Today, public schools face challenges that the founding fathers would never have imagined. School lunches, school safety and security, curricula, teachers' salaries, and attempts to finance private schools with public taxes are just a few of the major controversies that parents, teachers and school administrators have to address. The number of education-related bills introduced in Congress has been growing each year since the mid-1970s, signifying the fact that Americans are expecting the federal government to become involved. President Jimmy Carter believed in expanding the role of the federal government in the arena of public schooling so much that he created a cabinet-level position (the Department of Education) to implement measures that would ensure some consistency in the schools.

President Clinton announced that Congress would appropriate funding for 100,000 teachers across the United States and planned to "put a computer in every classroom." Conservative political leaders have criticized the Democrats' efforts to "nationalize" the public school system. Republicans respond that the solution is the creation of a voucher system, whereby parents could choose from among a variety of public or private schools. The voucher system plan is gaining widespread support among parents, despite claims from the teachers' unions that vouchers will serve only to re-segregate the public school system, thus wiping out fifty years of progress.

The Environment

Two significant factors relating to the environment make this policy arena particularly complicated. The first of these involves scientific data. The debate, even within the scientific community, on whether global warming is a public health issue, and whether or not the laws we have in place are sufficient to counteract any environmental damage is a continuous one. By this time, you know enough about government to know that if scientists cannot agree on something, politicians are certainly going to be hopelessly deadlocked. The second factor has to do with the lack of personnel and funds to ensure compliance and enforcement. Most environmental regulation relies on voluntary compliance and/or the oversight by state governments. Many of the states lack the resources necessary to regulate the multitude of industries, water districts, and chemical transporters involved in the sphere of hazardous waste.

The issue of pollution, particularly in the larger metropolitan areas, has been a concern since major environmental interest groups started forming in the mid-1950s. As a result of better science breeding increased awareness, coupled with pressure from the international community, President Nixon, in 1970, authorized the creation of the Environmental Protection Agency, which has since been renamed the U.S. Department of Environmental Protection. As is typical of all bureaucracies, this agency has expanded in its mission and scope to encompass an astonishing span of control with powers over any agency that affects land, air, or water.

This newly created agency was launched with new legislation to enforce, namely, the National Environmental Protection Act (1970) and the Clean Air Act of 1970. This second piece of legislation, among other things, was charged with monitoring and eventually enforcing its regulations on new car manufacturers. The next sweeping regulations came in 1980 with the passage of the Comprehensive Environmental Response Act, which established a "superfund" to finance the complete environmental cleanup of nearly 20,000 toxic waste sites.

There are widespread economic implications pertaining to environmental issues. Environmentalists contend that industries pollute the air and water at the expense of the environment, and should therefore reduce their hazardous emissions even at the expense of profits. On the other hand, many industrialists cite scientific data which refute the argument that human manufacturing is putting the environment at substantial risk. They argue that if forced to cut down production, many workers will have to be laid off and this would create economic problems. It appears that both arguments have some degree of merit, and indeed progress is being made.

Another contentious area of environmental policy is what to do with waste and harmful by-products of production. No one wants it in his or her neighborhood, or more specifically, no one wants it in his or her backyard. Political scientists have thus coined the term **"NIMBY,"** which stands for "not in my back yard." Everyone wants the new fire station and city park in their neighborhood, but no one wants the maximum-security prison the or pork rendering plant, much less the toxic waste dump. Throughout the country, ad-hoc interest groups spring up daily to express displeasure at the notion of having a biohazard waste on their block. The issue of NIMBY-ism can be used as a prime example of the expression used by many political scientists: All politics is local.

Unlike the other two policy arenas examined (public assistance and education), environmental policy has global implications. In many instances, the results of environmental damage caused by one nation have adversely affected other nations. For example, some Canadians have claimed that pollutants from heavy industries on the American east coast and Midwest have caused acid rain to fall in Canada. While all water contains some acid, it has been shown that rain that falls within certain regions of the nation contains a higher concentration of chemicals. The nitric acid comes from the sulfur that is created by coal mines and heavy industry. Although no studies have proven that acid rain is harmful, environmentalists have had a very hard time getting the issue on the agenda.

Even if the larger industrialized nations made a commitment to "clean up their acts," what could be done about the dozens of developing nations that over-pollute and fail to practice environmental responsibility? There are a good number of national and international organizations working on these and other important environmental issues. Through scientific research and breakthroughs, conservation training, and education, perhaps these issues will someday be resolved.

Major Environmental Laws Enacted by the Federal Government

The federal government has enacted many laws intended to protect environmental concerns ranging from the disposal of toxic waste to endangered species. In addition, all fifty states have passed laws in an effort to preserve the environment. The following are some of the major current federal laws affecting environmental regulation.

The Clean Air Act (1970)

The Clean Air Act is the comprehensive federal law which regulates air emissions from area, stationary, and mobile sources. This law authorizes the U.S. Environmental Protection Agency (EPA) to establish National Ambient Air Quality Standards to protect public health and the environment.

The Clean Water Act (1977)

This law gave the EPA the authority to set standards on an industry-by-industry basis and continued the requirements to set water quality standards for all contaminants in surface waters. The Clean Water Act makes it unlawful for any person to discharge any pollutant from a point source into navigable waters unless a permit is obtained.

The Comprehensive Environmental Response, Compensation, and Liability Act (CERCLA or Superfund) (1980)

CERCLA (pronounced SERK-la) provides a federal "Superfund" to clean up uncontrolled or abandoned hazardous waste sites as well as accidents, spills, and other emergency releases of pollutants and contaminants into the environment.

The Endangered Species Act (1973)

The Endangered Species Act provides a program for the conservation of threatened and endangered plants and animals and the habitats in which they are found. The U.S. Fish and Wildlife Service (FWS) of the Department of Interior maintains the list of 632 endangered species (326 are plants) and 190 threatened species (78 are plants). Species include birds, insects, fish, reptiles, mammals, crustaceans, flowers, grasses, and trees.

The National Environmental Policy Act (1969)

One of the first laws ever written that establishes the broad national framework for protecting our environment, its policy is to assure that all branches of government give proper consideration to the environment prior to undertaking any major federal action which significantly affects the environment.

The Pollution Prevention Act (1990)

The Pollution Prevention Act focused industry, government, and public attention on reducing the amount of pollution produced through cost-effective changes in production, operation, and raw materials use. Practices include recycling, source reduction, and sustainable agriculture.

The Safe Drinking Water Act (1974)

Established to protect the quality of drinking water in the U.S. This law focuses on all waters actually or potentially designated for drinking use, whether from above ground or underground sources. The Act authorized EPA to establish safe standards of purity and required all owners or operators of public water systems to comply.

The Toxic Substances Control Act (TSCA) (1976)

Enacted to test, regulate, and screen all chemicals produced or imported into the U.S. Many thousands of chemicals and their compounds are developed each year with unknown toxic or dangerous characteristics. To prevent tragic consequences, TSCA requires that any chemical that reaches the consumer market place be tested for possible toxic effects prior to commercial manufacture.

Source: United States Environmental Protection Agency, June 1999.

SUMMARY

Public policy can be defined as any course of action taken by the government that affects any segment of the public. The inquiry into public policy analysis represents a major subfield of political science. Given that there are literally thousands of public laws, rules, and regulations in effect today, policy analysts understand the importance of, and seek to understand, the dynamics that are part of every government action.

Perhaps the most important contribution to the field of public policy occurred when political scientists discovered that all policy, regardless of size or scope, evolves over similar stages. These stages are identified as agenda setting, formulation, adoption, implementation, and evaluation. By examining a public policy through such a model, we have been able to explain past events, shed light on current issues, and determine the best course for policy implications of the future.

Does the government have an obligation to get involved in a given policy arena? Does it take into consideration the thoughts and desires of all sides of the debate? Is the process by which public policies are made the most equitable? And finally, do the laws and rules enacted really address the problem that caused the action in the first place? These are some of the questions that public policy analysis seeks to answer.

KEY TERMS

Adoption
Agenda setting
Evaluation
Formulation
Implementation
Lone Star Card
Means test
NIMBY
Public policy
Sunset advisory committee

INTERNET SOURCES

a) http://www.policy.com
This site attempts to answer the question: What is public policy? It provides information on who, where, how, and when of public policy in general. Information on the federal government's policy-making process and

contemporary issues being discussed are included in this site as well as the process of government assistance to the public relative to different problems. Legal concerns and contacts are given.

b) http://www.ksg.havard.edu/~ksgpress/opin/

The Kennedy School of Government at Harvard University is responsible for maintaining this site. It provides information and several links on research data in regard to public policy issues.

c) http://www.cbo.gov/

The Congressional Budget Office (CBO) is responsible for maintaining this site. It provides information on the federal government's budget process, finances, laws, pending legislations, fiscal committees, actions taken on past and present budgets, etc.

d) http://www.whitehouse.gov/WH/EOP/omb

The Office of Management & Budget is the executive branch of government's equivalent of the CBO. This site provides information on the budget but from the point of view of the presidency. Federal government agency information, especially that directly responsible for the budget, is provided.

Chapter 14

American Foreign Policy

The Congress shall have power...To declare war, grant letters of marque and reprisal, and make rules concerning captures on land and water.
—*Constitution of the United States, Article I, Section 8.*

The President shall be Commander in Chief of the Army and Navy of the United States....He shall have Power, by and with the Advice and Consent of the Senate, to make Treaties...shall appoint Ambassadors......
—*Constitution of the United States, Article II, Section 2.*

INTRODUCTION

Foreign policy has always been a murky exercise and a number of factors shape its direction. Some are easily pointed to, but others are not so well defined. Only in times of war or near war have citizens of the United States interested themselves in it. Yet, our relations with foreign governments have an important influence on our lives in times of war and peace. Our jobs, general economy, travel, immigration, and pollution are all parts of foreign policy. This chapter will attempt to chart how it is made, by whom, and its history.

CITIZEN INTEREST IN FOREIGN POLICY

Foreign policy is a bundle of formal and informal positions which make up the official policy of the United States of America toward other countries. These policies are a combination of economic, moral, and military facets.

Americans have not been particularly attentive to foreign policy. Historically, this was due to our geography. The United States has been removed from much of the world's troubles. We are, in some sense, an "island nation," removed by the great oceans from Europe, Asia, and Africa. The United States has also had, for the greater part of this century, international borders which have provided us with stability. Having stable international borders both to our north and south, and great oceans to our west and east, has allowed us the luxury of attending primarily to domestic concerns.

Additionally, we have had a great amount of land which kept us occupied much of the time with westward movements of populations. This does not mean that top policy-makers have been isolated from the world. From the end of the nineteenth century, and for a hundred years thereafter, this country took care to keep the oceans open to our commerce and to maintain outposts essential to our security. However, except when engaged in the great world wars or in Vietnam, most Americans have been disengaged from foreign policy issues.

The United States has had the unique luxury of becoming a great world power and at the same time being labeled as isolationist. We increased our land area dramatically with the Louisiana Purchase early in the nineteenth century. In the mid-nineteenth century we added the immense land area of Alaska by purchasing it from Russia. The United States reached out to become a great power with the Mexican-American War, Spanish-American War, and the construction of the Panama Canal. We entered the First World War in Europe in 1917 and emerged as a major player on the world scene. With all of this tumult, most Americans were still able to enjoy a relatively peaceful day-to-day lifestyle. The Civil War, an internal struggle, has been the most violent and wrenching event ever for our people.

In 1940, at a time when great portions of the world were already at war in Asia and in Europe, the passage of military conscription, commonly known as the draft, passed Congress by only one vote.

Franklin Delano Roosevelt campaigned for office in 1940 partially on a political platform not to send American troops to war in Europe. More than two decades earlier, Woodrow Wilson also campaigned not to send American troops to Europe.

Both presidents eventually deployed troops to Europe to fight in the great wars. And their respective decisions were correct! But their early "promises" clearly reveal the feeling of most Americans that the wars of the world were none of our business.

Just before our entry into World War II, large portions of the American public were strongly against any involvement in European or Asian wars. Indeed, the famed aviator, Charles Lindbergh, spoke frequently against any involvement in faraway wars with peoples whom we know nothing about. Our entry into World War II and the public support for it was generated by the dramatic attack, in 1941, on our naval fleet in Hawaii. After that attack, the public became intimately involved with foreign affairs for the duration of the war.

Although most citizens have not been consistently interested in or involved with foreign affairs, there have always been exceptions. Various interest groups representing racial, ethnic, religious, and economic groupings have shown interest.

Immigrant groups coming to this country brought with them memories of and attachments to their homelands. They kept up with happenings in their countries of origin. Often they read foreign newspapers and listen to news programs of events in their former countries.

Various businesses and corporations trading or investing abroad have always had a stake and interest in foreign policy making. Likewise, businesses here at home have always been sensitive to how imported goods are treated. Tariffs and trade have always been major parts of domestic and foreign policies. In many areas, domestic and foreign policy issues often influence each other.

It could be said that for the greater part of this century, Americans, generally, have not been motivated or concerned with foreign policies. There have been notable exceptions when at war or during the Cold War. Citizens of this country have had the luxury of being able to concern themselves with their jobs, education, and their families.

It should be stressed at the outset that every citizen of the United States, individually or as a group member, has important constitutional rights. These rights also pertain to speaking out or organizing peacefully to affect foreign affairs.

MAKERS OF AMERICAN FOREIGN POLICY

There are formal and informal makers of our foreign policy. First, there are the official policy makers. The foremost is the president of the United States. The president can negotiate on behalf of the country and is the Commander in Chief. The president's roles in the conduct of foreign affairs have occasionally been in conflict with the will of Congress.

Other executive branch policy makers are the Secretary of State, National Security Adviser, National Security Council, ambassadors, the Central Intelligence Agency (CIA), the Federal Bureau of Investigation (FBI), and other intelligence and investigative agencies.

The **Secretary of State** is the official charged by Congress and appointed by the president of the United States to conduct relations with other countries. Some secretaries have made enormous contributions to foreign decision making. Others have been relatively minor players and have faded from history. Thomas Jefferson was our first Secretary of State. The office of **National Security Adviser** is a relatively new addition to foreign policy making after World War II. Perhaps the most well known is Henry Kissinger who held the post in President Nixon's administration.

Adding to these are the many committees and sub-committees of the United States Congress. The Senate Armed Services Committee, the House National Security Committee, the Senate Foreign Relations Committee, and the House International Relations Committee all have varying degrees of authority over foreign affairs.

The Senate must approve all presidential treaties and the appointment of ambassadors to foreign nations. And most important of all, Congress has the authority to appropriate money which can be used to affect any number of foreign policy decisions.

Our national government has established an elaborate array of foreign policy stations. In the State Department, headed by the Secretary of State, there are various sections, often referred to as "desks" assigned to geographic parts of the world. There are "desks" which have responsibility for North and South America, Asia, Africa, and Europe. These assignments are headed by assistant or deputy secretaries of state. There are also many career foreign service officers in the State Department who have worked for years implementing, advising, and executing policies.

Career foreign service officials also serve throughout the world in United States embassies in various capacities as well. They assist ambassadors in advice and implementation of policy.

Whether America has a comprehensive and coherent foreign policy is open to debate. Some contend that it is more reactive at times than following a planned design. It is most likely that we have had both. There were periods when we had a comprehensive and coherent plan in place and followed it through. At other times, we simply reacted to situations or crises as they occurred.

MAJOR FOREIGN POLICY ERAS

The best way to illustrate how American foreign policy is made and executed is to focus on prominent and well-known global events. There are many important foreign policy issues to explore prior to World War II, like those of President Woodrow Wilson in the early part of the twentieth century. A unique part of foreign policy was during the Civil War when other nations were scheming to exploit America's troubles in order to regain a foothold in this part of the world.

However, it may be best to focus on those policies that have had a direct and lasting effect on this generation. This portion will focus on exemplary policies since the end of World War II, when the United States found itself in a unique and powerful position in the world.

At the end of this war, much of Europe, and indeed other parts of the world, were destroyed. Of all the former great powers, prior to the war, only the United States truly emerged unscathed. Even those former powers who helped win the war, like Great Britain, were left in an inferior position, economically at least.

The United States, for a short time, had a monopoly on nuclear weapons. America was not directly affected by the war. It got involved in the war amidst an economic depression. It emerged as one of the greatest economic powers in history. Before the war, the United States pursued an isolationist foreign policy. It did not wish to be involved with world affairs. Americans were more interested in the building of a country. After the war, this country was faced with an important choice: Would we revert to our isolationist posture and turn our backs on the world, or would we assert our influence on world affairs?

Although the United States emerged as the preeminent world power after the war, there were many dangerous and watershed events to be faced. A united Soviet Union and our war ally, which was battered after the war, also emerged as a great world power. Its influence was felt throughout the world. Soviet troops occupied much of Eastern Europe. Additionally, communism, our main threat for decades, was potent in parts of the world.

The great European empires, especially those of the Dutch, French, and British, were now falling apart. The emerging new nations arising out of these expiring empires also posed a challenge to the United States. Indonesia gained its independence from the Dutch. French Indo-China emerged as an independent Vietnam, but not until after a bloody struggle involving both France, and later, the United States. India would gain its independence after years of struggle with Great Britain. After a struggle between Hindus and Muslims, an independent Pakistan entered the world stage. In the Middle East, an independent Israel emerged from the former British outpost of Palestine. These challenges and more occupied America's attention for most the twentieth century.

Again, how would America's foreign policy be shaped in light of these political earthquakes? Would America respond militarily or economically? What effect would other great powers have on America's policies? How would it respond to the ideological threat of communism?

One of America's most important foreign policies was formulated after the war. It was labeled the **containment policy**. It was the underlying basis of U.S. foreign and military policy since World War II. It was designed to contain the expansion of communist influence around the world. An agent of containment policy in Europe was the military alliance between the United States and the European allies—NATO, the **North Atlantic Treaty Organization**. Another aspect of containment, especially designed for Europe, was the **Marshall Plan**. It was an economic package named after an important Secretary of State and former World War II general, George Marshall. In 1947, Marshall proposed the European Recovery Program, under which the United States provided about $13 billion in aid to Europe. American economic aid thus became the key to Europe's economic revival.

Containment

After WWII, most of Europe was in shambles. Eastern Europe was under Soviet and communist domination. Western Europe was in economic ruin. The ideas of America's foreign policy makers were to extend economic aid to Western Europe in the hope that rebuilding their economies would stop communist expansion within and outside of Europe. In retrospect, it is considered a successful aid program. The Truman Administration focused on economic and even military assistance to Greece and Turkey in order to stop incipient guerilla movements and economic dislocation.

The containment plan against communism was geared toward a militant Soviet Union and China's expansionist program in the Pacific region by way of forming an umbrella organization named SEATO, the Southeast Asian Treaty Organization. NATO was to Europe what SEATO was to the Pacific world. Another alliance between the United States, New Zealand, and Australia was ANZUS, which stands for Australia, New Zealand, and the United States.

The military alliances of NATO, SEATO, and ANZUS were formed to contain communism. Economic aid, especially as embodied in the Marshall Plan, was the other prong in the policy of containment. In 1998, NATO was extended to Eastern Europe after the breakup of the Soviet Union and the demise of communism. SEATO and ANZUS, although still intact, have not been actively employed as before.

The above discussion shows that foreign policy is not only built around military affairs. Policies enacted in Europe at the end of World War II reveal the importance of economy as a vital foreign policy instrument. The United States foreign policy was severely tested at the end of the Second World War when China embraced communism and for several years, was battling a Japanese invasion, and involved in internal wars between various political factions. China was eventually taken over and ruled by a communist government hostile to the United States. Moreover, it was allied at the time with the Soviet Union.

The U.S. and Korea

The containment policy in Asia and Europe was severely tested by the Sino-Russian military and economic alliance when North Korea invaded the South in 1950. Chinese troops fought alongside the North Koreans. The United States military was deployed into combat under the auspices of the United Nations on the side of South Korea. Eventually, after bloody fighting, a truce was constructed between the two Koreas. Thousands of American troops still remain in South Korea with little prospect of being removed. Tensions between the two Koreas periodically flare up.

The Korean War tested American foreign policy intent in post-World War II era. The United States was unwilling to engage in an all-out war against China for fear of a possible use of nuclear weapons. Its goal was containment, and not total victory over the communist world. However, the containment policy was criticized by those who believed it was defeatist in nature. Their position was that America should go for an all-out victory when tested militarily.

The confrontation between supporters and opponents of containment policy culminated in the dismissal of **Douglas MacArthur** from his commanding post in Korea. General MacArthur wanted to march into mainland China during the Korean War. He was not content with merely pushing them back across the border of North Korea.

President Truman, as Commander in Chief, believed in containment. He realized that MacArthur was out of bounds by trying to disobey his orders to merely "contain" the North Koreans and their Chinese allies. The President eventually fired General MacArthur. The firing of a popular military general by the United States president reveals a different aspect of America's foreign policy options. Most foreign policy decisions are made in a more subtle and less visible manner.

The containment policy, Marshall Plan, Korean War, emergence of communism on Chinese mainland, Soviet domination of Eastern Europe, and the buildup of nuclear weapons led to what policy makers label the **Cold War**. This was a period when the United States and the Soviet Union were engaged in non-direct military confrontations globally, but fought each other through their proxy forces. The U.S. foreign policies until early 1990s were predominately structured around the Cold War.

The U.S. and Cuba
In the early 1960s, the Cold War theater shifted to Cuba. This was early in President John Kennedy's administration. The United States supported an invasion of Cuba by a group of Cuban exiles who despised Fidel Castro after he installed a communist regime in the country in 1959. Many Cubans who fled their country came to the United States without any monetary resources. Their dislike for Fidel Castro is still very much evident at the beginning of the twenty-first century. This relationship continues to influence U.S. foreign policy on Cuba.

In 1962, the United States came very close to a nuclear confrontation with the former Soviet Union. The Soviets, with Cuba's cooperation, installed nuclear weapons on Cuban soil. Since Cuba is only ninety miles away from American shores, President Kennedy and his advisers confronted the Soviets and their Cuban allies. This confrontation developed into what is referred to as the Cuban Missile Crisis. Soviet warships, carrying more missiles to install on Cuba, turned back after the United States mounted a sea blockade. Eventually, the Soviet missiles were removed from Cuba and the United States promised not to invade the island nation. After three decades, the relations between Cuba and the United States remained tense. Some members of Congress have expressed concerns on the continued tough stance against Cuba.

The United States policy toward Cuba reveals a multitude of factors: international, big power politics, and domestic pressures. These same factors impact American foreign programs and policies globally.

The U.S. and Indo-China
Another far-reaching foreign policy initiative involved the former French colony of Indo-China, later known as Vietnam. The French, after being militarily stalemated (some would say defeated) in their former outpost, requested assistance from the

United States. Initially, the United States sent a small cadre of military advisers which later grew by the mid-1960s into a major military commitment. The French signed a treaty that partitioned Vietnam into two countries, North and South.

The French eventually pulled out altogether leaving the United States with a major decision on whether or not to stay and if it did stay, to what extent. The Unites States eventually decided on a major commitment not to abandon South Vietnam (North Vietnam was already under communist domination) which was vulnerable to communism.

Vietnam is one of the most hotly debated issues of all times. America's foreign policy eventually supported a massive military and economic commitment in Vietnam. It was reasoned that since Vietnam is geographically close to China, and in a critical part of Asia, it should remain under American influence.

America's commitment in South Vietnam became a very controversial part of the Cold War. It brought about much debate, demonstrations in the United States for and against this policy, and a debate among our allies.

At the height of the Vietnam War, a great debate developed between Congress and the executive branch. Hearings were held in Congress over our conduct and legitimacy of the war. Some senators and representatives threatened to withhold financial appropriations for the continuation of the war.

Another argument was whether the U.S. military could effectively combat an indigenous force. Could the world's greatest military power fight against an effective guerilla army in Vietnam? Were the Vietnamese motivated more by communism or were they primarily supporting nationalistic and independent tendencies apart from any ideology? Even if Vietnam became communist in orientation, how would that influence other Asian countries? America's involvement in Vietnam ended in the early 1970s. Negotiations were tedious and prolonged. Eventually, a treaty was signed by the two Vietnams. American troops pulled out after being stalemated much like the French some years earlier.

No military engagement in this century has so much convulsed this country as the Vietnam War. There has not been greater citizen involvement in the foreign policy debate and formulation than Vietnam. Students who had never heard of Vietnam became very familiar with its geography, politics, and history. Americans became knowledgeable about Asia. Those who did not know the U.S. Secretary of State became very familiar with his name and face.

A major lesson from the Vietnam War is that Americans become interested in foreign policy when it directly affects them. Many college-age males received notices

of military induction. And many witnessed the effects of war on television. It is unfortunate that we become interested and knowledgeable about the policies of our country in foreign places only when we are directly involved, especially in war.

The U.S. and the Middle East

The 1950s and 1960s were periods of many foreign problems that demanded America's attention. In 1956, there was the Suez Canal crisis, involving our allies France, Britain, and Israel. All three invaded Egypt after that country blockaded the Suez Canal which, at the time, was vital to their interests. In the same year, Hungary, in eastern Europe, a Soviet satellite county, revolted. The **Hungarian Revolution** posed a dilemma for the United States. The Hungarian revolutionaries were asking for America's assistance. However, in order not to raise tensions, the United States decided not to intervene. The possible use of nuclear arsenals by the United States and the Soviet Union tempered U.S. policy. The Hungarian revolt was forcibly put down by Soviet tanks.

By refusing to assist the Hungarian revolutionaries, it seemed as if the United States was unwilling to support its allies in their political adventures. This action made America's allies dubious of its intentions and policies on other matters. The Suez crisis reveals the stress that foreign policy differences could engender among and between allies.

In 1967, while the Vietnam War was still raging, the Middle East crisis between Israel and its Arab neighbors was just starting. This engagement, known as the **Six-Day War**, again posed a dilemma for America's foreign policy. The United States had always supported Israel, but was also dependent on Mid-East oil which came from some of the Arab countries engaged in warfare with Israel. Stability in the Middle East was an important foreign policy goal.

Complicating matters at this time was the Soviet Union, which was arming several Arab nations in the region. Israel emerged victorious in the Six-Day War, but its aftermath left many issues unresolved.

In the 1970s, another group of international events demanded the United States' attention. In 1973, there was another Arab-Israeli confrontation called the **Yom Kippur War**. It ended with an Arab oil boycott and a massive increase in the price of oil. The United States was faced with long lines at the gas pump. However, America did not develop a different policy toward foreign oil imports. Our foreign policy did not make us any less dependent on oil imports. In fact, our dependence on oil imports increased from the 1970s to the end of the twentieth century.

In 1979, a tumultuous revolution occurred in Iran. The revolution resulted in an increase in the price of oil. America was humiliated by the taking of hostages in the United States embassy in Iran. Iran, under the Shah, had been a strategic partner of the United States. Thousands of United States citizens worked in Iran in military and oil industries. The Iranian revolution ended this partnership and alliance.

Also in 1979, the Soviet Union invaded Afghanistan. This invasion triggered an ominous guerilla movement, fueled by Islamic fundamentalism, to thwart the Soviets who were eventually defeated. However, the training and arming of the fundamentalists, with the backing of the United States, subsequently came back to haunt us in the form of the Taliban regime and global terrorism. This occurrence is known as **"blowback:"** when a desired action goes astray and results in unintended consequences detrimental to American foreign policy.

The revolution in Iran and the help we gave to Afghan fighters subjected our foreign policy to a critical internal review. The main ingredients of this review were: Should we have supported the Shah in Iran and Afghan fighters in prior years? Do we import too much oil? Should we have responded more forcefully in Iran after our embassy employees were taken hostage? What will be the future outcome of our actions around the world? And as always, should the United States take bold and major actions in various parts of the world or be a more low profile player in world affairs?

Reagan and American Foreign Policy

Our foreign policy in the 1980s saw a decided turn toward more defense expenditures and a strong military posture. This policy was driven by the election of Ronald Reagan as president. Reagan clearly turned American foreign policy toward not just containing communism, but defeating it! This was a dramatic change from previous policy. Reagan faced the Soviet Union and demanded that they dismantle the Berlin Wall, which was both a symbolic and real division between the communist and western democratic worlds.

The United States built up its defense to a point unmatched by the Soviets. The United States moved to support movements in Central America that we believed would help curtail communist expansionism. Further, the Reagan Administration bombed Libya believing it was behind the bombing of a club in Germany frequented by American servicemen. This administration also invaded the Caribbean island nation of Grenada believing that it was to be used as a staging ground for Cuban-Communist expansion.

Our new and bold foreign policy was not easily implemented. It brought forth controversies and debates between the executive and legislative branches. Some political leaders believed we were spending too much money on defense, and not enough on domestic programs. Others felt that our support of various anti-communist movements circumvented congressional directives.

However, Reagan's policies prevailed. Shortly after he left office, the Soviet empire began to crumble. The communist countries in Eastern Europe began to break away from their former master. Eventually, the Soviet Union itself broke apart. This was clearly one of the most triumphant moments for America's foreign policy objectives. The Cold War, which had so preoccupied and directed our foreign policy since the end of World War II had, for all practical purposes, ended. This did not mean, however, that the world was now safe or that foreign policy no longer would be stressed. The end of the Cold War simply meant that different challenges would now confront American foreign policy, and the nation would have to adapt to these changes.

Bush and American Foreign Policy

In 1991, Iraq invaded its neighbor, Kuwait. Both countries are rich in oil. The United States, in collaboration with its allies, particularly in that region, intervened militarily. The objective was to push Iraqi troops out of Kuwait and restore it to its rightful owners. The military confrontation with Iraq became known as the Gulf War.

However, there were more issues involved than simply freeing Kuwait of Iraqi troops. Saudi Arabia is a neighbor of Kuwait. Our fear was that Iraq, emboldened by its conquest of Kuwait, would move next on Saudi Arabia. That country has historically been an important source of oil to the world. Our foreign policy was turned to protecting our oil supplies as much as ridding Kuwait of Iraqi troops.

The Gulf War resulted in a complete victory for the United States and its allies that fought under the United Nations' auspices. Our foreign policy makers believed that fighting under the United Nations' resolutions would bring more support to what was essentially a war to which the Unites States had committed 500,000 troops.

Although the Gulf War was a major victory, Saddam Hussein, the Iraqi leader, was still in power. At the end of the twentieth century, Iraq and its ruler Saddam Hussein, still periodically presented troubles to our policy makers. The debate continued about whether we should have removed Hussein from power before declaring victory. But 2003 would bring about a new war against Iraq, resulting in the United States' occupation, and the final capture and removal of Saddam Hussein.

At the conclusion of the Gulf War, President George Bush said that a **"new world order"** was being created. This phrase has been much debated. But what the president meant was that the world would now be safer. Far away from the Middle East, the United States had invaded Panama, and removed its then ruler General Manuel Noriega in order to guarantee our interests in Central America and to curtail drug trafficking.

With the end of the Cold War, the United States has become the preeminent economic and military power in the world. The Gulf War exemplified this principle that the world would act, through the United Nations, if feasible, to put down aggression of one country against another. But if the United States' interests are threatened, it would not hesitate to act unilaterally.

As the Cold War ended, American foreign policy focused on economic issues. Foreign policies have never been free of economic considerations. But often they have been obscured in times of war or other similar events. Often, economic issues are intimately involved in foreign policy considerations. The Gulf War is very illustrative of this assumption.

Clinton and American Foreign Policy

President Clinton, continuing the policies of both Presidents Reagan and Bush, advocated for a free trade zone in the western hemisphere. The development of free trade under the North American Free Trade Association (NAFTA) was first an agreement between Canada and the United States.

President Clinton wanted to extend NAFTA to Mexico as well. The idea of free trade, and especially the agreement embodied in NAFTA, generated a great deal of debate between its supporters and detractors. Eventually, NAFTA was extended to Mexico.

President Clinton tried to include other South American nations in this agreement. However, in the late 1990s, Congress refused to give the president the negotiating authority he requested, and this slowed the incorporation of other countries into NAFTA. In early 2004, however, President George W. Bush initiated a new trade agreement between the United States and Central American nations called the Central American Free Trade Agreement (CAFTA).

There were other foreign policy dilemmas during the mid- to late-1990s. Questions involving the former Yugoslavia arose as ethnic fighting broke out. Haiti posed questions for foreign affairs specialists as well. The question was whether U.S. troops should be deployed to these countries. After much debate, and with different goals and durations in mind, troops were sent in.

These troops were defined as **"peace keeping"** and were not supposed to be directly involved in combat This posed another question: Should United States soldiers be used in places around the world in peace keeping roles?

George W. Bush and American Foreign Policy

As the twenty-first century began, United States foreign policy was suddenly confronted with a new and dangerous challenge: global terrorism. On September 11, 2001, the magnificent twin towers of the World Trade Center, in New York City, were attacked and destroyed by Arab terrorists who used hijacked planes as missiles.

American foreign policy makers were aware of the menace of global terrorism prior to September 11, 2001. Previously, there had been series of bombings of American embassies in several African countries. Terrorist attacks had been launched against a United States naval vessel in the port of Yemen. American military barracks in Saudi Arabia had been bombed as well. And even before the total collapse of the World Trade Center by hijacked planes, it had been attacked a few years earlier by car bombs. However, this first attack was not nearly as grave as the second attack on September 11, 2001.

Terrorism has been called a scourge of the world. It is destabilizing, unpredictable, and wreaks havoc on world economies. The events of September 11, 2001, led foreign policy makers to launch a war in Afghanistan where terrorist training took place under the leadership of a wealthy Saudi Arabian, Osama bin Laden. The Afghanistan war was launched to rid the country of the Taliban, a militant Islamic group that ruled the country.

At the end of 2001, the war in Afghanistan had been won. The United States had constructed a coalition of nations to fight terrorism in a variety of ways: economic, military, and political. The Taliban in Afghanistan had been routed and a new government installed. However, well into 2003, and the beginning of 2004, the United States and the coalition forces were in continual battle with the remnants of the Taliban regime. Also, several Afghan warlords were still operating in various parts of the land making it difficult for a unified and central government to organize. The trafficking in opium poppies was reported as rampant, thereby making it difficult to organize the economy and stabilize the government. The hope for Afghanistan was for a freely elected constitutional government, but many obstacles stood in the path of this goal.

By mid-2004, a new Afghan Constitution was in place. The search for Osama bin Laden continued, and Pakistan, Afghanistan's neighbor, seemed to be participating actively in the search. One of the most hopeful signs of 2004 was the election of Hamed Karzai as the country's new leader. It was a hopeful sign as women voted for the first time. However, with the Iraq war, Afghanistan was relegated to a secondary foreign policy position.

However, as President Bush consistently stated, the war against terrorism would take many years. It would not be just confined to Afghanistan, but would be a worldwide struggle. Foreign policy makers would have to ponder where and how to fight the war. Among the most frequently mentioned places were Iraq, Somalia, and Sudan.

The Bush Administration, led by its Secretaries of Defense, State, and the National Security Adviser began to make a strong case for going to war against Iraq. The Bush Administration's argument was based on allegations that Iraq possessed weapons of mass destruction and was a haven for and supporter of terrorists.

As the Administration made its case for war, various countries around the world, notably France and Germany, dissented. They argued that any military action and occupation must be consistent with United Nations format. Also, they argued that

Iraq could be contained, as in the past, without military invasion and occupation. Meanwhile, the Bush Administration obtained a resolution from the United States Congress allowing the President latitude in going to war, if necessary.

Around the world, and here in the United States as well, some demonstrations took place protesting the impending war. The Bush Administration went to the United Nations informing members of this global organization that Iraq was a bastion for terrorism and possessed weapons of mass destruction. The United States obtained a resolution from the United Nations calling on Iraq to disarm within a required time, failing which, there would be military action.

The United States, not convinced by actions of the United Nations arms inspections, asked for a second United Nations resolution authorizing military action. This resolution went unresolved and America went to war with a coalition comprised of Britain, and a host of other nations. The military action against Iraq was very swift. The Iraqi troops were defeated and the country occupied. Eventually, as 2003 came to an end, Saddam Hussein was captured alive and is awaiting trial.

The foreign policy of President George W. Bush is broad and challenging, focusing on making various countries in the world, especially in the Mid-East, more democratic and open. It is characterized as unilateralist rather than consigning decision making to international debate. With his re-election, Dr. Condolezza Rice was appointed new Secretary of State. Her first goal was to help "mend fences" with Europe. However, she would continue to strongly articulate the foreign policy goals of the administration.

Secretary of State Rice will be facing challenges on many fronts. Iran and North Korea's nuclear weapons may prove to be dangerous confrontations. Russia, under the leadership of Vladimir Putin, seems to be moving away from democratic trends to more authoritarian governance. In South America and the Caribbean, Venezuela, under President Hugo Chavez, may pose a challenge to our government. Cuba and its leader, Fidel Castro, are still major concerns to American policy makers.

The United Nations, under attack and investigation for having conducted a corrupt **"Oil for Food"** program, will continue to task American foreign policy. The $64 billion program was the largest U.N. humanitarian aid operation, running from 1996 to 2003 when Saddam Hussein was still in control. It allowed Iraqis to sell their oil, but to use the proceeds only for consumer and non-military goods. The United Nations was accused of corruption in this program, but also allowing some member countries with dictatorial and theocratic regimes to mold its policies.

The investigation, led by former U.S. Federal Reserve Chairman Paul Volcker, did not completely vindicate Kofi Annan, the Secretary-General of the United Nations. The findings faulted the secretary-general's management of the world body and his oversight of the scandal-ridden oil-for-food program. It also strongly criticized Kofi Annan's son, Kojo, who worked for a Swiss company, Cotecna Inspection S.A. that won the oil-for-food contract in 1998. Kojo Annan remained on the Cotecna payroll until 2004.

The makers of American foreign policy will be faced with strong challenges for many years. Two of the challenges are convincing other nations to join our war against terrorism, and keeping the American public engaged and interested.

GOALS OF AMERICAN FOREIGN POLICY

One of the most debated questions in the making of American foreign policy is its goals. Scholars of American foreign policy offer several alternative objectives of American foreign policy, which include national interest, national security, maintaining favorable trade relations, and promoting peace, human rights and democracy.

National Interest

National interest is a concept that is supposed to represent what is best for the country. However, it is a very subjective concept because different people define what is best for the country differently. By and large, the primary interest of every nation is its territorial security, its survival as a political unit, and the preservation of its core values and cultural identity.

National interests can change from generation to generation. Our allies in the world have changed. In both the First and Second World Wars, Germany was our enemy. After the Second World War, Germany became one of our most important allies.

National Security

National security involves defending the country against foreign invasion, and creating an international climate in which the United States can freely govern itself without threat from outside. During the Cold War era in the United States, national security referred to state security. The perceived global communist threat was to be countered and contained by military means. Security thinking revolved around nuclear weapons and deterrence strategy. Since the end of the Cold War, security has been perceived as international, rather than just national in scope. In addition, the exclusively military treatment of security issues has been challenged.

Trade Relations

Another goal of American foreign policy is to maintain favorable trade relations worldwide. Foreign trade provides the United States with indispensable resources such as oil, and raw and other precious materials. The United States has been promoting free and fair trade, and has played an important role in reforming international trade by signing the "Uruguay Round" of the General Agreement on Tariffs and Trade (GATT) in 1993. This led to the creation of the World Trade Organization in 1995.

Human Rights

America's trade policy is connected to human rights. Traditionally, the United States had thought about human rights in terms of civil and political rights. The primary threat to these rights comes from actions of governments. President Carter not only tried to put human rights at the center of his foreign policy, but also adopted a more expansive definition of human rights that included a concern for oppressive social and economic conditions. The current U.S.–Chinese human rights relations can be considered a return to the Carter Administration's definition of human rights, especially in the matters of child labor practices and the use of prison labor.

Democracy

Finally, promoting global democracy has been another objective of American foreign policy. Rhetorically, America has long championed democracy—from President Wilson's call to "make the world safe for democracy" to Robert Kennedy's pledge to "pay any price, bear any burden, meet any hardship, support any friend, oppose any foe to ensure the survival and success of liberty," to President Reagan's claim to "foster the infrastructure of democracy," and President Clinton's call for the U.S. to back democratic change and thus draw a "new map of freedom" around the world.

INTSTRUMENTS OF AMERICAN FOREIGN POLICY

Foreign policy makers not only must decide what goals to adopt, but also how to pursue them. There are several tools available to help pursue America's foreign policy objectives. Among them are diplomacy, covert action, and economic power.

Diplomacy

Diplomacy is closely identified with bargaining and negotiation. The most basic form of diplomacy is bilateral diplomacy in which two states interact with each other to solve common problems. Another type of diplomacy is summit diplomacy. Here the heads of state meet personally with one another. The most important Cold War summit conferences involved meetings between leaders of the United States and the Soviet Union. A third type of diplomacy is conference diplomacy. An example is the Uruguay Round of the GATT, which started in 1986 and ended in 1994. The conference resulted in further liberalized international trade.

Covert Action

Covert Action seeks results by altering the internal balance of power in a foreign country. Central to the techniques of covert action are clandestine support for individual organization, propaganda involving use of the media to influence perception of events, and assassination.

Economic Power

Economic embargo and foreign aid are two prominent economic instruments of American foreign policy. Imposition of economic embargo prohibits citizens from trading with one or several countries. It may apply only to certain products or a total prohibition of trade. The United States imposed a trade embargo on Iraq in 1991, which was lifted when Iraq complied with the U.N.'s terms for dealing with its nuclear power program.

Foreign Aid

Finally, foreign aid can be used as a means to promote American foreign policy goals. There are three categories of foreign aid. First is humanitarian aid. A good example of this is the Food for Peace Program. It makes surplus U.S. agricultural goods available to foreign countries. A second category of aid is economic development aid. The last type of foreign aid is foreign military sales. Through it the U.S. provides loans for the purchase of U.S. military equipment.

DOMESTIC CHALLENGES TO U.S. FOREIGN POLICY

In the making of United States foreign policy, there has been a tension between democratic institutions and policy makers. As discussed earlier in this chapter, we are a nation of many business and professional interest groups, immigrant groups, and varying constituent feelings. Also, Americans generally do not take much interest in foreign policy until a crisis develops. All of this greatly influences the foreign policy making among those charged with the responsibility.

What if the people do not view a foreign challenge as serious, but our policy makers do? How do we educate the public to take an event seriously? On the other hand, there may be times when the public wishes to take a stronger action than the policy makers think prudent or wise. If we were a simple dictatorship, foreign policy making would be made more easily without taking the will of the people into account.

What about the role of the media in foreign policy making? Many Americans influenced foreign policy commitments after watching television broadcasts. In Somalia, in the early 1990s, an American soldier was seen being dragged through the

---

Some Questions to Think About

As we enter a new century, there are important and new challenges to foreign policy-making in the United States.

1. Do we still need ambassadors, from this country to other countries in this new age of instant communications?
2. What should be our role in reining in terrorists?
3. Should the United States punish nations which assist countries we regard as potentially dangerous? Examples: Russia, China, or even some European nations who may aid Iran, Iraq, Libya or others in trade or weaponry.
4. What should be our overall foreign policy objective as we move forward in this new century?
5. Should the United States further reduce its military and defense expenditures? If so, by how much? If not, why not? Should the military forces and our defense expenditures be increased?
6. Are there any steps you believe should be taken to make our citizens more aware of foreign affairs?
7. Are you, as a student, aware of the many nations around the world? Are you familiar with our foreign policy toward them? If you are not aware, why not? Be frank. If you are aware, how did this come about?

> 8. Should the United States be an active participant in world affairs or be more isolationist?
> 9. Do you beleive in the lowering of trade barriers or the opening of our borders to goods and people?

streets by an angry mob. This sighting on television by the public compelled many to demand our government to "get out of Somalia!" Eventually, American troops were withdrawn from there. We had been there for a short time trying to "bring order" to warring groups and to help feed a hungry population.

Another classic case where the media influenced foreign policy was during the Vietnam War. During these years the television-viewing public could see the fighting, the "body bags," the bombings, and even interviews with combatants. This constant viewing on television certainly influenced Vietnam policies.

> ## Hypothetical Cases for Students to Assess
> 1. Two nations, both allies of the United States, have opposing interests. Greece and Turkey are two real examples of this dilemma. You are Secretary of State. How do you project foreign policy to these two countries or others in similar situations?
> 2. There is a country with important natural resources to the United States. It also is in an important geographical position where we can station troops in case of emergencies. However, this country is run by a dictatorial regime, oppresses its people, and is opposed by many human rights groups in this country. How would you direct foreign policy relative to this situation?
> 3. You wish to curtail the proliferation of nuclear weapons. Many countries in the world want to have and test them. They argue that the United States and other powers possess these weapons. How would you attempt to curtail this proliferation? What arguments would you make to these aspiring nuclear countries? How effective would they be?

> 4. You wish to further free trade in the world by expanding NAFTA. There are many domestic interest groups against this expansion. They argue that America would lose jobs to foreign countries. What would be your argument to bolster your economic policy agenda?
> 5. Many European nations in the coming years will make economic moves toward a common currency, open borders, and a general merging of their economies. As Secretary of State, how would you approach this new European economic arrangement? Do you believe it will be better or worse for United States interests? Explain your position.
> 6. A country in the Balkans region of Europe, Serbia, has tried to put down a revolt by ethnic Albanians, called Kosovars, in their Kosovo province. The Serbs have resorted to destroying homes, and thereby causing thousands of refugees to flee to other countries. The United States and its NATO allies intervene. Do you support such intervention? Why or why not? What conclusions do you reach about this episode in our foreign policy?

During the 1991 Gulf War, our policy makers were not as cooperative with the media as they were during Vietnam. The media were not able to maneuver as broadly or as easily as in Vietnam. This was partly due to the geography of the war, and our policy makers' wish to present the war in their own way and their own time as much as possible. There is no constitutional imperative for the government to assist the media in their information gathering and dissemination of news. The media were not as aggressive in the Gulf War as they were in Vietnam.

However, in the second Gulf War, or in the war against Iraq, the United States devised an innovative process whereby the media could have representatives embedded with the fighting forces themselves. This allowed for instant or "real time" reporting on television and radio. It paved the way for an entirely new method of covering military conflicts on the part of the United States Department of Defense.

The U.S. Congress often differs from the executive branch in foreign policy making. Very often members of Congress have to answer directly and immediately to constituent groups. "Why is my son being sent to Bosnia?" "Why are we sending all that foreign aid to those nations?" "Why don't we spend more on defense?" "Why do we spend so much on defense?" "Don't close down that Air Force base near my hometown; it provides many jobs for us!"

All of these questions and demands are real, and as a democratic nation Congress must respond to them. And occasionally, the wishes of Congress in response to their constituents is different from the overall perspective of the executive branch. Congress has the authority to appropriate money and declare war. The President of the United States is Commander in Chief and foreign policy leader. Further, Congress has the right to speak out on any event or policy as it sees fit, both as citizens and public officials.

It is easy to see how the Congress and the executive branch often disagree with each other in foreign policy making. Perhaps in the last three decades, the most important example of this conflict arose over Vietnam. Congress held public hearings in an attempt to change our foreign policy in Vietnam. It threatened to cut off appropriations, and finally passed a law dealing with war-making powers in order to curtail the president's authority to "make war" without congressional declaration.

In mid-2004, photos and stories were published in major American media outlets about the abuse of Iraqi prisoners held in custody as an outcome of the Iraqi war. Almost immediately, there were calls for congressional hearings about prisoner abuse and who bore the responsibility for the actions. Congressional hearings were held, the president denounced the abuses, and plans to curtail any possible further abuses were recommended.

However, there was criticism from some that the congressional hearings and outrage at the prisoner abuse were far out of proportion in comparison to what our enemies had done. Some held that the abuse of Iraqi prisoners was more in the line of humiliation and debasement, but not torture as some had described it.

The debate and comparison about what a democratic country can do in regard to prisoners rages on. Should a democracy be held to higher standards than other countries? Or, is there a time in war when a country, democratic in law and spirit, needs to fight for its survival without regard to its own or international standards?

Democracies are very often unable to clearly and concisely formulate and direct foreign policies. At times, our foreign adversaries try to take advantage of our open society, elections, and freewheeling media to tilt policy in their direction.

SUMMARY

The foreign policy of this country has been criticized as not being consistent, and not having a general purpose or direction. It is a reflection of our many diverse interests, goals, and peoples. Our power and prestige stand behind our foreign policies and are reflected by them. Hopefully, the reader has some greater sense of how foreign policy is made, its substance, and what it is as we move more fully into the next century.

KEY TERMS

- Balance of power
- Blowback
- Berlin wall
- Cold War
- Containment
- Covert action
- Cuban Missile Crisis
- Diplomacy
- Gulf War
- Hungarian Revolution
- Marshall Plan
- New World Order
- North American Free Trade Agreement
- Oil for food
- Six-Day War
- Suez Canal Crisis
- World Trade Organization

INTERNET SOURCES

a) http://www.state.gov/
This is the official site for the U.S. State Department. It catalogs activities of this federal government department relative to foreign policy. It provides information on country profiles, public assistance, legal issues, itinerary of the Secretary of State, etc.

b) http://www.defensellink.mil/
This site is similar to a) but relative to the Department of Defense or the Pentagon. It therefore provides information mainly on defense issues and events especially as they pertain to the international community.

c) http://www.odci.gov/cia/ciahome.html
The Central Intelligence Agency (CIA) maintains this site. It provides information on this agency's activities relative to foreign countries.

d) http://www.foreignrelations.org/
This site is maintained by the nongovernmental think tank, the Council on Foreign Relations (CFR). Information is provided on activities of this organization, analyses of major foreign policy decisions by past and present U.S. presidents, etc.

Appendix A
Founding Documents

THE DECLARATION OF INDEPENDENCE

Action of Second Continental Congress, July 4, 1776
The unanimous Declaration of the thirteen
United States of America

WHEN in the Course of human Events, it becomes necessary for one People to dissolve the Political Bands which have connected them with another, and to assume among the Powers of the Earth, the separate and equal Station to which the Laws of Nature and of Nature's God entitle them, a decent Respect to the Opinions of Mankind requires that they should declare the causes which impel them to the Separation.

WE hold these Truths to be self-evident, that all Men are created equal, that they are endowed by their Creator with certain unalienable Rights, that among these are Life, Liberty and the Pursuit of Happiness—That to secure these Rights, Governments are instituted among Men, deriving their just Powers from the Consent of the Governed, that whenever any Form of Government becomes destructive of these Ends, it is the Right of the People to alter or to abolish it, and to institute new Government, laying its Foundation on such Principles, and organizing its Powers in such Form, as to them shall seem most likely to effect their Safety and Happiness. Prudence, indeed, will dictate that Governments long established should not be changed for light and transient Causes; and accordingly all Experience hath shewn, that Mankind are more disposed to suffer, while Evils are sufferable, than to right themselves by abolishing the Forms to which they are accustomed. But when a long Train of Abuses and Usurpations, pursuing invariably the same Object, evinces a Design to reduce them under absolute Despotism, it is their Right, it is their Duty, to throw off such Government, and to provide new Guards for their future Security. Such has been the patient Sufferance of these Colonies; and such is now the Necessity which constrains them to alter their former Systems of Government. The History of the present King of Great-Britain is a History of repeated Injuries and Usurpations, all having in direct Object the Establishment of an absolute Tyranny over these States. To prove this, let Facts be submitted to a candid World.

HE has refused his Assent to Laws, the most wholesome and necessary for the public Good.

HE has forbidden his Governors to pass Laws of immediate and pressing Importance, unless suspended in their Operation till his Assent should be obtained; and when so suspended, he has utterly neglected to attend to them.

HE has refused to pass other Laws for the Accommodation of large Districts of People, unless those People would relinquish the Right of Representation in the Legislature, a Right inestimable to them, and formidable to Tyrants only.

HE has called together Legislative Bodies at Places unusual, uncomfortable, and distant from the Depository of their public Records, for the sole Purpose of fatiguing them into Compliance with his Measures.

HE has dissolved Representative Houses repeatedly, for opposing with manly Firmness his Invasions on the Rights of the People.

HE has refused for a long Time, after such Dissolutions, to cause others to be elected; whereby the Legislative Powers, incapable of the Annihilation, have returned to the People at large for their exercise; the State remaining in the mean time exposed to all the Dangers of Invasion from without, and the Convulsions within.

HE has endeavoured to prevent the Population of these States; for that Purpose obstructing the Laws for Naturalization of Foreigners; refusing to pass others to encourage their Migrations hither, and raising the Conditions of new Appropriations of Lands.

HE has obstructed the Administration of Justice, by refusing his Assent to Laws for establishing Judiciary Powers.

HE has made Judges dependent on his Will alone, for the Tenure of their Offices, and the Amount and Payment of their Salaries.

HE has erected a Multitude of new Offices, and sent hither Swarms of Officers to harrass our People, and eat out their Substance.

HE has kept among us, in Times of Peace, Standing Armies, without the consent of our Legislatures.

HE has affected to render the Military independent of and superior to the Civil Power.

HE has combined with others to subject us to a Jurisdiction foreign to our Constitution, and unacknowledged by our Laws; giving his Assent to their Acts of pretended Legislation:

FOR quartering large Bodies of Armed Troops among us;

FOR protecting them, by a mock Trial, from Punishment for any Murders which they should commit on the Inhabitants of these States:

FOR cutting off our Trade with all Parts of the World:

FOR imposing Taxes on us without our Consent:

FOR depriving us, in many Cases, of the Benefits of Trial by Jury:

FOR transporting us beyond Seas to be tried for pretended Offences:

FOR abolishing the free System of English Laws in a neighbouring Province, establishing therein an arbitrary Government, and enlarging its Boundaries, so as to render it at once an Example and fit Instrument for introducing the same absolute Rules into these Colonies:

FOR taking away our Charters, abolishing our most valuable Laws, and altering fundamentally the Forms of our Governments:

FOR suspending our own Legislatures, and declaring themselves invested with Power to legislate for us in all Cases whatsoever.

HE has abdicated Government here, by declaring us out of his Protection and waging War against us.

HE has plundered our Seas, ravaged our Coasts, burnt our Towns, and destroyed the Lives of our People.

HE is, at this Time, transporting large Armies of foreign Mercenaries to compleat the Works of Death, Desolation, and Tyranny, already begun with circumstances of Cruelty and Perfidy, scarcely paralleled in the most barbarous Ages, and totally unworthy the Head of a civilized Nation.

HE has constrained our fellow Citizens taken Captive on the high Seas to bear Arms against their Country, to become the Executioners of their Friends and Brethren, or to fall themselves by their Hands.

HE has excited domestic Insurrections amongst us, and has endeavoured to bring on the Inhabitants of our Frontiers, the merciless Indian Savages, whose known Rule of Warfare, is an undistinguished Destruction, of all Ages, Sexes and Conditions.

IN every stage of these Oppressions we have Petitioned for Redress in the most humble Terms: Our repeated Petitions have been answered only by repeated Injury. A Prince, whose Character is thus marked by every act which may define a Tyrant, is unfit to be the Ruler of a free People.

NOR have we been wanting in Attentions to our British Brethren. We have warned them from Time to Time of Attempts by their Legislature to extend an unwarrantable Jurisdiction over us. We have reminded them of the Circumstances of our Emigration and Settlement here. We have appealed to their native Justice and Magnanimity, and we have conjured them by the Ties of our common Kindred to disavow these Usurpations, which, would inevitably interrupt our Connections and Correspondence. They too have been deaf to the Voice of Justice and of Consanguinity. We must, therefore, acquiesce in the Necessity, which denounces our Separation, and hold them, as we hold the rest of Mankind, Enemies in War, in Peace, Friends.

WE, therefore, the Representatives of the UNITED STATES OF AMERICA, in GENERAL CONGRESS, Assembled, appealing to the Supreme Judge of the World for the Rectitude of our Intentions, do, in the Name, and by Authority of the good People of these Colonies, solemnly Publish and Declare, That these United Colonies are, and of Right ought to be, FREE AND INDEPENDENT STATES; that they are absolved from all Allegiance to the British Crown, and that all political Connection between them and the State of Great-Britain, is and ought to be totally dissolved; and that as FREE AND INDEPENDENT STATES, they have full Power to levy War, conclude Peace, contract Alliances, establish Commerce, and to do all other Acts and Things which INDEPENDENT STATES may of right do. And for the support of this Declaration, with a firm Reliance on the Protection of divine Providence, we mutually pledge to each other our Lives, our Fortunes, and our sacred Honor.

The United States Constitution

We the People of the United States, in Order to form a more perfect Union, establish Justice, insure domestic Tranquility, provide for the common defence, promote the general Welfare, and secure the Blessings of Liberty to ourselves and our Posterity, do ordain and establish this Constitution for the United States of America.

Article I.

Section 1.

All legislative Powers herein granted shall be vested in a Congress of the United States, which shall consist of a Senate and House of Representatives.

Section 2.

Clause 1: The House of Representatives shall be composed of Members chosen every second Year by the People of the several States, and the Electors in each State shall have the Qualifications requisite for Electors of the most numerous Branch of the State Legislature.

Clause 2: No Person shall be a Representative who shall not have attained to the Age of twenty five Years, and been seven Years a Citizen of the United States, and who shall not, when elected, be an Inhabitant of that State in which he shall be chosen.

Clause 3: Representatives and direct Taxes shall be apportioned among the several States which may be included within this Union, according to their respective Numbers, which shall be determined by adding to the whole Number of free Persons, including those bound to Service for a Term of Years, and excluding Indians not taxed, three fifths of all other Persons. The actual Enumeration shall be made within three Years after the first Meeting of the Congress of the United States, and within every subsequent Term of ten Years, in such Manner as they shall by Law direct. The Number of Representatives shall not exceed one for every thirty Thousand, but each State shall have at Least one Representative; and until such enumeration shall be made, the State of New Hampshire shall be entitled to choose three, Massachusetts eight, Rhode-Island and Providence Plantations one, Connecticut five, New-York six, New Jersey four, Pennsylvania eight, Delaware one, Maryland six, Virginia ten, North Carolina five, South Carolina five, and Georgia three.

Clause 4: When vacancies happen in the Representation from any State, the Executive Authority thereof shall issue Writs of Election to fill such Vacancies.

Clause 5: The House of Representatives shall choose their Speaker and other Officers; and shall have the sole Power of Impeachment.

Section 3.

Clause 1: The Senate of the United States shall be composed of two Senators from each State, chosen by the Legislature thereof, for six Years; and each Senator shall have one Vote.

Clause 2: Immediately after they shall be assembled in Consequence of the first Election, they shall be divided as equally as may be into three Classes. The Seats of the Senators of the first Class shall be vacated at the Expiration of the second Year, of the second Class at the Expiration of the fourth Year, and of the third Class at the Expiration of the sixth Year, so that one third may be chosen every second Year; and if Vacancies happen by Resignation, or otherwise, during the Recess of the Legislature of any State, the Executive thereof may make temporary Appointments until the next Meeting of the Legislature, which shall then fill such Vacancies.

Clause 3: No Person shall be a Senator who shall not have attained to the Age of thirty Years, and been nine Years a Citizen of the United States, and who shall not, when elected, be an Inhabitant of that State for which he shall be chosen.

Clause 4: The Vice President of the United States shall be President of the Senate, but shall have no Vote, unless they be equally divided.

Clause 5: The Senate shall choose their other Officers, and also a President pro tempore, in the Absence of the Vice President, or when he shall exercise the Office of President of the United States.

Clause 6: The Senate shall have the sole Power to try all Impeachments. When sitting for that Purpose, they shall be on Oath or Affirmation. When the President of the United States is tried, the Chief Justice shall preside: And no Person shall be convicted without the Concurrence of two thirds of the Members present.

Clause 7: Judgment in Cases of Impeachment shall not extend further than to removal from Office, and disqualification to hold and enjoy any Office of honor, Trust or Profit under the United States: but the Party convicted shall nevertheless be liable and subject to Indictment, Trial, Judgment and Punishment, according to Law.

Section 4.

Clause 1: The Times, Places and Manner of holding Elections for Senators and Representatives, shall be prescribed in each State by the Legislature thereof; but the

Congress may at any time by Law make or alter such Regulations, except as to the Places of choosing Senators.

Clause 2: The Congress shall assemble at least once in every Year, and such Meeting shall be on the first Monday in December, unless they shall by Law appoint a different Day.

Section 5.

Clause 1: Each House shall be the Judge of the Elections, Returns and Qualifications of its own Members, and a Majority of each shall constitute a Quorum to do Business; but a smaller Number may adjourn from day to day, and may be authorized to compel the Attendance of absent Members, in such Manner, and under such Penalties as each House may provide.

Clause 2: Each House may determine the Rules of its Proceedings, punish its Members for disorderly Behaviour, and, with the Concurrence of two thirds, expel a Member.

Clause 3: Each House shall keep a Journal of its Proceedings, and from time to time publish the same, excepting such Parts as may in their Judgment require Secrecy; and the Yeas and Nays of the Members of either House on any question shall, at the Desire of one fifth of those Present, be entered on the Journal.

Clause 4: Neither House, during the Session of Congress, shall, without the Consent of the other, adjourn for more than three days, nor to any other Place than that in which the two Houses shall be sitting.

Section 6.

Clause 1: The Senators and Representatives shall receive a Compensation for their Services, to be ascertained by Law, and paid out of the Treasury of the United States. They shall in all Cases, except Treason, Felony and Breach of the Peace, be privileged from Arrest during their Attendance at the Session of their respective Houses, and in going to and returning from the same; and for any Speech or Debate in either House, they shall not be questioned in any other Place.

Clause 2: No Senator or Representative shall, during the Time for which he was elected, be appointed to any civil Office under the Authority of the United States, which shall have been created, or the Emoluments whereof shall have been encreased during such time; and no Person holding any Office under the United States, shall be a Member of either House during his Continuance in Office.

Section 7.

Clause 1: All Bills for raising Revenue shall originate in the House of Representatives; but the Senate may propose or concur with Amendments as on other Bills.

Clause 2: Every Bill which shall have passed the House of Representatives and the Senate, shall, before it become a Law, be presented to the President of the United States; If he approve he shall sign it, but if not he shall return it, with his Objections to that House in which it shall have originated, who shall enter the Objections at large on their Journal, and proceed to reconsider it. If after such Reconsideration two thirds of that House shall agree to pass the Bill, it shall be sent, together with the Objections, to the other House, by which it shall likewise be reconsidered, and if approved by two thirds of that House, it shall become a Law. But in all such Cases the Votes of both Houses shall be determined by yeas and Nays, and the Names of the Persons voting for and against the Bill shall be entered on the Journal of each House respectively. If any Bill shall not be returned by the President within ten Days (Sundays excepted) after it shall have been presented to him, the Same shall be a Law, in like Manner as if he had signed it, unless the Congress by their Adjournment prevent its Return, in which Case it shall not be a Law.

Clause 3: Every Order, Resolution, or Vote to which the Concurrence of the Senate and House of Representatives may be necessary (except on a question of Adjournment) shall be presented to the President of the United States; and before the Same shall take Effect, shall be approved by him, or being disapproved by him, shall be repassed by two thirds of the Senate and House of Representatives, according to the Rules and Limitations prescribed in the Case of a Bill.

Section 8.

Clause 1: The Congress shall have Power To lay and collect Taxes, Duties, Imposts and Excises, to pay the Debts and provide for the common Defence and general Welfare of the United States; but all Duties, Imposts and Excises shall be uniform throughout the United States;

Clause 2: To borrow Money on the credit of the United States;

Clause 3: To regulate Commerce with foreign Nations, and among the several States, and with the Indian Tribes;

Clause 4: To establish an uniform Rule of Naturalization, and uniform Laws on the subject of Bankruptcies throughout the United States;

Clause 5: To coin Money, regulate the Value thereof, and of foreign Coin, and fix the Standard of Weights and Measures;

Clause 6: To provide for the Punishment of counterfeiting the Securities and current Coin of the United States;

Clause 7: To establish Post Offices and post Roads;

Clause 8: To promote the Progress of Science and useful Arts, by securing for limited Times to Authors and Inventors the exclusive Right to their respective Writings and Discoveries;

Clause 9: To constitute Tribunals inferior to the supreme Court;

Clause 10: To define and punish Piracies and Felonies committed on the high Seas, and Offences against the Law of Nations;

Clause 11: To declare War, grant Letters of Marque and Reprisal, and make Rules concerning Captures on Land and Water;

Clause 12: To raise and support Armies, but no Appropriation of Money to that Use shall be for a longer Term than two Years;

Clause 13: To provide and maintain a Navy;

Clause 14: To make Rules for the Government and Regulation of the land and naval Forces;

Clause 15: To provide for calling forth the Militia to execute the Laws of the Union, suppress Insurrections and repel Invasions;

Clause 16: To provide for organizing, arming, and disciplining, the Militia, and for governing such Part of them as may be employed in the Service of the United States, reserving to the States respectively, the Appointment of the Officers, and the Authority of training the Militia according to the discipline prescribed by Congress;

Clause 17: To exercise exclusive Legislation in all Cases whatsoever, over such District (not exceeding ten Miles square) as may, by Cession of particular States, and the Acceptance of Congress, become the Seat of the Government of the United States, and to exercise like Authority over all Places purchased by the Consent of the Legislature of the State in which the Same shall be, for the Erection of Forts, Magazines, Arsenals, dock-Yards, and other needful Buildings;—And

Clause 18: To make all Laws which shall be necessary and proper for carrying into Execution the foregoing Powers, and all other Powers vested by this Constitution in the Government of the United States, or in any Department or Officer thereof.

Section 9.

Clause 1: The Migration or Importation of such Persons as any of the States now existing shall think proper to admit, shall not be prohibited by the Congress prior to the Year one thousand eight hundred and eight, but a Tax or duty may be imposed on such Importation, not exceeding ten dollars for each Person.

Clause 2: The Privilege of the Writ of Habeas Corpus shall not be suspended, unless when in Cases of Rebellion or Invasion the public Safety may require it.

Clause 3: No Bill of Attainder or ex post facto Law shall be passed.

Clause 4: No Capitation, or other direct, Tax shall be laid, unless in Proportion to the Census or Enumeration herein before directed to be taken.

Clause 5: No Tax or Duty shall be laid on Articles exported from any State.

Clause 6: No Preference shall be given by any Regulation of Commerce or Revenue to the Ports of one State over those of another: nor shall Vessels bound to, or from, one State, be obliged to enter, clear, or pay Duties in another.

Clause 7: No Money shall be drawn from the Treasury, but in Consequence of Appropriations made by Law; and a regular Statement and Account of the Receipts and Expenditures of all public Money shall be published from time to time.

Clause 8: No Title of Nobility shall be granted by the United States: And no Person holding any Office of Profit or Trust under them, shall, without the Consent of the Congress, accept of any present, Emolument, Office, or Title, of any kind whatever, from any King, Prince, or foreign State.

Section 10.

Clause 1: No State shall enter into any Treaty, Alliance, or Confederation; grant Letters of Marque and Reprisal; coin Money; emit Bills of Credit; make any Thing but gold and silver Coin a Tender in Payment of Debts; pass any Bill of Attainder, ex post facto Law, or Law impairing the Obligation of Contracts, or grant any Title of Nobility.

Clause 2: No State shall, without the Consent of the Congress, lay any Imposts or Duties on Imports or Exports, except what may be absolutely necessary for executing it's inspection Laws: and the net Produce of all Duties and Imposts, laid by any State on Imports or Exports, shall be for the Use of the Treasury of the United States; and all such Laws shall be subject to the Revision and Controul of the Congress.

Clause 3: No State shall, without the Consent of Congress, lay any Duty of Tonnage, keep Troops, or Ships of War in time of Peace, enter into any Agreement or Compact with another State, or with a foreign Power, or engage in War, unless actually invaded, or in such imminent Danger as will not admit of delay.

ARTICLE II.

Section 1.

Clause 1: The executive Power shall be vested in a President of the United States of America. He shall hold his Office during the Term of four Years, and, together with the Vice President, chosen for the same Term, be elected, as follows

Clause 2: Each State shall appoint, in such Manner as the Legislature thereof may direct, a Number of Electors, equal to the whole Number of Senators and Representatives to which the State may be entitled in the Congress: but no Senator or Representative, or Person holding an Office of Trust or Profit under the United States, shall be appointed an Elector.

Clause 3: The Electors shall meet in their respective States, and vote by Ballot for two Persons, of whom one at least shall not be an Inhabitant of the same State with themselves. And they shall make a List of all the Persons voted for, and of the Number of Votes for each; which List they shall sign and certify, and transmit sealed to the Seat of the Government of the United States, directed to the President of the Senate. The President of the Senate shall, in the Presence of the Senate and House of Representatives, open all the Certificates, and the Votes shall then be counted. The Person having the greatest Number of Votes shall be the President, if such Number be a Majority of the whole Number of Electors appointed; and if there be more than one who have such Majority, and have an equal Number of Votes, then the House of Representatives shall immediately choose by Ballot one of them for President; and if no Person have a Majority, then from the five highest on the List the said House shall in like Manner choose the President. But in choosing the President, the Votes shall be taken by States, the Representation from each State having one Vote; A quorum for this Purpose shall consist of a Member or Members from two thirds of the States, and a Majority of all the States shall be necessary to a Choice. In every Case, after the Choice of the President, the Person having the greatest Number of Votes of the Electors shall be the Vice President. But if there should remain two or more who have equal Votes, the Senate shall choose from them by Ballot the Vice President.

Clause 4: The Congress may determine the Time of choosing the Electors, and the Day on which they shall give their Votes; which Day shall be the same throughout the United States.

Clause 5: No Person except a natural born Citizen, or a Citizen of the United States, at the time of the Adoption of this Constitution, shall be eligible to the Office of President; neither shall any Person be eligible to that Office who shall not have attained to the Age of thirty five Years, and been fourteen Years a Resident within the United States.

Clause 6: In Case of the Removal of the President from Office, or of his Death, Resignation, or Inability to discharge the Powers and Duties of the said Office, the Same shall devolve on the Vice President, and the Congress may by Law provide for the Case of Removal, Death, Resignation or Inability, both of the President and Vice President, declaring what Officer shall then act as President, and such Officer shall act accordingly, until the Disability be removed, or a President shall be elected.

Clause 7: The President shall, at stated Times, receive for his Services, a Compensation, which shall neither be encreased nor diminished during the Period for which he shall have been elected, and he shall not receive within that Period any other Emolument from the United States, or any of them.

Clause 8: Before he enter on the Execution of his Office, he shall take the following Oath or Affirmation:—"I do solemnly swear (or affirm) that I will faithfully execute the Office of President of the United States, and will to the best of my Ability, preserve, protect and defend the Constitution of the United States."

Section 2.

Clause 1: The President shall be Commander in Chief of the Army and Navy of the United States, and of the Militia of the several States, when called into the actual Service of the United States; he may require the Opinion, in writing, of the principal Officer in each of the executive Departments, upon any Subject relating to the Duties of their respective Offices, and he shall have Power to grant Reprieves and Pardons for Offences against the United States, except in Cases of Impeachment.

Clause 2: He shall have Power, by and with the Advice and Consent of the Senate, to make Treaties, provided two thirds of the Senators present concur; and he shall nominate, and by and with the Advice and Consent of the Senate, shall appoint Ambassadors, other public Ministers and Consuls, Judges of the supreme Court, and all other Officers of the United States, whose Appointments are not herein otherwise provided for, and which shall be established by Law: but the Congress may by Law vest the Appointment of such inferior Officers, as they think proper, in the President alone, in the Courts of Law, or in the Heads of Departments.

Clause 3: The President shall have Power to fill up all Vacancies that may happen during the Recess of the Senate, by granting Commissions which shall expire at the End of their next Session.

Section 3.

He shall from time to time give to the Congress Information of the State of the Union, and recommend to their Consideration such Measures as he shall judge necessary and expedient; he may, on extraordinary Occasions, convene both Houses, or either of them, and in Case of Disagreement between them, with Respect to the Time of Adjournment, he may adjourn them to such Time as he shall think proper; he shall receive Ambassadors and other public Ministers; he shall take Care that the Laws be faithfully executed, and shall Commission all the Officers of the United States.

Section 4.

The President, Vice President and all civil Officers of the United States, shall be removed from Office on Impeachment for, and Conviction of, Treason, Bribery, or other high Crimes and Misdemeanors.

ARTICLE III.

Section 1.

The judicial Power of the United States, shall be vested in one supreme Court, and in such inferior Courts as the Congress may from time to time ordain and establish. The Judges, both of the supreme and inferior Courts, shall hold their Offices during good Behaviour, and shall, at stated Times, receive for their Services, a Compensation, which shall not be diminished during their Continuance in Office.

Section 2.

Clause 1: The judicial Power shall extend to all Cases, in Law and Equity, arising under this Constitution, the Laws of the United States, and Treaties made, or which shall be made, under their Authority;—to all Cases affecting Ambassadors, other public Ministers and Consuls;—to all Cases of admiralty and maritime Jurisdiction;—to Controversies to which the United States shall be a Party;—to Controversies between two or more States;—between a State and Citizens of another State;—between Citizens of different States,—between Citizens of the same State claiming Lands under Grants of different States, and between a State, or the Citizens thereof, and foreign States, Citizens or Subjects.

Clause 2: In all Cases affecting Ambassadors, other public Ministers and Consuls, and those in which a State shall be Party, the supreme Court shall have original Jurisdiction. In all the other Cases before mentioned, the supreme Court shall have appellate Jurisdiction, both as to Law and Fact, with such Exceptions, and under such Regulations as the Congress shall make.

 Clause 3: The Trial of all Crimes, except in Cases of Impeachment, shall be by Jury; and such Trial shall be held in the State where the said Crimes shall have been committed; but when not committed within any State, the Trial shall be at such Place or Places as the Congress may by Law have directed.

Section 3.

Clause 1: Treason against the United States, shall consist only in levying War against them, or in adhering to their Enemies, giving them Aid and Comfort. No Person shall be convicted of Treason unless on the Testimony of two Witnesses to the same overt Act, or on Confession in open Court.

 Clause 2: The Congress shall have Power to declare the Punishment of Treason, but no Attainder of Treason shall work Corruption of Blood, or Forfeiture except during the Life of the Person attainted.

ARTICLE IV.

Section 1.

Full Faith and Credit shall be given in each State to the public Acts, Records, and judicial Proceedings of every other State. And the Congress may by general Laws prescribe the Manner in which such Acts, Records and Proceedings shall be proved, and the Effect thereof.

Section 2.

Clause 1: The Citizens of each State shall be entitled to all Privileges and Immunities of Citizens in the several States.

 Clause 2: A Person charged in any State with Treason, Felony, or other Crime, who shall flee from Justice, and be found in another State, shall on Demand of the executive Authority of the State from which he fled, be delivered up, to be removed to the State having Jurisdiction of the Crime.

 Clause 3: No Person held to Service or Labour in one State, under the Laws thereof, escaping into another, shall, in Consequence of any Law or Regulation therein, be discharged from such Service or Labour, but shall be delivered up on Claim of the Party to whom such Service or Labour may be due.

Section 3.

Clause 1: New States may be admitted by the Congress into this Union; but no new State shall be formed or erected within the Jurisdiction of any other State; nor any State be formed by the Junction of two or more States, or Parts of States, without the Consent of the Legislatures of the States concerned as well as of the Congress.

Clause 2: The Congress shall have Power to dispose of and make all needful Rules and Regulations respecting the Territory or other Property belonging to the United States; and nothing in this Constitution shall be so construed as to Prejudice any Claims of the United States, or of any particular State.

Section 4.

The United States shall guarantee to every State in this Union a Republican Form of Government, and shall protect each of them against Invasion; and on Application of the Legislature, or of the Executive (when the Legislature cannot be convened) against domestic Violence.

ARTICLE V.

The Congress, whenever two thirds of both Houses shall deem it necessary, shall propose Amendments to this Constitution, or, on the Application of the Legislatures of two thirds of the several States, shall call a Convention for proposing Amendments, which, in either Case, shall be valid to all Intents and Purposes, as Part of this Constitution, when ratified by the Legislatures of three fourths of the several States, or by Conventions in three fourths thereof, as the one or the other Mode of Ratification may be proposed by the Congress; Provided that no Amendment which may be made prior to the Year One thousand eight hundred and eight shall in any Manner affect the first and fourth Clauses in the Ninth Section of the first Article; and that no State, without its Consent, shall be deprived of its equal Suffrage in the Senate.

ARTICLE VI.

Clause 1: All Debts contracted and Engagements entered into, before the Adoption of this Constitution, shall be as valid against the United States under this Constitution, as under the Confederation.

Clause 2: This Constitution, and the Laws of the United States which shall be made in Pursuance thereof; and all Treaties made, or which shall be made, under the Authority of the United States, shall be the supreme Law of the Land; and the Judges in every State shall be bound thereby, any Thing in the Constitution or Laws of any State to the Contrary notwithstanding.

Clause 3: The Senators and Representatives before mentioned, and the Members of the several State Legislatures, and all executive and judicial Officers, both of the United States and of the several States, shall be bound by Oath or Affirmation, to support this Constitution; but no religious Test shall ever be required as a Qualification to any Office or public Trust under the United States.

ARTICLE VII.

The Ratification of the Conventions of nine States, shall be sufficient for the Establishment of this Constitution between the States so ratifying the Same.

done in Convention by the Unanimous Consent of the States present the Seventeenth Day of September in the Year of our Lord one thousand seven hundred and Eighty seven and of the Independence of the United States of America the Twelfth In witness whereof We have hereunto subscribed our Names,

AMENDMENTS TO THE CONSTITUTION

CONSTITUTION OF THE UNITED STATES ARTICLES IN ADDITION TO, AND AMENDMENT OF THE CONSTITUTION OF THE UNITED STATES OF AMERICA, PROPOSED BY CONGRESS, AND RATIFIED BY THE LEGISLATURES OF THE SEVERAL STATES, PURSUANT TO THE FIFTH ARTICLE OF THE ORIGINAL CONSTITUTION

AMENDMENT I.

Congress shall make no law respecting an establishment of religion, or prohibiting the free exercise thereof; or abridging the freedom of speech, or of the press; or the right of the people peaceably to assemble, and to petition the Government for a redress of grievances.

AMENDMENT II.

A well regulated Militia, being necessary to the security of a free State, the right of the people to keep and bear Arms, shall not be infringed.

Amendment III.

No Soldier shall, in time of peace be quartered in any house, without the consent of the Owner, nor in time of war, but in a manner to be prescribed by law.

Amendment IV.

The right of the people to be secure in their persons, houses, papers, and effects, against unreasonable searches and seizures, shall not be violated, and no Warrants shall issue, but upon probable cause, supported by Oath or affirmation, and particularly describing the place to be searched, and the persons or things to be seized.

Amendment V.

No person shall be held to answer for a capital, or otherwise infamous crime, unless on a presentment or indictment of a Grand Jury, except in cases arising in the land or naval forces, or in the Militia, when in actual service in time of War or public danger; nor shall any person be subject for the same offence to be twice put in jeopardy of life or limb; nor shall be compelled in any criminal case to be a witness against himself, nor be deprived of life, liberty, or property, without due process of law; nor shall private property be taken for public use, without just compensation.

Amendment VI.

In all criminal prosecutions, the accused shall enjoy the right to a speedy and public trial, by an impartial jury of the State and district wherein the crime shall have been committed, which district shall have been previously ascertained by law, and to be informed of the nature and cause of the accusation; to be confronted with the witnesses against him; to have compulsory process for obtaining witnesses in his favor, and to have the Assistance of Counsel for his defence.

Amendment VII.

In Suits at common law, where the value in controversy shall exceed twenty dollars, the right of trial by jury shall be preserved, and no fact tried by a jury, shall be otherwise re-examined in any Court of the United States, than according to the rules of the common law.

AMENDMENT VIII.

Excessive bail shall not be required, nor excessive fines imposed, nor cruel and unusual punishments inflicted.

AMENDMENT IX.

The enumeration in the Constitution, of certain rights, shall not be construed to deny or disparage others retained by the people.

AMENDMENT X.

The powers not delegated to the United States by the Constitution, nor prohibited by it to the States, are reserved to the States respectively, or to the people.

AMENDMENT XI.

The Judicial power of the United States shall not be construed to extend to any suit in law or equity, commenced or prosecuted against one of the United States by Citizens of another State, or by Citizens or Subjects of any Foreign State.

AMENDMENT XII.

The Electors shall meet in their respective states, and vote by ballot for President and Vice-President, one of whom, at least, shall not be an inhabitant of the same state with themselves; they shall name in their ballots the person voted for as President, and in distinct ballots the person voted for as Vice-President, and they shall make distinct lists of all persons voted for as President, and of all persons voted for as Vice-President, and of the number of votes for each, which lists they shall sign and certify, and transmit sealed to the seat of the government of the United States, directed to the President of the Senate;—The President of the Senate shall, in the presence of the Senate and House of Representatives, open all the certificates and the votes shall then be counted;—The person having the greatest number of votes for President, shall be the President, if such number be a majority of the whole number of Electors appointed; and if no person have such majority, then from the persons having the highest numbers not exceeding three on the list of those voted for as President, the House of Representatives shall choose immediately, by ballot, the President. But in choosing the President, the votes shall be taken by states, the representation from each state having one vote; a quorum for this purpose shall consist of a member or members from two-thirds of the states, and a majority of all the states shall be necessary to a choice. And if the House of Representatives shall not choose a President whenever the right of choice shall devolve upon them, before the fourth day of March next following, then the Vice-President shall act as President, as in the case of the death or other constitutional disability of the President.—The person having the greatest number of votes as Vice-President, shall be the Vice-President, if such number be a majority of the whole number of Electors appointed, and if no person have a majority, then from the two highest numbers on the list, the Senate shall choose the Vice-President; a quorum for the purpose shall consist of two-thirds of the whole number of Senators, and a majority of the whole number shall be necessary to a choice. But no person constitutionally ineligible to the office of President shall be eligible to that of Vice-President of the United States.

AMENDMENT XIII.

Section 1.
Neither slavery nor involuntary servitude, except as a punishment for crime whereof the party shall have been duly convicted, shall exist within the United States, or any place subject to their jurisdiction.

Section 2.
Congress shall have power to enforce this article by appropriate legislation.

AMENDMENT XIV.

Section 1.
All persons born or naturalized in the United States, and subject to the jurisdiction thereof, are citizens of the United States and of the State wherein they reside. No State shall make or enforce any law which shall abridge the privileges or immunities of citizens of the United States; nor shall any State deprive any person of life, liberty, or property, without due process of law; nor deny to any person within its jurisdiction the equal protection of the laws.

Section 2.
Representatives shall be apportioned among the several States according to their respective numbers, counting the whole number of persons in each State, excluding Indians not taxed. But when the right to vote at any election for the choice of electors for President and Vice President of the United States, Representatives in Congress, the

Executive and Judicial officers of a State, or the members of the Legislature thereof, is denied to any of the male inhabitants of such State, being twenty-one years of age, and citizens of the United States, or in any way abridged, except for participation in rebellion, or other crime, the basis of representation therein shall be reduced in the proportion which the number of such male citizens shall bear to the whole number of male citizens twenty-one years of age in such State.

Section 3.
No person shall be a Senator or Representative in Congress, or elector of President and Vice President, or hold any office, civil or military, under the United States, or under any State, who, having previously taken an oath, as a member of Congress, or as an officer of the United States, or as a member of any State legislature, or as an executive or judicial officer of any State, to support the Constitution of the United States, shall have engaged in insurrection or rebellion against the same, or given aid or comfort to the enemies thereof. But Congress may by a vote of two-thirds of each House, remove such disability.

Section 4.
The validity of the public debt of the United States, authorized by law, including debts incurred for payment of pensions and bounties for services in suppressing insurrection or rebellion, shall not be questioned. But neither the United States nor any State shall assume or pay any debt or obligation incurred in aid of insurrection or rebellion against the United States, or any claim for the loss or emancipation of any slave; but all such debts, obligations and claims shall be held illegal and void.

Section 5.
The Congress shall have power to enforce, by appropriate legislation, the provisions of this article.

AMENDMENT XV.

Section 1.
The right of citizens of the United States to vote shall not be denied or abridged by the United States or by any State on account of race, color, or previous condition of servitude.

Section 2.
The Congress shall have power to enforce this article by appropriate legislation.

Amendment XVI.
The Congress shall have power to lay and collect taxes on incomes, from whatever source derived, without apportionment among the several States, and without regard to any census or enumeration.

Amendment XVII.
The Senate of the United States shall be composed of two Senators from each State, elected by the people thereof, for six years; and each Senator shall have one vote. The electors in each State shall have the qualifications requisite for electors of the most numerous branch of the State legislatures.

When vacancies happen in the representation of any State in the Senate, the executive authority of such State shall issue writs of election to fill such vacancies: Provided, That the legislature of any State may empower the executive thereof to make temporary appointments until the people fill the vacancies by election as the legislature may direct. This amendment shall not be so construed as to affect the election or term of any Senator chosen before it becomes valid as part of the Constitution.

Amendment XVIII.

Section 1.
After one year from the ratification of this article the manufacture, sale, or transportation of intoxicating liquors within, the importation thereof into, or the exportation thereof from the United States and all territory subject to the jurisdiction thereof for beverage purposes is hereby prohibited.

Section 2.
The Congress and the several States shall have concurrent power to enforce this article by appropriate legislation.

Section 3.
This article shall be inoperative unless it shall have been ratified as an amendment to the Constitution by the legislatures of the several States, as provided in the

Constitution, within seven years from the date of the submission hereof to the States by the Congress.

AMENDMENT XIX.

The right of citizens of the United States to vote shall not be denied or abridged by the United States or by any State on account of sex.

Congress shall have power to enforce this article by appropriate legislation.

AMENDMENT XX.

Section 1.

The terms of the President and Vice President shall end at noon on the 20th day of January, and the terms of Senators and Representatives at noon on the 3d day of January, of the years in which such terms would have ended if this article had not been ratified; and the terms of their successors shall then begin.

Section 2.

The Congress shall assemble at least once in every year, and such meeting shall begin at noon on the 3d day of January, unless they shall by law appoint a different day.

Section 3.

If, at the time fixed for the beginning of the term of the President, the President elect shall have died, the Vice President elect shall become President. If a President shall not have been chosen before the time fixed for the beginning of his term, or if the President elect shall have failed to qualify, then the Vice President elect shall act as President until a President shall have qualified; and the Congress may by law provide for the case wherein neither a President elect nor a Vice President elect shall have qualified, declaring who shall then act as President, or the manner in which one who is to act shall be selected, and such person shall act accordingly until a President or Vice President shall have qualified.

Section 4.

The Congress may by law provide for the case of the death of any of the persons from whom the House of Representatives may choose a President whenever the right of choice shall have devolved upon them, and for the case of the death of any of the persons from whom the Senate may choose a Vice President whenever the right of choice shall have devolved upon them.

Section 5.
Sections 1 and 2 shall take effect on the 15th day of October following the ratification of this article.

Section 6.
This article shall be inoperative unless it shall have been ratified as an amendment to the Constitution by the legislatures of three-fourths of the several States within seven years from the date of its submission.

AMENDMENT XXI.

Section 1.
The eighteenth article of amendment to the Constitution of the United States is hereby repealed.

Section 2.
The transportation or importation into any State, Territory, or possession of the United States for delivery or use therein of intoxicating liquors, in violation of the laws thereof, is hereby prohibited.

Section 3.
This article shall be inoperative unless it shall have been ratified as an amendment to the Constitution by conventions in the several States, as provided in the Constitution, within seven years from the date of the submission hereof to the States by the Congress.

AMENDMENT XXII.

Section 1.
No person shall be elected to the office of the President more than twice, and no person who has held the office of President, or acted as President, for more than two years of a term to which some other person was elected President shall be elected to the office of the President more than once. But this Article shall not apply to any person holding the office of President when this Article was proposed by the Congress, and shall not prevent any person who may be holding the office of President, or acting as President, during the term within which this Article becomes operative from

holding the office of President or acting as President during the remainder of such term.

Section 2.
This article shall be inoperative unless it shall have been ratified as an amendment to the Constitution by the legislatures of three-fourths of the several States within seven years from the date of its submission to the States by the Congress.

AMENDMENT XXIII.

Section 1.
The District constituting the seat of Government of the United States shall appoint in such manner as the Congress may direct:

> A number of electors of President and Vice President equal to the whole number of Senators and Representatives in Congress to which the District would be entitled if it were a State, but in no event more than the least populous State; they shall be in addition to those appointed by the States, but they shall be considered, for the purposes of the election of President and Vice President, to be electors appointed by a State; and they shall meet in the District and perform such duties as provided by the twelfth article of amendment.

Section 2.
The Congress shall have power to enforce this article by appropriate legislation.

AMENDMENT XXIV.

Section 1.
The right of citizens of the United States to vote in any primary or other election for President or Vice President, for electors for President or Vice President, or for Senator or Representative in Congress, shall not be denied or abridged by the United States or any State by reason of failure to pay any poll tax or other tax.

Section 2.
The Congress shall have power to enforce this article by appropriate legislation.

AMENDMENT XXV.

Section 1.
In case of the removal of the President from office or of his death or resignation, the Vice President shall become President.

Section 2.
Whenever there is a vacancy in the office of the Vice President, the President shall nominate a Vice President who shall take office upon confirmation by a majority vote of both Houses of Congress.

Section 3.
Whenever the President transmits to the President pro tempore of the Senate and the Speaker of the House of Representatives his written declaration that he is unable to discharge the powers and duties of his office, and until he transmits to them a written declaration to the contrary, such powers and duties shall be discharged by the Vice President as Acting President.

Section 4.
Whenever the Vice President and a majority of either the principal officers of the executive departments or of such other body as Congress may by law provide, transmit to the President pro tempore of the Senate and the Speaker of the House of Representatives their written declaration that the President is unable to discharge the powers and duties of his office, the Vice President shall immediately assume the powers and duties of the office as Acting President.

Thereafter, when the President transmits to the President pro tempore of the Senate and the Speaker of the House of Representatives his written declaration that no inability exists, he shall resume the powers and duties of his office unless the Vice President and a majority of either the principal officers of the executive department or of such other body as Congress may by law provide, transmit within four days to the President pro tempore of the Senate and the Speaker of the House of Representatives their written declaration that the President is unable to discharge the powers and duties of his office. Thereupon Congress shall decide the issue, assembling within forty-eight hours for that purpose if not in session. If the Congress, within twenty-one days after receipt of the latter written declaration, or, if Congress is not in session, within twenty-one days after Congress is required to assemble, determines by two-thirds vote of both Houses that the President is unable to discharge the powers and duties of his office, the Vice President shall continue to discharge the same as Acting President; otherwise, the President shall resume the powers and duties of his office.

AMENDMENT XXVI.

Section 1.
The right of citizens of the United States, who are eighteen years of age or older, to vote shall not be denied or abridged by the United States or by any State on account of age.

Section 2.
The Congress shall have power to enforce this article by appropriate legislation.

AMENDMENT XXVII.
No law, varying the compensation for the services of the Senators and Representatives, shall take effect, until an election of Representatives shall have intervened.

THE FEDERALIST NO. 10

The Union as a Safeguard Against Domestic Faction

To the People of the State of New York:
Among the numerous advantages promised by a well-constructed Union, none deserves to be more accurately developed than its tendency to break and control the violence of faction. The friend of popular governments never finds himself so much alarmed for their character and fate, as when he contemplates their propensity to this dangerous vice. He will not fail, therefore, to set a due value on any plan which, without violating the principles to which he is attached, provides a proper cure for it. The instability, injustice, and confusion introduced into the public councils, have, in truth, been the mortal diseases under which popular governments have everywhere perished; as they continue to be the favorite and fruitful topics from which the adversaries to liberty derive their most specious declamations. The valuable improvements made by the American constitutions on the popular models, both ancient and modern, cannot certainly be too much admired; but it would be an unwarrantable partiality, to contend that they have as effectually obviated the danger

on this side, as was wished and expected. Complaints are everywhere heard from our most considerate and virtuous citizens, equally the friends of public and private faith, and of public and personal liberty, that our governments are too unstable, that the public good is disregarded in the conflicts of rival parties, and that measures are too often decided, not according to the rules of justice and the rights of the minor party, but by the superior force of an interested and overbearing majority. However anxiously we may wish that these complaints had no foundation, the evidence of known facts will not permit us to deny that they are in some degree true. It will be found, indeed, on a candid review of our situation, that some of the distresses under which we labor have been erroneously charged on the operation of our governments; but it will be found, at the same time, that other causes will not alone account for many of our heaviest misfortunes; and, particularly, for that prevailing and increasing distrust of public engagements, and alarm for private rights, which are echoed from one end of the continent to the other. These must be chiefly, if not wholly, effects of the unsteadiness and injustice with which a factious spirit has tainted our public administrations.

By a faction, I understand a number of citizens, whether amounting to a majority or a minority of the whole, who are united and actuated by some common impulse of passion, or of interest, adverse to the rights of other citizens, or to the permanent and aggregate interests of the community.

There are two methods of curing the mischiefs of faction: the one, by removing its causes; the other, by controlling its effects.

There are again two methods of removing the causes of faction: the one, by destroying the liberty which is essential to its existence; the other, by giving to every citizen the same opinions, the same passions, and the same interests.

It could never be more truly said than of the first remedy, that it was worse than the disease. Liberty is to faction what air is to fire, an aliment without which it instantly expires. But it could not be less folly to abolish liberty, which is essential to political life, because it nourishes faction, than it would be to wish the annihilation of air, which is essential to animal life, because it imparts to fire its destructive agency.

The second expedient is as impracticable as the first would be unwise. As long as the reason of man continues fallible, and he is at liberty to exercise it, different opinions will be formed. As long as the connection subsists between his reason and his self-love, his opinions and his passions will have a reciprocal influence on each other; and the former will be objects to which the latter will attach themselves. The diversity in the faculties of men, from which the rights of property originate, is not less an insuperable obstacle to a uniformity of interests. The protection of these faculties is the first object of government. From the protection of different and unequal faculties of acquiring property, the possession of different degrees and kinds of property immediately results; and from the influence of these on the sentiments and views of the respective proprietors, ensues a division of the society into different interests and parties.

The latent causes of faction are thus sown in the nature of man; and we see them everywhere brought into different degrees of activity, according to the different circumstances of civil society. A zeal for different opinions concerning religion, concerning government, and many other points, as well of speculation as of practice; an attachment to different leaders ambitiously contending for pre-eminence and power; or to persons of other descriptions whose fortunes have been interesting to the human passions, have, in turn, divided mankind into parties, inflamed them with mutual animosity, and rendered them much more disposed to vex and oppress each other than to co-operate for their common good. So strong is this propensity of mankind to fall into mutual animosities, that where no substantial occasion presents itself, the most frivolous and fanciful distinctions have been sufficient to kindle their unfriendly passions and excite their most violent conflicts. But the most common and durable source of factions has been the various and unequal distribution of property. Those who hold and those who are without property have ever formed distinct interests in society. Those who are creditors, and those who are debtors, fall under a like discrimination. A landed interest, a manufacturing interest, a mercantile interest, a moneyed interest, with many lesser interests, grow up of necessity in civilized nations, and divide them into different classes, actuated by different sentiments and views. The regulation of these various and interfering interests forms the principal task of modern legislation, and involves the spirit of party and faction in the necessary and ordinary operations of the government.

No man is allowed to be a judge in his own cause, because his interest would certainly bias his judgment, and, not improbably, corrupt his integrity. With equal, nay with greater reason, a body of men are unfit to be both judges and parties at the same time; yet what are many of the most important acts of legislation, but so many judicial determinations, not indeed concerning the rights of single persons, but concerning the rights of large bodies of citizens? And what are the different classes of legislators but advocates and parties to the causes which they determine? Is a law proposed concerning private debts? It is a question to which the creditors are parties on one side and the debtors on the other. Justice ought to hold the balance between them. Yet the parties are, and must be, themselves the judges; and the most numerous party, or, in other words, the most powerful faction must be expected to prevail. Shall domestic manufactures be encouraged, and in what degree, by restrictions on foreign manufactures? are questions which would be differently decided by the landed and the manufacturing classes, and probably by neither with a sole regard to justice and the public good. The apportionment of taxes on the various descriptions of property is an act which seems to require the most exact impartiality; yet there is, perhaps, no legislative act in which greater opportunity and temptation are given to a predominant party to trample on the rules of justice. Every shilling with which they overburden the inferior number, is a shilling saved to their own pockets.

It is in vain to say that enlightened statesmen will be able to adjust these clashing interests, and render them all subservient to the public good. Enlightened statesmen will not always be at the helm. Nor, in many cases, can such an adjustment be made at all without taking into view indirect and remote considerations, which will rarely prevail over the immediate interest which one party may find in disregarding the rights of another or the good of the whole.

The inference to which we are brought is, that the causes of faction cannot be removed, and that relief is only to be sought in the means of controlling its effects.

If a faction consists of less than a majority, relief is supplied by the republican principle, which enables the majority to defeat its sinister views by regular vote. It may clog the administration, it may convulse the society; but it will be unable to execute and mask its violence under the forms of the Constitution. When a majority is included in a faction, the form of popular government, on the other hand, enables it to sacrifice to its ruling passion or interest both the public good and the rights of other citizens. To secure the public good and private rights against the danger of such a faction, and at the same time to preserve the spirit and the form of popular government, is then the great object to which our inquiries are directed. Let me add that it is the great desideratum by which this form of government can be rescued from the opprobrium under which it has so long labored, and be recommended to the esteem and adoption of mankind.

By what means is this object attainable? Evidently by one of two only. Either the existence of the same passion or interest in a majority at the same time must be prevented, or the majority, having such coexistent passion or interest, must be rendered, by their number and local situation, unable to concert and carry into effect schemes of oppression. If the impulse and the opportunity be suffered to coincide, we well know that neither moral nor religious motives can be relied on as an adequate control. They are not found to be such on the injustice and violence of individuals, and lose their efficacy in proportion to the number combined together, that is, in proportion as their efficacy becomes needful.

From this view of the subject it may be concluded that a pure democracy, by which I mean a society consisting of a small number of citizens, who assemble and administer the government in person, can admit of no cure for the mischiefs of faction. A common passion or interest will, in almost every case, be felt by a majority of the whole; a communication and concert result from the form of government itself; and there is nothing to check the inducements to sacrifice the weaker party or an obnoxious individual. Hence it is that such democracies have ever been spectacles of turbulence and contention; have ever been found incompatible with personal security or the rights of property; and have in general been as short in their lives as they have been violent in their deaths. Theoretic politicians, who have patronized this species of government, have erroneously supposed that by reducing mankind to a perfect equality in their political rights, they would, at the same time, be perfectly equalized and assimilated in their possessions, their opinions, and their passions.

A republic, by which I mean a government in which the scheme of representation takes place, opens a different prospect, and promises the cure for which we are seeking. Let us examine the points in which it varies from pure democracy, and we shall comprehend both the nature of the cure and the efficacy which it must derive from the Union.

The two great points of difference between a democracy and a republic are: first, the delegation of the government, in the latter, to a small number of citizens elected by the rest; secondly, the greater number of citizens, and greater sphere of country, over which the latter may be extended.

The effect of the first difference is, on the one hand, to refine and enlarge the public views, by passing them through the medium of a chosen body of citizens, whose wisdom may best discern the true interest of their country, and whose patriotism and love of justice will be least likely to sacrifice it to temporary or partial considerations. Under such a regulation, it may well happen that the public voice, pronounced by the representatives of the people, will be more consonant to the public good than if pronounced by the people themselves, convened for the purpose. On the other hand, the effect may be inverted. Men of factious tempers, of local prejudices, or of sinister designs, may, by intrigue, by corruption, or by other means, first obtain the suffrages, and then betray the interests, of the people. The question resulting is, whether small or extensive republics are more favorable to the election of proper guardians of the public weal; and it is clearly decided in favor of the latter by two obvious considerations:

In the first place, it is to be remarked that, however small the republic may be, the representatives must be raised to a certain number, in order to guard against the cabals of a few; and that, however large it may be, they must be limited to a certain number, in order to guard against the confusion of a multitude. Hence, the number of representatives in the two cases not being in proportion to that of the two constituents, and being proportionally greater in the small republic, it follows that, if the proportion of fit characters be not less in the large than in the small republic, the former will present a greater option, and consequently a greater probability of a fit choice.

In the next place, as each representative will be chosen by a greater number of citizens in the large than in the small republic, it will be more difficult for unworthy candidates to practice with success the vicious arts by which elections are too often carried; and the suffrages of the people being more free, will be more likely to centre in men who possess the most attractive merit and the most diffusive and established characters.

It must be confessed that in this, as in most other cases, there is a mean, on both sides of which inconveniences will be found to lie. By enlarging too much the number of electors, you render the representatives too little acquainted with all their local circumstances and lesser interests; as by reducing it too much, you render him unduly attached to these, and too little fit to comprehend and pursue great and national objects. The federal Constitution forms a happy combination in this respect; the great and aggregate interests being referred to the national, the local and particular to the State legislatures.

The other point of difference is, the greater number of citizens and extent of territory which may be brought within the compass of republican than of democratic government; and it is this circumstance principally which renders factious combinations less to be dreaded in the former than in the latter. The smaller the society, the fewer probably will be the distinct parties and interests composing it; the fewer the distinct parties and interests, the more frequently will a majority be found of the same party; and the smaller the number of individuals composing a majority, and the smaller the compass within which they are placed, the more easily will they concert and execute their plans of oppression. Extend the sphere, and you take in a greater variety of parties and interests; you make it less probable that a majority of the whole will have a common motive to invade the rights of other citizens; or if such a common motive exists, it will be more difficult for all who feel it to discover their own strength, and to act in unison with each other. Besides other impediments, it may be remarked that, where there is a consciousness of unjust or dishonorable purposes, communication is always checked by distrust in proportion to the number whose concurrence is necessary.

Hence, it clearly appears, that the same advantage which a republic has over a democracy, in controlling the effects of faction, is enjoyed by a large over a small republic,—is enjoyed by the Union over the States composing it. Does the advantage consist in the substitution of representatives whose enlightened views and virtuous sentiments render them superior to local prejudices and schemes of injustice? It will not be denied that the representation of the Union will be most likely to possess these requisite endowments. Does it consist in the greater security afforded by a greater variety of parties, against the event of any one party being able to outnumber and oppress the rest? In an equal degree does the increased variety of parties comprised within the Union, increase this security. Does it, in fine, consist in the greater obstacles opposed to the concert and accomplishment of the secret wishes of an unjust and interested majority? Here, again, the extent of the Union gives it the most palpable advantage.

The influence of factious leaders may kindle a flame within their particular States, but will be unable to spread a general conflagration through the other States. A religious sect may degenerate into a political faction in a part of the Confederacy; but the variety of sects dispersed over the entire face of it must secure the national councils against any danger from that source. A rage for paper money, for an abolition of debts, for an equal division of property, or for any other improper or wicked project, will be less apt to pervade the whole body of the Union than a particular member of it; in the same proportion as such a malady is more likely to taint a particular county or district, than an entire State.

In the extent and proper structure of the Union, therefore, we behold a republican remedy for the diseases most incident to republican government. And according to the degree of pleasure and pride we feel in being republicans, ought to be our zeal in cherishing the spirit and supporting the character of Federalists.

Publius.

THE FEDERALIST NO. 51

Checks and Balances

To the People of the State of New York:

To what expedient, then, shall we finally resort, for maintaining in practice the necessary partition of power among the several departments, as laid down in the Constitution? The only answer that can be given is, that as all these exterior provisions are found to be inadequate, the defect must be supplied, by so contriving the interior structure of the government as that its several constituent parts may, by their mutual relations, be the means of keeping each other in their proper places. Without presuming to undertake a full development of this important idea, I will hazard a few general observations, which may perhaps place it in a clearer light, and enable us to form a more correct judgment of the principles and structure of the government planned by the convention.

In order to lay a due foundation for that separate and distinct exercise of the different powers of government, which to a certain extent is admitted on all hands to be essential to the preservation of liberty, it is evident that each department should have a will of its own; and consequently should be so constituted that the members of each should have as little agency as possible in the appointment of the members of the others. Were this principle rigorously adhered to, it would require that all the appointments for the supreme executive, legislative, and judiciary magistracies should be drawn from the same fountain of authority, the people, through channels having no communication whatever with one another. Perhaps such a plan of constructing the several departments would be less difficult in practice than it may in contemplation appear. Some difficulties, however, and some additional expense would attend the execution of it. Some deviations, therefore, from the principle must be admitted. In the constitution of the judiciary department in particular, it might be inexpedient to insist rigorously on the principle: first, because peculiar qualifications being essential in the members, the primary consideration ought to be to select that mode of choice which best secures these qualifications; secondly, because the permanent tenure by which the appointments are held in that department, must soon destroy all sense of dependence on the authority conferring them.

It is equally evident, that the members of each department should be as little dependent as possible on those of the others, for the emoluments annexed to their offices. Were the executive magistrate, or the judges, not independent of the legislature in this particular, their independence in every other would be merely nominal.

But the great security against a gradual concentration of the several powers in the same department, consists in giving to those who administer each department the necessary constitutional means and personal motives to resist encroachments of the others. The provision for defense must in this, as in all other cases, be made commensurate to the danger of attack. Ambition must be made to counteract ambition. The interest of the man must be connected with the constitutional rights of the place. It may be a reflection on human nature, that such devices should be necessary to control the abuses of government. But what is government itself, but the greatest of all reflections on human nature? If men were angels, no government would be necessary. If angels were to govern men, neither external nor internal controls on government would be necessary. In framing a government which is to be administered by men over men, the great difficulty lies in this: you must first enable the government to control the governed; and in the next place oblige it to control itself. A dependence on the people is, no doubt, the primary control on the government; but experience has taught mankind the necessity of auxiliary precautions.

This policy of supplying, by opposite and rival interests, the defect of better motives, might be traced through the whole system of human affairs, private as well as public. We see it particularly displayed in all the subordinate distributions of power, where the constant aim is to divide and arrange the several offices in such a manner as that each may be a check on the other that the private interest of every individual may be a sentinel over the public rights. These inventions of prudence cannot be less requisite in the distribution of the supreme powers of the State.

But it is not possible to give to each department an equal power of self-defense. In republican government, the legislative authority necessarily predominates. The remedy for this inconveniency is to divide the legislature into different branches; and to render them, by different modes of election and different principles of action, as little connected with each other as the nature of their common functions and their common dependence on the society will admit. It may even be necessary to guard against dangerous encroachments by still further precautions. As the weight of the legislative authority requires that it should be thus divided, the weakness of the executive may require, on the other hand, that it should be fortified. An absolute negative on the legislature appears, at first view, to be the natural defense with which the executive magistrate should be armed. But perhaps it would be neither altogether safe nor alone sufficient. On ordinary occasions it might not be exerted with the requisite firmness, and on extraordinary occasions it might be perfidiously abused. May not this defect of an absolute negative be supplied by some qualified connection between this weaker department and the weaker branch of the stronger department, by which the latter may be led to support the constitutional rights of the former, without being too much detached from the rights of its own department?

If the principles on which these observations are founded be just, as I persuade myself they are, and they be applied as a criterion to the several State constitutions, and to the federal Constitution it will be found that if the latter does not perfectly correspond with them, the former are infinitely less able to bear such a test.

There are, moreover, two considerations particularly applicable to the federal system of America, which place that system in a very interesting point of view.

First. In a single republic, all the power surrendered by the people is submitted to the administration of a single government; and the usurpations are guarded against by a division of the government into distinct and separate departments. In the compound republic of America, the power surrendered by the people is first divided between two distinct governments, and then the portion allotted to each subdivided among distinct and separate departments. Hence a double security arises to the rights of the people. The different governments will control each other, at the same time that each will be controlled by itself.

Second. It is of great importance in a republic not only to guard the society against the oppression of its rulers, but to guard one part of the society against the injustice of the other part. Different interests necessarily exist in different classes of citizens. If a majority be united by a common interest, the rights of the minority will be insecure. There are but two methods of providing against this evil: the one by creating a will in the community independent of the majority that is, of the society itself; the other, by comprehending in the society so many separate descriptions of citizens as will render an unjust combination of a majority of the whole very improbable, if not impracticable. The first method prevails in all governments possessing an hereditary or self-appointed authority. This, at best, is but a precarious security; because a power independent of the society may as well espouse the unjust views of the major, as the rightful interests of the minor party, and may possibly be turned against both parties. The second method will be exemplified in the federal republic of the United States. Whilst all authority in it will be derived from and dependent on the society, the society itself will be broken into so many parts, interests, and classes of citizens, that the rights of individuals, or of the minority, will be in little danger from interested combinations of the majority. In a free government the security for civil rights must be the same as that for religious rights. It consists in the one case in the multiplicity of interests, and in the other in the multiplicity of sects. The degree of security in both cases will depend on the number of interests and sects; and this may be presumed to depend on the extent of country and number of people comprehended under the same government. This view of the subject must particularly recommend a proper federal system to all the sincere and considerate friends of republican government, since it shows that in exact proportion as the territory of the Union may be formed into more circumscribed Confederacies, or States oppressive combinations of a majority will be facilitated: the best security, under the republican forms, for the rights of every class of citizens, will be diminished: and consequently the stability and independence of some member of the government, the only other security, must be proportionately increased. Justice is the end of government. It is the end of civil society. It ever has been and ever will be pursued until it be obtained, or until liberty be lost in the pursuit. In a society under the forms of which the stronger faction can readily unite and oppress the weaker, anarchy may as truly be said to reign as in a state of nature, where the weaker individual is not secured against the violence of the stronger; and as, in the latter state, even the stronger individuals are prompted, by the uncertainty of their condition, to submit to a government which may protect the weak as well as themselves; so, in the former state, will the more powerful factions or parties be gradually induced, by a like motive, to wish for a government which will protect all parties, the weaker as well as the more powerful. It can be little doubted that if the State of Rhode Island was separated from the Confederacy and left to itself, the insecurity of rights under the popular form of government within such narrow limits would be displayed by such reiterated oppressions of factious majorities that some power altogether independent of the people would soon be called for by the voice of the very factions whose misrule had proved the necessity of it. In the extended republic of the United States, and among the great variety of interests, parties, and sects which it embraces, a coalition of a majority of the whole society could seldom take place on any other principles than those of justice and the general good; whilst there being thus less danger to a minor from the will of a major party, there must be less pretext, also, to provide for the security of the former, by introducing into the government a will not dependent on the latter, or, in other words, a will independent of the society itself. It is no less certain than it is important, notwithstanding the contrary opinions which have been entertained, that the larger the society, provided it lie within a practical sphere, the more duly capable it will be of self-government. And happily for the republican cause, the practicable sphere may be carried to a very great extent, by a judicious modification and mixture of the federal principle.

    Publius.

Appendix B

The Government and the Community:
A Coordinated Response to Hate Crime in America

Hate crimes...leave deep scars not only on the victims, but on our larger community. They weaken the sense that we are one people with common values and a common future. They tear us apart when we should be moving closer together. They are acts of violence against America itself.
—Remarks by President Clinton during his Radio Address on Hate Crime, Saturday, June 7, 1997.

A hate crime is the embodiment of intolerance—an act of violence against a person or property based on the victim's race, color, gender, national origin, religion, sexual orientation, or disability. With the rash of arsons at African-American churches in the South in the past couple of years, more attention has been given to this problem. However, this phenomenon is not new.

> From Romans' persecution of Christians and Nazis' "final solution" for the Jews to the "ethnic cleansing" in Bosnia and genocide in Rwanda, hate crimes have shaped and sometimes defined world his-

tory. In the United States, racial and religious bias largely have inspired most hate crimes. As Europeans began to colonize the New World in the 16th and 17th centuries, Native Americans increasingly became the targets of bias-motivated intimidation and violence. During the past two centuries, some of the more typical examples of hate crimes in this Nation include the lynchings of African Americans, cross burnings to drive black families from predominantly white neighborhoods, assaults on homosexuals [gays, lesbians, bisexuals], and the painting of swastikas on Jewish synagogues.[1]

The official statistics maintained by the Federal Bureau of Investigation (FBI) illuminate but still understate the problem. In response to the passage of the Hate Crime Statistics Act of 1990, the attorney general designated the FBI's Uniform Crime Reporting Program to develop and implement a data collection system for its nearly 17,000 voluntary law enforcement agency participants. This act (amended in 1994 to include crimes motivated by bias against persons with disabilities) defines hate crimes as acts in which individuals are victimized because of their "race, religion, sexual orientation, or ethnicity."[2]

During 1996, 8,759 bias-motivated criminal incidents were reported to the FBI by 11,354 law enforcement agencies in 49 states and the District of Columbia. Of the 8,759 incidents, 5,396 were motivated by racial bias; 1,401 by religious bias, 1,016 by sexual-orientation bias; 940 by ethnicity/national origin bias; and six by multiple biases.[3]

The collection of the data is only as good as the ability of a given jurisdiction to identify and maintain a record of bias-motivated crime and provide this information to the FBI. As training of law enforcement officials improves in this area, so will law enforcement officials' ability to discern and detect bias-motivated crime. Further, victims of these crimes hesitate to report because of the nature of the crime and their uncertainty of police response. Experts in the area believe that this problem will increase as society becomes more diverse.

Hate crimes are more likely than other crimes to lead to acts of brutal violence. Assaults causing physical injury occur in 74 percent of bias crimes versus 29 percent of nonbias crimes. Hate crimes are more likely than other criminal activity to be committed by several individuals acting as a group. Hate crimes are also more likely to be committed by strangers, unlike most crimes against persons which are usually committed by someone the victim knows. The majority of hate crimes in this country are committed by young males, typically persons younger than 20.

Last year, our office prosecuted five persons for placing a cross on the lawn of a black man in Gresham, Ore.[4] Few hate crimes engender as much fear as cross-burning. In addition to terrorizing the victim, the crime alarmed and outraged the community. Quick response by the Gresham Police Department, the Federal Bureau of Investigation, the U.S. attorney's office, and the Justice Department's Civil Rights Division led to the filing of federal civil rights conspiracy charges against the five offenders. All five pled guilty and received federal prison sentences. The case is a textbook example of how local and federal authorities can work in a cooperative manner to combat hate crimes. Our community has also suffered a church arson, the defacing of Jewish cemeteries and places of worship, and attacks on our gay and lesbian neighbors.

On Nov. 10, 1997, President Clinton convened the first White House Conference on Hate Crime to focus the nation on one of its enduring and challenging problems: "conquering the forces of hatred and division that still exist in our society...." This conference was attended by representatives from all governmental levels of law enforcement, national organizations that have historically challenged bigotry based on race, national origin, religion, sexual orientation, or disability, scholars and researchers, the unsung heroes who have stood up against hate crime in communities around the country. Kris Olson and Charles Moose were Oregon's delegates. In addition to calling national attention to the problem of hate crimes, this conference also provided the President with an opportunity to highlight effective law enforcement and educational strategies and announce new federal initiatives to prevent and punish hate crimes. One of the legislative initiatives is to expand the principal federal hate crimes statute to include hate crime causing bodily injury based on sexual orientation, gender, or disability. Furthermore, this new legislation, introduced by Sens. Kennedy and Spector, would also make illegal any act of force based on prohibited characteristics and leading to bodily injury, even if the act did not interfere with federally protected activities.

A central aspect of this renewed effort by the federal government to address the problem of hate crimes is to establish a local hate crimes working group in each federal district. These working groups would represent a federal, state, and local partnership to ensure close coordination on hate crimes investigations and prosecutions among responsible law enforcement agencies; promote training of police, investigators, and prosecutors in identifying and dealing with hate crimes; encourage victims to report hate crimes; and educate the public about the harm they cause.

This office has been participating in a group known as Coalition Against Hate Crimes since the President's Hate Crime Conference. The convener of this group is a representative of the American Jewish Committee. Currently, this coalition has representatives from a variety of advocacy organizations principally based in Portland, but also from Salem and Eugene, Ore. Both the office of the U.S. attorney and the FBI have regularly sent representatives to their meetings. We have also sponsored speakers from "Facing History and Ourselves" and the Community Relations Service of the U.S. Department of Justice.

The coalition is still in an early stage of determining the course of action that it will take to address hate crime, although the principal focus of the discussions to date has been about a need to establish an effective network of advocates and government officials, develop education initiatives directed at primary and secondary school-age children, as well as a public education campaign to address the intolerance, hate, and bigotry that still exists within our communities. Our office will continue to participate in this coalition, as we develop a comprehensive district-wide plan that includes improved efforts among various law enforcement agencies to use federal and state criminal and civil laws and to seek enhanced sanctions whenever possible. We will also seek out creative ways to combine with community groups concerned with the problem of hate crime, to encourage more victims to report, and—most importantly—to educate the public, but especially our children, about prejudice, violence, intolerance, and discrimination.

Source: "The Government and the Community" by Kristine Olson, et al. from *The Federal Lawyer*, October 1998, pp. 47–48.

NOTES

[1] Bureau of Justice Assistance, *A Policymaker's Guide To Hate Crimes*, ix (March 1997).

[2] This definition of hate crimes fails to address hate crimes against women. Further, this definition does not measure the deeper sense of the severity of hate crimes or their impact on individual victims, their families, and communities. The definition in the federal Hate Crimes Sentencing Enhancement Act of 1994, does include women and persons with disabilities.

[3] Criminal Justice Information Services Division, FBI, *Hate Crime Statistics* 1996, 5 (1997).

[4] There are several Federal statutes providing jurisdiction to prosecute hate crimes. The federal criminal civil rights statutes provide for prosecution of conspiracies to interfere with federally protected rights. 18 U.S.C. 241, the use of force or threat of force to injure or intimidate someone in the enjoyment of specific rights (such as voting, employment, education, use of public facilities) 18 U.S.C. 245, and criminal housing interference, 42 U.S.C. 3631. In addition, the Church Arson Protection Act of 1996 amended the criminal civil rights statues to facilitate prosecutions of racially motivated arsons and other acts of desecration against houses of worship. 18 U.S.C. 247. Federal prosecutors can also seek enhanced penalties against persons who commit federal criminal offenses motivated by bias.

Appendix C

Glossary

Affirmative action—Plan or program to remedy the effects of past discrimination in employment, education, or other activity and to prevent its recurrence.

Articles of Confederation—It was the first constitution to govern the new nation of America. It established thirteen independent states which were loosely overseen by a central government of limited power.

Anti-federalists—"Ancestors" of today's Democrats, initially opposed ratification of the U.S. Constitution, opposed the creation of a strong national government and were supported by farmers and those working in agriculture.

Aristotle—Greek political thinker who was born in Stagira, in Northern Greece. His most celebrated work is *The Politics*.

Authority—The right to exercise power.

Autocracy—Any system of government in which political power and authority are exercised by a single individual.

Balance of power politics—The world powers are kept from going to war against one another by balancing one nation against another.

Bill of Rights—The first ten amendments to the Constitution, concerned with basic freedoms.

Bureaucracy—Any administrative system that carries out policy on an everyday basis, uses standardized procedures, has a hierarchy, and is based on a specialization of duties.

Bureaucrat—One who works in a bureaucratic organization.

Cabinet—Executive-level bureaucracies comprised of fourteen departments, each headed by a secretary appointed by the president.

Capitalism—Based on the principle of "laissez faire" or "let alone," this means there should be a minimum intervention by government in economic affairs.

Categorical Grants—Federal aid to the states and localities to be used for specific projects.
Caucus—A closed meeting of party leaders to select party candidates.
Certiorari—An order given to a lower court by a higher court to send up the record of a case for a review.
Civil laws—The code regulating conduct between private persons.
Civil liberties—Individual rights clearly outlined in the first ten amendments to the United States Constitution.
Cloture—A vote to end filibuster in the Senate by requiring approval of sixty senators.
Communism—An economic system based on government ownership of means of production.
Confederal system—A voluntary association of sovereign states, where major powers belong to member states and the central government has only minor powers.
Containment policy—A policy adopted in 1947 by the Truman Administration to build "situations of strength" around the periphery of the Soviet Union and Eastern Europe in order to contain communist power within its existing boundaries.
Constitution—A fundamental law that establishes the framework of government, assigns the powers and duties of governmental agencies, and establishes the relationship between the people and their government.
Continental Congress—A political institution, made up of delegates representing the colonies, first convened in 1774 to protest the British treatment of the colonies and eventually became the central government of the United States.
Convention—Gathering of delegates who nominate a party's presidential candidate.
Criminal laws—Behavior prohibited by state law which is punishable by imprisonment.
Devolution revolution—The demand for responsibility to be given to the states over federal government and its agencies.
Direct democracy—Individuals make political decisions for themselves.
Diversity of citizenship jurisdiction—Power of the federal courts to hear cases involving citizens of different states.
Domestic policy—Exists to deliver goods and services to people who are perceived to be, or perceive themselves to be, in need.
Due process of law—Protection against arbitrary deprivation of life, liberty, or property.
Easton, David—A political scientist who defines politics as the authoritative allocation of values.
Economic policy—Deals with the effects of taxation, public spending, and money management.
Elastic clause—Article I, Section 8, describes the implied powers of Congress.
Electoral college—Representatives of the states who officially elect the president.

Elitism—A theory of decision making in which views American politics as understand in terms of those with wealth.
Empirical statement—Factual statement.
En banc—"By all."
Exclusionary rule—Evidence gathered through illegal or unreasonable means is not admissible in federal trials nor, under the Fourteenth Amendment, in state trials.
Ex-post facto laws—Retroactive criminal laws.
Federal question jurisdiction—Power of a court to hear a case based on an alleged violation of federal law.
Federal system—There is a division of powers between the central government and member states. The flow of power is two-directional: from federal government to its member states, and vice versa.
Federalists—"Ancestors" of today's Republicans, supported ratification of the U.S. Constitution, a strong national government, and were generally supported by the affluent citizens whose interests were business, industry, manufacturing, and trade.
Filibuster—Allows unlimited debate on a bill in the Senate and is often used to "talk a bill to death."
Foreign policy—External American goals for which the nation is prepared to commit its resources.
Gerrymander—A process of drawing district boundaries to help increase the chance of a candidate from a particular political party or a particular group get elected.
Government—Consists of institutions established to make and enforce laws.
Government corporation—Government entities that are set up to be run as corporations.
Hatch Act—A law which prohibits federal employees from engaging in political activity while on duty or while acting under the color of office.
Ideology—A coherent set of beliefs guiding people's attitude toward government.
Indirect democracy—Individuals have the right to elect their representatives and they will make political decisions on behalf of the voters.
Implied powers—All laws which are necessary and proper for carrying out the forgoing powers.
Incumbent—One who holds an office.
Independent agencies—Exist to regulate an industry or major government program which does not fall under any of the cabinet departments.
Individualistic political culture—The ultimate objective of politics is not so much to create a better public life, but rather to get things for yourself and your group.
Influence—The ability to persuade others to accept certain things or behave in certain ways.
Joint committees—Composed of members from both houses. Joint committees help the two houses come together to work on compromises on bills or resolutions.

Judicial activism—Actions by the courts which go beyond the role of the judiciary as interpreter of the law and adjudicator of disputes.
Judicial review—The power of the federal courts to declare federal and state acts unconstitutional.
Legitimacy—General public acceptance of governments' right to make and enforce decisions.
Libel—Written defamation of one's character.
Liberals—Those who favor government regulation of business and government spending for social programs.
Lobbyists—Hired by special interest groups to communicate with the appropriate governmental authorities about those groups' needs, and to influence the government's decisions as they affect the groups. Provide the interest groups with access to the government.
Locke, John—English philosopher and politician whose political theory influenced the writing of the American Declaration of Independence and the Consitution.
Majority leader—Party leader on the floor of the House. The majority leader assists the speaker in scheduling legislation and deciding party strategy in floor debates.
Marshall Plan—A proposal made by the Secretary of State, George C. Marshall, in 1947, for a vast program of American economic aid to reconstruct the war-devastated economics of Western Europe.
Minority leader—The minority party's principal spokesman and strategist.
Moralistic political culture—Politics is seen as a way of improving life, and people have a strong sense that they should participate.
National Security Council—Works closely with the President on foreign policy matters. Consists of the President, Vice-President, Secretary of State, Secretary of Defense and National Security Advisor.
Natural rights—Rights that no person or society can take away.
Normative statements—Require ethical or moral judgments, identify one outcome as better than another.
Paine, Thomas—British-born pamphleteer who published *Common Sense* in 1776. It pleaded the case for American independence at a time when few Americans were prepared to adopt this policy openly.
Patronage—A system of rewarding jobs to those close to or those who supported the President or other high government officials.
Pendleton Act (1883)—A law that eliminated most patronage-based hiring and promoting in federal government employment.
Plato—A Greek political thinker who was born in Athens. His most celebrated work in politics is *The Republic*.
Pluralism—A theory of decision making which views American politics as best understood in terms of the interaction, conflict, and bargaining of groups.

Polis—A Greek term for city-state. Classical Greek political thinkers considered individuals as part and parcel of city-state.
Political Action Committees—Committees set up by and representing corporations, labor unions, and special interest groups and that raise and spend campaign contributions on behalf of candidates or causes.
Political culture—Widely shared political values among members of a political community.
Political science—A discipline within social sciences that uses scientific method to study that aspect of human behavior involving power and authority.
Political party—An organized group that seeks to influence the government through winning elections.
Political socialization—A process by which people acquire their orientation towards the political world.
Political system—A set of institutions and activities that link together government, politics, and public policy.
Poll tax—A tax paid as a condition for voting.
Popular sovereignty—Political power and authority rests with the people.
Power—The ability of individuals to control the behavior and actions of others using means ranging from influence to force or coercion.
Primary matching payments—Available during the nomination season to candidates who raise $5,000 in at least twenty states in contributions of no more than $250. Once candidates meet this, they will receive public funds to match the first $250 of each private contribution they raise during the presidential primary election season up to a predetermined spending ceiling.
Prior restraint—The government's power to prevent publication of an article.
Public good—The social choice that represents the best outcome for society as a whole rather than for some subset of the population.
Public policy—Any course of action taken by the government that affects any segment of the public.
Reapportionment—The 435 congressional districts are reallocated by Congress among the states, every ten years following the publication of national census, in terms of gains or losses in population.
Regulatory policies—Control private behavior to protect the general public.
Redistricting—The state legislature draws the boundary lines for each congressional election district so that legislature districts are all approximately equal in population.
Reserved powers—The powers of the states under the Tenth Amendment.
Satare decisis—The legal doctrine that says precedent should guide judicial decision making.
Select committees—Temporary committees established for a particular purpose, such as to research a problem or to conduct an investigation.

Self-oriented interest group—Seek to benefit their own groups.

Slander—Spoken defamation of one's character.

Social contract—Government derives its power from the consent of the people and government is instituted among people to protect and promote life, liberty and property.

Soft money—Expenditures by political parties for party "building" activities such as voter registration and voter mobilization.

Speaker of the House—The presiding officer of the House of Representatives. The post combines the duties of presiding officer with those of leading the majority party.

Standing committee—Permanent committee. They are specialized in particular areas and deal with bills related to those areas.

Strict construction—This belief argues that the Court is bound by the words of the Constitution and interpretations which can clearly be found or implied by those words.

Suffrage—The right to vote.

Sunset review—Laws that call for a periodic review of government agencies and programs to determine if they are still necessary.

Sunshine laws—Reforms that require some government agency meetings and discussions to be open to the press and to the public.

Tort reform movement—This reform movement's objective was to place a cap on punitive damages.

Traditionalist political culture—Politics is not seen as a way to further the public good, but to maintain the status quo.

Unconventional acts of participation—Acts of participation not allowed by law.

Unitary system—Concentrates power in the central government; power flows from center to constituents.

Weber, Max—Recognized that overall government efficiency depended on the structure of the agencies charged with performing the function.

Whips—They assist the floor leaders of both parties. They inform members about upcoming key votes, attempt to "whip up" support for the party position on important roll call votes, and work to maintain party unity.

Whistle-blowers—Government employees who make public accounts of waste or fraud.

White primaries—Primary elections open only to white voters.

Writ of certorari—A procedural device for discretionary review of cases issued by the court when at least four of the nine justices agree that the case should be reviewed.

Writ of mandamus—To perform acts required by law to officers of the United States.

Index

Adoption, 313, 316, 323, 359, 363
Advice and consent, 43, 97, 193, 218, 325, 360
Affirmative action, 298–299, 389
Agency, 65
Agenda setting, 146–147, 154, 309, 311, 316, 323
American Equal Rights Association (AERA), 294
American Female Moral Reform Society, 293, 305
Amicus Curiae, 110, 126, 251, 296
Anti-Federalists, 39, 40, 116, 117, 126, 130, 389
Appellate jurisdiction, 241, 245, 246, 251, 362
Articles of Confederation, 34, 36, 39, 48, 49, 51, 130, 389
At-Large election, 188
Authoritarianism, 21, 22, 28
Authority, 9

Balance of power, 343, 348, 389
Balancing decisions, 257
Berlin Wall, 336, 348
Bicameral legislature, 38, 188
Bills of attainder, 42
Black Codes, 285, 305
Blanket primary, 88–89, 99
Block grant, 62–63, 65–66, 68
Blowback, 335, 348
Bureaucracy, 15, 67, 143, 145, 182, 219–236, 240, 389

Cabinet, 210–211, 217–218, 224–229, 231, 233–234, 389, 391
Capital crime, 240, 270, 311
Capitalism, 24, 26, 28, 235, 389
Categorical grant, 62, 65, 68, 390
Caucus, 87–89, 99, 120–121, 147, 168, 183, 195, 197, 200, 218, 390
Caucus-Convention, 197, 218
Censure, 174, 175, 188
Centralized federalism, 58, 61, 68
Charismatic legitimacy, 10, 28
Checks and balances, 17, 40–41, 49, 153, 228, 381
Chief of state, 193, 213, 218
City-state, 2, 4–6, 28, 393
Civil liberties, 106–107, 253–280, 390
Clear and present danger, 260, 277
Closed primary, 88, 99
Cloture, 179, 188, 390
Cold War, 327, 332–333, 336–337, 341–342, 348
Committee of the whole, 178, 188
Communism, 24, 26, 28, 330–333, 335, 390
Concurrent powers, 53, 68
Concurrent resolutions, 181
Concurring opinion, 247, 251
Confederal system, 19, 21, 28, 36, 51, 390
Conference committee, 179, 180, 182, 189

395

Conservatism, 14, 28, 256
Constitution, 17
Constitutional Convention, 34, 36–37, 49, 130
Containment, 330–332, 348, 390
Convention, 39, 120, 121, 197, 199, 200, 206, 207, 218
Cooperative federalism, 58, 60–61, 68
Corporate PACs, 126
Covert action, 342, 343, 348
Criminal law, 55, 240, 251, 390, 391
Cuban Missile Crisis, 332, 348

Declaration of Resolves, 34, 49
Declaration of Rights and Grievances, 49
Declaratory Act of 1766, 34, 49
Delegated powers, 42, 58, 68
Democracy, 21
Democracy's watchdog, 124, 125, 130, 154
Devolution revolution, 58, 62–63, 68, 390
Diplomacy, 9, 86, 342, 348
Dissenting opinion, 251, 273
Diversity of Citizenship, 242, 251, 390
Dual federalism, 58–60, 68–69
Dual primary, 88, 89, 99
Due process, 45, 47, 55, 248, 266, 267, 274, 275, 277, 299, 365, 367, 390

Electoral vote, 48, 74, 194, 198–199, 201–204, 208, 209, 218, 293
Empirical analysis, 28
En banc, 244, 251, 391
Equal time rule, 140, 154
Evaluation, 314
Ex post facto law, 54, 55, 69, 358, 391
Exclusionary rule, 266, 277, 391

Fairness doctrine, 140, 141, 154
Federal Election Campaign Act (FECA), 94
Federal Election Commission, 97
Federal question, 242, 391
Federal system, 19, 20, 29, 41, 51, 66–68, 242, 285, 383, 384, 391
Federalism, 51–70
Federalist, 39–40, 49, 116–117, 126, 130, 164, 380, 391

Felonies, 176, 240, 251, 357
Fifth branch of government, 145, 154
Filibuster, 178–179, 184, 189, 390–391
First Continental Congress, 34, 49
Formula grant, 65, 69
Formulation, 312, 316, 323, 334
Franchisement, 99, 286
Franking privilege, 174, 182, 189
Freedom of Information Act, 143, 154
"Fruit from a poisonous tree" doctrine, 266
Full faith and credit clause, 55, 56, 69

General elections, 94, 99
General revenue sharing (GRS), 62, 66
Gerrymandering, 164, 166, 188–189
Government, 9
Government corporation, 229, 234, 391
Grant-in-aid, 60, 61, 68
Great Compromise, 38, 49, 160
Great Society, 61, 64, 232, 234, 278
Gulf of Tonkin Resolution, 212, 218
Gulf War, 138–139, 151, 195, 212–213, 336–337, 345–346

Hard money, 92, 99
Hatch Act, 232, 234, 391
Head Start, 232, 234
Horse race journalism, 147, 154
Hungarian Revolution, 334, 348
Hyperpluralism, 26–29

Ideological parties, 123, 126
Ideology, 12, 391
Impeachment, 42–43, 176–78, 189, 192–193, 214–218, 237, 241, 354, 360–362
Implementation, 313, 329
Implied power, 42, 49, 52–53, 68, 390, 391
Incumbent, 74, 111, 164, 165, 391
Independent agency, 226–228, 234
Influence, 9
Infotainment, 136, 154
Initiative, 23
Interest groups, 103–128, 135–136, 188, 230, 260, 319–320, 327, 343, 346, 392
Interstate compacts, 55, 56, 68

Interstate rendition, 55, 56, 68
Intolerable Acts, 34, 49
Iron triangle, 230, 234
Issue ads, 99

Jacksonian Democrats, 117, 126
Jim Crow laws, 74
Joint committee, 181, 184, 186, 189, 391
Joint resolutions, 181
Judicial activism, 238, 249, 251, 392
Judicial restraint, 238, 249, 251
Jurisdiction, 242–246

Laissez faire, 24, 29, 389
League of United Latin American Citizens (LULAC), 106, 292
Legislative rule, 222, 234
Legitimacy, 9
Legitimacy by habit, 10, 29
Legitimacy by procedures, 10, 29
Legitimacy by results, 10, 29
Libel, 44, 140, 142, 256, 263, 277, 392
Literacy test, 74–77, 99, 284
Lobbying, 109–110
Lone Star Card, 317, 323
Loose construction, 249, 251

Majority leader, 182, 392
Malapportionment, 163, 189
Mark-up session, 177, 189
Marshall Plan, 330–332, 348, 392
Matching grant, 65, 68
McCain-Feingold Act, 260, 277
Means test, 315, 316, 323
Minority leader, 182, 392
Miranda Rights, 268, 277
Misdemeanors, 43, 176, 193, 240, 251, 361
Monarchy, 5, 21, 22, 28, 33, 35, 36, 130, 193
Monica Lewinsky scandal, 215, 218
Muckrakers, 131–132, 153, 154

National Association for the Advancement of Colored People (NAACP), 106, 110, 282
National Convention, 120–121, 197, 199200, 206, 263

National Farm Workers Association (NFWA), 292
National Organization for Women (NOW), 106, 296
National Performance Review, 233, 234
National Woman Suffrage Association (NWSA), 295
Necessary and proper clause, 42, 53, 58, 68
New Deal, 60, 64, 231, 317
New federalism, 58, 61–63, 68–70
New World Order, 337, 348
News leaks, 144, 154
NIMBY, 67, 320
Normative analysis, 28
North American Free Trade Agreement (NAFTA), 337

Oil for Food, 340, 348
Open primary, 88, 99
Oral argument, 243, 247, 251
Original jurisdiction, 241, 242, 245, 251, 361
Overspecialization, 221, 232, 234

Packaged news, 149, 154
Pairing technique, 164, 165, 188
Partisan gerrymandering, 164, 188
Party dealignment, 122, 126
Party realignment, 122, 126,
Patronage, 230, 231, 234, 392
Pendleton Act, 231, 234, 392
Platform, 118, 121, 123, 200, 218, 327
Pluralism, 26, 27, 392
Pocket veto, 179, 188
Political action committee (PAC), 91
Political culture, 18–19
Political socialization, 18
Politics, 1–7
Poll tax, 74, 75, 393
Popular vote, 23, 95, 96, 120, 121, 201, 203, 204, 205, 208, 209, 218, 237
Populism, 14, 15, 28
Power, 9
President *pro tempore,* 179, 183–184, 188, 354, 373
President's cabinet, 210–211, 224, 225, 234

Presidential preference primary, 197, 200, 218
Primary election, 87–89, 95, 99, 147, 206, 393
Privileges and immunities, 43, 47, 55, 56, 69, 274, 362
Progressive Voters' League, 284, 305
Project grant, 65, 69
Provisional ballot, 79, 80, 99
Public figures, 142, 152, 154
Public Policy, 309–324
Publius, 40

Racial gerrymandering, 164, 166, 188
Rational ignorance, 83, 99
Rational-legal legitimacy, 10, 29
Reapportionment, 160–62
Recall election, 22, 29, 87, 90, 99
Recess appointment, 251
Reconstruction Acts, 286, 305
Redistricting, 162–166, 188, 393
Referendum, 22, 23, 29
Reform Party, 95, 120, 123, 196, 218
Reinventing government, 222, 233, 234
Reprimand, 174, 175, 189
Reserved powers, 46, 53, 58, 69, 393
Right-of-rebuttal rule, 140, 154
Rule of four, 247, 251
Rules Committee, 178, 189

Scientific method, 7, 8
Second Continental Congress, 35, 49
Secretary, 224
Select committee, 184, 186, 189, 393
Separation of powers, 37, 41, 49
Seventeenth Amendment, 47, 74, 160, 189
Shield laws, 142, 154
Simple resolution, 181, 189
Six Day War, 334, 335, 348
Social contract, 16–17, 29, 394
Social values, 12, 29, 104, 118
Socialism, 24, 29
Soft money, 93, 94, 99, 260, 394
Southern Christian Leadership Conference (SCLC), 106, 283
Special election, 89–90, 99
Spin doctor, 133, 154
Spoils system, 231, 234

Stamp Act of 1765, 33, 49
Stare decisis, 239, 251
Starr Report, 216, 218
State of the Union Address, 43, 193, 213, 214, 218
Statutory law, 238, 248, 251
Student Nonviolent Coordinating Committee (SNCC), 286
Subcommittee, 184, 189
Suez Canal crisis, 334, 348
Suffrage, 294–295
Sugar Act of 1764, 33, 49
Sullivan Principle, 142, 154
Sunset Advisory Committee, 314, 323
Sunset law, 233, 234
Sunshine law, 233, 234, 394
Supremacy clause, 43, 49, 57, 240, 248
Suspect classifications, 282
Suspect criteria, 282, 305

Tea Act, 34, 49
Third parties, 119, 122–123, 126
Townsend Revenue Act, 34, 49
Trial balloons, 144, 154

Unitary system, 19, 20, 29, 51, 394
United Farm Workers of America (UFWA), 292
Universal suffrage, 73, 76, 99, 113

Values, 6, 12
Vote concentration, 165, 189
Vote diffusion, 165, 189

War on Poverty, 61, 64, 69, 232
War Powers Act, 212, 218
Whigs, 117, 126
Whip, 183, 189, 394
Whistle-blower, 232, 234
White primary, 74, 75, 76, 77, 99
Whitewater, 192, 214–215, 218
Winner-take-all, 120, 201, 218
World Trade Organization (WTO), 114
Writ of certiorari, 246, 247, 251
Writ of habeas corpus, 54, 55, 69, 358
Written briefs, 247, 251

Political Chaos

INTRODUCTION

Political Chaos is a computer game designed specifically for first-year American government or political science students in four-year and community college settings. The purpose of this game is to assist these students in comprehending information provided in texts recommended for introductory government courses. It will also enable students to put such textbook information to practical use by helping to resolve the problems presented in Chaos Community. A thorough understanding of the materials taught in these introductory government courses is essential in enjoying this game, and being able to accumulate the required points for an excellent grade.

It is assumed that law and order have broken down in Chaos Community. Its leaders are incapable of preventing the anarchy from ravaging this once-peaceful society. Individuals now constitute a law unto themselves, especially leaders of various ethnic, racial, religious, and other social groups. Drastic measures must be taken to avoid civil war.

As a student currently taking a government or political science course, your task is to help salvage Chaos from destruction. Your responsibilities are to:

1. Assist Chaos Community in picking a leader acceptable to a majority of the people;

2. Suggest a political system that must be approved by a majority of Chaosites; and

3. Recommend a system of government that would enable Chaosites to fairly distribute the goods in their society.

Game Rules

1. Whatever decision a student makes must be acceptable to a majority of Chaosites.
2. Every decision must be fair, just, and ultimately lead to a civil society.
3. No group can dominate or oppress others.
4. The chosen leader for Chaos must be acceptable to all groups.

Playing and Scoring the Game

Five leadership categories have been provided:

1. Racial/ethnic
2. Religious
3. Elitist
4. Radical
5. Neutral

Also given are combinations of different governmental systems made up of key political terms and phases generally found in all U.S. government recommended textbooks. The student's responsibility is to match the various leadership categories with each of the political systems provided.

Let's assume you decide that a leader from a "*Racial/ethnic*" group would be the most qualified person to prevent warfare in Chaos Community. Your next action is to select the type of governmental system this particular leader could introduce in order to achieve peaceful coexistence for Chaosites. For instance, if you decide that "*laissez-faire, direct democracy, and Hobbesian absolute monarchy*" is likely to prevent warfare in Chaos, you match this selection with the leader of your choice. You are therefore strongly advised to read through each combination of political systems or terminologies before making a final selection.

To further simplify the problem for the player, Chaosites have been categorized into three decision groups as follow:

1. Majority agreement (MA): a majority of Chaosites who accept a player's choice for a governmental system.

2. Majority disagreement (MD): a majority of Chaosites who reject a player's choice for a governmental system.
3. Conditional majority agreement (CA): a majority of Chaosites who accept a player's choice for a governmental system, but on condition that other requirements are provided. Each decision choice made must be acceptable to only one of these groups.

A player is awarded 10 points (+10) if a majority of Chaosites approve his choice for a political system; minus 10 points (–10) if they disapprove; and zero if they arrive at a conditional majority agreement. A player must accumulate at least 300 Majority Agreement (MA) points considered necessary to avert a civil war in Chaos. Players should ensure that they obtain a computer printout indicating their score level to help their instructor record whatever credit has been appropriated for this section of the game.